WITHDRAWN

THE MAN IN THE STREET

The Man in the Street

THE IMPACT OF AMERICAN PUBLIC OPINION

ON FOREIGN POLICY

BY THOMAS A. BAILEY

*"The man in the street does not know
a star in the sky."*—EMERSON.

GLOUCESTER, MASS.
PETER SMITH
1964

PREFACE

WHY DO WE BEHAVE like Americans in regard to the outside world?
This is the basic question that the present volume attempts to answer,
and in so doing it is a pioneering enterprise. Several general books have been
written on what we currently think about domestic and (somewhat incidentally) foreign affairs, but so far as the author is aware no effort has been made
on a wide scale to correlate the "what" with the "why," the present with the
past. The treatment is broadly interpretative and, like many other path-
breaking endeavors, is suggestive rather than exhaustive. The author hopes
that some of the areas here opened will be further cultivated by later settlers.
The topical rather than the narrative approach seemed desirable, even at the
cost of some slight but inevitable duplication.

A warning regarding perspective must be posted. Singling out special
topics for individual chapters may lead to the impression that those topics
were more important to the American public than they really were. Singling
out foreign affairs for concentrated treatment may lead to the impression
that overseas lands loomed larger in our thinking than they actually have.
Singling out the American people for special consideration may lead to the
impression that we are more blameworthy than others. American nature reveals no marked differences from human nature.

The following colleagues graciously read and helpfully commented on
parts of the manuscript relating to their special interests: Claude A. Buss,
George J. Hall, John J. Johnson, Ralph H. Lutz, Adolph F. Meisen, and
Clifford F. Weigle. Edith R. Mirrielees, Professor Emeritus of English at
Stanford University, and editor of the *Pacific Spectator*, cheerfully assumed
the task of reading and criticizing the entire manuscript. I am also indebted
to her for permission to republish the material that appeared as "Finnish
Facts" in the *Pacific Spectator*. William A. Lydgate, editor of the American
Institute of Public Opinion, also read the entire manuscript, and made many
valuable suggestions as to a proper interpretation of the polls. Dr. Alden Jami-
son gave me special permission to use his manuscript doctoral dissertation
at Harvard University, entitled, "Irish-Americans: The Irish Question and
American Diplomacy, 1895–1921." Numerous students have contributed useful ideas, and I am particularly indebted to Jacob M. Bellig, Malcolm C.
Hanna, Albert G. Pickerell, and J. D. Williams. My wife, Sylvia Dean Bailey,
helpfully criticized a substantial portion of the manuscript and read proof.

STANFORD UNIVERSITY
June, 1947

THOMAS A. BAILEY

v

CONTENTS

CHAPTER ONE

THE SOVEREIGN CITIZEN

"Public opinion in a democracy wields the scepter."
—CHARLES EVANS HUGHES

1

NERO murdered his mother and his divorced wife and did many other diabolical deeds with complete impunity, but he was forced to give up his ambition to become an actor when the Roman populace reacted unfavorably to his efforts. The Pharisees attempted to lay unfriendly hands on the Apostles, but they were compelled to desist when an angry murmur rose from the multitude. These are but two early examples, and by no means the earliest ones, of the sovereign power of an aroused public.

The British economist John Stuart Mill, writing in 1859 on liberty, concluded: "In politics it is almost a triviality to say that public opinion now rules the world." A year earlier Abraham Lincoln, debating with Senator Douglas on the issue of limiting slavery, declared: "With public sentiment on its side, everything succeeds; with public sentiment against it, nothing succeeds." And a dozen years later Charles Dudley Warner, perhaps with tongue in cheek, opined: "Public opinion is stronger than the Legislature, and nearly as strong as the Ten Commandments." Actually, it is often stronger than the Ten Commandments.

All governments, whatever their nature, rest on the foundation stone of public opinion. The Scottish philosopher David Hume observed as long ago as 1741: "As force is always on the side of the governed, the governors have nothing to support them but opinion." The yellowing scroll of history reveals few if any instances when a ruler flagrantly and persistently defied the will of his subjects without courting disaster. Even dictators are keenly aware of their servitude to public opinion, and this explains why they are at such pains to propagandize their people into supporting arbitrary rule. Hitler had to deceive the German nation through Dr. Goebbels' lie factory, and Mussolini and Stalin and other dictators of recent vintage had to employ similar chicanery. Censorship and propaganda are the unconscious compliments that despots pay to the potency of public opinion.

All this seems like an attempt to prove the obvious, but the truth is that millions of people are still unconvinced. Public opinion is so apathetic and preoccupied, so changeful and impulsive, so ill-informed and misinformed, that critics are apt to sneer at its power. Yet a giant who is fickle and ignorant still has a giant's strength, and may use it with frightful effect.

Another source of skepticism is that public opinion is awkward to describe, elusive to define, difficult to measure, and impossible to see, even though it may be felt. James Russell Lowell once remarked that popular

1

sentiment was like the pressure of the atmosphere: one could not see it but "all the same, it is sixteen pounds to the square inch." The British Foreign Secretary Sir Samuel Hoare had never seen public opinion when, in 1935, he plotted with the French premier to sacrifice Ethiopia on the altar of Italy's imperial ambitions. But when the backfire of public resentment blew him out of office, he could not deny its force. An angered electorate is an awesome thing.

In a dictatorship, the masses must be deceived; in a democracy, they must be educated. In either case, they must be courted if public programs are to be carried through. If Mr. Average American wants to get a glimpse at the power behind the officeholder's chair, all he has to do is pick up a mirror and look into it.

2

The most powerful nation in the world today is the United States, and consequently the most powerful body of public opinion in existence is formed by the American people. What the government in Washington does or fails to do in the field of foreign affairs will depend largely on the wishes of our citizens, and what our citizens demand or fail to demand will affect mightily the destiny of this planet.

A vexatious problem here at home, such as housing or unemployment, touches the Man in the Street more immediately than one abroad. For this reason there is normally much more popular pressure on Washington for action regarding internal affairs than foreign affairs.

The sovereign American people may influence their government either positively or negatively. The classic example of positive action may be found in 1898, when the masses rose and cried out for war against Spain with such overwhelming insistence that the amiable McKinley dared not deny their demands.

Negative pressure is much less obvious but no less potent. Fear as to how the people may react has often caused the President and the State Department to recoil from a contemplated course. When the United States minister in Mexico City, James Gadsden, was negotiating in 1853 for the strip of southwestern territory that bears his name, he suggested that the State Department supply him with money for bribing certain Mexican officials. He was informed from Washington that such funds could be provided only by Congressional action, and that the resulting stench would be undesirable. Similarly, the ingrained distrust of the average American for entangling alliances, combined with his hereditary dislike of England, has repeatedly caused the State Department to draw back from a closer understanding with Downing Street, lest the news leak out and recoil disastrously upon the administration.

The Harding landslide of 1920 was falsely interpreted as a tremendous mandate against the League of Nations, and Republican administrations for the next decade, paralyzed by their prodigious plurality of 7,000,000 votes, shunned the League as they would a leper. The cautious Republican politician would invite no similar rebuke from a presumably wrathful electorate.

By the early 1930's it was clear to all discerning students of finance that the debts owed us by our associates in World War I were uncollectible. The alternatives were cancellation or just not getting the money. But the almighty taxpayer, knowing that he would have to foot the bill in either case, bristled up at the slightest suggestion of cancellation. The officials in Washington had to keep crying for the moon, many of them knowing perfectly well they were crying uselessly, except in so far as they were usefully placating the public.

3

How does the citizen actually exert pressure on his government? He may send letters, telegrams, and petitions to his congressman, his senator, or his President, but his most formidable bludgeon is the ballot. As Oliver Wendell Holmes put it,

> The freeman, casting with unpurchased hand
> The vote that shakes the turret of the land.

The President fears the electorate, although he may not respect it. He is the head of a great political party first; the director of foreign affairs second or perhaps third. With a natural desire for the endorsement of reelection, he is bedeviled by his eligibility for a second term and, in the days of Franklin Roosevelt, for a third and a fourth. If he offends or defies the voter, he may be repudiated at the polls.

A war with France in 1800 would have been good for the party but bad for the country, and President John Adams, courageously ignoring the clamor of the crowd for blood, patched up existing disputes and gave the nation peace. He suspected that he was committing political suicide when he boldly put patriotism above party, and the event proved him correct. He was defeated for reelection in 1800, and never thereafter held public office. A century later, in 1898, war with Spain over Cuba was good for the party but bad for the country. President McKinley, yielding to the clamor of the crowd for blood, gave the country war. He was triumphantly reelected in 1900. In all fairness it must be added that the two cases are only roughly parallel, but in each instance there was tremendous pressure from the mob and an awareness in the White House of the political penalties and preferments involved. Someone has urged that we award medals to public servants who show courage above and beyond the call of politics.

Even if the President does not care about his own personal fortunes, as Cleveland notoriously did not, he cannot without the basest ingratitude be indifferent to the fortunes of the party that gave him immortality. Scores of Congressmen and other elected officials ride into office on the coattails of a popular President, and their careers are jeopardized if their titular leader needlessly antagonizes the ballot casters.

The Chief Executive is usually more exposed to public pressure regarding major issues of foreign policy than is the Congress and the State Department. He is one; they are many, and some of them are entrenched behind bureaucratic barriers.* His name and White House residence are well known, and the ordinary voter can easily send him a postal card, a letter, or a telegram. The names of the bureaucrats may not be known, and their addresses present difficulties. The President is elected every four years; the bureaucrats often have life tenure under civil service. The pressure may therefore converge upon the Executive Mansion with fearful force, as was notably true when McKinley had to take sleeping powders while pondering the fateful decision of war or peace with Spain.

A Frenchman in the days of the Revolution is supposed to have dashed to his window, when he heard the mob go roaring by, and to have cried: "There go my followers. I must follow them. I am their leader." Like this legendary Frenchman, the President must seem to follow public opinion, or at least not get too far out in front of it, for he will then be sniped at from the rear. Franklin Roosevelt's Quarantine Speech of 1937, defiantly delivered in the isolationist capital of America (Chicago), evoked such an uproar from the noninterventionist camp as to force a hasty retreat.

One British statesman, so it is said, would have made fewer political blunders "if he had only ridden more in omnibuses." The President does not ride the busses at all, and if the people have not indicated their desires, he must anticipate their reaction to his moves. His touch must be sure, for if he guesses wrong, his political life may be forfeited. Franklin Roosevelt had no directive from the American public when in 1938 he boldly declared at Kingston, Ontario, that the United States would help defend Canada against foreign invasion; nor when in the pre-Pearl Harbor days of 1941 he dramatically took over the defense of Iceland from Great Britain. But both of these strokes were aimed at the security of the United States, and the President assumed that the American people would support him, as the Gallup polls later revealed that they did in overwhelming measure. Roosevelt was a successful leader because he was generally clever enough to lead in a direction where the masses were willing to go.

4

The State Department likewise fears the hands that cast the ballots. If it blunders, the administration may be swept out, including the Secretary of State and other top men in the Department.

William H. Seward, who served with distinction during the Civil War,

---

* A strong president, like Franklin Roosevelt, is usually his own Secretary of State in critical matters, but this fact is not generally known. Much of the criticism directed at the State Department in the early 1940's could better have been aimed at the President.

was the first Secretary of State to conduct foreign relations with a keen eye to the necessity of informing and placating public opinion. He published diplomatic papers with unusual frequency, and inaugurated the annual series of official documents which for recency and completeness far surpasses anything put out by other foreign offices. His master stroke came in 1861 with the handling of the *Trent* affair. The United States naval officer who seized two Confederate commissioners from the British mail steamer *Trent* was clearly in the wrong, but his bold wrenching of the lion's tail was ecstatically popular in the North. The Lincoln administration dared not keep the prisoners, lest England declare war; it was unwilling to turn them loose, lest the populace get out of hand. But after passions had cooled, the Confederate envoys could be released, and public opinion was to some extent mollified when in a clever note Seward congratulated the British on having finally accepted the principles for which we had vainly fought them in 1812. Seward's specious discourse was clearly more of a sop to public opinion than a contribution to international law.

The Secretary of State and his associates need to know at all times what the public is thinking, for a policy cooked up in a closet and served suddenly to the people will often produce indigestion, mild or acute. The Department acknowledged the need of entering into more satisfactory diplomatic relations with the American masses when in 1944 it set up the Division of Public Liaison, which analyzes opinion polls, newspaper editorials, Congressional debates and other indexes of popular thinking. The policy officers of the State Department, rather than make a decision blindly, have on occasion arranged for confidential public opinion polls. The precaution is a wise one, for Congress, responding to the outraged voter, may cripple the Department by slashing the annual appropriation.

The average citizen, instead of complaining that the State Department has no policy, could better say: "Let's give the Department a policy." Public pressure can force a policy upon an unwilling administration, as was true of the neutrality legislation of the 1930's, but the administration can hardly force a major policy upon an unwilling people, as Franklin Roosevelt attempted to do in his Quarantine Speech. When there is a strong and articulate public opinion, the Department may move with the assurance that it will not be left out on the end of a limb. When opinion is confused, or when the issue is minor and no public opinion exists regarding it, the Department must make its decisions more or less blindly, and on a guess-and-pray basis. These are the occasions when it has the greatest latitude, and some seemingly minor decisions, regarding which the people were apathetic, have drawn us deeper and deeper into the international quicksands. Commitments in the 1940's to support the Nationalist government of China against the Communists, while fraught with grave dangers, passed virtually unnoticed in the United States.

Congressmen fear the electorate even more than the President does, for they have only two sure years of political life as compared with his four. If President McKinley kept his ear to the ground for rumblings from the grass-roots, Congressman Claghorn keeps his political antennae spread for every current from his constituents. The late Senator Norris records that in 1917 a number of his colleagues told him they did not favor the war resolution against Germany, but they dared not vote against it, so strong was the pressure from their districts. "The conscience of Congress," as one writer puts it, "is peculiarly responsive to large numbers." In more recent years it has also become markedly responsive to Gallup polls.

The national opinion surveys reveal that in the pre-1941 era the people were many months in advance of Congress on such burning issues as lifting the arms embargo and instituting compulsory military training. With the air of a discoverer, one recent writer concludes that during the years from 1935 to 1943 "public opinion was, on the average, between one and two years ahead of Congress." More than fifty years earlier, and without benefit of Gallup polls, Lord Bryce observed that public opinion "leads" the politicians, not vice versa. A Washington publisher has defined a politician as one who is only six months behind popular sentiment.

What is so surprising or reprehensible about these lags? It is certainly more in keeping with the democratic ideal that the people should push a reluctant Congress into war than that the Congress should pull a reluctant people into war. As the famous Wickersham report on prohibition concluded in 1931: "We expect legislation to conform to public opinion, not public opinion to yield to legislation." A national opinion poll in 1946 showed that only two out of ten people thought that congressmen should rely on their own judgment: they are public servants and they should obey the will of their masters as a beast of burden responds to the rein. (Actually, five out of ten citizens thought that the Congressmen did rely on their own judgment.)

The caution of the average congressman is quite understandable. He is badgered and confused by lobbyists, and he is often unable to distinguish public opinion from pressure opinion. When in doubt he had better play safe. He is also a candidate for reelection; the Gallup pollee is not. He must stand up and be counted when the votes are taken in Congress; the Gallup pollee remains anonymous, and for this reason can enjoy the luxury of a more unselfish or more moral attitude. As Francis Bacon long ago observed: "Do not wonder if the common people speak more truly than those of higher rank; for they speak with more safety."

A United States senator is in a much more comfortable position than his colleague in the House. He is elected for six years, and only one third of the entire membership of the Senate comes up for reelection every two years. The individual voters have notoriously short memories; it is difficult for them to hold a grudge against a senator for some vote on foreign policy, especially if they do not know his name, which often they do not. Domestic affairs are normally more important than foreign affairs to the ordinary American, and even if he dislikes the record of his senators on foreign policy, he may still vote for them if they are sound on free silver or the tariff on lemons. Sometimes the senator rises high enough in state politics (like Hiram W. Johnson of California) or serves long enough in the Senate (like William E. Borah of Idaho) to become an "institution," in which case the voters are apt to overlook his idiosyncrasies regarding such minor matters as foreign affairs, and keep him on for the good he has done. Many of the senators are from Southern poll tax districts, where less than the ordinary amount of interest is shown in foreign policy.

Ensconced behind the six-year term, the Senate has to a surprising degree been deaf to the voice of public opinion. "God made the world in seven days," remarked a South Carolina newspaper at the height of the League of Nations struggle in 1919, "but he didn't have a senate to deal with." Yet when an aroused citizenry speaks in stentorian tones, even the proud Solons come to heel. Although one senator sneered at the Kellogg-Briand pact of 1928 as an "international kiss," and another spoke of "throwing peace paper wads at the dogs of war," so great was the tidal wave of public approval that the treaty was passed with only one dissenting vote and with no formal reservations. When the American people in 1945 arose as almost one man to demand the United Nations Charter, isolationist senators grew quiet or clambered onto the bandwagon, and the much-feared opposition melted away before the hot breath of public opinion.

6

A purposeful public has on numerous occasions actually forced the President and the State Department to move, sometimes against their better judgment.

In 1803 a rising tide of Western resentment over the closure of the Mississippi prodded President Jefferson into a course that led to the purchase of Louisiana. In 1809, with public opinion so hostile that the very foundations of government trembled, Jefferson was forced to bring about a repeal of the embargo on shipping. In 1854 an enraged North halted the pro-Southern President Pierce in his design to wrest Cuba from the palsied grasp of Spain. In 1893 an aroused nation compelled Cleveland to abandon his plans to restore the dusky Hawaiian queen to her throne. In 1898 the war-mad masses forced the nation into an unnecessary clash with Spain, in spite of McKinley, Mark Hanna, and Big Business. (It was a victory for Main Street rather than Wall Street.) In 1921 a determined citizenry insisted upon the Washington Disarmament Conference, for which a lackadaisical President Harding received more than his just share of praise. In 1928 an organized and inspired public kicked Secretary Kellogg into immortality by forcing him to negotiate the Kellogg-Briand pact, for which at the outset he revealed little enthusiasm but for which he ultimately received the Nobel Peace Prize.

During the years from 1935 to 1937, a peace-obsessed public opinion drove through Congress and foisted upon the administration "permanent" neutrality legislation, as though one could legislate permanence in a world of change. In 1943, when Franklin Roosevelt shamelessly rewarded the Tammany politician "Ed" Flynn with the nomination of minister to Australia, a scandalized public, usually indifferent to such plum passing, compelled a withdrawal of the appointment. Australia, then defended by American boys and facing a Japanese invasion, was much too vital to be used as a political football; besides, many citizens confused Mr. Flynn with the actor of that name, whose alleged amours were enlivening the headlines of a prurient press.

The sovereign voter may not only compel his elected servants to do his bidding, but by defying his own government he may turn laws and treaties into dead letters, with consequent international friction.

Certain parts of the treaty of peace with England in 1783, specifically those having to do with debts and loyalists, were so unpopular in some sections of the country that they were openly nullified.* During the Texas revolution of 1835–1836, the Canadian rebellion of 1837, and the Irish-Fenian invasions of Canada in the 1860's and 1870's, public sympathy was so overwhelmingly favorable to the rebels that the federal officials found it difficult or impossible to enforce the neutrality laws. In some instances government agents brazenly joined with the revolutionists in violating the statutes which they had sworn to uphold. The mid-century American filibustering expeditions, notably those of López in Cuba and Walker in Central America, were warmly applauded in the expansionist and slave-holding South, so much so that the federal officials were unable to secure juries that would convict even the most flagrant violators of our national laws. A half-century later the people of the Pacific Coast, determined to hold the dike against an Oriental inundation, deliberately flouted the treaties and statutes of the United States so as to compel the Washington government to adopt exclusion.

The force of American opinion is felt not only at home but abroad. Foreign statesmen study our national crosscurrents with meticulous care, and not infrequently shorten sail rather than risk shipwreck.

The explosive rising of the Westerners in 1803 against the Spanish and French was not lost on Paris when Napoleon sold us Louisiana. American wrath in 1844 over British machinations in Texas was a clear storm warning that Downing Street had better go more slowly. The swelling demand to throw the French out of Mexico in 1867 presumably hastened their going; and the uproar against German brutality during the Venezuela intervention of 1902 certainly had a similar result. The British whitened their blacklist of

---

* A South Carolina Loyalist who had brutally murdered his Whig neighbors was so ill-advised as to return home, and when freed by the courts he was lynched by a mob, contrary to the treaty.

American firms in 1916 when they saw how offensive it was to us, and they came to terms with Ireland in 1921 partly, although not primarily, out of a desire to reduce the chronic inflammation of Anglo-American relations resulting from the Irish problem.

World War II came to an end with the American people quite favorably disposed to cooperation with the Soviet Union. But the Kremlin, either not recognizing the importance of American public opinion or not understanding how to deal with it, or possibly both, doggedly pursued a course which rapidly alienated American sympathy. President Truman's sensational proposal, in March, 1947, for support of Greece and Turkey received strong public backing, and the nation embarked upon a course which seemed inimical to the interests of the Soviets and possibly to the cause of world peace.

7

The President and the State Department have on occasion disregarded or even defied a strong majority opinion, but not frequently, and then not too openly. Such defiance is easier in war time, for the government can then hide behind the shield of secrecy. During World War II our continued relations with Fascist-tainted Vichy France, to say nothing of other dubious dealings, were highly unpopular among American liberals. But Washington apologized for these disturbing bedfellows by pleading military necessity, and as a consequence our people were more tolerant than they otherwise would have been.

If the public is rather evenly divided on a given issue, the government may occasionally support what appears to be a minority group. When President Washington angered the pro-French faction in America by issuing his neutrality proclamation in 1793, and when he infuriated the same partisans by sponsoring John Jay's unpopular treaty with Britain in 1795, he may have sided with the minority, but in any event the issue was close and the clatter great. The earlier incident, so Mark Sullivan surmises, inspired Kipling's immortal "If."

When the American people favor a proposed step by a large majority, but with only weak intensity, they may be disregarded by the State Department with relative impunity. After the Sino-Japanese "incident" flared forth in 1937, American sentiment promptly sided with underdog China, although there was a vast amount of indifference. But by 1939, when the issues had sharpened, the opinion polls showed that our people were only 2 per cent pro-Japanese while 74 per cent pro-Chinese. By 1940 the nation was 90 per cent favorable to an embargo on munitions for the Japanese aggressors.

This overwhelming display of solicitude did not stampede the Roosevelt administration, which stubbornly declined to halt the flow of war materials to Japan until three full years after the Marco Polo Bridge incident. The President reasoned that an invocation of the Neutrality Act of 1937 would cut off munitions from both Japan and China, and we wanted China to get her trickle. Also, as was later revealed, Roosevelt feared that strong measures against Japan would drive her into a premature descent upon the Dutch East Indies.

No democratic government on earth can long resist a 90 per cent public opinion, provided it is unified and intense. American sympathy for China was widespread but not intense; we sympathized but we sympathized luke-warmly. The Far East was far away and the Great Depression was close at hand. The Roosevelt administration was fully aware of these facts, and con-sequently felt free to pursue what it regarded as a farsighted program.

A major blunder of American foreign policy in the 1930's, certain critics have claimed, was committed by a designing pro-Catholic clique in the State Department. Putting their loyalty to the Pope first, they allegedly defied American opinion in 1937 by refusing to permit the shipment of arms to demo-cratic, Loyalist Spain, which as a consequence fell to the Fascist-supported Franco. If the will of our people had not been thwarted, so it is said, the Spanish preview of World War II would not have come off, and possibly not even World War II itself. The advocates of this interpretation point out that public opinion, according to the Gallup polls, rose from 65 per cent favorable to the Spanish Loyalists in 1937 to 76 per cent favorable by the end of 1938.

These figures are arrived at by the totally misleading practice of disregard-ing the neutral or no-opinion vote. Actually, in February, 1937, a Gallup poll discovered that the American people were 22 per cent pro-Loyalist, 12 per cent pro-Franco, 26 per cent neutral, and 40 per cent without opinion. The significant thing about this tally is not that the pro-Loyalists outnumbered the pro-Francoites by nearly two to one, but that a strong majority, despite the clamor of the pro-Franco Catholics and pro-Loyalist liberals, had no opinion.* They did not know; they did not care; they were confused as to what it was all about ("I haven't been able to figure it out"); they were con-vinced that no true democracy could come out of this Communist-Fascist cauldron; and above all they were still under the spell of the then current neutrality-at-any-price obsession. The Roosevelt administration, by declining to take active interventionist measures for one side or the other, was merely responding to the wishes of the people. Significantly, the joint resolution forbidding arms shipments to both Spanish loyalists and rebels passed Con-gress in 1937 by a count of 80 to 0 in the Senate and 403 to 1 in the House. This thunderous vote went even beyond the Gallup polls in revealing that we were not pro-Loyalist or pro-Franco but pro-stay out of war.

* The "no opinion" vote dropped from 66 per cent to 52 per cent by February, 1938, according to Gallup, but it was still a clear majority.

8

The dangers of flying in the face of public opinion are so apparent that in time of crisis the administration is strongly tempted to resort to deception rather than to defiance.

Some deception is comparatively harmless. When President Madison, in his message to Congress in 1815, congratulated the nation (and incidentally his own administration) on its glorious prosecution of the inglorious War of 1812, he was merely glossing over one of the most disgraceful episodes in our history. When Secretary Marcy in 1855 deliberately deleted damaging passages from his published correspondence describing the attempt to grab Cuba, he was merely trying to whiten his name with posterity, which he succeeded in doing until 1928, at which time a lynx-eyed scholar sharply blackened it. When President Wilson told an inquisitorial Senate committee in 1919 that he had never heard of the notorious secret treaties before reaching the Paris conference, he was presumably trying to smooth the path for the ratification of the Treaty of Versailles. Presidents have claimed achievements for themselves, such as the results of disarmament conferences, which a candid examination of the facts would not support. Theodore Roosevelt was a past master at leading and misleading public opinion by magnifying minor issues and minifying major ones. But such episodes were usually political gestures, designed to make or at least to save votes.

More serious was the deception practiced by President Polk in 1846. He ordered an armed detachment into an area in southern Texas to which the Texans had a highly debatable claim. The Mexicans were provoked into an attack, as Polk expected and rather hoped they would be, and then he triumphantly announced that "American blood" had been shed on "American soil." The people of the United States, even those of the opposition Whig party, arose to avenge this wanton assault, and we were off for the Halls of the Montezumas. Crude young Representative Abraham Lincoln repeatedly taunted the President for this fraud; he wanted to know the exact spot on *American* soil where blood had been shed. If Polk had been writing history instead of making it, he would have said that the Mexican troops were goaded into shedding the blood of those whom they regarded as invaders of their soil. This would have been a good deal nearer the truth than his wordy misrepresentation.

Franklin Roosevelt repeatedly deceived the American people during the period before Pearl Harbor. When he warned them against the aggressors, he was branded a sensationalist. When he pointed to the perils of storm-cellar neutrality, he was branded an interventionist. When he urged adequate armaments, he was branded a warmonger. He was faced with a terrible trilemma. If he let the people slumber in a fog of isolation, they might well fall prey to Hitler. If he came out unequivocally for intervention, he would be defeated in 1940, or shelved for a candidate more willing to let the masses enjoy their fool's paradise. If he was going to induce the people to move at all, he would have to trick them into acting for their best interests, or what he conceived to be their best interests. He was like the physician who must tell the patient lies for the patient's own good. Congresswoman Clare Boothe Luce missed the point entirely when she violently charged, in the campaign of 1944, that Roosevelt "lied us into a war because he did not have the political courage to lead us into it." The latter course would have been fool-hardy rather than courageous. The country was overwhelmingly noninter-ventionist to the very day of Pearl Harbor, and an overt attempt to lead the people into war would have resulted in certain failure and an almost certain ousting of Roosevelt in 1940, with a consequent defeat for his ultimate aims.

9

The embattled democracies in 1939 needed our munitions, and it was to our interests as well as theirs to lift the arms embargo. In a memorable mes-sage to the special session of Congress, Franklin Roosevelt urged that we return to international law, though actually we had never abandoned it: the arms embargo was purely domestic legislation. He dramatically declared that the embargo policy of Jefferson's day had resulted in the burning of the predecessor of the Capitol building from which he was then speaking, though actually the embargo-nonintercourse policy of that time came within a few days of preventing war. Like Polk in 1846, Roosevelt was making history rather than writing it, and he was doing it effectively. Dr. Gallup found a sharp increase of five points in the majority sentiment for lifting the arms embargo following the President's appearance before Congress.

Roosevelt's spectacular transfer of fifty overage United States destroyers to the British, in September, 1940, was difficult to defend on any legal grounds, but Attorney General Jackson dutifully built up a case, much of which hinged on the placement of a comma in the relevant federal statute. The destroyer deal, to say nothing of other acts of unneutrality, was further defended by a shyster-like appeal to an international law that had largely been trampled to death under the hobnailed boots of the belligerents. When the Lend-Lease Act was being debated in 1941, its foes insisted that the munitions would have to be convoyed and convoy would mean war. But the specter of convoy was then unpopular, and administration spokesmen brushed it aside: one thing at a time. Thus sympathy for the democracies led to Lend-Lease, Lend-Lease led to convoy, convoy led to shooting, and shooting led to war.

The noninterventionists cried out against war, and because they were in a strong majority some color of legality had to be found for every question-able step that was taken. Lend-Lease almost certainly would not have been passed, at least not as it was and when it was, if the people could have foreseen that the scheme would lead so inexorably to hostilities.* After the bill was safely approved, Roosevelt himself quietly issued the orders to convoy.

The President was also anxious to make it appear, again with the isolationist masses in view, that the aggression was coming from Germany. After a U-boat had fired two torpedoes at the United States destroyer *Greer*, Roosevelt went on the air and declared that henceforth the Navy would repel the piratical acts of these seagoing "rattlesnakes" and defend freedom of the seas by firing first. (Actually, freedom of the seas in the American tradition was not involved at all.) Again Roosevelt's dramatic methods brought results; Dr. Gallup found a strong majority in favor of shoot-at-sight. Yet more than a month after the event the Navy Department revealed that the *Greer* had been trailing the U-boat for three and one-half hours and broadcasting the latter's position to nearby British destroyers when the submarine turned and attacked.

Roosevelt either knew these facts or he did not know them. If he knew them, he deliberately deceived the American people; if he did not, he handled a critical situation with inexcusable precipitancy.

A president who cannot entrust the people with the truth betrays a certain lack of faith in the basic tenets of democracy. But because the masses are notoriously shortsighted, and generally cannot see danger until it is at their throats, our statesmen are forced to deceive them into an awareness of their own long-run interests. This is clearly what Roosevelt had to do, and who shall say that posterity will not thank him for it?

Deception of the people may in fact become increasingly necessary, unless we are willing to give our leaders in Washington a freer hand. In the days of the horse and buggy we could jog along behind our billowy barriers with relative impunity, but in the days of the atomic bomb we may have to move more rapidly than a lumbering public opinion will permit. Just as the yielding of some of our national sovereignty is the price that we must pay for effective international organization, so the yielding of some of our democratic control of foreign affairs is the price that we may have to pay for greater physical security.

* A majority favored Lend-Lease, no doubt for defensive purposes; but a majority of those with opinions believed that it would not result in having to send an American army abroad.

CHAPTER TWO

CHILDREN OF THE CRUCIBLE

"America is God's Crucible, the great Melting-Pot where all the races of Europe are melting and re-forming! . . . God is making the American."—ISRAEL ZANGWILL, 1908

1

THE MAN IN THE STREET either came to America from a foreign land or is descended from men and women who did. If he is white, his forebears emigrated from Europe or its environs. If he is black, they were imported from Africa. If he is yellow, they came from Asia. If he is red, they also came from Asia, across what is now the Bering Strait, millennia ago.* But whether white, black, yellow, or red, Americans are all transplanted Asiatics, Africans, or Europeans, predominantly Europeans.

This is a fact of supreme importance to anyone who would understand the logic and illogic of American foreign policy. The famed melting pot has now bubbled along merrily for many decades, but even today about one American in four was born abroad or has at least one parent who was born abroad. And these figures do not take into account the undeniable influence of foreign-born grandparents. There is still much force in the old saying: "Scratch an American and you will find a foreigner." Sometimes one does not even have to scratch him.

The United States, more than any other great power, is a racial league of nations on a continental scale. Woodrow Wilson not only regarded America as a living demonstration of the workability of his hemispheric League of Nations, but he glimpsed a divine purpose in the American experiment. "America," he said, "was created to unite mankind." But the United States failed mankind in 1920, partly because forces less than divine were pursuing selfish ends, and partly because, as the builders of the tower of Babel discovered, in a multiplicity of tongues there is much confusion. The Chicago *Tribune* in 1921, pointing to more than 800,000 foreign-born Chicagoans, queried: "Why go abroad for a League of Nations?"

The foreign daubs on the national canvas are not only numerous and variegated, but relatively fresh. As age is reckoned among nations, the United States is hardly more than a lusty adolescent. When George Washington took the presidential oath in 1789, the infant republic numbered but 4,000,-000 souls; scarcely more than a century and a half later our population had skyrocketed to some 140,000,000. The first great increment of post-1789 immigration, that from Ireland and Germany, was not thrown upon our shores until the 1840's; and the tidal wave from southern Europe did not begin to

* The part-Indian Will Rogers liked to twit the General Society of Mayflower Descendants by saying that his ancestors greeted theirs at Plymouth Rock.

swirl past the Statue of Liberty until the 1880's. Within the memory of men still living the great bulk of European immigration reached the American haven.

Why did they come? Mainly because the "great caravan of the discontented" was made up of unfortunates who were maladjusted or otherwise unhappy. Most of them, underprivileged and land-starved, no doubt sought economic betterment in the Land of the Second Chance. Those of their countrymen who had enough of this world's goods were generally content to stay where they were. "Dukes don't emigrate," so the saying goes, except when fleeing the guillotine. Others were washed upon our shores by the wars and revolutions of Europe. Irish victims of British tyranny or Jewish victims of Russian butcheries saw in America the historic "asylum of the oppressed of every nation." * The bitterness that they brought in their hearts, despite the magic of the melting pot, has not completely faded away.

The undigested immigrant has been made more indigestible by his natural tendency to herd with fellow nationals in already stinking slums. For such persons a smelting pot rather than a melting pot is needed. New York City, which has been jokingly referred to as Uncle Sam's most troublesome island population, is perhaps the most polyglot center in the world today. It boasts more Italians than Rome, one half again as many Irishmen as Dublin, and four times as many Jews as Palestine. "We would not advise Karl and Zita to come to America," remarked a Southern newspaper in 1921, "but they might do very well in New York."

The transplanting of Jewish ghettos and Little Italys to New York and other eastern areas has enabled foreign groups to maintain their identity with great persistence, to support foreign newspapers and radio programs, to organize mass meetings for transatlantic causes, and above all to use their voting power to club public officials into doing their will. In concentration there is strength.

2

The foreigner in American diplomatic history is commonly referred to as "the hyphenate." The term was early seized upon by Theodore Roosevelt, who in a speech in 1895 inveighed against "the hyphenated Americans—the German-American, the Irish-American, or the native-American." "Be American, pure and simple," he exhorted.

Hyphenism rose to a high pitch after the outbreak of war in 1914, when the nationals of the Allied Powers and the Central Powers turned America into a verbal battleground. "United we stand, hyphenated we fall," sagely observed the Toledo *Blade*. Woodrow Wilson was well aware of this weak-

---

* In 1946, forty-eight Estonians, unwilling to endure Soviet tyranny, daringly crossed the Atlantic to America in small boats. Their entry was illegal, but rather than return them for punishment, President Truman, in keeping with American tradition, arranged to have them remain.

ness, for a few weeks before the shot at Sarajevo he told a Washington audience: "Some Americans need hyphens in their names, because only part of them has come over; but when the whole man has come over, heart and thought and all, the hyphen drops of its own weight out of his name." The red-blooded Theodore Roosevelt, for one of the few times in his life, agreed with Wilson. "When two flags are hoisted on the same pole," he insisted, "one is always hoisted undermost. The hyphenated American always hoists the American flag undermost."

The plight of the hyphenate has seldom aroused the sympathy of those other Americans whose fathers were fortunate enough to come on earlier if smaller ships. The immigrant is a stranger in a strange land. Set down in a country with a different language, folkways, traditions, aspirations, prejudices, and social conventions, he is expected to blend his soul with that of an alien people, and feel no stirrings of interest in the fate of the Old Country. Usually relegated to the status of a second-class citizen, frequently segregated in slums with expatriates of his own nationality, often cheated and bilked by American sharpers, always severed from his native land and not fully adopted by the land of his choice, he may be pardoned for developing a sense of lonesomeness and homesickness which cause him to minimize the unwholesome features of his native hearth while magnifying the attractive. The wonder is that he has not been more securely attached to his ancestral womb by an umbilical hyphen three thousand miles long.*

Millions of birds-of-passage immigrants have come to the promised land of America with no thought but to make money and return, whether to Sicily as wealthy bootleggers or to China as retired laundrymen. Millions have thus returned, and while in America they have felt no urge to sever the ties of their foreign allegiance. Theodore Roosevelt once referred to such people as merely changing "hog-troughs."

But the average immigrant came with the intention of shaking the dust of Europe off his feet forever. He had the makings of a loyal citizen, but in many cases even he had immigrated physically rather than spiritually. "You can take a man out of a country," someone has said, "but you can't take a country out of a man." George Washington voiced this distrust when in 1777 he requested only "natives" for his bodyguard, an order which apparently is the basis for the better known: "Put none but Americans on guard tonight."

Human nature being what it is, millions of imported Americans cannot be indifferent to the fate of the Old Country when the mother continent becomes cursed with one of its periodic convulsions. A large proportion of our hyphenates are refugees from traditionally troubled lands, such as Ireland and Poland. This partly explains why they came in large numbers, why so many of them were well schooled agitators, and why an upheaval abroad brings

* On Labor Day, 1942, the Washington Office of War Information arranged for broadcasts from Moscow, Vt., to the older Moscow. Similar messages went from Athens, Pa.; Amsterdam, N.Y.; Warsaw, N.C.; Oslo, Minn.; Berlin, Pa., and other American namesakes of European capitals.

a corresponding if less violent upheaval in the United States. Some phases of Europe's most important political, diplomatic, and military battles have been fought on our shores, three thousand miles away.

When the European volcano erupted in 1914, German-Americans urged a course upon the Washington government favorable to the Fatherland; Anglo-Americans urged a course favorable to the Mother England. When Czechoslovakia was betrayed to Hitler in 1938, Czechs in the United States reacted bitterly; when Finland was attacked by Russia in 1939, Finns in the United States sought intervention for their homeland. After the outbreak of World War II in 1939, the United States proved to be an ideal base from which the various governments-in-exile, such as the Polish, the Dutch, and the Czech, could gather supplies and distribute propaganda.*

3

We can sympathize with the solicitude of the hyphenate for the fate of his native land, but we can hardly applaud his actions when they are designed to embroil the land of his adoption.

The immigrant presumably comes here because of all the nations on earth he feels that America has the most to offer. This is what one wit had in mind when he said that immigration is the sincerest form of flattery. The hyphen is a guest within our house; he accepts our hospitality. Common decency decrees that one refrain from embarrassing one's host or using his house for plots that will bring it down in flames. More than that, as Woodrow Wilson discerned, the immigrant has a special sense of obligation. The native-born American lives here because he has no choice; the foreign-born American lives here because he made a choice. Disloyalty is even more unlovely in the immigrant than in the native.

But when the melting pot bubbles, often with European faggots under its bottom, the scum rises to the top. America is the land of pressure groups, and among the more powerful and militant organizations are those formed by hyphenates to promote some foreign cause. In many instances the hyphenated American minorities are better organized to achieve their special purposes than are native American majorities. It is not unusual for the Washington government, under such compulsion, to make decisions that are more conducive to the interests of foreigners than of Americans.

The foreign born not only recognize the value of organization but appreciate the potency of the ballot box. A study made in 1944 revealed that proportionately more hyphenates go to the polls than do native Americans, among whom the percentage of stay-at-home voters is notoriously high.

Why this unusual interest? First, the foreigner, being a member of a

* The foundations of the Czechoslovakian Republic were laid during 1917–1918 by Czech expatriates in the United States, many of whom were concentrated in the Pittsburgh and New York areas.

minority group, is acutely conscious of having to use every effective tool for the protection of his interests. Second, the novelty of casting the ballot, and the newness of one's responsibility as a citizen, combine to bring out the vote. The average native American—preoccupied, confused, indifferent— is more inclined to remain at home.

4

The Germans are numerically the most important non-English element in our population. The census of 1940 listed 5,236,000 born in Germany, or with at least one parent born in Germany.* Although intelligent, energetic, and somewhat clannish, the Germans have generally exerted less influence on the Washington government than the Irish, whom they outnumber, primarily because their strength is diffused throughout the nation.

The German-Americans, though active in domestic politics, did not bring powerful influence to bear upon the conduct of our foreign relations until 1914. The explanation is that Germany did not become unified until as late as 1871, and she avoided protracted general wars until the guns went off in 1914. Until then, disputes between the Fatherland and the United States were generally lacking in headline importance.

After the brutal invasion of Belgium in 1914, the great body of German-Americans made no attempt to conceal their sympathies. So noisy were their demonstrations that the Houston *Post* could observe: "Germany seems to have lost all of her foreign possessions with the exception of Milwaukee, St. Louis and Cincinnati." Vociferous German groups in America demanded of the Washington government that it break the British blockade, embargo the shipment of munitions to the Allies, and otherwise assist the Prussian war lords. The *Wall Street Journal* was provoked to remark: "Our citizens of German extraction could do with a little more extracting;" while the Brooklyn *Eagle* concluded: "When your true Hun leaves the Fatherland he doesn't emigrate; he hyphenates."

The high command in Berlin was evidently counting on Germans in America to neutralize the United States if the latter should enter the war, for Foreign Minister Zimmermann in Berlin told our Ambassador Gerard that there were "500,000 German reservists who would rise in arms. . . ." Gerard's ringing answer (as recorded by himself) was: "We have five hundred thousand and one lamp posts in America, and that is where the German reservists will find themselves if they try any uprising."

When the clash finally came, the German-Americans showed a surprising loyalty to their adopted land. The more rabid hyphenates wisely grew silent or were bulldozed into submission. The German-language press was viewed with understandable suspicion by native Americans, and the suppression of some of these journals prompted the Brooklyn *Eagle* to say: "More than one

* Population figures herein given are generally taken from the 1940 census.

German-language paper has got out its last sedition." A considerable number of German hyphenates, forbidden to praise the Fatherland, sought satisfaction in abusing the British, who have always been fair game in America. After the Armistice the German-American pack was soon in full cry, and the baying was no less violent for having been so long pent up. The leaders concentrated their attacks on the punitive features of the Treaty of Versailles and the allegedly British-dominated League of Nations. The members of the Senate, notably those from the Middle West, were not unaware of the voting power that lay behind these demands. By 1921 the German-Americans had so far recovered their voices that they could hold a huge mass meeting in New York to protest against alleged outrages committed by French colored troops upon the German women of the Rhineland.

As the next two decades passed, and as the premonitory rumblings of World War II could be heard, one needed no clairvoyant gifts to perceive that the German-American problem was far less formidable than it had been in 1914. Tens of thousands of native Germans had died; others had been assimilated; others had been excluded by the immigration barriers of the 1920's; others with Nazi leanings had left for the Reich; and others, comprising the great body of German-Americans, were repelled by Hitler's brutalitarianism. The pro-Nazi Bundist movement in the United States, despite its noise and fanaticism, attracted so few followers as to be regarded as something of a joke.

But the German-Americans were still to some extent German at heart. Public opinion polls from 1937 to 1940 showed that in comparison with other Americans they were somewhat more favorable to a return of German colonies to Hitler; less favorable to a declaration of war on Germany; more favorable to a retention of the arms embargo; more inclined to believe the news reports from Berlin; more convinced that Germany would win the war; more desirous of running food through the British blockade to German-occupied countries. The tales in 1945 of German atrocities at corpse camps like Buchenwald and Belsen were received with the most doubt in those areas of the Middle West where German-Americans were concentrated. In all these opinion polls the German vote was not more than slightly out of line with the national average, but the residuum of attachment to the Fatherland was unmistakable.

The behavior of this huge hyphenate group has on the whole been gratifyingly good, particularly when we consider that our two greatest wars have been fought with Germany. The conduct of German-Americans in 1917–1918 was commendable; in 1941–1945 it was almost beyond reproach. In these two great acid tests, the Germans have done much to vindicate our faith in the melting pot.

5

By far the most conspicuous hyphenate group until at least 1921 was composed of the Irish-Americans. Less numerous than the Germans, they were more vocal, more zealous, more bitter. Their not unjustified venom against England is a recurring motif in American history.

A sprinkling of Irish refugees fled to America after the bloody failure of the rebellion of 1798, and a number of them became newspaper editors, in which capacity they belabored Britain. But the Emerald Isle did not move across the Atlantic until the 1840's, when the terrible potato blight drove tens of thousands of starving Irishmen to the New World. Embittered, destitute, and crowded into the slums of Boston and New York, they overtaxed the assimilative capacity of the melting pot. Long before the present decade there were more persons of Irish blood in America than in Ireland.

These fugitives from Erin's Isle were for various reasons able to exercise an influence out of all proportion to their numbers. They herded into politically important eastern cities, where in close local or national elections they held the balance of power. The leaders of our great political parties, emulating the male black widow spider, felt an irresistible impulse to woo the Irish vote, while at the same time fearing it. The Hibernian hyphenates pressed their advantage without mercy, tyrannizing over office holders and demanding (and getting) anti-British demagoguery.

The Irish-Americans had a genius for political organization (as Tammany Hall attests), a well developed capacity for politics at the local level, and few scruples about using the ballot box for their own ends. "Vote early and often" was a well recognized practice of the Irish wardheeler. (In fairness it must be added that corruption in America was not a monopoly of immigrants.)

The Irish also had an unparalleled capacity for keeping alive the centuries-old hatred of England. The atrocities perpetrated by Cromwell's troops some three hundred years earlier seemed as fresh in Irish memories as the verdure of their native isle. Hatred of the English was one thing that could be transplanted across the Atlantic without deterioration, and the Hibernians of Boston have often been described as more Irish than the Irish. As far as England was concerned, once an Irishman, always an Irishman, even though a naturalized American citizen.

The Irish-Americans had a Cause—the independence of Ireland from her oppressor—and they agitated unceasingly until 1921, when the goal was finally attained. The six counties of Protestant North Ireland remained British, and although the Irish-Irish still demand this unredeemed birthright, the Irish-Americans generally feel that the great battle has been won. But until 1921 the clamor for independence never abated on either side of the Atlantic.

Finally, the Irish Paddies loved agitation, and were vociferous in promoting it in a rich brogue, especially when under the spell of the proverbial flask.

"The Irishman is never at peace except when he is fighting," runs an old Irish saying.

The net result of all this was an oversized hornets' nest. The German-Americans naturally reacted when Germany was in serious trouble, but the Irish-Americans made it their business to stir up trouble between the United States and Great Britain with the avowed purpose of snatching Irish independence from the fiery furnace of an Anglo-American conflict. "England's danger is Ireland's opportunity" is an ancient Irish proverb; and "professional Irishmen" on both sides of the Atlantic sought to create danger if none existed. The sons of the shamrock had no scruples about embroiling their adopted land if they could free their native land, and the same spirit could be found among second- or third-generation Americans born of Irish parents. The Irish Mr. Dooley (Finley Peter Dunne) was wont to refer to "Americans of all nationalities"; and Thomas Fitch once heard an Irishman say: "Every man loves his native land whether he was born there or not."

The Irish-Americans undoubtedly had well founded grievances against Great Britain, and they carried on their crusade in the British Dominions as well as in the United States. But it was one thing to agitate for their aspirations under the British Union Jack, and quite another to abuse the privileges of American citizenship.

6

A quick glance at a few of the more dramatic episodes in Anglo-American relations will illuminate the observations just made.

At the close of the American Civil War, Irish Fenians in the United States brazenly raised money and drilled recruits for an invasion of Canada. So awesome was the Irish vote, and so bitter was Northern feeling against the British aristocrats for their recent sympathy toward the South, that the federal authorities interfered with the Fenian invasions only belatedly and half-heartedly.

In 1886 the Senate refused to include dynamiters in an extradition treaty with England. Thus we would shield Irish-Americans who, unworthily donning the disguise of United States citizenship, returned to Erin, dynamited public buildings, and then fled to the protective petticoats of their adopted mother.

In 1888, when President Cleveland sent a sensational anti-British message to Congress, he was deluged with telegrams from the Rileys, Murphys, and Ryans, who blessed him for his "devotion to old Erin." In the same year the platforms of both political parties expressed sympathy for Irish home rule, as though that were legitimate business of the United States.° During the ensuing presidential campaign the high-tariff Republicans sought Irish votes

---

° In 1888, when a visiting British statesman, Joseph Chamberlain, became engaged to the daughter of Cleveland's Secretary of War, the secret had to be carefully guarded until after the presidential election of that year, lest the Irish vote be alienated.

by accusing the low-tariff Democrats of being tools of free-trade England. The charge was repeatedly made: "The only time England can use an Irishman is when he emigrates to America and votes for free trade."

In 1896 the Republicans solicited Irish support for their presidential candidate, William McKinley, with a pamphlet entitled: *How McKinley Is Hated in England.*

In 1897 Irish pressure contributed powerfully to the defeat of the Anglo-American general arbitration treaty, which, through Hibernian spectacles, looked like the beginnings of an alliance with Erin's oppressor. Among the antitreaty lobbyists in the Senate building on the day of the final vote was Michael Davitt, one of the most active Irish nationalists in the British Parliament.

At the turn of the century an alliance with Britain was much discussed, but the very thought of such a marriage was enough to cause Irish-Americans to become apoplectically profane. Secretary of State Hay complained in 1900 that every senator whom he met burst out: "For God's sake, don't let it appear we have any understanding with England." Hay felt that his loyalty was suspected because he did not say: "To hell with the Queen!" at every breath. When Queen Victoria died the next year, the Tammany mayor of New York won Irish acclaim when he resolutely refused to lower the city flag to half staff. Those who did not follow his example in other cities were branded as "half-mast mayors" and marked well for future reprisals at the polls.

The dignified United States Senate in 1919 overwhelmingly and gratuitously passed a resolution looking toward Irish home rule. The British press was calloused to this type of Yankee impertinence, but if Parliament had reciprocated by passing a resolution in favor of Philippine home rule a torrent of denunciation would have gushed from the American press. As the Dallas *News* slyly remarked in 1921: "We are so interested in the independence of Ireland that the Philippines will have to wait."

The mountebank Big Bill Thompson won the mayoralty of Chicago by an anti-British appeal to Irish and other foreign voters. He promised to purge the textbooks of pro-British influences, and to make the King of England keep his "blasted snout" out of Chicago politics, as though the royal nose would voluntarily seek the atmosphere of the stockyards. This "Third War with England" was greeted elsewhere with derision, and the Detroit *News* proposed as a history questionnaire: "What British propagandist was it who disguised himself as Mrs. O'Leary's cow and started the Chicago fire?"

7

Irish-American vigilantes have been traditionally on the lookout to see that American ambassadors and other spokesmen in England have not expressed sentiments too friendly to the Mother Country. Ambassadors Bayard

and Page both got into hot water with the Irish for their Anglophile effu-
sions,* but the restive-mouthed Admiral Sims rather overdid things in 1921
when in a London speech he condemned the obstructionism of the Irish-
Americans during the recent war. He charged:

> They are like zebras, either black horses with white stripes, or white horses with
> black stripes. But we know they are not horses—they are asses, but each of these
> asses has a vote, and there are lots of them. One inconvenience of a republic is that
> these jackass votes must be catered to.

The resulting Irish uproar was a thing to behold, and the outspoken Admiral
was promptly recalled to receive his official reprimand.

The Sims fusillade was fired in the year when Ireland attained home rule,
and since then, with the disappearance of the Cause and with the simmering
of the melting pot, the power and fervor of the Irish hyphenate have waned.
Prime Minister De Valera and his seemingly pro-Nazi neutrality were unpopular even in certain Irish-American quarters, particularly after Pearl
Harbor. Yet various public opinion polls taken during World War II revealed
that Irish-Americans were substantially more Ireland-conscious than the
average American. Early in 1942 Dr. Gallup reported that while only half
of our citizens were aware of Eire's neutral status, over 80 per cent of the
Irish-Americans were properly informed. Irish-Americans were consistently
and markedly less favorable than the rank and file to the following propositions: that Eire provide Britain with submarine bases; that De Valera dismiss
Japanese and German agents; and that Eire enter the war at the side of
England. One Irish pollee declared in 1941 that the German-British fight was
only twenty-five years old, but that the Irish-British fight had been going on
"for near 700 years. That's what we Irish got to remember."

The significant thing about these figures is not that the Irish-Americans
were ahead of the average American in their sympathy for Ireland, but that
in every one of these instances an Irish-American majority was ultimately
found on the same side as the larger American majority.

The persistence of a certain amount of sentiment for Eire, though waning,
is to be expected. In 1946 a number of Irish-American organizations went
on record as opposing the huge loan to Great Britain. The trend seems to be
for the Hibernian organizations gradually to lose their identity and to merge
with those other groups whose chief stock in trade is anti-British agitation.
The day may not be far distant when the Irish vote, in matters pertaining to
foreign affairs, will have completely lost its fearsome effect on public servants
in Washington.

* A safe rule for American envoys was to keep quiet, speak on innocuous subjects, or insult
the British. When Bayard in 1895 made the mistake of expressing friendly sentiments, he
was branded by one Buffalo paper as "the most popular Englishman ever born in the
United States."

CHAPTER THREE

CRACKS IN THE MELTING POT

"[The question is] whether . . . we are to continue as a separate
nation at all or whether we are to become merely a huge polyglot
boarding-house and counting house, in which dollar-hunters of
twenty different nationalities scramble for gain, while each really
pays his soul-allegiance to some foreign power."
—THEODORE ROOSEVELT, 1917

1

THE GERMAN-AMERICANS and the Irish-Americans, while the most
important hyphenate elements in the past, are becoming increasingly less
numerous and hence less influential. The spotlight has been or is being stolen
from them by other groups, most of whom came to America within the past
fifty or sixty years. Conspicuous among these are the Jewish-Americans, who
in some ways are the most formidable foreign bloc in the United States today.

The Jews in America number about 4,700,000 or approximately one third
of the world's Jewish community. Five boroughs of New York City alone
contain about 2,000,000, or four times the Jewish population of Palestine.
The American metropolis is today the undisputed capital of world Jewry.

The Jew is a racial rather than a national hyphen, if one may use the
term "race" popularly. The German-American completely loses his European
traits and identity by the second or third generation, but not so the Jewish-
American. His grandparents may have been Polish-Americans or Russian-
Americans or German-Americans, but he is still a Jew and will continue to
be one. There is and can be little crossing over the racial line. In this sense
the Jewish hyphenate group is the only one with an assured future.

The Jewish-Americans are a powerful voting bloc, partly because the mass
of them are concentrated in important urban areas, and partly because they
are a self-conscious minority and hence keenly alive to any developments,
at home or abroad, that will bring further woe to them or to their compatriots.
Like the Irish, to whom they present a number of striking parallels, they have
a Cause—in this case the cause of a pitilessly persecuted minority. Specifically, the Jewish-Americans seek to allay anti-Semitism at home, of which
there is a disquieting amount; to succor persecuted brethren abroad; and to
set up—at least this is the goal of the Zionist faction—a new Canaan in Palestine. Their influence, though substantial, is less effective than it would be
if they had the talent of the Irish for political organization, leadership, and
agitation.

Some persecution of European Jews continued throughout the nineteenth
century, but in the early 1900's a series of bloody pogroms—bloody at least
for those times—broke out in Rumania and Russia. Jews fortunate enough
to be in America were naturally anxious to relieve the distress of relatives

abroad, and they deluged the Washington government with appeals for intervention. If Rumanians wanted to lynch fellow countrymen of Jewish extraction, that was no more the business of the United States, from a narrowly legalistic point of view, than it was the business of Rumania if Americans wanted to lynch fellow countrymen of Negro extraction. But the Congressional elections of 1902 were approaching, and the Jewish vote was coveted, so Secretary Hay sent a protest to Bucharest which was widely read in American synagogues and which may have helped the Republican ticket. Hay cynically wrote: "The Hebrews—poor dears! all over the country think we are bully boys."

In 1911, following refusals by the Russian government to honor passports issued to American Jews, the United States abruptly terminated its commercial treaty with Russia, a slap that was administered in response to Jewish-American pressure. The irritated Russian Foreign Minister stated that if the Americans felt so strongly about anti-Semitism, he was willing to consider transferring all Jews in Russia to the United States.

2

The horrible mistreatment of the Jews by the Nazis made all previous butcheries look like mere bargain-counter brawls. A public opinion poll in the United States during 1935 disclosed that, especially among Jews, the German government was the least popular in the world. The usual pressure was brought to bear on the State Department for intervention; Mayor La Guardia of New York (himself of Jewish extraction) stirred up an international incident when in 1937 he publicly branded Hitler as "that brown-shirted fanatic"; and after unprecedentedly ferocious attacks on German Jews in 1938, President Roosevelt publicly denounced Germany and recalled the United States ambassador from Berlin "for consultation." These latest outrages caused support in America for a boycott of German goods to jump sharply, and one national poll found that disapproval of Nazi atrocities was almost unanimous.

But humanity, unlike charity, often begins abroad rather than at home. On the question of admitting some of these persecuted Jews to the United States, one public opinion poll in 1938 found the nation less than 8 per cent favorable, although Jewish-Americans were 70 per cent favorable. The opposition among native Americans may be explained by active or latent anti-Semitism, and more particularly by overcrowded occupations and continuing unemployment. Surprisingly enough, one fourth of the Jewish-Americans were opposed to unbarring the immigration gates. They no doubt were worried about unemployment and the danger of provoking a really serious anti-Semitic movement in the United States. "The world is divided into two groups of nations," as Dr. Chaim Weizmann is alleged to have said, "those which want to expel the Jews and those which do not want to receive them."

After the outbreak of World War II, Jewish-Americans were conspicuous among those urging interventionist measures against Nazi Germany. The isolationist Charles A. Lindbergh, speaking at Des Moines, Iowa, in 1941, listed the three most influential warmongering groups as the Roosevelt administration, the Jews, and the British. A Gallup poll put the Jews in fifth place, although only one respondent in sixteen even mentioned them.

When the war ended in 1945, Jewish interest in a national haven in Palestine reached a new high point. Eight out of ten Jewish-Americans, as contrasted with three out of ten native Americans, were aware of the political status of the Holy Land. In the late spring of 1946, we were overwhelmingly in favor of having 100,000 Jewish refugees enter Palestine, but by a similarly overwhelming majority we were unwilling to help the British troops protect them against the infuriated Arabs. We much preferred to let the infant United Nations organization grasp the Palestinian nettle.

The British found it desirable to exclude crowded Jewish refugee ships from Palestine waters, within sight of the Promised Land, and these heart-rending expulsions aroused much bitterness in America. On October 4, 1946, at the height of the Congressional campaign, President Truman issued a statement urging the immediate admission of 100,000 Jews to Palestine. British Foreign Secretary Bevin, who later claimed that he was making encouraging progress in composing Arab-Jew differences, begged that Truman's pronouncement be withheld, but he was informed that if it was not issued Thomas E. Dewey, New York gubernatorial aspirant, would come out with a "competitive statement." Dewey, presumably not unaware of his large Jewish constituency, actually trumped Truman's card two days later when he demanded the admission of "several hundreds of thousands." Some months thereafter Bevin explained with much heat to Parliament that his promising negotiations had been ruined by American local politics. One may doubt this oversimplified explanation of the breakdown without in the slightest doubting the injection of our politics. There was something grimly humorous about attempting to force Jews whom we would not receive upon Arabs who wanted them even less than we did, and with far better reasons.

The air was still ringing with charges of British brutality and perfidy when, in the summer of 1946, the proposed loan of $3,750,000,000 to Great Britain came before the House of Representatives for a final vote. A group of Jewish-American congressmen, among whom Representative Celler of New York was conspicuous, spectacularly turned against the bill. Other Jewish leaders, like Representative Sol Bloom of New York, while in no way condoning British policy in Palestine, insisted that the loan had nothing to do with Zionism, and that the best interests of the United States required affirmative action. The bill was finally approved despite Jewish opposition, but if the result had been otherwise we would have had a striking illustration of the harm that can be done when the hyphenate hoists his own flag above that of his adopted country.

3

Italian-Americans constitute our largest foreign-born immigrant group, and including those with at least one parent born abroad, they rank next to the Germans as the largest hyphenate element. But their influence has not been in proportion to their numbers, partly because of diffusion, lack of organization, and the absence of able leadership. Most important of all, they have revealed a less intense interest in the fate of the Old Country than have some other hyphenates. Relations between Italy and the United States have generally been good, or at any rate uneventful, and the Italian-Americans have therefore been under little compulsion to make their voices heard.

The lynching of eleven Italian Blackhanders in New Orleans (1891) deeply angered Italian-Americans, but the tempest quickly blew over. Italy and the United States were wartime associates from 1917–1918, but Wilson's inability to satisfy Italian Adriatic aspirations aroused wide hostility to him and the League of Nations. A conspicuous leader of the protesting Italian-Americans was the fiery Fiorello H. La Guardia, of Jewish-Italian descent, destined to be the "Little Flower" and mayor of New York. Senator Henry Cabot Lodge of Massachusetts, the "scholar in politics," likewise espoused the claims of Italy to Yugoslavia's port of Fiume, possibly with his huge Italian-American constituency in mind. He was advised by his friend Henry White that Yugoslavia's claim was much sounder; but there were not enough Yugoslavs in Massachusetts to make it politically profitable for the scholarly senator to see the error of his ways.

The rise of the strutting Mussolini in the 1920's and 1930's aroused a feeling of satisfaction and pride among a vast number of Italian-Americans. Studies made of the Boston Italians reveal that they listened to the short-wave radio broadcasts from Rome, swallowed Fascist propaganda wholesale, and made heroes of the Pope, the King, Mussolini, Colonel Charles A. Lindbergh, and Senator Burton K. Wheeler. These American isolationist leaders were popular because they favored leaving Europe to the tender mercies of the dictators. Yet when war came in 1939 the Italian-Americans seem not to have brought any great amount of pressure on Washington to pursue a noninterventionist policy favorable to Italy.

While the Italian-Americans were not violent in their pro-Axis sympathies, they revealed, like the Germans, a substratum of attachment to the Old Country. In 1939 and 1940 they ranked with the Germans and Russians as the groups least desirous of having the United States declare war on Germany; and they ranked with the Germans as the group least willing to have the arms embargo repealed in favor of the democracies. After Mussolini stabbed France in the back and came in for the jackal's share of the loot, a plurality of Italian-Americans believed that the British would ultimately triumph, although a considerable sprinkling, larger in fact than could be found anywhere else, thought that Italy would win.

After Pearl Harbor, unnaturalized Italians in America became enemy aliens, but their conduct was so exemplary that within a year they were relieved of the customary restrictions. Large numbers of Italian-Americans now disapproved of Mussolini and his ill-starred alliance with Hitler, and for this reason the Roosevelt administration had to move slowly when in 1943 it recognized the Fascist-blackened Badoglio government. Roosevelt also deemed it necessary, with the Italian and Catholic voters in view, to handle the assault on Rome with extreme circumspection, and to issue a full explanation of the reasons for attacking the Monte Cassino Abbey. But by this time the sons of the Italian-Americans were fighting on bomb-pocked Italian soil, and in the conflict of loyalties their parents did not find it too difficult to put their own flesh and blood first. Blood was thicker than hyphenism.

4

Polish-American spokesmen have extravagantly claimed some 6,000,000 adherents in America, with tremendous voting power. The actual figures in 1940 were 2,905,000, counting both the foreign born and those with at least one parent foreign born. Next to the Germans and Italians, the Polish-Americans were the largest foreign-born group in our population.

Until recent years the Polish elements in this country have not been influential, although Americans hold in grateful memory the contributions of Pulaski and Kosciusko during our War for Independence. The reasons are not far to seek. First, the Poles did not begin to come in large numbers until near the turn of the century. Second, like the Italians they are somewhat inert politically, preoccupied with their own heavy labors, degraded to the status of inferior citizens, and widely diffused throughout the industrial and agricultural areas of the East and the Middle West. As the Irish of Central Europe, they had a Cause—the departitioning of Poland—but by the time they got their roots firmly planted in America the goal of Polish independence was won by the treaty settlement of 1919.

After the frightful German Blitzkrieg into Poland of 1939, followed by Stalin's invasion from the east, the Cause again sprang to life, and America became one of the ideological battlegrounds for Polish zealots. From Polish headquarters in London the anti-Russian government-in-exile spread propaganda among Poles in the United States designed to thwart cooperation with Russia and the Russian-sponsored Polish regime. This was dangerous business, particularly after Pearl Harbor, for we were then at war on the same side as Russia, and cooperation with the Kremlin was imperative if the war was to be won.

The Crimean Charter of 1945—drafted on Black Sea shores by Roosevelt, Churchill, and Stalin—decreed that about one third of Poland would be lopped off in the east, and that compensating German territory would be found in the west. An anguished cry arose from Polish patriots in the United States. Congressman O'Konski of Wisconsin, supported by Congressman

Lesinski of Michigan, assailed the "crime of Crimea" as a "stab in the back" for Poland and as a "second Munich." But the deal stood.

The Polish-Americans turned out to be the most important hyphenate element in the Roosevelt-Dewey campaign of 1944. This was a wartime election, and by common consent issues of foreign policy were soft-pedaled. But neither candidate could resist the traditional temptation to pander to the hyphenates. In Irish-Italian Boston, Roosevelt made a gracious reference to the Irish and Italians; in Scandinavian Minneapolis, Dewey expressed the hope that the Scandinavian nations would not be left out of the proposed concert of world powers. Dewey, in his Pulaski Day speech, appropriately expressed his dissatisfaction with existing secret arrangements regarding Poland, and implied that the Poles would fare better under his administration. The Communist *Pravda* blared back from Moscow that Polish reactionary groups were using the United States for "their own dirty blackmailing machinations."

The Poles have a passion for liberty, and as the affairs of Poland are smooth or troubled the Poles in America are silent or vocal. Polish-Americans wield too many votes to be ignored, and they are more than ordinarily sensitive to slights.° Oratorical flowers must be placed at the shrine of Polish liberty on appropriate days. In 1944, on the occasion of the 153rd anniversary of the adoption of the Polish constitution, an impressive verbal barrage was laid down on the floor of Congress. The speakers included 147 senators and congressmen (including Congressmen Wasielewski and Sadowski), and they extolled Pulaski, Kosciusko, and others for a total of 222 columns of fine print in the *Congressional Record*. Pulaski and Kosciusko were undoubtedly dead, but Joseph Kaszubowski of the American-Polish Associations, allegedly representing 2,000,000 persons of Polish descent, was definitely not.

5

A listing of all the hyphenate groups in America would be both monotonous and overwhelming. Let those who think that this country is truly Americanized go to the index of the *Congressional Record* and count the scores of associations and societies of foreign name which command Congressmen to subserve the interests of some foreign land.

A hasty glance at the brief but crowded years of World War II is highly instructive. The Czechs in America labored for a restoration of their temporarily defunct republic; the Graeco-Americans solicited relief and intervention; the Finnish-Americans sought sympathy and assistance against Russia; Scandinavian-Americans resented the rape of their mother countries by Hitler; the Franco-Americans clamored for a recognition of De Gaulle; the Estonians, Latvians, and Lithuanians besought a restoration of their national

---

° Several years ago the radio announcer Lowell Thomas was berated by a Polish-American listener for his failure to do full justice to the batting prowess of "Whitey" Kurowski, star third baseman of the St. Louis Cardinals.

identity; the Chinese-Americans bespoke American relief, intervention, and support; the Korean-Americans panted for independence; Hungarian-Americans agitated for a return of the territory handed over to Rumania; the Armenian-Americans pleaded for a restitution of their independent status; the Yugoslavs demanded Trieste from Italy and the Italian-Americans demanded that Italy be allowed to keep Trieste; the Spanish-Americans urged that Franco be left alone; and the British-Americans worked for succor, intervention, and a substantial loan. This depressing list is by no means exhaustive.

In the midst of the hyphenate uproar following the outbreak of World War I, the British ambassador in Washington wrote disgustedly: "America is no nation, just a collection of people who neutralize one another." As the student thumbs back through the earlier pages of our history, and remembers the multitongued clamor of the years since Versailles, he is almost tempted to ask if there is any place in the American scene for the interests of American-Americans.

No mention has thus far been made of the most numerous hyphenate group of all, the Afro-Americans, who constitute about one tenth of our population. They are racial hyphenates rather than national hyphenates, for they have long since lost any foreign nationality. Yet when Mussolini in 1935 invaded the black Kingdom of Ethiopia, the sympathies of the American Negroes, in so far as they had any, were with their colored brethren. One Afro-American aviator, the colorful Hubert Fauntleroy Julian ("Harlem's Black Eagle"), achieved some notoriety by volunteering for service with Emperor Haile Selassie, but he was an outstanding exception. In World War I the German propagandists made some headway among the Negroes with the hoary promise of "forty acres and a mule"; and in World War II one opinion poll discovered that the Japanese propaganda against the white man, though not accepted by anywhere near a majority of our Negroes, met with substantially more sympathy among the blacks than among the whites, and for obvious reasons. To most Americans God is a Nordic, and the black and yellow do not fit into our color scheme.

6

In illiberal Protestant circles it is common to find Catholics regarded as religious hyphenates, and in fairness to the vast body of loyal American Catholics this accusation must be examined.

There is undeniably a much higher proportion of foreigners among Catholics than among the rank and file of Americans, owing to the fortuitous fluctuations of recent immigration. The Irish in the 1840's gave the Catholic Church its first great influx of communicants; and the late-coming New Immigration from southern Europe, beginning on a huge scale in the 1880's and 1890's, added enormously to the numbers of the Church.

The Catholic clergy in America are also undeniably members of a hierarchy which is centered in the Vatican, and as a consequence they look across the Atlantic to Rome for spiritual leadership. The Catholic layman naturally feels this overseas attachment much less keenly, or not at all, particularly if he is a second- or third-generation American. But Protestants in the United States, notably those of a more ignorant cast, widely believe that Catholic "papists" cannot be loyal citizens. The Catholic and "wet" Governor Alfred E. Smith probably could not have defeated Hoover for the presidency in 1928 even if he had been Protestant and "dry," but he was definitely handicapped by the popular prejudice that, if made President, he would owe allegiance to the Pope first and to the American flag second. Governor Smith was at pains to deny such a charge, but he probably convinced no considerable number of bigots. We have thus far had no Catholic or Jew in the White House, and while we may have at some time in the future, the cards are definitely stacked against those who were not born Protestants and Nordics.

The presence of so many Roman Catholics among hyphenates, like the Irish-Americans and Polish-Americans, has caused the Protestant-American, in many cases unfairly, to connect the Church with the aspirations of these foreign groups. The pro-Franco stand of the more conservative Catholics since 1936 may be attributed to religious rather than to national grounds. The same is true of the bitter anti-Communist bias of the Church since the Bolshevist uprising of 1917. During World War II the Catholics in the United States were naturally nervous about possible bombing attacks on the Vatican, and the Roosevelt administration went out of its way to avoid desecrating holy ground.

If the hyphenate—say a Polish-American—is both a national and a religious hyphenate, he is less likely to lose his double hyphenism. The United States has traditionally been a Protestant and a north European country, and the Catholic immigrant from southern Europe, feeling the ostracism of both racial and religious prejudice, has been prone to draw apart and seek solace in hyphenated organizations and in the church of his fathers. There is ideally no place in the American pattern for citizens of inferior rank, but if we insist on creating them by our snobbery and prejudice, we must share the blame if they resist the processes of Americanization. American persecutions of Baptists, Catholics, and Mormons, to say nothing of discriminations against Jews, remain blots on the national escutcheon, and while less vicious than those of many other countries, they have chilled the melting pot at home and branded us as Pharisees abroad.

7

The existence of a great foreign fungus has beyond any doubt seriously hampered the formulation and execution of a rational and national foreign policy.

Hyphenism, as already noted, has consistently placed us at the mercy of events abroad; foreign convulsions become our convulsions. On the other hand, a few of the smaller hyphenate groups have persistently pulled in the direction of isolationism. Scandinavians in the Middle West have long insisted that if their native countries were able to preserve neutrality, the United States, sheltered by an ocean moat, ought to do as well.

The diplomatic position of our statesmen has often been weakened by the existence of powerful and vocal hyphenate organizations, pulling and hauling in all directions. In times of crisis, foreign governments have confidently counted on the disruptive influence of this non-American element. The Kaiser and Hitler and Hirohito all hoped and expected that the famed melting pot would crack wide open if the United States went to war. The Republican presidential candidate in 1920, Warren G. Harding, told a visiting delegation that we could not meddle abroad because such interference would merely split America into discordant camps. But the very complexity of the problem has in some measure proved our salvation. The hyphenates, by getting on different sides of the same fence, have on occasion succeeded in cancelling each other out, and have thus enabled the Washington government to pursue a genuinely American policy.

Hyphenism has also confused foreign governments as to the true intentions of our State Department. The British, in the nineteenth century, could never be sure whether we were twisting the lion's tail for the delight of Irish-Americans, or whether we meant business. This uncertainty almost led to tragic consequences in 1895 during the British-American dispute over Venezuela.

The hyphenated voter has also made cowards of our political leaders. Whether the orator extols Leif Ericsson, Christopher Columbus, Casimir Pulaski, or Carl Schurz will depend on the constituency that he is wooing. In Scandinavian Minnesota he will praise Ericsson; in Italian Chicago he will praise Columbus. Even so courageous a presidential candidate as Charles Evans Hughes wobbled and descended to the mumbo jumbo of double talk in the campaign of 1916. To the Anglo-Americans he seemed to say that he would "act tough" with the Kaiser; to the German-Americans he seemed to say that he would not. Politicians have even been known to take diametrically opposite stands in different parts of the country, but the nation-wide radio hookup has made such a practice more dangerous.

The proverb says that there is never any great loss without some small gain, and the cancer of hyphenism has conferred at least one minor advantage. The people of the United States have been forced by the uproar from the immigrants in their midst to take a keener interest in the affairs of the outside world. This interest has seldom, if ever, been as active as it should be, but at any rate the hyphenates unwittingly have done their part. While we have Americanized the Europeans, they to some extent have Europeanized us.

8

Hyphenism has so long been a part of the American scene that the average citizen takes it for granted. If anything, we have been too tolerant of it, despite unseemly and not infrequent nativist or antiforeign outbursts. Someone has well said that our immigrant population uses seventy-six languages and dialects with which to curse the institutions of the United States and to promote overseas aspirations. If a large body of American immigrants in Moscow were to make demands on the Kremlin in the interests of their native land, one wonders how long they would remain unliquidated.

Much of the blame for the persistence of hyphenism rests not on wicked foreigners but on unscrupulous Americans. The native American demagogue has consistently courted the foreign groups by cursing their enemies; praising their leaders, living and dead; and making them conscious not only of their hyphen but of their political potency. If the hyphenate had been less appealed to as a hyphenate in the past, he would be more of an American today. "One of the needs of the United States," remarked the Pittsburgh *Post* in 1921, "is to Americanize the politicians who cater to the hyphenate vote." But regardless of who is to blame, we can now see the folly of hustling the immigrants off their ships and into the polling booths before they are trained to discharge their new responsibilities.

National hyphenism, as distinguished from racial or religious hyphenism, is dying out and will ultimately pass away. There is scarcely any business in the United States with less of a future than the foreign-language newspaper. The melting pot is now being fed by a trickle instead of by a torrent, and among certain nationalities fewer immigrants are dripping in at the top than are leaking out at the bottom and flowing back to the Old Country. Unless there is a radical lifting of the present immigration bars, which seems highly improbable, the hyphenate groups can expect no appreciable renewal of strength. As the melting pot continues to bubble, and as the hearse continues to roll to the graveyard with the remains of the foreign born, the violent passions and prejudices of hyphenism will fade. Intermarriage between members of hyphenate groups blots out transatlantic attachments, especially among the second generation, who tend to be ashamed of their ancestral land and to scorn its language and folkways. A last stand of hyphenism is seen in the tendency for several different groups to collect together in some camp—say the anti-Russian or anti-British camp—rather than to continue their separate identity. But even this final bastion will fall, and the United States may become completely sovereign in foreign affairs.

Considering the vigor and tenacity of hyphenism, one may well marvel that the American people have generally been able to unite behind a reasonably consistent foreign policy. To a surprising degree we have risen above the anemic loyalties of transplanted citizens, and brought unity out of disunity. But we have achieved our goals with difficulty, and with our feet always in the water. We still have a long road to travel, but as regards the immigrant within our gates we may hope with Emerson that "one day we will cast out the passion for Europe by the passion for America."

CHAPTER FOUR

THE TORCH OF DEMOCRACY

"Liberty has still a continent to live in."—HORACE WALPOLE, 1779

1

THE MAN IN THE STREET is the proud citizen of a democratic republic, the first one in modern times to be established and perpetuated on a vast scale. This indeed may be regarded as our most significant contribution to Western civilization.

The patriotic American is perhaps shocked to learn that his form of government was once an uncertain experiment. When the Declaration of Independence was proclaimed in 1776, there had already been modern republics of a sort. But they had all perished, except mountain-girt Switzerland, which still flourishes; and they had all started on a tiny scale. "Democracy," wrote Voltaire in 1764, "seems suitable only to a very little country."

The attempt of the Founding Fathers to set up a democracy on a continental basis seemed to Europeans a daring and indecent defiance of the laws of political gravitation. Experience and reason alike cried out that the monstrosity could not work; it must collapse. A consciousness that the eyes of a critical world were upon us warped the thinking of our people and leaders for many decades. Abraham Lincoln, in the midst of the gravest crisis yet to confront the Union, referred to the Civil War as testing the principle whether "any nation so conceived and so dedicated can long endure."

But European observers were more than curious and critical; they were downright hostile. The monarchs of Europe feared that a dangerous precedent was being established. If the American experiment in human liberty should succeed, then their oppressed subjects, straining at their chains and pointing to the blessings of republicanism, might demand the same thing for themselves. This is precisely what happened. For more than a century the guiding star of foreign constitutionalists and revolutionists was the United States of America. The great English Reform Bill of 1867, by which England became a political democracy, followed by two years the end of our Civil War, which proved, despite the century-old vilification of British Tories, that the American venture could "endure." * The battles for British democracy were fought hardly less on the bloody fields of Virginia than on the carpeted floors of Parliament.

For more than a century and a half, the United States of America, detesting despotism in any guise, has been the bane of monarchs and dictators. We began as the world's ugly duckling; we ended as the world's overshadow-

* Ambassador Walter Hines Page in 1915 found some British Tories secretly rejoicing at America's unwillingness to fight over the *Lusitania*; this was further proof to them that democracies are degenerate.

ing eagle. The foes of human liberty sneered at us and jeered at us, from the days of Lord Sheffield to those of Benito Mussolini, who excoriated "the stinking corpse of democracy." Their hatred and fear of us grew with our power and with their corresponding impotence; they plotted to keep us out of Texas, Cuba, Florida, and practically every other area into which we wished to expand. They schemed to succor the South during the Civil War; and the success of the Confederacy was prayed for by the enemies of freedom in Europe. A consciousness of foreign hostility in fact helped steel the North to a last-ditch defense of the Union.

The democratic experiment finally succeeded in spite of, and perhaps to some extent as a result of, the hatred of foreign monarchies, and we mocked them with prosperity and contentment. The republican virus spread from its culture bed in America to the four quarters of the earth. The most dangerous "ism" unloosed on the modern world, at least until 1917, was American republicanism.

The tables were sharply reversed when Bolshevist Russia embarked upon its vast adventure into the unknown. The economic and social royalists of America, like the economic and social royalists of nineteenth century Europe, prayed for the failure of the Russian experiment, for if it succeeded the underprivileged of America might demand the same dubious blessings for themselves. Like democratic America, Russia became the pride of radicals; the fear of aristocrats. "The Russian experiment proves nothing," sneered one conservative American newspaper, "except that when the train turns over the upper berths are lowers." Just as the European powers plotted to keep us out of Florida, Texas, and Cuba, so we later joined with the other powers to keep the communistic colossus caged and confined, and we gave aid and comfort to his enemies. Yet in spite of our opposition, and no doubt in part as a result of it, the Soviet experiment waxed strong. The *Ohio State Journal* in 1927 could well have been a British quarterly in 1830 jeering at America when it observed: "One of the most annoying things about Soviet Russia is that she's still managing to get along."

The ostracism of the Soviet Union resulted in the development or accentuation of certain disagreeable national traits; the ostracism of the United States had a similar effect. We grew more militantly antimonarchical, more prorevolutionary, more zealous for democracy, more resentful of outside interference, more suspicious of foreigners, more isolationist, and more arrogant. One example will suffice. A distinguished visitor from monarchical Britain stopped at an American home in the 1830's, and when one of the boys refused to obey his mother, the father, instead of rebuking him, remarked proudly: "A sturdy republican, sir."

2

The United States began as an oasis of democracy in a Sahara of absolutism, and it won its independence from an allegedly brutal monarch, George

III. These twin facts stimulated a powerful antimonarchical prejudice in the United States. Tom Paine likened the well-meaning George III to a "common murderer, a highwayman, or a house-breaker," while Thomas Jefferson in the Declaration of Independence gave classic form to his bill of indictment, which was customarily read at Fourth of July celebrations all over the land.°
Mark Twain was merely voicing a deep American aspiration when he had Huck Finn say to Nigger Jim: "Sometimes I wish we could hear of a country that's out of kings." As late as 1917, the Philadelphia *Press*, in the one-down-and-more-to-go spirit, could gloat: "The Czar has abdicated. Next."

Distrust of Catholicism in America stems partly from a tendency among Protestants to associate the papacy with monarchy. Historically there is a close connection. A Connecticut newspaper in 1830 reported that the crowned heads of Europe were scheming to establish a monarchy in the United States, and that the Catholic religion was to be one of their tools. A Catholic presidential candidate in 1928, Alfred E. Smith, was attacked on the ground that as Chief Executive he would take orders from a foreign potentate.

Antipathy to "effete monarchies" may also be seen in our dislike of hereditary titles, and this antipathy still constitutes a minor psychological barrier in the path of better relations with Britain. Dictatorship and monarchy are closely associated in the public mind, and it is not surprising that much of the opposition to a third term for Franklin Roosevelt was based on the allegation, whether sincere or synthetic, that repeated reelection would prove an entering wedge for tyranny.

The true American democrat is scandalized by the thought that men should be elevated to high office by the accident of birth, often in a degenerate and diseased line, rather than by merit or by the votes of the people. When Jefferson was in Europe in the 1780's, he amused himself by calling the roll of ruling kings, and then noting that they were all fools, hogs "in body as well as in mind," or completely insane. He concluded that this is what would happen to any race of animals if they were kept in idleness, fed on a rich diet, permitted to gratify all sexual appetites, and discouraged from thinking. "There is not a crowned head in Europe," he wrote proudly in 1788, "whose talents or merits would entitle him to be elected a vestryman by the people of any parish in America."

In 1902, when Prince Henry of Prussia, the brother of the Kaiser, came to America on a good-will tour, Representative Wheeler of Kentucky protested heatedly against the cost of the receptions. "What difference does it make whether he is Prince Henry or not?" he demanded. "There are thousands of citizens of the republic following the plow as noble, as honest, as intelligent as Prince Henry or as Prince Anybody Else." The rough-riding Theodore Roosevelt, for all his catholicity of taste, had little respect for his hereditary counterparts in Europe. He referred to the Tsar as "a preposterous little

---

° The French observer, Alexis de Tocqueville, attended a Fourth of July celebration at Albany in 1831. He found the oration contemptible, the militia parade ludicrous, but the reading of the Declaration one of the most thrilling experiences of his life.

creature," and was profoundly distrustful of the gyrations of the Kaiser, whom he dubbed an "autocratic zig-zag," though later conceding that the proud Prussian was the only one of the entire batch who could carry his own ward in the land of the free and the home of the strenuous.

When in 1914 the German hosts burst into Belgium, the current campaigns of ridicule against the cloven-hoofed Kaiser, both in cartoons and in editorials, reached a new high—or rather a new low. The hereditary House of Hohenzollern, though partially shackled by a Constitution, was bitterly assailed, while the Kaiser with his withered arm, and the Crown Prince with his cringing manner, became objects of indecent vilification. The latter in particular was represented as a weak, degenerate, treacherous, contemptible wretch. "The belief grows," wrote the Pittsburgh *Post* in 1918, "that the Crown Prince has a face which only the Kaiser could love."

Contrast the reception of Adolf Hitler by the American public. As late as the early 1930's he did not attract a great deal of attention. He was a ranting, screaming demagogue, and the American people have traditionally taken both their politics and religion with a good deal of shouting. He was something of a clown, with his plastered-down hair and Charlie Chaplin mustache, and the American people have long tolerated a good deal of buffoonery in both their politics and religion. For a while the toothbrush mustache was the focus of much interest. In 1933, when Hitler became associated with President Hindenburg as Chancellor, the Chicago *Tribune* quipped:

"Hindenburg Has Only One Request to Make of Hitler—Headline. Bet a nickel we know what it is. Mein Gott in Himmel, shave it from the face off, your funny mustache already."

The joking faded away after Hitler's incredibly brutal anti-Jewish butcheries; he was no longer a laughing matter. Compared with him the much-cursed Kaiser was an upstanding Christian gentleman, but ·even after Pearl Harbor Chancellor Hitler was treated with considerable respect. By this time the American people were more adult in international relations than they had been in 1917,° and they realized that childish attacks on Hitler's person would not contribute in the slightest degree to the collapse of his thousand-year empire. But the fact is as inescapable as it is unpalatable that Hitler was more in accord with American tradition than the monarchical Kaiser. From frustrated housepainter to Chancellor of Germany, master of Europe, and architect of more human misery than any other man living or dead—that is an epic of which Horatio Alger never dreamed. When Hitler returned to his native Austria in 1938 with a mechanized army, a Middle Western newsman came up with the inspired headline: "Local Boy Makes Good." Decent Americans might condemn Hitler for his methods, but they could scarcely suppress a sneaking admiration for his results. To a nation of success-worshipers, and

° In 1917 the German language and German opera were banned, and Hamburg steak became Liberty steak and the German measles Liberty measles. We did not do these stupid things in 1941–1945; rather, we learned the language of our enemies. Opinion polls showed that the public was overwhelmingly against repeating the follies of 1917–1918.

to a nation of antimonarchists, there was something appealing about a lone figure who attained the heights, not by the accident of birth, but by the accidents of politics and intrigue.

3

The contempt of the average citizen for monarchy has led to certain excesses which, to those unfamiliar with the American experience, seem silly.

The practice of diplomacy was perfected in Europe at monarchical courts, long before the American Republic was ever born, and diplomatic procedures and habiliments still smack of their ancient origins. When President Franklin Roosevelt referred to Joseph P. Kennedy as "my ambassador" at the Court of St. James's, he was speaking by the book, for to this day the ambassador is regarded as the emissary of the ruler, just as Louis XVI had "his" ambassadors. The average American has long been prone to regard the foreign service as an unnecessary, extravagant, and deleterious appendage of degenerate monarchs. This partly explains why we have rewarded our representatives with poor pay and equipment, and why on occasion we have entrusted our diplomatic affairs to cooky-pushing characters whom we would not tolerate as local aldermen.

Secretary of State Marcy, a political spoilsman who had never set foot in Europe, formalized in 1853 our contempt for the "trappings" of European courts. He decreed that American ministers should thereafter appear at diplomatic functions in black evening clothes, rather than in resplendent gold braid and ostrich-plumed uniforms. Some embarrassing incidents occurred when the American envoy was confused with the waiters, but our minister in England avoided this affront by wearing a dress sword. If Marcy's decree was designed to promote admiration for the democratic simplicity of America, it defeated its ends: the American minister stood out like a black sheep. In Berlin the proud British envoy cuttingly asked the American minister, in the presence of many listeners, why the representatives of the United States appeared at court "all dressed in black, like so many undertakers." The thoroughly American retort was:

"We could not be more appropriately dressed than we are—at European courts, where what we represent is the Burial of Monarchy."

Marcy's order left some latitude, but simple attire for American diplomats was the rule until well into the twentieth century. In the 1920's the journalistic Ambassador George Harvey was widely criticized when he appeared at the Court of St. James's clad in monarchical knee breeches. Referring both to his attire and his indiscreet utterances, the New York *American* suggested as a motto: "Shorter speeches and longer pants." Ambassador Andrew W. Mellon, whose calves were less than bulging, cut an even less handsome figure when he donned similar garb. In 1932, when William G. McAdoo was campaigning for the United States Senate in California, he ringingly informed a small-town audience: "When we send Americans abroad we ought to insist that they wear good old American pants." The resulting applause was warmer than that greeting any other part of his speech. This was quite in keeping with American tradition, for in the early days of the Republic uniforms of any kind for civilians were not popular, even among policemen: the uniform suggested too strongly the royal lackey.

In the 1850's we sent as Minister to Spain a refugee French revolutionist by the name of Pierre Soulé. By temperament and background he was exquisitely unfitted for the task, and after provoking a duel with the monarchical French ambassador in Madrid, he succeeded in shooting him in the thigh. The less sober newspapers of the United States, far from condemning such disgraceful goings on, rejoiced that this exhibition of "American grit" would do the "lackeys of despotism some good."

Woodrow Wilson struck a refreshing note in his Fourteen Points when he demanded an end of secret diplomacy. In the popular mind secret diplomacy is associated with monarchical machinations, and Wilson's forthright declaration seemed like a significant step in the direction of democratizing foreign affairs. Failure to attain the goal did not invalidate the ideal.

4

The American people have naturally applauded the downfall of monarchy, especially where it was longest and most despotically established. The outbreak of the French Revolution in 1789, which we regarded as a second chapter of our own, was greeted with extravagant rejoicing in the United States. Royal Exchange Alley in Boston, among others, was promptly changed to Equality Lane. The fate of our good ally, Louis XVI of France, and his frivolous Queen, Marie Antoinette, is instructive. We thought well enough of the one to name Louisville, Kentucky, after him, and of the other to name Marietta, Ohio, after her. Yet when the guillotine was erected, and monarchical heads began to roll monotonously into executioners' baskets, our more liberty-loving citizens tossed their caps with loud huzzas. When the stupid but well-meaning King went the way of all monarchical flesh, together with his comely consort, one Pittsburgh sheet could gloat: "Louis Capet has lost his caput." The more sensible liberals, like Thomas Jefferson, regretted the gore, but realistically concluded that revolutions are not made with rosewater, and that a few thousand aristocratic heads were but a cheap price to pay for the triumph of human liberty. Monarchs, like our trees, would have to be chopped down if they stood in the path of progress.

The Latin-American revolutions against Spanish monarchy inspired similar if less frenzied sentiments. Again we felt that imitation of our own revolution was the sincerest form of flattery; and there can be no doubt that the Declaration of Independence, smuggled into Spanish-American ports with other propaganda literature, proved to be highly subversive. Although our assistance to the struggling patriots of the New World was on the whole more oratorical than practical, no one could mistake our hostility to Spanish monarchy and our sympathy for Latin-American republicanism. The Monroe Doctrine, issued a few years later, was a warning to monarchical Europe to keep its hand off Latin America and let republicanism run its natural course.

The Canadians, strange as it may seem today, were long an object of our concern and pity. Their Union Jack was but the red rag to the antimonarchical Yankee bull. We have never been able to understand why these people, so much like us in many other respects, did not have enough gumption to get rid of the heirs of our George III, or why they permit even the remnants of royal trappings to color their way of life.

To mention in order all major antimonarchical disturbances abroad is merely to list those periods when the American people openly lauded or assisted embattled revolutionaries. The Greek revolt of the 1820's revived classical languages and architecture, and studded the land with the place names of the heroic Hellenes, including Ypsilanti, Michigan. We rejoiced over the European revolutionary outbursts of 1830 and 1848, and expressed deep disappointment when they were stamped out. Rebels with prices on their heads, from Ireland to Hungary, fled to our shores and were feted like conquering heroes. Thomas Meagher, fugitive leader of the abortive Irish rebellion of 1848, was borne in a carriage on the backs of an Irish mob in New York, and later wined and dined by the President. Louis Kossuth, the dynamic Hungarian exile, was likewise officially greeted in Washington, and touched off a craze the like of which may be found nowhere else among the more bizarre chapters of American history. Secretary of State Daniel Webster, possibly overstimulated by champagne, so far forgot the diplomatic proprieties at a Kossuth banquet as to hope for the establishment of "our American model upon the Lower Danube."

5

Other revolutionary outbursts should be briefly noted. When the "citizen king" of France, Louis Philippe, was deposed in 1848, and the Second Republic was established, the American minister in Paris was the first to recognize the new government, for which he was duly commended from Washington. When the selfsame French Republic was overthrown by Napoleon III, the American envoy for a time refused to attend his weekly receptions.

Dr. Sun Yat-sen appropriately plotted revolution against the Chinese empire while enjoying the protection of the American flag in Hawaii, and when he finally proclaimed the Republic in 1912, the United States was the first of the great powers to extend formal recognition. Yet so great was the internal confusion in China that the Boston *Transcript* was moved to remark: "The United States appears to have recognized the Chinese Republic without waiting for the Chinese people to do it themselves."

The Russian upheaval of 1917 was greeted in America with the usual acclaim. We were then on the eve of accepting the German U-boat challenge, and the prospect of fighting for democracy at the side of autocratic Russia had rather chilled our enthusiasm. Now all was different. Many of our citizens wishfully believed that the exhausted Russians not only would remain in the war, but with the dynamism of a new democracy would fight harder than ever.

The Russian Revolution, like the French Revolution, suddenly took an ugly turn, and the bewhiskered Bolshevists landed on top. "Well, if Russia is lost to us, all right," rationalized the Kansas City *Star.* "We never did want to make the world safe for the Bolshevik kind of democracy anyway." We cared even less for the dictatorship of the proletariat than for that of the Tsar. In 1917 it took us only seven days to recognize the new revolutionary government; it took us fifteen years to recognize the Soviet regime. In 1917 we were among the first of the great powers to act; in 1933 we were the last. Thus are the first last, and the last first.

The neutrality obsession of the 1930's wrought a change in our thinking, and in 1937 we departed from one of our dearest traditions when we formally refused to send arms to the Spanish Republic in its death struggle with the Fascist Franco. Yet a majority of Americans with opinions favored the Spanish republicans, and several hundred American volunteers fought Franco under the banner of the appropriately named George Washington and Abraham Lincoln brigades. Liberals in America applauded this heroic defense of democracy on foreign soil, while conservatives frowned at clasping hands with "Communist" Russia in such an enterprise. After we entered World War II, and commissions were being awarded by the army and navy, some American veterans of the Spanish campaign were penalized. Their great sin had been to fight Fascism too soon.

The sympathy of the American people has invariably gone out to democracies whenever they have become involved in war with monarchies or dictatorships. Instinctively we sense the real foe. In 1914 our hearts were with the Allies; there was much more real democracy on their side, despite the temporary incubus of Tsarist Russia. In 1939 our hearts were with the democracies against the dictators, so much so that we deliberately changed our neutrality laws, openly flouted our neutral obligations, and ultimately took a course that led directly to war rather than permit the torch of democracy to flicker out.* As far as the American is concerned, whenever a democracy is threatened by a dictator, the democracy must be right. The Man in the Street cannot escape a century and a half of his history.

* A typically American gesture was made in 1942, when the Nazis erased the Czechoslovakian town of Lidice from the map. The name was promptly adopted by a Federal Housing Project in Illinois.

6

The hatred of the average American for monarchy has by no means been confined to remote areas. Where we have had a chance to snatch territory from royal hands, we have invariably used the antimonarchical argument as an excuse for taking it.

Louisiana was no less a bargain in 1803 because the flags of Spanish Bourbonism and Bonapartist despotism were to be replaced by the Stars and Stripes. The Floridas would have fallen ultimately into the capacious basket of Manifest Destiny, but the harvesting process was stimulated by the provocative presence of royalist Spain. The American people in 1867 did not share Secretary Seward's enthusiasm for the glaciers and walruses of Alaska, but Senator Sumner, in his great speech supporting the purchase, appealed with unerring instinct to American prejudice when he argued that the transfer would banish one more monarchical banner from this continent. Secretary Seward remarked to a friend on March 30, 1867, that by one of the strangest coincidences of history, the flags of two monarchs were being withdrawn from the New World on the same day: that of the Russian Alexander II from Alaska, and that of the French Napoleon III from Mexico.

Hawaii was an independent republic when annexed in 1898, but one should not forget that when President Cleveland, distressed by the improper use of American troops in overthrowing Queen Liliuokalani in 1893, sought to restore the deposed potentate to the throne of the Kamehamehas, he was forced to retreat before the outburst of popular indignation. The Atlanta *Constitution*, possibly with an eye to the approaching election, sternly reminded him that the "Democratic party has not been in the habit of restoring monarchies anywhere." *

When the Philippine persimmon fell into our laps in 1898, we had no real desire for it, but we recoiled from the prospect of turning it back to the frightful misrule of monarchical Spain. We had entered the war to free Cuba from Bourbon barbarities, and succeeded in doing so. As Senator Cannon of Utah put it: "The hand of God moved this country to destroy in Cuba the divine right of kings and establish there the diviner right of the people." Puerto Rico was something of an afterthought, but McKinley took it partly because he wanted to make a clean sweep of the rotting rule of Spain. From the floor of Congress came the cry: "These murderous, treacherous, bull-fighting hyenas" should be made to furl their "dirty flag" and leave the Western Hemisphere.

Our zeal for expelling monarchical flags has met with extraordinary success. Except for Britain, which is royalist in name only, there is no foreign-grown monarchy or dictatorship in the Western World today. The United States bought out Russia in 1867, forced out France in 1867, and drove out Spain in 1898. "Spain's reigny season in Cuba is about over," rejoiced the

---

* In 1947 we attempted to bolster the illiberal Greek monarchy against the Soviets, but here security ranked ahead of antimonarchism.

Chicago *Journal* shortly before our invasion was launched. We also purchased the Danish West Indies in 1917 from the government of King Christian X of Denmark. It would be erroneous to say that the antimonarchical principle was uppermost in all or perhaps any of these transfers, but it would be just as erroneous to suggest that the result was not in keeping with the most deep-seated aspirations of the American people.

The annoyance provided by a monarchy-tainted Canada has long since ceased to trouble us, but it was a factor to be reckoned with throughout much of the nineteenth century. Among a large body of Americans the conviction was unshakable that Canada would inevitably be annexed to the United States, with a consequent removal of the British flag. The purchase of Alaska was all the more palatable to annexationists because it was in the nature of a pincers attack on Canada; ultimately the intervening territory would be squeezed into our outstretched hands. A few ardent annexationists argued that we ought not to bother with Alaska at all; it could easily be scooped in when we took over all of Canada. In 1867 the House of Representatives passed a resolution deploring the formation of the Dominion of Canada as a step toward strengthening monarchy. The Canadians were careful to use the word "Dominion" rather than "Kingdom," partly because they did not want to provoke the anti-British and antimonarchical hotheads in the United States.

7

The average American has long had a sense of mission. He believes that God Almighty set aside this empty continent so that the United States, freed from the shackles of European despotism, might become an inspiration to the world. The American regards himself as one of God's chosen people, the custodian of the great democratic ideal.* The hostility of foreign monarchs and dictators has merely caused him to tend the altar flame more zealously. He is an active proselyte for his democratic theology, much as the Russians are for theirs, although his zeal is less than theirs, and even less now than it was in the nineteenth century. He is a tired and somewhat disillusioned liberal, but he still holds aloft the torch. In the nineteenth century the United States was on the march; today it is on the defensive, content to be the conservator of the democratic tradition. Our future tends more and more to be in the past. The Soviet Union, on the other hand, is on the march; it is revolutionary; its future lies in the future.

Our bland faith in democracy as a kind of political cure-all has propagated a cluster of illusions and delusions, some of which have caused us no little trouble and expense.

We take it for granted that all people should have our brand of democracy, regardless of whether they want it or are equipped to make it work. We for-

---

* Emerson in 1849 wrote: "Only the English race can be trusted with freedom." William Allen White added in 1899: "Only Anglo-Saxons can govern themselves."

get that democracy is the most difficult form of government to operate, and that it assumes on the part of the citizenry a high degree of intelligence, interest, and experience. Many foreign peoples are too inert or unintelligent to govern themselves, and they find it much easier to leave the affairs of state to a dictator. They prefer it that way.

We take it for granted that a democratic form of government can be imposed from above. Woodrow Wilson in 1918 indicated to the German people that if they would overthrow their Kaiser and democratize their government, they might expect a decent peace treaty. Without enthusiasm, and with the conscious thought of erecting a lightning rod to fend off Allied wrath, the Germans brought the Weimar Republic into being, only to have it loaded down with both the incubus of defeat and the Treaty of Versailles. The republic might have collapsed anyhow, but no democratic government can succeed unless the people themselves, of their own volition, want to make it succeed. Even then it may fail.

We take it for granted that a democracy can be made to work in any latitude. But as Senator Pettigrew observed near the turn of the present century, a banana and self-government cannot grow on the same piece of land. This is an exaggeration, but it underscores a profound truth. We have repeatedly tried to teach people in the tropics our democratic ways—the people of the Philippines, Haiti, Santo Domingo, and elsewhere. Woodrow Wilson vowed, in the midst of his earnest efforts to bar bloody-handed dictators from the presidency of Mexico: "I am going to teach the South American republics to elect good men!" Walter Hines Page echoed the same sentiment with more brutality when he wrote about "shooting men into self-government." But such efforts on our part among the "lesser breeds" have met with scant appreciation. A good many of us have learned by now, after much toil and trouble, that an idiot can put on his trousers easier than a wise man can for him.

We take it for granted that other people, when they want democracy, necessarily want our brand. We forget that democracy means one thing in China, another in Russia, and still another in the United States. The question is not only one of ideology but of definition.

We take it for granted, or at least we have in the past, that all other peoples want us to free them from their autocratic chains in order that they may have democracy. In 1812, just prior to invading Canada, we assumed that the Canadians were chafing under the British yoke, and that they needed only the encouragement of our presence to thrust it off completely. The bombastic proclamation of General Hull as he invaded Upper Canada in 1812, and the no less bombastic proclamation of General Taylor as he invaded Mexico in 1846, indicate that the Americans regarded themselves as emancipators rather than conquerors.

The same delusion arose afresh in 1837 at the time of the Canadian uprisings, and thousands of Americans swore a solemn oath to destroy all authority of "Royal origin" and "never to rest till all tyrants of Britain cease to have any dominion or footing whatever in North America. . . . So help me God." Likewise, when American filibusterers in the 1850's invaded Cuba under López and Central America under Walker, they looked upon themselves as liberators who were bringing liberty and republicanism to a people who were panting for such blessings. Both adventurers sadly overestimated the degree of panting.

By a curious inversion, the peoples of Russia and other dictator countries have been led to think of the American serfs as groaning under a capitalistic yoke and suffering from intolerance, racial persecutions, misgovernment, and corrupt politics, and crying for deliverance from whatever "ism" the critic happens to be assailing.

8

The zeal of the American democrat for his faith has led him into a number of inconsistencies, and has developed a peculiar blindness to those inconsistencies.

We have been accused of being friendly to one absolutism and unfriendly to another. Specifically, we recognized the revolutionary Mexican monarchy in 1822, while refusing to recognize that imposed on Mexico by France in the 1860's. The answer is that while we have been charitable toward homegrown despotism, we have been consistently hostile to monarchies imposed upon the Americas by outsiders. We felt kindly toward the Emperor Dom Pedro II of Brazil, a liberal and highly moral man—"a Queen Victoria in breeches." * But when he was overthrown by the coup of 1889, and a republic rose on the ruins of kingship, we felt that mere personalities, no matter how eminent or benevolent, should not be allowed to impede the march of democracy.

Dictators without number have sprouted from the fertile soil of Latin America, and some of them for narrowness and meanness could match the choicest of Europe. Yet on the whole we have been tolerant of them because they were products of this hemisphere, and we have been especially tolerant if they "played ball" with the United States. During World War II, the "good" dictators like Trujillo of Santo Domingo and Vargas of Brazil were those who cooperated with the United Nations; the "bad" dictators were those who did not. The test of virtue was utilitarian rather than totalitarian.

We have long deprecated royalty, but the sixty-four-year reign of Queen Victoria, who brought to monarchy an unusual degree of dignity, morality, and enlightenment, weakened the foundations of our prejudice. As *Puck* (New York) put it in 1897, the sixtieth year of the reign:

> For this we'll say:—if we *had* to
> Obey a Queen just so,
> We guess we'd rather she were you
> Than any one we know.

* Dom Pedro made a splendid impression during his visit to the United States in 1876. One editorial described him as "Our Yankee Emperor," and a leading San Francisco daily referred to him as one man who had "given respectability to the trade of king."

By 1939 we had so far forgotten our hatred of George III that we could over-whelmingly approve the visit of George VI and his Queen to the United States. Among the favored female few who were to be presented to the junketing royalty, the burning question of etiquette was "to curtsy or not to curtsy." But among the masses of the people, as Dr. Gallup ascertained, eight out of ten decreed that the women should bow (not curtsy), and that the men should shake hands (not bow). "I wouldn't bend my knees to anybody," declared one respondent. "It isn't America." Another suggested: "Shake hands. Every man's a king in this country." Another true American advised: "Just slip them a mitt—they're just a man and woman to us." The average American probably would like to see Britain abolish kingship, and this feeling increased after Edward VIII was forced to surrender his throne before he could marry the American divorcée whom he loved.

We have in the past felt a righteous impulse to interfere in other peoples' civil wars, to buy the bonds of Cuban and Irish revolutionaries, and to sponsor raiding parties into the territory of our friendly neighbors. But when British investors bought Confederate bonds, when the British governing class openly favored the South, and when Confederate raiders operated against us from Canadian soil, our resentment against the Mother Country led to the brink of war. Someone has remarked that we sympathize with everybody's revolutionists but our own.

9

We assume that our democracy is perfect, whereas it is highly vulnerable to criticism. Our practices have actually fallen far short of our professions. As Tacitus put it in Roman times: "It is easier for a republican form of government to be applauded than realized."

Our political democracy unfortunately has many unlovely blots on its record. Obvious items are mistreatment of our Indian wards; an exhausting Civil War; disorderly, crooked, and bloody elections; incompetence and graft in civil administration; well oiled and ruthless political machines; and loud-mouthed and ignorant demagogues. This is by no means the whole indictment, but one need not overprove the point. We have certainly done much to disappoint the high hopes of our friends, and we have fallen so far short of our ideals, even with many priceless advantages on our side, that our critics have accused us of betraying the cause committed to our care.

Our social democracy undeniably presents many inconsistencies. We decry hereditary titles, but seek them in exclusive organizations. We decry aristocracy, yet we set up an aristocracy of wealth and the social register. The wholesale marrying off of the daughters of American millionaires to impecunious foreign noblemen, near the turn of the century, was a minor international scandal, and led to protests against bartering away the American birthright for a "mess of peerage," and to the suggestion that the floral emblem of decadent nobility be the marigold. We protest against foreign

pogroms and preach the equality of the Declaration of Independence, yet
we have a submerged nation of blacks, the victims of poll taxes, black ghettos, race riots, and lynching. We proclaim the doctrine of religious freedom,
but the Ku Kluxers and other hooded hoodlums have practiced both racial
and religious intolerance, especially at the expense of Negroes, Catholics,
and Jews. We preach the doctrine of equality before the law, but are guilty
of palpable miscarriages of justice, especially among foreign immigrants,
Negroes, and others of the economically and socially underprivileged groups.
The story is told of a French visitor who, on first seeing the Statue of Liberty,
remarked: "We also erect statues to our illustrious dead."

These criticisms, while containing much force, do not recognize the fact
that the merits of our democracy far outweigh its faults, which at least are
on the surface and visible. Democracies elsewhere have their closeted skele-
tons; despotisms elsewhere are not for us. Theodore Roosevelt concluded in
1905: "The more I see of the Tsar, the Kaiser, and the Mikado, the better I
am content with democracy."

One may well argue that the cause of democracy will be best served if,
instead of trying to force it on other nations, we make it succeed so well in
America that other nations will demand it for themselves.

10

As the American people have donned long pants, they have become less
fanatical about the democratic ideal. They are not so sure as they once were
that it is a magic formula. They fought a great war from 1917 to 1918 to make
the world safe for democracy, and when it was over the world was less safe
for democracy than it had been at any time in the past half century or so. In
World War II the average American was content just to make the world safe.

In the adolescent days of the Republic, we were nervous and uncertain,
not knowing whether the great experiment would collapse of its own weight,
not knowing whether outside monarchs would let it succeed. The more un-
sure we were of ourselves, the louder we extolled the virtues of democracy.
Conscious of our weaknesses, we were hypersensitive to foreign criticisms,
especially those from monarchical Britain; and even so friendly an observer
as Charles Dickens could, by his *American Notes,* stir up a veritable tempest
of denunciation. "Our backs is easy ris," he later had an American character
say in *Martin Chuzzlewit.*

A hundred years later all had changed. We were paying huge fees to British
lecturers, and we sat patiently and respectfully before them while they mum-
bled scarcely intelligible insults at the United States. Then we applauded
them to the echo. In 1933 the incomparable George Bernard Shaw was given
a tremendous ovation by a sell-out crowd in the Metropolitan Opera House.
He said:

You have set up in New York harbor a monstrous idol which you call Liberty. The only thing that remains to complete that monument is to put on its pedestal the inscription written by Dante on the gate of Hell: "All hope abandon, ye who enter here."

In 1830, when the American citizen proclaimed with strident emphasis that we were a great people, his bluster did not fully conceal an undertone of doubt. We had not yet "arrived." Now the American does not have to say it, either in a loud or a soft voice. He simply takes it for granted, and so does everyone else. We may not have made a great success of democracy, but we have made a great nation—at least in wealth, power, and influence.

The American people will no doubt continue to feel a lively solicitude for the cause of democracy abroad, but they will have to strike a sensible middle course between doing nothing at all and charging forth to attack hydra-headed antidemocratic forces all over the world. What shall it profit a nation if, to preserve democracy abroad, it launches out upon a course which debilitates and bankrupts its democracy at home? Henry Clay, at the time of the mid-century European revolutions, warned his countrymen not to extinguish their own altar flame in their enthusiasm for lighting others beyond the sea. His warning could well be pondered a century later.

CHAPTER FIVE

THE SPIRIT OF SPREAD-EAGLEISM

"Most Americans are born drunk. . . . They have a sort of perma-
nent intoxication from within, a sort of invisible champagne. . . .
Americans do not need to drink to inspire them to do anything."
—G. K. Chesterton, 1931

1

The Yankee has long been recognized, especially abroad, as a boastful,
aggressive, swaggering fellow, not given to hiding his light under a bushel.
He is proud of his nation and its unparalleled achievements, and he feels a
sort of pitying contempt for that nineteen twentieths or so of the world's
population so unlucky as to have been born in foreign climes.* If we want
to know within rough limits how we appear to outsiders, all we have to do
is to note the condescension of the Californian toward his less sun-kissed
brethren in the other forty-seven states. Emerson remarked many years ago
that the American eagle is a good deal of a peacock.

Yet cultured Americans have long tempered their boastfulness with gratitude for our many advantages, whether of liberty, equality, or opportunity.
"My God!" exclaimed Jefferson in 1785, "how little do my countrymen know
what precious blessings they are in possession of, and which no other people
on earth enjoy." Margaret Fuller wrote from Europe in 1846: "The American
in Europe, if a thinking mind, can only become more American." And Emerson summed it up admirably when he said: "We go to Europe to be Americanized."

But among less intelligent Americans gratitude is often submerged by
crasser impulses. The boastfulness of American tourists abroad has long given
foreigners an unfair picture of the great mass of our countrymen who pursue
their daily tasks in less of a holiday spirit. The traveling "misrepresentatives"
of the United States were perhaps at their worst during the boom days of the
1920's. The more flamboyant tourists in France, showing their scorn for the
inflated French currency, would plaster franc notes on their suitcases or on
the sides of their train compartments. One French cartoon in 1928 had a nou-
veau riche American businessman say as he viewed the outstanding landmark
of Paris: "I have a good mind to buy this Eiffel Tower and set it up on my
country place."

American boastfulness has declined as we have had more to boast about,
but to this day we can hardly be classified as shrinking violets. A poll was
taken in England shortly after the close of World War II in an effort to
determine why the British were noticeably cooling toward their transatlantic

* Dr. Gallup in 1946 found that only one American in one hundred preferred to live elsewhere, which is a striking result when one considers the large number of foreign-born.

kinsmen. Among the reasons given were: "mean to be top dog," "take too much credit for winning the war," "too dictatorial," "too big for their boots."

Why did the American develop his offensive bravado? At the outset he was keenly aware that his was a crude, pioneering civilization, but that a mighty nation was in the making. In an attempt to stretch a bridge from the realities of the moment to the probabilities of the future he sought psychological compensation in loud and somewhat disagreeable talk. He cared nothing for the glory that was Greece or the ruins that were Rome. He had no deep roots in the American past; he came here full grown, and hardly waited to step off the boat before beginning to hack a dent in the wilderness. The vastnesses of America forced him to measure up to the challenge; what were mountains in Europe were mounds in America; what were rivers in Europe were rills in America. "Sunset" Cox once heard an American who probably had never seen Italy sneer at the destructive power of its most famous volcano. "Talk about Vesuve! Niag'll put her out in three minutes."

2

Nothing was more firmly implanted in the American mind than the assurance that the United States would one day be a great and populous nation. The hand of God could be seen in it, especially in New England, and more particularly in Massachusetts. The Almighty, as Emerson put it, had sifted a continent through a giant colander, and had deposited the choice residue of liberal and adventuresome spirits in the new Canaan. With sleepless hand He had guided the destinies of His hand-picked people. As late as 1889 a centennial sermonizer could proclaim: "If ever there were a nation favored of Heaven, and under the special protection of Almighty God, that Nation is the United States of America." During the imperialistic upsurge at the turn of the century, the flamboyant Senator Beveridge was convinced that God had "marked us as His chosen people, henceforth to lead in the regeneration of the world."

We were not only a Providence-protected race but a fertile one. On the eve of the American Revolution we were doubling our population every twenty-three years—pulling ourselves up by our birth-rate bootstraps. Contemporaries referred to our "brave propagating Fellows," and one of our earliest indoor sports was to calculate the future numbers of the Republic. One American concluded in 1770 that we would have 96,000,000 inhabitants by 1866; another estimated 1,280,000,000 by A.D. 2000. Senator Seward in 1850 reasoned that there would be 200,000,000 Americans by 1950. The historian-philosopher John Fiske made the "extremely moderate statement" in 1885 that by 2000 "the English race in the United States will number at least six or seven hundred millions." *

---

* Recent estimates by census officials indicate that a peak of 164,585,000 will be attained in 1990, after which there will be a tapering off.

Such mathematical computations fired us with a sense of inevitable destiny. In the infant days of the Republic, when our wilderness experiment seemed to be tottering, we could derive much comfort from the almost certain assurance that we would one day be populous and powerful. Time was on our side, and Washington and Jefferson and the other Founding Fathers deliberately adopted the policy of postponing the settlement of foreign disputes, for they knew that the longer we waited the more certain we were to work our will. The American birth rate—"multiplication table" one congressman called it—was long regarded as a first line of defense.

The fertility and optimism of the Americans were further proof of their youthfulness of spirit and body. "America," said Emerson, "is a country of young men." And he wrote in 1841: "We think our civilization near its meridian, but we are yet only at the cock-crowing and the morning star." During the full flush of Manifest Destiny in the 1840's, a French statesman, thinking to compliment Senator Cass on the achievements of the young democracy, asked, "If such is the youth of the republic, what will be its old age?" He was startled by the proud reply: "Sir, it will have no old age." Such cocksureness later inspired Oscar Wilde to sneer: "The youth of America is their oldest tradition. It has been going on now for three hundred years."

When the European tourist came to America in the 1820's, and was asked to admire a "city" which consisted of a few log cabins set down in a malarial swamp, he did not know whether to burst out laughing or to humor his guide as one humors a lunatic. If foreigners complained of having to sleep three or four to a bed in hotel rooms, sometimes with umbrellas raised over them for protection against a leaking roof, the reply would be, "Just you wait. It won't be long now before we have *real* hotels." The visitor, nearsightedly, saw only what lay before him; the American, farsightedly, peered into the future. To the Englishman the American was an incurable braggart; to the American the Englishman was an incorrigible bigot.

One of the most popular early American card games was "brag," a forerunner of poker. Without too much in his hand, and with a good deal of self-assurance, the clever player might do well. Mark Twain must have been thinking of his fellow Americans when he said in 1887: "All you need in this life is ignorance and confidence, and then Success is sure."

3

A basic ingredient of the American ego was the consciousness that we were carrying the banner of republicanism in a democratic El Dorado. We thought of ourselves as uniquely liberty-loving. Zealots with a sense of destiny, earnest and well-meaning though they may be, are frequently disagreeable.

American bumptiousness during the nineteenth century was largely a defense mechanism against the hostility of European aristocrats toward our wilderness experiment. We were regarded as the scum and offscourings of

Europe; even American food and grass were allegedly so deficient in proper nutriment that both men and animals were stunted. The wily Benjamin Franklin asked all the guests at a Parisian dinner party to stand, and to the mortification of the assembled nobility the Americans towered over them.

We were determined to show the effete rulers of Europe that we were "some pumpkins." A mid-century British traveler heard a Maine Yankee say: "Well, now, I declare I know'd it; we air a great people, and bound to be tolerable troublesome to them kings."

The inaugural addresses of the Presidents, especially the early ones, abounded in superlatives. Our democratic government was not only a good system, but the best ever devised. It was the "strongest government on earth" (Jefferson), the "noblest structure of human wisdom" (Polk), or the "best form of government ever vouchsafed to man" (Cleveland). Not only were we "happy and prosperous," but we enjoyed "unexampled prosperity" (John Adams), a "height never before attained" (Madison), "a fortunate condition, without parallel" (Van Buren).

American pride was also fed by the growing servitude of Europe to our foodstuffs and raw materials. As the Civil War approached, the Southerners, knowing how desperately British textile mills needed their fiber, loudly proclaimed, "Cotton is King." This implied that, if war came, the starving English factory hands would force the London government to break the Northern blockade and release the cotton. But such paper calculations failed to work out as planned. In the early days of the conflict the British had an oversupply of cotton and an undersupply of grain, and were more worried about King Wheat from the North than King Cotton from the South. Bondage to our waving fields of grain has continued to the present day: in the last two world wars America was the hope of famine-stricken lands the world over.

The bumptiousness of the American is but another name for the natural optimism and self-confidence of a nation on the march. We have faith in the future, in progress, in the American dream. We are professional optimists and boosters, with "boosters' clubs" and similar organizations. One reason why we early developed the habit of exaggeration was the necessity of persuading people to come to the unpeopled United States. The pessimist has no proper place in the American scene; pessimism is a species of treason to the nation. "Remember, my son," advised the banking magnate J. Pierpont Morgan, "that any man who is a bear on the future of his country will go broke." The great depression of the 1930's was a soul-searing experience, and for once our people faltered before unseen forces which they were unable to overcome with brute force. One of the great contributions of Franklin Roosevelt was to restore confidence in ourselves and in our nation's destiny.

The American early accustomed himself to big ideas; his was a big continent, with big tasks and big obstacles. The obstacles he surmounted or thrust aside; he killed both trees and Indians with equal ruthlessness. He built the Erie Canal, the transcontinental railroad, the Panama Canal (which Bryce called "the greatest liberty Man has ever taken with Nature"), the Empire State Building, the Grand Coulee Dam. The saga of America cannot be told without repeated use of superlatives like "biggest," "costliest," "longest," "deepest," "highest." The "tall story" is one of the most typical forms of American humor; Paul Bunyan rather than George Washington is in a very real sense the national hero. Someone has said that it is impossible to tell the truth about America without lying. We have long accustomed ourselves to doing the impossible; the United States is the story of the impossible.

Where big tasks had to be done, and done in a hurry, the American could not cultivate too tender a conscience. "Teddy" Roosevelt "took" the Panama Canal Zone, an act which was quite European, but he publicly boasted about it, an act which was quite American. Even Hitler was usually more discreet.

4

The spirit of American superiority has been assiduously kept alive by the pronouncements of our statesmen and educators. In 1899 William Jennings Bryan could aver: "Great has been the Greek, the Latin, the Slav, the Celt, the Teuton, and the Anglo-Saxon, but greater than any of these is the American, in whom are blended the virtues of them all." President Harding in 1922 modestly told a Muskingum College audience that we "have contributed more to human advancement in a century and a half than all the people of the world in all the history of the world."

The nineteenth century historian, George Bancroft, in his popular multi-volume history of the United States, unblushingly says of the American people at the time of the Revolution: "They were more sincerely religious, better educated, of serener minds, and of purer morals than the men of any former republic." Not to be outdone, the historian John Clark Ridpath acclaimed the new Republic as "the grandest Republican government in the world." At various times and in various places our schools have been forbidden to teach that the government of the United States is inferior to that of any other country.

The perspiring Fourth of July orator, who used to hold forth interminably at the annual observances of the national holiday, and who in some areas still does, was a professional stimulator of the American ego. He filled the air with eagles, Star-Spangled Banners, sovereign people, the glorious achievements of the past, and the still more glorious dreams of the future.

The school textbooks, whether geography or history, were written by Americans for Americans. Geography was primarily American; some other countries existed vaguely in the outer darkness; and the United States was larger than all the rest of the universe put together. The history books were no less inflationary. "We were taught every day and in every way," reminisced T. L. Nichols in 1864, "that ours was the freest, the happiest, and soon to be the greatest and most powerful country in the world."

The patriotic history textbook, closely under the scrutiny of nationalistic organizations, has traditionally emphasized the drum-and-trumpet phases of our history. Unlike other less fortunate nations, we did not evolve from the shadowy past but on a specific day tore ourselves from the side of the Mother Country. If the birth of America was a glorious event, then the war which made it possible must also have been a glorious event. We "whipped" the British in the Revolutionary War (with the help of the French and others), and we "whipped" them again during the War of 1812. There is some doubt about who "whipped" whom in the second war, but in any event we were aided by the Napoleonic diversion and Europe's exhaustion.

Such unpalatable qualifications, even if known to the patrioteering textbook writer, could well be omitted in the interests of popularity and pay, and through a dangerous misreading of our history we have developed the legend that we "twict licked" the British empire singlehanded, and could do it again, if need be, with one hand tied behind our backs. The "never lost a war" tradition was a source of considerable comfort to us in 1898, in 1918, and especially in 1941, when the conflict was almost lost before we got into it, and when we were up against the Japanese, who boasted a similar tradition.

All nations pervert the truth in the interests of patriotism, and although we have sinned much less than some others, and are sinning less now than fifty years ago, there is still room for reform. We laugh when we read in British textbooks that the British won the battle of Waterloo, in German textbooks that the Germans won it, and in French textbooks that it was all a mistake. Yet in 1938 Arthur Walworth published his *School Histories at War*, in which he compared the American textbook accounts of our foreign wars with the corresponding accounts in the textbooks of our former enemies. Our descriptions of the War of 1812 differ so sharply from those of the Canadians as to create some doubt as to whether the same conflict is being discussed in both cases. The other side commonly had the bigger force and the more guns, but our side won heroically in the face of great odds.

5

The blind optimism of the American regarding the military prowess of his country will ever be a source of wonder to the student of our history.

On the eve of the American Revolution, many Massachusetts patriots were sure that the minutemen of their colony could singlehandedly repel the British. The war hawks of 1812 looked forward to the invasion of Canada with similar optimism. Thomas Jefferson wrote that it was "a mere matter of marching"; Henry Clay, a "brag" expert, boasted that the militia of Kentucky alone could turn the trick. Not to be outdone by a brash Westerner, one New England congressman asserted that the militia from his state alone could conquer Canada. They all failed.

In 1823, without an army or navy of any consequence, and from a capital which had been burned only nine years earlier by the British, we squared our adolescent shoulders and through the memorable manifesto of Monroe warned England, France, Spain, Austria, Prussia, Russia, and all others who might be interested to stay away from the Americas. Fortunately for us, the British, who did have a navy, were also interested in keeping the other powers away.

In 1844, while quarreling with Britain over the Oregon country, we extravagantly and belligerently demanded everything up to 54° 40', the present southern tip of the Alaska panhandle. Countless thousands of our superpatriotic citizens who shouted themselves hoarse with the slogan "Fifty-four forty or fight" had not the remotest idea where or what 54° 40' was. Countless thousands had no conception of what they were up against, and those who had even a faint glimmering did not much care. Actually, we still had a contemptibly weak navy, and Britannia ruled the waves. "Some skeery folks talk about the navy of England," asserted one boastful Southerner, "but who cares for the navy? Others say that she is *mistress* of the ocean. Suppose she is—ain't we master of it? Who's afeerd?"

In 1846, while on the brink of conflict with England over Oregon, we plunged enthusiastically into war with Mexico. The cry of the hour was "Ho! For the Halls of the Montezumas," despite the solemn warning of the London *Times* that the conquest of so huge an area by "a State which is without an army and without credit" was "a novelty in the history of nations." Yet American valor, enterprise, intelligence, and good luck carried the day against the weak and disorganized Mexican opposition, and peace was dictated near the Halls of the Montezumas. There was no living with the American after these exhilarating triumphs, and one Yankee boasted to a visiting Briton that history did not record bigger battles than the assault on Chapultepec, nor mightier campaigns than the one which had crushed Mexico. (Americans have never been distinguished for their interest in or knowledge of world history.) Another Yankee, swelled by these victories, remarked to an Englishman: "Your little isle, sir, would make a pretty addition to this fine country!"

In 1895 we jumped with both feet into a rather inconsequential boundary controversy between Great Britain and Venezuela. Secretary Olney virtually demanded of the British that they submit the dispute to arbitration. "To-day," wrote Olney with true American spirit, "the United States is practically sovereign on this continent, and its fiat is law upon the subjects to which it confines its interposition." Its "infinite resources" and "isolated position" made it "master of the situation and practically invulnerable as against any or all other powers." President Cleveland supported his Secretary up to the hilt, and the nation screamed for war despite the fact that we had only three major ships in our entire navy as against fifty for Britain. The bellicose young

Theodore Roosevelt thirsted for hostilities, and while he assumed that the British fleet would devastate our coastal cities, he was confident that the rest of the country would rise up and invade Canada. The dispute was finally settled without shooting, but through no fault of American fire-eaters.

In 1917 we were reluctant to accept the challenge of the German undersea corsairs, for much of our youthful hot-bloodedness had cooled. But once in the fight, we displayed an energy that astonished and overthrew the German war lords. Woodrow Wilson reminded a Kansas City audience in 1919 that it took only "half as long" to train the American Army as any other, "because you had only to train them to go one way." When our troops reached England the badly battered Britons did not relish the Yankee witticism that A.E.F. meant After England Failed. And when the war was won the American doughboys immodestly, but with typically American self-assurance, declared: "The Yanks did it," and then tried to determine which branch of our service had actually done it. To British and French and others, all of whom for two and one-half years had been bleeding themselves white while the Americans were making money and then making up their minds to do something about the German menace, such arrogance was infuriating. Most Britons and Frenchmen were quite willing that the Yankee should gratify as speedily as possible his oft-repeated desire to return "to God's country."

In World War II the visiting GI's in England were on the whole less blatant, partly because they were somewhat more sophisticated, but their boastfulness and loud preference for "the Land of the Free" did not contribute to their popularity. They repaid the centuries-old British condescension with compound interest. One disgusted Briton found our servicemen "overpaid, oversexed, and overbearing." Yet, all things considered, the American boys made a not unfavorable impression.

6

The Man in the Street assumes that democracy (especially *his* democracy) is less warlike than monarchies or dictatorships, and that if one wishes to decrease the likelihood of war one must seek to build American-modeled democracies on the ashes of absolutism.

This may all be true, but there is scant support for it in the historical record. The distinguished Russian-American sociologist, Pitirim A. Sorokin, concludes that we are more bellicose than the Russians, and for proof he states that from 1775 to 1933, a period of one hundred fifty-eight years, we were at war for seventy-seven years. To arrive at this preposterous figure Mr. Sorokin has to include the century-long Indian campaigns, as well as the landings of the marines in Nicaragua, Cuba, and Haiti.

Excluding two undeclared wars, and other minor clashes with both Indians and foreigners, we have actually fought since independence a total of five major wars, which is enough for any peace-loving people—especially the last two conflicts. One could easily compile a list of twenty or so crises in American history which took the nation to the very verge of war, and from which we were not extricated by any efforts on the part of our more red-corpuscled citizens. Especially during the nineteenth century, when we were most irritated by foreign criticism and were most conscious of our inferiority, we developed a dangerous chip-on-the-shoulder attitude regarding affronts to our flag, to our territory, and to the persons of our citizens. Governor William H. Seward was no doubt thinking of this my-country-right-or-wrong attitude when in 1848 he complained: "Democracies are prone to war, and war consumes them."

Bent on forcible annexation, we twice invaded Canada (1775 and 1812), and the marvel is that we did not try a third or fourth time. We invaded Mexico on a full-dress basis in 1846–1848, and again informally several times, notably in the bandit-chasing foray of Pershing in 1916–1917. We fought England only twice, but those who in 1814 signed the Treaty of Ghent scarcely dared hope that the one hundredth anniversary of unbroken peace would one day be celebrated.

We entered upon all our wars with a boastfulness that was matched only by our unpreparedness. "On to Canada," "Ho! For the Halls of the Montezumas," "On to Richmond," "On to Cuba," "On to Berlin," and "On to Tokyo" were successively shouted with an enthusiasm that was in direct ratio to ignorance of the obstacles involved.

The events before Pearl Harbor are still painfully fresh in the national memory. "We can whip any country in the world," proclaimed a United States senator in the 1930's. Then, with a slight indication of misgiving, he added: "I know we can do it, and if we cannot, then let us get an army and navy that can." An opinion poll early in 1941 revealed that a majority were confident that Hitler could never conquer us, even though France had fallen and our defenses were dangerously inadequate. Congressmen were declaring that it would be a simple matter to sail on to Tokyo, and one can hardly blame the layman for reaching this conclusion when the admirals themselves were openly estimating that it would take only a few weeks to "polish off" the entire Japanese Navy.

The sneak attack at Pearl Harbor jolted us a bit, but not nearly as much as it should have. We knew that our fleet had been damaged, but, thanks to official falsehoods, we did not know that every capital ship in Hawaii had been sunk or immobilized. Even if we had known it, we would still have retained a vast amount of cocksureness. The reports of the *Time, Life,* and *Fortune* correspondents located in various American cities on December 7, 1941, have been brought together in one book, and they are most revealing. In New Orleans the Southerners were saying, "We can lick 'em hands down." In Chicago people were saying, especially the young men, "Well, we've got to whip the whole world—and we can do it." In Denver the correspondent summed up the general attitude: "Everybody is keenly interested but very few are excited, some are mad. Nobody is afraid."

In May, 1942, when we were clearly losing the war, *Fortune* found 85.7 per cent of the American people absolutely certain we would win, while only 0.7 per cent felt sure that we would never gain a decisive victory over the Axis. When one considers our then desperate plight, the large number of German-Americans, and the admitted margin of error in polling techniques, these figures are simply incredible. But there they are, glaring evidence of our illiteracy in military affairs, and a glowing tribute to our traditional faith in ourselves.

7

James Russell Lowell suggested in the 1840's that our loud talk about Manifest Destiny was half ignorance "an' t'other half rum." The average citizen would be less arrogant if he knew more about the facts of international life.

The American people in early 1945 believed that the Russians were securing most of their war materials through our Lend-Lease agencies rather than from their own factories. This of course was far from the truth. The Russians, on the other hand, annoyed us greatly by minimizing the importance of Lend-Lease; the jeep was commonly regarded in the Soviet Union as a remarkable Russian invention. We have not yet learned that allies (including the United States) seldom show real and enduring gratitude toward one another.

Poll takers in both Canada and the United States asked the people in 1943 what nations had done the most to win the war. The results are illuminating.

In Canada		In U. S.	
Russia	50 per cent	U. S.	55 per cent
Britain	42	Russia	32
China	5	Britain	9
U. S.	3	China	4

While the Canadians no doubt were thinking of the actual fighting thus far, and while the Americans were probably thinking of war production or potential war production, the high rating that the American gave himself was completely in character.

In the spring of 1945, with the end of the war in sight, our people ranked the United States as the most influential nation in the world, with 75 per cent; Russia next, with 10 per cent; and Britain third, with 7 per cent. We were serenely confident that we would have a lion's share in shaping the postwar world, though other nations were less sure. The more ignorant the American, the more inclined he was to take on the job of running the universe, and the more insistent he was that we be allowed to do it all by ourselves.

A hurried glance at these figures does much to explain why we have often failed to win friends and influence people in foreign lands. A disquieting residue of the ancient "lick all creation" spirit remains, but most of it has evaporated as we have grown more secure and more mature. During World

War II, when the German Focke-Wulf airplane was a fearsome foe, an American aircraft manufacturing company, paraphrasing the popular song, "Who's Afraid of the Big Bad Wolf," published an advertisement of one of its planes with the caption, "Who's Afraid of the Big Focke-Wulf." An officer near the fighting front hung the page on a bulletin board, and wrote below it, "I am," with his initials. Every man in the squadron followed suit. The tale may be legendary, but we were then big enough so that we were not afraid to admit that we were afraid.

As our nation has become an overshadowing colossus, we have been less prone to wear our honor on our sleeves. We are less sensitive to slights and affronts; less easily provoked into war. Far from worrying about what the rest of the world thinks about us, we have developed toward foreign nations an indifference and "don't-give-a-damn" attitude which are hardly less annoying than our earlier swagger. We no longer have to convince people in piercing tones that we are going to be a great nation; that our democracy is not going to collapse; that the Union is going to hang together; that we are going to have big cities and tall buildings. All of these things have come, and more too, so many in fact that in the managing of them we have little time or energy to worry about the outside world. But a certain unshakable confidence in America and the American way remains.

8

Disagreeable though bumptiousness may be, it contributed powerfully to making America formidable and then great. The boyish optimism of the average citizen has on the whole been an asset rather than a liability when tremendous tasks had to be tackled. Deliberation is the first cousin of cowardice. The more one knows about the obstacles one is up against, whether in domestic or foreign affairs, the more inclined one is to hesitate, weigh all factors, and then move cautiously, if at all. But that is not the American way; if it had been, many of our gigantic projects would still be blueprints.

Remember the days of Pearl Harbor. Our fleet had been destroyed. China had been cut off from the outer world. Russia was desperately repelling the invader from the gates of Moscow. Britain was near the end of her tether, and German submarines were devastating both our overseas and coastwise shipping. But supported by an overwhelming public opinion, the Roosevelt administration, though far more keenly aware of these perils than the ordinary voter, coolly and confidently went ahead with long-range plans for victory. As Franklin Roosevelt told Congress, with an outward-thrust jaw, "We will gain the inevitable triumph—so help us God."

Undeterred by defeat, the high officials in Washington worked out elaborate plans for training officers to govern a still triumphant Germany and Japan. An enormous sum was secretly set aside for perfecting the atomic bomb. The fleet was raised from the ooze of Pearl Harbor to join in the crushing of

Japan. "I will return," said General MacArthur as he was forced from Manila in March, 1942. To realistic observers this sounded a bit like American boasting; to the unrealistic average American it seemed like a simple statement of fact. Less than three years later General MacArthur did return.

The coolness and imperturbability of Franklin Roosevelt, though unwarranted by the desperate situation of 1941–1942, were among his strongest assets, and they cannot fail to command admiration today. When in 1940, as France was about to fall, he urged a 50,000-airplane program, some of his staunchest supporters expressed skepticism, and the criticism of his political foes was biting. Such a goal was impossible, even for a nation which is a story of the impossible. Yet the "stinking corpse" of democracy rose to its feet to smite the dictators hip and thigh. From July, 1940, through July, 1945, the American people actually delivered 297,000 airplanes—six times the impossible. If they and their forebears had not for several centuries been vying with Paul Bunyan, they might have recoiled from the task and never done it. We took both defeat and victory, and branded them imposters.

As we come to learn more about foreign peoples, their strengths and their limitations, and as we become more keenly aware of our own, perhaps we shall do less stupendous things. But until then do not sell the American people short; they never have themselves. America is not only a place but a state of mind.

CHAPTER SIX

THE UNGUARDED RAMPARTS

"The spirit of this country is totally adverse to a large military force."
—THOMAS JEFFERSON, 1807

1

THE MAN IN THE STREET, like men in other streets all over the world, is deeply concerned about anything that affects his security against foreign invasion and domination. He responds to a clear threat to his safety more quickly than to any other stimulus in the field of foreign affairs.

The British were willing to fight and actually did fight in 1914 rather than see a hostile Germany occupy the trans-channel ports of Belgium; the Japanese were willing to fight and actually did fight in 1904 rather than permit Manchuria to pass under the control of Tsarist Russia. Other great powers have set up security danger zones, and the United States is no exception. Jefferson was prepared to ally the United States with Great Britain to fight France in 1803 rather than see the mouth of the Mississippi fall into the clutches of Napoleon. We repeatedly made it clear in the nineteenth century that we would permit no hostile foreign power to acquire Cuba, which lies dangerously athwart our Gulf and Isthmian shipping routes. But the real jugular vein of American seapower, as well as the key to a commercial empire, is the Panama Canal. The Washington government has long been able to count on overwhelming popular support for any necessary measure, including war, designed to keep dangerous intruders at a safe distance.

The derisive term "dollar diplomacy" is highly misleading, especially when applied to our activities in the banana republics of the Caribbean during the first decades of the present century. "Life-Line Diplomacy" would be better terminology, for we were more concerned with the security of our communications than with the security of our investments. Our protectorates over Cuba and Panama; the numerous landings of the marines; the warning given to Japan in 1912 regarding Magdalena Bay, in Lower California; the leasing of the Nicaraguan canal route in 1916, with base sites at both ends—all these are episodes in the same drama. The list could be greatly expanded, but one might add our purchase of the Danish West Indies in 1917 at a hold-up price and in the face of a potential German occupancy; our desire for bases on the Ecuadorian Galápagos Islands (temporarily gratified by our Latin-American ally during World War II); and our reluctance to relinquish these bases as well as others granted temporarily by Panama during the same conflict.

2

The ordinary citizen, occupied with his daily labors and diversions, is not easily aroused by a foreign danger unless there is some immediacy to the threat, or unless the threat is directed at a life-line area, like the Caribbean Zone, where not even a potential lodgment may be tolerated. During the nineteenth century the naval men, whose business it is to take a long-range view, repeatedly urged the acquisition of bases in Santo Domingo and Haiti. But such schemes came to naught, largely because the coveted spots were not in danger of falling into the grasp of some unfriendly power.

For many decades naval experts like Captain A. T. Mahan urged that we annex the Hawaiian Islands as an outer defense bastion for the Pacific Coast, but their pleas went unheeded. In 1893 we would not even take Hawaii as a gift. But in 1898 the scene rapidly shifted. The unhampered trip of the Spanish Admiral Cervera from Spain to Cuba highlighted the desirability of having island fenders some two thousand miles off our Pacific Coast, and we began to see with increasing clarity that if the United States did not take Hawaii the Japanese would be glad to do so. The security argument had been just as valid three decades before, but a wartime object lesson was needed to drive home the real peril. Hawaii proved its worth in World War II as a Gibraltar for the defense of the Pacific Coast, and as an advance base for the crushing of Japan. The story would make less pleasant reading for Americans if the Japanese had been allowed to take over in 1898.

We annexed other areas because a threat to our security was posed by actual or potential foreign machinations. Texas and California are the best examples. Perhaps the fundamental reason why we reluctantly took the Philippines was the fear that an international scramble for them would create a situation inimical to our peace and safety.

As modern mechanical miracles have annihilated both time and distance, the fringe of our safety zone has vastly widened. Just before and during our entrance into World War II, we became interested for security reasons in Greenland, Iceland, the Azores,* the Canaries, and Dakar, on the bulge of Africa across from the bulge of Brazil. After securing temporary bases on some of these places, notably Iceland, we were loath to leave them. When the war ended, we were determined to retain control over the Japanese-held steppingstones in the Pacific, so dearly purchased with American blood, and finally secured them as a mandate on our terms. We were disturbed to learn after Yalta that Churchill and Roosevelt had promised to return the Japanese Kurile Islands to Russia; we feared that these outposts might one day be used as bombing bases against the United States. At the close of World War II, several nations began to display a lively interest in the frozen

---

* More than six months before Pearl Harbor, President Roosevelt, fearing German occupation of the Portuguese-owned Azores, ordered Admiral Stark (May 22, 1941) to assemble a task force of 25,000 men to seize them. The order was cancelled on June 22, the day Hitler attacked Russia.

wastes of Antarctica, and the Byrd expedition of 1946, whatever the official explanation, was generally regarded as a security enterprise. The rumored uranium deposits there were an object of interest, not only because we coveted them for the manufacture of our own atomic bomb, but also because we wanted to keep them out of the hands of future foes.

3

We fought every one of our foreign wars primarily or partially for reasons of security. The "War Hawks" of 1812 were largely concerned with removing the British-succored Indians from their frontier. The American people wanted California in 1846, and fought Mexico to get it, partly because of the presumed necessity of forestalling British and French designs on that sun-bathed land. We plunged into war with Spain in 1898 basically to free Cuba from Spanish brutality, but also to safeguard our physical security. Continued disorders in the Island invited international complications, with the danger of a foreign lodgment; and the nearness of this gigantic pesthouse jeopardized the health of our people.

The war with Germany in 1917 was largely a war of security. German U-boats were actually sinking American ships crossing the Atlantic life line; and while theoretically we could have kept out of the conflict by withdrawing our flag from the danger zones, as we did under the Neutrality Act of 1939, neither national honor nor security would at that time permit such a cowardly course. A belief was current in the United States, and Allied propagandists harped skillfully on this string, that if the Allies collapsed, the conquest-mad Kaiser would turn his millions of spiked helmets upon us and our Monroe Doctrine. Ambassador George Harvey bluntly told a British audience in 1921 that we fought "solely to save the United States of America. We were afraid not to fight." An uproar of dissent arose from that vast body of Americans who had been indoctrinated with Wilsonian idealism to believe that they were motivated by less selfish aims. At all events, in 1917, as in 1941, it seemed better to fight when we could have allies than to wait and face the might of Germany alone.

The ordinary American was slow to recognize the rising menace of Hitlerism, but the same thing may be said of his British cousin in England, who was living on the future firing line. Yet our people must be credited with having been much further ahead in their desire for adequate military preparedness than their representatives in Congress. As early as 1935, seven voters in ten favored building up the army and navy, and this percentage steadily increased as the European war clouds darkened. Though pinched by a depression, and fully aware that more armaments meant more taxes, the average citizen was willing to sacrifice for security. Those congressmen who work on the cynical principle that one must never vote for a tax bill or against an appropriation bill sorely misjudged the American people, who from the days of the Declaration of Independence have valued their liberties above dollars.

The American preparedness program rocked along on a business-as-usual basis until the Munich crisis of 1938 ripped aside the veil from Hitlerian ambitions. Congress accelerated the pace somewhat but did not respond with an all-out effort until the fall of France in 1940 brought an almost hysterical reaction. We feared that if Britain foundered we would have to face the wrath of Hitler alone, probably from a flanking movement based in Latin America. By overwhelming majorities we branded Hitler a liar when he declared that as far as he was concerned South America was "as far away as the moon."

We proceeded to put into operation the first peacetime conscription act in our history; we indicated an overwhelming willingness to fight in order to keep Germany out of the Caribbean area; we admitted the Latin-American republics to a defensive copartnership under the Monroe Doctrine; and we cast aside the fiction of neutrality when Roosevelt transferred fifty "overage" destroyers to Britain and received from her a string of eight base sites ranging from Newfoundland to British Guiana. This was a double-barreled security measure of epochal importance, and as such was supported by the American public, despite the irregularity of secret and unauthorized presidential action. The fifty destroyers would enable Britain to keep afloat; the eight bases, which otherwise might fall into Axis hands, would enable us to keep our potential enemies farther away from the North American mainland.

The Lend-Lease Act of 1941, by which we virtually declared war on the Axis, was presented to Congress and the American people as a security measure. We would "grubstake" those who would protect us by continuing to resist our potential enemies. The official title of this momentous measure was "An Act Further to Promote the Defense of the United States."

The passion for security has led us to seek strange bedfellows. In 1778 we did not like Catholics and monarchists and foreign entanglements, yet we made a binding military alliance with the Catholic monarch of France. There seemed to be no other way to achieve our independence and security. As a British historian has written, when one's house is on fire one does not inquire "too curiously into the moral antecedents of those who hand the water-buckets." In 1941 we were distrustful of the Soviet Union, and millions of our citizens were convinced that Russia was a menace to our economic, political, social, and religious structure. But the threat to our external security from Hitler seemed much more menacing than the threat to our internal security from Stalin, so we accepted Russia as an ally a good deal more heartily than she did us.

4

The American citizen presents a puzzling contradiction. He sets great store by security, but he has generally been reluctant to take adequate measures to insure it until his enemy is on the threshold. We have been seriously unprepared for every war we have ever fought, though we were less unprepared for World War II than for any of the previous ones, a statement which may give a better idea of how painfully unready we were for the others. Our armed forces were in relatively good shape on the eve of Pearl Harbor, primarily because we had been unofficially in the conflict many months before the official blow-up came. Yet the American tradition has been to declare war first, and prepare for it later.

Physical separation from both Europe and Asia has contributed powerfully to the American coldness toward military preparedness. For generations we enjoyed the luxury of a comfortable sense of security, ensconced as we were behind two mighty ocean moats, each one of which used to be worth at least the British Navy, though costing the taxpayer nothing. In the nineteenth century the wars of Europe seemed distant and unreal, a kind of dim rumbling on the other side of the seas.

The troubled Mother Continent was not only far away but during most of our national history it was divided into uneasy balances of power. Seldom was any one nation free to invade the United States without fear that some vengeful foe would deliver a fatal stab in the back. In 1812 we declared war on England, expecting that Napoleon would continue to tie up British forces while we invaded semidefenseless Canada. Napoleon did what we expected of him for about two years,* but we failed to do what we expected of ourselves. In the era before World War I Germany resented our Monroe Doctrine, but so nicely was her strength balanced with that of Britain that she could not risk coming over and chastising the upstart Yankee.

If England's extremity was traditionally Ireland's opportunity, so were Europe's distresses a fertile field for American diplomatic successes. By taking advantage of the preoccupations of European powers with hostile neighbors, and by playing one off against the other, American statesmen during the formative years of the Republic were able to fashion a noteworthy succession of bloodless diplomatic victories. Europe's distresses were in fact our first line of defense. Why should a poor and struggling nation burden itself with huge armaments when by fishing in troubled waters it could attain security without additional cost to the taxpayer? Thus another prop was thrust under the unpreparedness illusion.

Even more important was our rare good fortune in having weak neighbors both north and south. During the colonial era we did have powerful French and Spanish neighbors, and their aggressiveness in leading Indians upon our frontier wrote many a blood-stained chapter. But during the national

* The news of Napoleon's victory at Lützen, in 1813, was received with great rejoicing among administration supporters in Washington.

period we never knew what it was to live next to a powerful, ambitious, and frustrated nation. We have had frustrated neighbors, but not powerful and frustrated ones. To the south, we have not had to fear Mexico; she has had to fear us. To the north, we have not had to fear Canada; she has had to fear us. The witty French ambassador in Washington, Jules Jusserand, once remarked that America was lucky among nations: on the north, a weak neighbor; on the south, a weak neighbor; on the east, fish; on the west, fish.

Enjoying the boon of nonaggressive neighbors, we have not had to build up costly Maginot lines against them. During the 1920's we were totally unable to understand why the French, suffering from a security psychosis, were maintaining the most powerful army in Europe. We could not appreciate the fears of the French cleric Abbé Dimnet, who sadly remarked at the end of World War I: "My house was in the hands of the Germans in 1814, again in 1870, and again in 1914. I pray God that He will make it impossible that it shall ever be in their hands again." His ancestral home fell into their hands again in 1940.

Until the air age dawned, we were the only major power not exposed to an immediate attack on vital territory by at least one powerful foe. In the early 1930's we maintained a peacetime army which ranked about nineteenth among those of the world, just ahead of Portugal's. When an American general told a French statesman, some time after the disastrous Franco-German war of 1870–1871, that our army numbered only 25,000 men, he probably expected to be complimented on the pacific disposition of our people. Instead, the Frenchman replied: "What good neighbors the United States must have!"

Yet we have had some narrow escapes. France in 1803 almost moved into Louisiana in force; Texas in the 1840's might have become a Europe-supported transcontinental republic; and France in the 1860's might have established her puppet Maximilian in Mexico. The most ominous threat was the Civil War, when the United States threatened to break into two snarling republics, with the European powers, taking advantage of the Balkanization of North America, playing one set of antagonists against the other, while they bade defiance to the Monroe Doctrine. The American people were fortunate enough to be spared this fate.

5

Habitual unpreparedness is in part a heritage from our Anglo-Saxon past, and in part the result of our unhappy experiences with British redcoats before and after the days of the so-called Boston Massacre. Like the British, we are distrustful of large standing armies in time of peace; a standing army is a standing invitation to a would-be dictator to mount a charger and stage a military coup. Like the British, whose point of view Kipling has immortalized, we have never entertained too high a regard for the regular soldier in time of peace; he is usually not the kind of person we want our daughters to meet. Like the British, we have regarded the navy as the first line of defense, and as the favored branch of the service. Battleships cannot march inland and set up a dictatorship.* Battleships can hold off the enemy while the nation leisurely goes about raising and training an army. Both the Americans and the British have developed a tradition of "muddling through," and there is a measure of truth in the legend that the British lose every battle except the last.

The American is an individualist, and he sets great store by human freedom. His spirit recoils from conscription, without which huge citizen armies are impracticable, and the liberty-loving British have revealed the same antipathy. After we were forced into war with Germany in 1917, George Creel of the Committee on Public Information publicly rejoiced that we had been unprepared. His remark was widely misunderstood and bitterly criticized, but what he meant to say was that unpreparedness characterizes a freedom-loving, liberty-cherishing, nonaggressive, nonmonarchical people. Not until 1940, after the tragedy of France, were we stunned into casting aside an age-old prejudice and passing our first peacetime conscription act.

Many of the immigrant outcasts from Europe who sought American shores in the nineteenth century came from conscript countries, where they or their relatives had served in the army, and they wanted no part of it. Some of these refugees undoubtedly came for the primary purpose of evading service, and those who later returned to the lands of their birth often involved the Washington government in annoying diplomatic controversies.

Until the Great Depression of the 1930's, America was short of manpower. With forests to be felled, and mines to be dug, and railroads to be built, it seemed little short of sacrilegious to thrust able-bodied men into uniform and have them shoulder muskets instead of axes.

The United States today is the richest of the nations, but we were relatively poor in our youth. With land all over the world going begging, we had little that anyone else coveted: no rich cities to plunder or put under ransom. When a man is poor, he does not have to latch his door at night or set a guard over his children; when he becomes rich, he has to lock up his valuables and take precautions against kidnaping. When we became rich, we carried over some of the carefree habits of our less lush years. What a colossal prize the cities and factories and mines of America would have been for Adolf Hitler!

The penny-pinching habits of an earlier day have been hard to shake off. "Battleships and cruisers go out of date too fast," remarked a landlocked Kansan in 1935. "Better save the money." On the whole we have regarded the army, navy, and diplomatic service as necessary evils. Like the little Japanese tree growing in a flower pot, we have traditionally given them just enough nourishment to keep them alive, but not enough to keep them strong

---

* Jefferson wrote in 1786: "A naval force can never endanger our liberties, nor occasion bloodshed; a land force would do both."

and flourishing. In matters of preparedness we have been penny wise and pound foolish; we have habitually underdone rather than overdone. Then we find ourselves in a war that costs over $350,000,000,000, a war which almost bankrupts us and which we almost lose, a war which conceivably could have been prevented if a small portion of its final cost had been used to build a military establishment which would have given the dictators pause. It seems cheaper in the long run to count on a future war and not get it, than to count on none and get one. Significantly, our more wealthy citizens are more willing to pay taxes for military preparedness: they have more to pay with and more to lose should the invader come.

The curse of politics has likewise hampered a realistic preparedness program. The party out of power consistently opposes in normal times any program sponsored by the administration, particularly where the disbursement of large sums is to be in the hands of political foes. The Republicans in the 1930's regularly fought the preparedness proposals of Franklin Roosevelt, and then in the presidential campaigns of 1940 and 1944 condemned him for having been caught unprepared. It is the business of the opposition party to oppose, and there is every reason to believe that the Democrats would have done the same thing if the tables had been reversed.

Sectionalism also enters into the picture. The less one feels exposed to danger, the less one is concerned about preparedness. In prenatal days those colonies, like Maryland, which were farthest removed from the French-Canadian fighting front, were most laggard and niggardly in their contributions to the common cause. In 1915 the East, which felt more vulnerable to the German menace, was much more enthusiastic about fighting than the Far West; in 1940 the East, which was more exposed to German submarine and bombing raids, showed far greater interest in preparedness than the Middle West. In 1927 the Portland (Maine) *Express* predicted: "The United States will build the world's greatest navy whenever somebody invents a gun that will shoot from the Coast to Kansas."

6

Just as we have not had to worry about aggressive neighbors, so we have not had to concern ourselves with long-range plans for aggression against powers which possessed something that we wanted. From the very dawn of our national existence we have been a "have" nation, with enormous untrodden areas into which to expand, and consequently without any problem of "living room" for our population. Although we invaded Canada in 1812 and Mexico in 1846, we did so at a time when we still held vast unoccupied areas, and the real bases of our demand for those two wars must be sought elsewhere than in immediate land hunger. Each of our nineteenth century conflicts, even those of presumed conquest, was taken in stride, which in itself is prima facie evidence of the lack of far-visioned aggressive plans.

A dictator may build up a huge army for clearly thought out but unannounced purposes of aggression, as Hitler did in the 1930's. A democracy will not tolerate the expense of a great military establishment if there is no clear necessity for its use, either for purposes of defense or offense. One of the most interesting aspects of American naval history is that the advocates of a big navy, in order to get a modest-sized navy, have had to prop up a potential foe, even where none existed. At the turn of the present century, Congress was frightened into making appropriations by the bogey of the German Navy, even though it was checkmated by that of Britain; later, the Japanese Navy was used for the same purpose. Ironically, the Germans and the Japanese during the same period used the alleged menace of the American Navy to "shake down" reluctant legislators. No nation can have a naval race all to itself.

The American people over the years were in general too deeply absorbed in the back-breaking task of taming a continent to give much attention to either defense or aggression. At times our military and naval defenses were allowed to fall into an alarming state of decay. So decrepit was the navy in the 1870's that Admiral Porter was reminded of the dragons which the Chinese used to paint on their forts to frighten the enemy away. The New Navy of the 1880's and 1890's was brought into being in the face of the most determined opposition, and not until a new interest in foreign affairs had brought faint glimmers of outer-world mindedness. The distinguished American naval writer, Captain A. T. Mahan, whose *The Influence of Sea Power upon History, 1660–1783* (1890), was avidly read by British, German, and Japanese officers, failed to receive recognition as an honored prophet in his own country until he had become a world figure. The preparedness campaign of 1915, inspired by German ruthlessness in Belgium and on the high seas, encountered the most vehement opposition, including that at first of the pacifist-inclined President Wilson. We belatedly passed a conscription law in 1940, and a year later—four months before Pearl Harbor—this was renewed and extended with only one vote to spare, although the debate was complicated by the issue of keeping faith with the men already drafted.

In purely local matters of public health and safety, we are notoriously negligent; how then can we be expected to take a long-range view of preparedness? At times we have even regarded it as a laughing matter. "Secretary [of the Navy] Wilbur says the Navy is unready for war," quipped the *New Yorker* in 1929. "By an amusing coincidence there is no war ready for the Navy." Ten years later there was, and the navy was still unready.

The professional pacifists have increased the confusion by getting things as badly out of focus in their way as the professional preparedness zealots have in theirs. Unfortunately, as a Southern newspaper noted in 1916, "a soft head always seems to go with a soft heart." The pacifists, although not numerous, have been extremely vocal, well organized, and well financed, largely through the generosity of a millionaire philanthropist, Andrew Carnegie. Earnest pacifists have argued that armaments bring war (which is debatable), and that total disarmament, even on a unilateral basis, would bring peace (which is naïve). Another stock pacifist argument is that if we build up a big military machine our militarists will want to start shooting just to see how the shiny new toy will work. While it is perhaps true that a few of the younger and more daring spirits crave action, junior officers are seldom in a position to start wars. The charge of deliberately causing bloodshed is moreover a libel upon the responsible officers of the service, whose primary concern is to have the tools that will enable them to do the job expected of them, rather than court certain death. To accuse our generals and admirals of "starting wars" is equivalent to accusing the fire department of starting fires so that the personnel may see how far the new hose on the big red engine will squirt water.

7

The supreme self-confidence of the American has led him to sneer at elaborate military preparations. Brought up fighting Indians, he developed an exaggerated idea of his military prowess with the squirrel rifle; accustomed to brushing aside tremendous obstacles, he became a devotee of the cult that everything would come out all right. The "War Hawks" of 1812 voted for war, and then voted down naval preparations. During the pre-1917 preparedness agitation, the professional pacifist William Jennings Bryan proclaimed that if the need arose a million men would spring to arms between sunrise and sunset. Once in a war we have consistently counted upon an early and victorious ending. "The American people never carry an umbrella," said Alfred E. Smith in 1931. "They prepare to walk in eternal sunshine."

America was a gamble, and the American was and is a born gambler. He gambled his life against the Indians, the elements, disease, and wild animals and reptiles. He gambled his crops against drought, heatwaves, prairie fires, and dust storms; against frosts and blizzards; against floods and cyclones; against locusts, grasshoppers, and boll weevils; against erosion and soil exhaustion; against low prices, high railroad rates, and high interest rates. Often he has gambled his national fortunes without too much in his hand. President Polk backed "Fifty-four Forty" against the might of the British Navy in 1845–1846, while undertaking no corresponding naval preparations. President Cleveland backed the claims of Venezuela against the might of the British Navy in 1895–1896, while undertaking no serious naval preparations. Sometimes the bluff has backfired, as against Germany in 1917 and Japan in 1941, but on the whole we have done some remarkable things with a penny-ante hand.

Lady Luck has been our greatest and most consistent ally, and she has been on our side so often that we have almost come to regard her as a first line of defense, along with the oceans and Europe's distresses. We blundered into fever-infested Cuba in 1898, to the tune of "There'll Be a Hot Time in the Old Town Tonight." The Spanish fleet obligingly ran out to destruction before yellow fever could do its deadly work, and the war came to a victorious end. Someone has well said that both God and the Spaniards fought on the side of the United States. The unfriendly Bismarck was moved to growl a version of the old saying: "God looks after drunks, children, and Americans."

We were lucky to come off as well as we did in 1783 and in 1814; we were lucky to invade Mexico as expeditiously as we did in 1846–1848; we were lucky to preserve the Union in 1861–1865. (Even the elements cooperated, as in World War I and World War II, to bring bumper grain crops.) In 1917, despite prolonged warning, we entered upon hostilities with Germany, proceeded to pass (with full debate) a conscription law six weeks later, and finally got an army to France (chiefly in Allied ships), while our Allies were holding the enemy at bay. The war was almost lost twice after we got into it: in the spring of 1917, when submarine attacks took an appalling toll; in the spring of 1918, when the Germans almost broke through to Paris in their final desperate drive. The Kansas City *Star* remarked in 1915: "The United States would have no difficulty about defending itself in a war with a great Power if the enemy would only agree to postpone the fighting until the second year."

In 1941, despite another prolonged warning, we were plunged into war after suffering the most devastating naval defeat in our history. If Stalingrad had not held, if El Alamein had not held, if Guadalcanal had not held, if the Battle of Midway (thanks to the "cracking" of the secret Japanese code) had not been won—if, if, if—the conflict could well have been lost. Yet we won, not because of our unpreparedness, but in spite of it, and because the Allies held back the enemy while we forged our armor and buckled it on.

8

Chance has been described as another name for human ignorance and shortsightedness, and if this is true our military fortunes, so far as the public is concerned, have been left largely at the mercy of chance. But Luck is a fickle goddess, and by the law of averages cannot dwell in our camp forever. When our good fortune turned and the Great Depression descended in the 1930's, the American was more baffled by it than by any other major obstacle that had yet confronted him: he could not see it and grapple with it. Also, as one Georgia newspaper said in 1931: "A depression is harder to lick than a foreign enemy because there is nobody to hold it while we get ready."

Luck has not only been on our side in wartime, but with the characteristic ingratitude of republics, we have refused to give her credit for her help. Our textbooks prove that we not only won all of our wars but that we did so all by ourselves. We whipped the "master race" twice, in 1918 and again in 1945; and oh, yes! there were some other nations in there botching up the job until we showed them how to do it. We might not be so sadly unprepared next time if our textbooks would place less emphasis on our glorious victories and more on our chronic unpreparedness, our dismal defeats, our narrow escapes, the contributions of allies, the intervention of the oceans, the assistance provided by the world situation, and the blessings of good fortune. But such a textbook would probably not get adoptions, and the author and publisher would not make the same mistake a second time.

The capacity of the human race to forget misery and disgrace, while making life more endurable, does not conduce to military preparedness in a democracy. Our only smashing land victory in the War of 1812 that was not set up by naval power came with Andrew Jackson's exhilarating triumph over the British at New Orleans. The battle was actually fought after the treaty of peace had been signed, and Jackson escaped disaster by a narrow margin. If the British had only thrown a slightly stronger force across the river in their flanking attack, he probably would not have become president of the United States or possibly of anything else. But it was a great victory, and if a nation is going to win only one great victory, the aftertaste is more pleasant if success comes with the last battle rather than the first. For more than a century the rejoicing over New Orleans drowned out our earlier ineptitudes and failures, and contributed powerfully to the legend that we beat England to her knees and extorted a victor's peace.

"Remember Pearl Harbor" was a thoroughly un-American slogan. No nation likes to remember its disgraces, and Americans are less prone to than most. In time of war we prepare for war, and when it ends we tend to forget all about it, thus reversing the maxim: "In time of peace prepare for war." In 1917, when we were bogged down in the early confusion of World War I, the Brooklyn *Eagle* aptly remarked, "Prepare at leisure, repent in haste." The military men begged for a high-class army after both World War I and World War II; they knew perfectly well that they had better strike while the memory of recent unpreparedness was hot. They failed after World War I, when the nation lapsed back into its customary coma; they had a much better chance of success after World War II, when the atom bomb served as a potent reminder. A strong majority of the voters favored peacetime conscription in the months after the atomic awfulness of Hiroshima, Nagasaki, and Bikini. The average citizen has learned a good deal in recent years, and he has learned it the hard way, but the future will tell whether he has learned enough.

9

A basic weakness of American foreign policy is the inability of our people to recognize the intimate relationship between military power and foreign affairs. This weakness is not confined to the Man in the Street; the men on the Potomac at times seem no less blind. A kind of superstitious horror has sprung up against the realities of "power politics," despite Bismarck's dictum: "Political questions are questions of power."

Why do we have armed forces? Negatively, for self-defense and security; positively (and correlatively) to uphold policies. The long scroll of history reveals that whenever the policies and ambitions of two nations collide, the one able to muster the greater physical force prevails. Theodore Roosevelt understood this principle well. His policy was to speak softly and carry a Big Stick; if you had the Big Stick, you could work your will without shouting; if you did not have it, you could shout and not work your will. Theodore Roosevelt also said that he never took a position in foreign affairs that he could not ultimately back up by force, and he scolded his successor Taft for trying to halt Japan in Manchuria with a barricade of State Department notes. To do the job, Roosevelt pointed out, Taft would need a navy as powerful as Britain's then was, and an army as powerful as Germany's then was.

Woodrow Wilson, with strong pacifist leanings, and with a pacifist secretary of state and a pacifist secretary of war, did not appreciate the potency of the Big Stick; instead, as someone quipped, he made Big Faces. His bluffing worked for a while, as long as it was to the interest of Germany to respect it, but then the bluff was called and we found ourselves in the conflict. If in 1914 or even 1915, Wilson had thrown his full weight behind a formidable army and merchant marine, and a properly equipped navy, he might have dissuaded the German war lords in 1917 from provoking the United States into battle. Again we were penny wise and pound foolish.

Franklin Roosevelt understood as well as his distant cousin the value of the Big Stick, but partisan politics and a parsimonious Congress denied him the physical force with which to back up his Far Eastern demands. By 1941 the only alternatives seemed to be to leave Japan alone or resort to bluff, and the bluff finally boomeranged on the day of Pearl Harbor.

Everything is relative, and the size of a nation's armed forces should depend on the policy it proposes to uphold. To clamor for a navy three or four times larger than all the fleets of the rest of the world put together seems out of line with reality. The slogan, "A navy second to none," makes sense only if a nation's defense requirements and foreign policy require a navy second to none. The legend has grown that a second-best navy is like a second-best hand in a poker game; yet some remarkable bluffs have been engineered with second-best hands. The German Navy in World War I and the Italian and Japanese navies in World War II had high nuisance value. In World War II much Allied naval strength was diverted to watch the German high seas fleet, even after it had been secretly demobilized for about two years.

The naval needs of the United States have grown with its growth. When we had only one coast, we needed only a small navy; when we acquired two coasts, we needed a modest-sized navy; when we annexed Hawaii, Guam, the Philippines, and Puerto Rico, we needed a strong navy; when we undertook to halt Japan in China we needed a huge navy; when we sought to stamp out Axis dictatorship in two hemispheres, we needed (and built) a colossal, seven-ocean navy.

The tail should never wag the dog, and one must never forget that armaments are made (or should be) for policies, not vice versa. The armed forces should be the handmaidens of foreign affairs. We must first define our policies, and then amass powerful enough units to uphold them. It naturally follows that unless we have a clearly defined foreign policy, we cannot have an intelligent military and naval policy. In fairness to the fighting men, we ought to tell them what our foreign policy is, what they will be expected to defend or uphold in time of war, and then give them the equipment with which to complete the assignment. Instead, we have traditionally kept them in the dark as to what was expected of them, and if they asked for the bare minimum of tools we branded them warmongers. In the darkest days of 1942 we had only one aircraft carrier and one modern battleship in the vast Pacific Ocean, not counting those resting on the bottom of Pearl Harbor, and not counting smaller craft.

10

President Wilson's Secretary of the Navy once asked the Secretary of War for some minor cooperation, and was told: "You run your show and I'll run mine." One of the most sensible proposals to come out of Washington in recent years was the one to merge—or at least to coordinate—not only the army and the navy but the State Department as well. The disaster at Pearl Harbor was plainly due to a breakdown of liaison among the three departments. Nor was this the last instance. In 1946 the State Department was trying to "talk tough" to Russia, while the army and navy were being demobilized with indecent haste.

The American citizen must be educated to an awareness of the intimate connection between preparedness and foreign policy. The great naval act of 1916 was not a case of too little and too late, but too much and too late and of the wrong kind.[*] Only one of the capital ships that might have backed up Wilson's demands on Berlin in 1917 was completed by 1921, three years after the armistice, and most of these were scrapped under the terms of the Washington Disarmament Conference of 1921–1922. In the 1930's we lagged far behind in building up the naval strength to which we had been entitled by treaty arrangements, and when Congress belatedly began to vote huge appropriations for supplying the deficiencies, the United States appeared to be accelerating in an unfriendly manner the current arms race. We put off fortifying Guam for so long in the 1930's that an eleventh-hour program was opposed as a seemingly hostile act aimed at Japan.

The public must also be educated to its responsibilities in wartime. After giving our military men the tools, we should let them do the job for which they are trained without joggling their elbows. Clemenceau uttered a great truth when he said that war is much too important to be left to the soldiers,

[*] Late in 1915 the Washington *Post* remarked: "A good navy is to be built within the next five years. Foreign foes will please be patient."

but it is also too important to be left to ignorant if well-meaning civilians.

A sober analysis of our military history reveals that on a number of occasions we came near the brink of disaster because of ill-advised public pressure. When Admiral Cervera's fleet left Spain in 1898 for the West Indies, and panic seized our Atlantic seaboard, public opinion forced the Navy Department to detach some warships from places where they were most needed to areas where they were least needed. If the Spanish fleet had been stronger, the tale might well have had a less happy ending. In 1943, when our forces were so weak that our high command had decided to concentrate on Hitler, a loud get-Hirohito-first group threatened to force a change of policy and thus prolong or even lose the war. Instances could be multiplied, including the agitation during World War II for a second front several years before this gigantic and hazardous operation could be undertaken with a reasonable prospect of success. There should be enough public discussion so that the generals may know what losses will be tolerated in achieving certain objectives, but the layman should leave highly technical problems to those trained to understand them.

We have learned a good deal from the remorseless tutelage of recent events, and we are not likely to slip back completely into the pre-1930 stupor. At the end of World War II we expected another world conflict within twenty-five or fifty years; we continued to favor peacetime conscription; we were unwilling to give up our atomic bomb until it was properly internationalized; and we were determined not to be caught again, as at the time of Pearl Harbor, with our planes down. But human nature being what it is, especially American human nature, the events of the postwar years will have to be critical indeed if we are going to retain the same deep solicitude for continued defense that we had when the war ended with a bang after Nagasaki. The noise and stench of battle are all too quickly forgotten.

CHAPTER SEVEN

THE AMERICAN WAY IN WAR

"It would be not merely foolish but wicked for us as a nation to agree to arbitrate any dispute that affects our vital interest or our independence or our honor."—THEODORE ROOSEVELT, 1911

1

THE EXPERIENCE of the American people, as earlier noted, gives little support to the popular fallacy that democracies are less likely to provoke war than other forms of government. We are undeniably more peace-loving than other nations in the sense that we plunge into war without adequate preparation. Someone has well said that we are a warlike but unmilitary people.

The brutal truth is that the citizens of a democracy are at times the hardest and most unreasonable bargainers. Without give and take there can be no successful international negotiation in peacetime, and the American people, not properly appreciating this principle, are likely to demand all take and no give. The masses of any country are less prone to prevision than the leaders of an absolutist government. While a dictator may provoke a war with Machiavellian motives, he is less apt than the mob to embark upon a war of impulse or passion. Hitler appeared to be an exception when he attacked Poland in a fit of exhausted patience, but up to that point his plans had certainly been laid with diabolical cunning.

A further glimpse at the record is rewarding. In 1812 England was a monarchy (though the last bulwark of constitutionalism in Europe), and she did not want war with us, but our "War Hawks" got out of hand and we found ourselves fighting at the side of the Hitler of the Napoleonic era. In 1898 the Spanish monarchy did not want war with us, and was doing all it decently could to avert hostilities, but public pressure in America forced President McKinley's hand. Both of these conflicts, aggressively declared by the American democracy upon a reluctant monarchy, were wars of impulse, and as such could theoretically have been avoided.

One may conclude that during certain periods democracies have been known to fight more often, more irrationally, and over more trivial causes than certain contemporary monarchies. Much more depends on circumstances than on form of government. A designing dictator will fight when his interests are vitally touched; the masses of a democracy will demand war (and get it) when they think, whether correctly or not, that their interests are critically threatened. The citizens of a democracy may be oversensitive on points of national honor, they may be subject to the terrifying whims of mob psychology, but, unlike the dictator, they cannot engage in a mass conspiracy against the peace. A mass conspiracy is a contradiction in terms.

If the American nation has been more pacific than others, the basic explanation is not to be found in our form of government. We are an amalgam of other peoples, and logic does not indicate that the melting pot has made us either more warlike or less warlike than the racial strains from which we have been fused. There is nothing about the air, water, or soil of America that demonstrably changes the innate impulses of human nature.

Much depends on opportunity and incentive. The Swiss, boasting the oldest of living democracies, once excelled as professional soldiers; now they excel as hotelkeepers. England, first as a monarchy and then as a democracy, has been embroiled in countless wars. Sweden is now a democracy, but under the monarchical Gustavus Adolphus and Charles XII the Swedes were the scourge of Europe. A Swede is a Swede, whether he lived in Stockholm under Gustavus II or in Minneapolis under Roosevelt II.

The provocations that drive other people to fight have on the whole been strikingly absent from America. With enormous acreage, we have never felt the pressure of overpopulation, like Japan and Italy. With seemingly inexhaustible natural resources, we have never felt the pressing urge for raw materials, like England and Germany. With a tremendous virginal endowment, we have seldom felt the impulse to conquer just for the sake of conquering. A formidable list could be made of the areas we might have peacefully annexed or forcibly seized if we had been more grasping, and it would include all of Mexico, Canada, Cuba, Haiti, Santo Domingo, and Greenland. We finally did take over Hawaii (1898) and the Virgin Islands (1917), but both of these places could have been acquired much sooner.

2

We as a people are prone to pass through national moods, some pacific, some bellicose. Other countries do the same thing. In 1870 the French shouted, "On to Berlin!" In 1939 they groaned, "Why die for Danzig?"

All of our foreign wars, including the one for independence, began in the spring of the year, except that of 1941, when the devastating assault at Pearl Harbor left Congress no choice. The poet might almost have said that in the springtime men's fancies lightly turn to thoughts of fighting.

Historically, our war moods have tended to have a cyclical recurrence. Our major conflicts have been spaced about a generation apart, with the young bloods whooping it up for hostilities.[*] The youthful devotees of Mars are not only more energetic, adventuresome, and hotheaded, but, having had no war of their own, they become weary hearing their fathers and grandfathers win the previous one singlehanded.

Thus we have had recurring fits of bellicosity. In the 1890's, with reconstruction ended, the transcontinental railroads built, the Indians sent to the Happy

[*] Except in 1939–1941, when the disillusionment of the 1930's was conspicuous among youths of college age.

Hunting Grounds or to reservations, the last free land in quantity dispensed, the memories of the Civil War dimmed, the international atmosphere tense with land-grabbing, we simply had to fight somebody—or so it seemed. We were bursting with pent-up power, and we responded naturally to the elemental laws of physical expansion. From 1891 to 1895, a period of four years, we came close to fighting three different powers: Italy, Chile, and Britain. The various quarrels were finally patched up, but we were not to be denied in 1898, when we took it out on a fourth, Spain. If we had fought England in 1895, as we almost did, Spain certainly would have lingered longer in Cuba, and might conceivably be there today.

We have had periods of national exaltation or grandeur. In the 1840's, when Manifest Destiny was epidemic, we were intoxicated with the idea of spreading our republican institutions, by arms if necessary, from the aurora borealis to the Southern Cross. Mexico had the misfortune to be in our way, and we expended our energy on her.

We have had periods of irrationality. Our grievances against England were less acute in 1812 than they had been at any time since 1807, yet we unsheathed the sword. The *Maine* explosion of 1898 was the incident that touched off the Spanish-American powder magazine, and we rushed into the conflict shouting: "Remember the *Maine*, to hell with Spain." Yet to this day we do not know how, by whom, or under what circumstances the fatal spark was ignited.

Then we have had periods of spiritual depression, frequently preceded by economic doldrums. The imperialistic upsurge at the turn of the century proved to be an expensive escapade. The war to make the world safe for democracy and to end wars, fought and concluded with such high hopes in 1917–1918, produced a harvest of smoke and ashes. The fruit of victory proved to be the apple of discord and disillusionment.

A lost generation of young people wandered aimlessly during the depression years of the 1930's between the war that had been fought and the war that was coming, and they brought a dash of defeatism to the American spirit that its younger days had never known. This cynicism, deepened by the Great Depression, contributed powerfully to the head-in-the-sands neutrality legislation of the 1930's. In the Far East, where the mad men of Tokyo were on the rampage, we were willing that the Open Door should be slammed shut rather than risk war. There was strong sentiment for turning tail, pulling all troops out of China, and warning Americans to stay there at their own risk.

In 1898 no earthly power could hold us back from war with Spain; in 1937 the picture was entirely different. As the war lords of Nippon ran amok in China, American businesses were ruined; American property was confiscated and destroyed; American missions were wrecked; American citizens were slapped, stripped, and slaughtered. Yet the hitherto proud American eagle merely cowered and glowered. The Far East was too far away, and the Great Depression was too close at hand. Why should we be "suckered" into fighting

China's battles? In 1898 the explosion on the *Maine* was matched by an explosion of public opinion; in 1937 the sinking of the *Panay* by Japanese aviators aroused no comparable reaction. Yet there never was the slightest doubt as to how or by whom the American gunboat was destroyed.

Early in 1945, after the conflict had been fought and Japan's imperialistic gangsterism had been laid bare, a national opinion poll revealed an incredible state of mind. Eight persons out of ten still believed that on the day of Pearl Harbor the President should have been making every effort to keep the nation out of war.

3

Conceptions of national honor have changed with our changing moods. In the days of our youth, we had a well developed inferiority complex, and were hypersensitive to any affront to our nation or people. The impressment of American seamen from American ships flying the American flag on the high seas was an outrage not to be borne. But the years marched on, and by 1916 the mood of the hour was: "He kept us out of war." The Democratic keynoter at the national convention in St. Louis repeatedly brought the delegates to their feet with his long list of instances when we had not fought to avenge insult.

One of the hoariest tricks of monarchs is to whip up a foreign war scare behind which to divert attention from empty stomachs and stolen liberties. Such devices have not been absent from the repertoire of democratic governments. When President Harrison in 1892 used an unnecessarily harsh tone toward Chile in connection with the killing of American sailors in the *Baltimore* riot, he was accused, whether correctly or not, of having the coming election in view. In 1895, during the Venezuela crisis with England, certain bellicose congressmen openly asserted that hostilities would be a good thing: war would submerge the economic and social discontent of the country.

Franklin Roosevelt has often been accused by isolationists and Republicans of leading the nation into war so as to cover up the failures of the New Deal. Proof of such a contention is lacking. But it is a fact that after nearly a decade of depression, the war brought unparalleled prosperity, as could have been predicted. It is a fact that Roosevelt told the newsmen in 1943 that the slogan "New Deal" was out of date, and suggested a change to something like "Win the War." It is a fact that the national opinion polls revealed that if there had been no war in 1944 Roosevelt could not have triumphed over the Republican candidate.

In the absence of proof no fair-minded person would accuse Roosevelt of having deliberately provoked Pearl Harbor so as to cut loose from the burden of the New Deal, and thus insure his reelection. But whether he planned it that way or not, it worked out that way, and he would have been a little less than human if, in view of the necessity of halting the dictators, he did not secretly rejoice at the outcome.

What the moods of the future will be no man can safely predict. But we have had our bellicose outbursts in the past; and who can say that we shall not have them in the future? When the Yugoslavs in 1946 shot down and killed several American airmen, a New York newspaper suggested that we might drop at least one atomic bomb somewhere in Yugoslavia just to show these young upstarts that we were pretty tough people. This kind of talk was of course irresponsible, as was the contemporary suggestion that since we had the atomic bomb and Russia did not, we had better pick a fight with her and knock her out before she got too strong and began the inevitable war with us. In 1947 a Congressional Committee was told by ex-Governor George H. Earle, of Pennsylvania, former United States minister to Bulgaria and Turkey, that because we would not wipe out Russia with atomic bombs, she would wipe us out within five years, and that not 10 per cent of our people would survive.

Such views were not endorsed by majority opinion in the United States, but they had a most disquieting effect in the Soviet Union. We Americans know that we are nice people and that we have the best of intentions; we know that we do not want anybody's territory and that we have no intention of picking wars. We know that others ought to trust us to do the right thing with the atomic bomb. But do the Russians and all other foreign peoples also know this?

The Soviets profess to fear the United States, and we know that their fears are ridiculous. Yet we are tremendously powerful, and we are a democracy. Democracies, including our own, pass through moods that are as unpredictable as the way of a man with a maid. Democracies can be and have been taken over by dictators. We have had our bellicose outbursts in the past, and although we are now more adult, there is no absolute assurance that we shall not have them again in the future.

4

Loyal Americans have long felt complacent about the record of their government in contributing to the pacific settlement of international disputes.

It is undeniable that the United States (with England) pioneered in the establishment of modern arbitration when we negotiated and ratified Jay's treaty. It is undeniable that our government has presented a considerable number of disputes to arbitral tribunals, notably in the case of the Geneva award of 1872. It is undeniable that we have taken the lead in mediating disputes between foreign powers, conspicuously so when in 1905 Theodore Roosevelt induced the Russians and the Japanese to stop their blood-letting.

American political figures like Root, Taft, and Bryan have shown aggressive leadership in promoting general arbitration treaties. The "cooling off" pacts of Secretary Bryan commanded much less respect at home than they deserved, largely because Bryan himself did not command too much respect.* Other American statesmen—men like Theodore Roosevelt, Woodrow Wilson, and Frank B. Kellogg—have won more Nobel peace prizes than their contemporaries elsewhere. Distinguished American jurists—men like Root, Moore, Hudson—took the lead in establishing the World Court at the close of World War I, and the new World Court at the close of World War II.

This looks like an impressive record, and it is, relatively. But there is another side of the ledger. While we have consented to arbitrate a number of disputes, usually of minor importance, we have repeatedly refused to arbitrate other cases where the issue of peace or war was at stake. For example, we declined to arbitrate the Oregon boundary with Britain and the Alaska boundary with Canada. The Oregon dispute was finally settled by mutual agreement, but only after we had skated near the brink of bloodshed; and the Alaska boundary was adjusted by a highly unsatisfactory pseudo-arbitration arrangement. We declined to arbitrate the *Maine* case in 1898, and it led to war. In 1896 we forced Britain at pistol's point to arbitrate a boundary dispute with Venezuela; in 1913 we flatly declined to arbitrate our Panama Canal tolls dispute with Britain. The sauce of arbitration was evidently good for the British goose but not for the American gander.

The Senate eviscerated and then rejected a general arbitration treaty with England in 1897, and by so doing sacrificed American leadership of the movement. Subsequent arbitration or "cooling-off" treaties were ineffective, or watered down by the Senate, or equipped with senatorial escape hatches, which meant, as one newspaper put it in 1908, that we would have to arbitrate "only in cases where we don't care to fight." We ran out on the League of Nations (after sponsoring it), and we refused to adhere to the League-connected World Court (after sponsoring it), except on our own terms, which were unacceptable to the other powers. We would go into the "League Court," as one Southern paper put it, only if we could "go in with our fingers crossed." † When the Senate struck the final blow in 1935, the irreconcilable Senator Borah uttered a fervent, "Thank God!" while the no less irreconcilable Senator Hiram W. Johnson declared: "This is one of the happiest days of my life. The Senate has averted a serious danger to our beloved republic."

Chastened by World War II, we actively sponsored a new world court in 1945. But when the Senate took final action in 1946, even the most ardent advocates of the new tribunal united with an overwhelming number of their colleagues to attach the inevitable emasculating reservations. We reserved the right to withhold from adjudication any question which we regarded as domestic, and this covered a great deal of territory. We were to be the judges of what the judges should judge. Again we were going into things with our fingers crossed.

* The Memphis *Commercial-Appeal* jeered in 1914: "Secretary Bryan's completed arbitration treaties with Switzerland, Denmark, and Uruguay take a great load off our minds. The thought of war with them was terrible."

† The New York *Evening Post* jibed in 1929: "If a resolution indorsing the Ten Commandments were introduced in the Senate it would be loaded down with 110 reservations."

The ordinary citizen is not responsible in a positive sense for all of these unfortunate failures. When the State Department refused to arbitrate questions touching national honor, the American people were undoubtedly behind their government. But the Senate at times has been less definitely in line with public opinion. One cannot speak with complete assurance for the pre-Gallup era, but popular majorities were almost certainly favorable to both the League (in some form) and to the World Court (with reservations) when each failed of approval by the Senate. The more responsive House of Representatives in 1925 passed a resolution favoring the World Court by a majority of 303 to 28. The Senate, for reasons indicated in an earlier chapter, is less amenable to public pressure, particularly in regard to treaties. "If there is anything in the world which will make a United States Senator fight," opined a Virginia newspaper in 1929, "it is a peace pact."

5

But in a negative sense the Man in the Street is responsible for our many failures in the pacific settlement of disputes. If he had appreciated the importance of the World Court; if he had thrown himself wholeheartedly behind it; if he had spoken with singleness of purpose for affirmative action, there seems no doubt that he would have prevailed, as he did in the case of the United Nations Charter. When the corpse of the World Court was dragged from the senatorial bull ring in 1935, the *Christian Science Monitor* observed that the result was "a victory for ignorance, prejudice—and apathy." And the greatest of these was apathy. A majority of the American people clearly favored the Court, but they did not favor it hard enough. The country dozes, while the Senate disposes.

The path of good will is seldom exciting, and the ordinary citizen, bred to the journalistic principle that good news is no news, is somewhat repelled by the whole drab subject of arbitration. The cause of peace lacks color and drama, unlike war, with its roll of drums and blare of trumpets. "Peace has its victories no less than war," wrote Kin Hubbard, "but it doesn't have as many monuments t' unveil." After the exhilarating successes of the Spanish-American War, the American people were bored by the disarmament proposals of the Hague Peace Conference of 1899, and it is perhaps significant that the best known of our delegates was the distinguished naval officer and author, Captain A. T. Mahan. The Hague Conference of 1899 was criticized in the press for not even having "disarmed criticism"; the second one (that of 1907) was disrespectfully referred to as the "Vague Peace Conference."

Arbitration seems unappealing for another reason: it apparently does not touch the average person directly, like tax reduction. A more serious objection is the possibility that we might lose. If the arbitration is a fair one, and the issues are closely drawn, our chances are about fifty-fifty. This is the basic reason why we are reluctant to arbitrate such vital questions as tariff barriers and immigration dikes.

The more powerful we have become, the less enthusiastic we have been about resorting to the courts. Arbitration in the past has frequently been the first (and last) defense line of small nations. Our earliest major move toward arbitration, in Jay's treaty of 1794, came at a time when we were so weak that there was no sensible alternative. After we became strong, we became more indifferent: we could twist the arms of the small powers and have our own way. So why risk the hazards of adjudication? It is perhaps more than coincidental that the year before we overwhelmed Spain and burst onto the stage as a world power, we rejected our first general arbitration treaty, that of 1897 with England. Yet on the whole we have been willing to arbitrate small issues with great powers; it is not easy to push them around, and besides it costs too much to fight them. In such cases we prefer settlement by men around a table rather than by men around a gun.

One may conclude that the record of the United States in arbitration leaves something to be desired. With the usual weaknesses of human nature, we have been more enthusiastic about having others arbitrate. "Arbitration is like international law," remarked the New York *World* in 1916, "something that the other fellow ought scrupulously to respect." Although we have submitted a number of issues to arbitration, one can scarcely point to a single instance when, if we had lost, we would have been seriously discommoded. Significantly, we have never subjected to the hazards of arbitration a single controversy involving our security in the Caribbean defense zone. Our general attitude in such disputes was summed up by the Philadelphia *Ledger* in 1897, when Japan was protesting against our treaty for absorbing the Hawaiian Islands: "The United States does not propose to arbitrate the annexation of Hawaii with any power but itself."

6

Once we have found ourselves in armed conflict, the weaknesses of democratic processes have been underscored and magnified. Democracy is better geared for the victories of peace than for the victories of war. An earlier chapter has dealt with our chronic unpreparedness, and with the dangers of ignorant pressure from a panicky and ill-informed public. Certain additional defects must be mentioned.

The war-declaring power is in the hands of Congress, which is alleged to be a deliberative body, but no great deliberative body can move with either secrecy or dispatch. On the eve of Pearl Harbor President Roosevelt knew perfectly well that the Japanese were preparing to strike, and if he had been a dictator he would have thrown them off balance by striking first. He in fact seriously considered doing so. But since he was not a dictator, and since an aggressive act on his part would have disrupted the nation, he had to sit quietly and wait for the prospective enemy to choose the time and place of attack.

Another weakness is no less glaring. The average citizen does not understand that in time of war the diplomatic front is often more important than the military front, and that the ordinary methods of diplomacy must frequently be thrown to the wolves of expediency. The State Department continued diplomatic relations from 1940 to 1942 with the Fascist-tinged government of Vichy France, primarily to pave the way for the surprise invasion of North Africa. The American people obviously did not know that such plans were in the making, and just as obviously their government could not reveal its secret. Hence a constant yammering was directed at the State Department for maintaining relations with the puppet Pétain, but when the invasion was sensationally launched, most of the red-faced critics grew silent.

Modern wars are coalition wars, and the average American does not want to entrust the lives of his sons to a foreign generalissimo. In World War I General Pershing bitterly and successfully resisted the efforts of the French to have American troops used as replacements; whatever the cost, he was going to have a separate command. This decision could have lost the war, but as usual luck was on the side of the United States. Not until the spring of 1918 did the Allies subordinate themselves to a supreme command; and in World War II they never did succeed in doing so.

Another wartime embarrassment is the quadrennial convulsion of the presidential election. Nations which enjoy the parliamentary form of government, like Great Britain, can avoid this distraction. But in the United States elections come not by the crisis but by the calendar, and the calendar is no respecter of wars. At critical times in the past, when our undivided energy should have been concentrated on winning the conflict, we have had to lay aside the tools of the warrior for the tools of the politician. Elections came most inopportunely in 1812, in 1864, and in 1944, but in all these cases the administration survived, partly on the Lincolnian principle that one should not swap horses in the middle of the stream. In 1812 and 1864 a victory for the opposition might have proved disastrous; in 1944, when there was some talk of laying aside the Constitution for the duration, a victory for the Republicans would have been awkward rather than disastrous.

7

Disunity is a demon which to some extent always hampers democracies in wartime. Dictatorships have developed effective if brutal methods of silencing ordinary dissent. But free speech and free press are among our most priceless birthrights, and we have never willingly submitted to arbitrary control.

The value of unity hardly needs proof, but a glance at the past is rewarding. Our worst-fought war was the one in which we were most disunited

(War of 1812), and our best-fought war was the one in which we were most united (World War II).

The nation was badly disrupted in 1812, with the opposition Federalists, concentrated in New England, condemning the approach of "Mr. Madison's War." President Madison knew this, but he flung forward the torch in the hope that the patriotic impulses of the people would cause them to rise and seize it. He was rudely disillusioned, and we fought with one section of the country, New England, either immobilized or actively assisting the enemy. To lead a disunited people into war in the hope that war will unify them is as risky as marrying a drunkard in the hope that marriage will reform him. In the Mexican War the opposition of the Whigs was not at first formidable, but it swelled as the conflict progressed. One Ohio congressman expressed the sentiments of many Whig brethren when he branded the conflict as "illegal, unrighteous, and damnable." In the closing stages of the fighting, the Whig newspapers called upon Congress to vote down supplies for the armies in the field, thus forcing our troops to evacuate Mexico or surrender. The opportune conclusion of peace helped forestall such a disaster.

The Civil War was not a foreign war, but a series of civil wars within a big one. Yet there were die-hard Unionists in the South and irreconcilable Copperheads in the North.

The Spanish-American War, though not welcomed by the moneyed interests, was too spontaneous, too short, and too uninterruptedly successful to permit the formation of a formidable dissenting group.

In 1917 the country finally accepted the U-boat challenge with a high degree of unity. The Kaiser was sinking our ships on the high seas, and we have seldom been so dead to the promptings of honor as to take this kind of thing lying down. As the Philadelphia *North American* put it, on the eve of formal action by Congress: "The difference between war and what we have now is that now we aren't fighting back." The votes in both houses of Congress were overwhelming, and most of the rather negligible opposition was concentrated in the German-immigrant Middle West. But the German-Americans, despite fears to the contrary, generally proved themselves loyal— or at any rate discreet.

President Wilson was a discerning student of American history, and he knew better than to lead a disunited nation into war. In one of his letters of the predeclaration period he noted that only two Princeton men had ever been elected President, Madison and himself, and he was not going to repeat Madison's blunder. He was determined not to ask Congress for a declaration until public opinion was unmistakably for it, and his decision doubtless was wise, though many of his critics accused him of leaning over backward.

On the early morning of Pearl Harbor Day, the country was seriously at cross-purposes. A colossal majority wanted to keep out of war, although a bare majority was willing to risk war rather than see Britain go down. The America Firsters, with Colonel Lindbergh as the leading spokesman, had a formidable following, though it fell somewhat short of a simple majority.

If the Japanese had continued their push toward the Dutch East Indies without attacking American soil, the Roosevelt administration would have encountered great difficulty in getting a war resolution through Congress. Even if such a measure had passed, it would have been approved by a disruptively close margin, and only after long and costly delay.

The Japanese, who thus far had been successfully counting on disunity to paralyze American policy, did the one thing needful to unify the nation. The aerial torpedoes that sank the American fleet at Pearl Harbor no less successfully sank America Firstism. The nation rose in one hour as one man in a demonstration of unanimity unequalled in all our history. "The only thing now to do," asserted isolationist Senator Wheeler, "is to lick hell out of them." The battleships sunk in Hawaii were a cheap if unnecessary price to pay for American unity.

Hitler and Mussolini likewise obliged. They declared war on us and spared us the agony and disunity of a prolonged debate, during which professional Anglophobes undoubtedly would have objected to fighting a war for British imperialism. Other shortsighted souls would have said that since only the Japanese had attacked us we should wage a private war against them in the Pacific. (The get-Hirohito-first groups took essentially this line anyhow.) As it turned out, only one dissenting vote was cast against the three war resolutions in both houses of Congress.

Future presidents of the United States, whether from Princeton or not, will do well to remember one priceless lesson. If they plan to lead this nation into war against a formidable foe, they should have the backing of not a mere majority, nor of a strong majority, but of an overwhelming majority. A percentage of 51 or 55 will almost certainly bring disaster; 90 per cent may bring victory.

8

Handicapped as our democracy has been in wartime by individualism and free speech, how have we managed to muddle through?

One answer is that as our conflicts have become more gigantic, our people have become more mature. World War II is instructive. Although there was considerable agitation for breaking relations with Vichy France, for rushing aid to MacArthur at Bataan, for "getting" Hirohito first, and for starting a second front prematurely, these pressures came from a minority small enough to be ignored, or from a group whose intensity of feeling was not at a dangerously high pitch. One poll revealed that a strong majority of our people, even those on the Pacific Coast during the month or so after Pearl Harbor, realized that the Germans were a greater menace than the Japanese. If in ancient Greek times men, rather than walls, made the city strong, so in modern American times our greatest national resource is an intelligent people.

We also have energy, imagination, Yankee inventiveness, industrial knowhow, unprecedented wealth, and tremendous national resources. In 1918, as in 1942, the outcome could not be doubted once the American people were given the time to swing their industrial colossus into the scales.

Above all—and dictators present and future please note well—we have the resourcefulness and dynamism of a free people who are still on the march, even though their breathless pace may have slackened. Democracy has its faults in war, but some of these are by-products of its virtues.

CHAPTER EIGHT

THE GREAT GAME OF POLITICS

Ez to my principles, I glory
In hevin' nothin' o' the sort;
I aint a Whig, I aint a Tory,
I'm jest a canderdate, in short.
—JAMES RUSSELL LOWELL, 1846

1

THE AMERICAN is a political animal. In the pre-Revolutionary era Benjamin Franklin observed that we are a nation of politicians, and from that day to this politics have been one of our greatest indoor and outdoor sports.

Politics unfortunately hamper an intelligent and far-visioned control of our foreign policy, although by any standard of logic and patriotism they should not. Nothing should be more nonpartisan than foreign affairs; what is good for the entire nation is good for both parties, because each major party represents roughly one half of our population. Senator Henry Cabot Lodge once declared in a memorable speech that politics stop at the three-mile line. Possibly he meant to say that politics *should* stop at the three-mile line, for during the League fight he gave a deplorable demonstration of how partisan advantage may be put above national welfare.

The brutal fact is that the supreme objective of the politician is to keep his party in power and himself in office. Macaulay made no original discovery when he noted in 1842 that the time-serving politicians "think much more about the security of their seats than about the security of their country." Some years ago a United States senator observed that unusual activity in the room of the Committee on Foreign Relations indicated that a presidential election was in the offing. The politician will of course vehemently attack Ambrose Bierce's definition of politics as "the conduct of public affairs for private advantage"; he pays liberal lip service to the welfare of the nation. But the true politician thinks nothing of insulting a friendly power if by so doing he can score a point for his party or himself in the political game.

Until 1913 the Republican legislature of California held back from passing an alien land law offensive to the Japanese, lest it embarrass the Republican administration in Washington. But as soon as Woodrow Wilson and his fellow Democrats took up the reins, the Sacramento legislature kicked over the apple cart and precipitated an international crisis with Tokyo. Four years later we were in the midst of a desperate war with Germany, but this emergency brought no complete "adjournment" of politics. The Toledo *Blade* complained: "Too many members of Congress are fighting to have the world made safe for reelection." During the postwar years, the demagogic Mayor (Big Bill) Thompson of Chicago insulted the British for the obvious purpose of harvesting anti-British votes. Even where politics are not so blatantly involved, they are suspected of being involved.

2

Politics figured more offensively in foreign affairs during the morning years of the Republic than during recent times. The conservative, pro-British Federalists lined up against the democratic, pro-French Republicans, and epithets like "poison-sucking salamanders" were the order of the day. This was a precarious period in our history, and the only one when each of the two great political parties tied its fortunes to the tail of some European kite. George Washington was moved to deplore such violence of partisan spirit, and in his "Farewell Address" condemned the practice of making the interests of some foreign country the primary concern of our domestic politics. We have had numerous and bitter party battles since then, but we have never again divided along the lines of predilection for or prejudice against some overseas land.* The primary function of the opposition party—in fact an indispensable function in a healthy democracy—is to criticize and even oppose every major proposal brought forward by the party in power. Oftentimes congressmen who personally favor an achievement in foreign affairs, as was true of the annexation of Texas in 1845, vote against their personal convictions so as loyally to subserve party strategy. The political admiral of Gilbert and Sullivan could well have been a member of the United States Congress:

> I always voted at my party's call,
> And I never thought of thinking for myself at all.
> I thought so little, they rewarded me
> By making me the Ruler of the Queen's Navee!

Partisan criticism may easily overstep reasonable bounds, even though a searching examination of administration proposals by opponents in Congress is perhaps the best means of exposing defects. In 1888 the Senate was Republican and the Chief Executive was a Democrat when President Cleveland submitted a fisheries treaty with England. "We cannot allow the Democrats to take credit for settling so important a dispute," remarked a leading Republican senator, and he and his colleagues forthwith made a political football of the pact in order to gain votes in the impending presidential election. They even took the then extraordinary step of throwing open the galleries so that the public might enjoy the fun. In 1896, on the eve of the heated election of that year, Republican majorities in Congress, seeking to embarrass President Cleveland, passed a resolution favoring recognition of Cuban belligerency.

The most spectacular illustration of politics in foreign affairs is provided by the protracted struggle over the League of Nations. Wilson was a Democrat; the Senate was Republican. The stage was set for trouble. Before the Treaty of Versailles was even completed, the Republican senators in Wash-

* A latter-day minor exception is the loyalty of American Communists to Moscow.

ington drew up a Round Robin proclaiming their opposition to the yet unborn League of Nations, and doing so with the specific intent of weakening Wilson's hand in the current negotiations in Paris. Two prominent Republicans (presumably Senators) secretly explained to the British ambassador in Washington that in opposing the treaty they would have to attack England savagely, but they wanted the British government to know that they really meant nothing by it. One Republican newspaper in Ohio was quite realistic when it remarked: "Our great party is for anything calculated to advance the noble cause of world peace that the Democrats won't get the credit for." Yet if the Republican Hughes had defeated the Democratic Wilson in 1916, as he almost did, and had brought back a Hughes League from Paris, the Democrats almost certainly would have found plenty of flaws in it. As one disgusted citizen remarked to a Gallup poll taker in 1935: "It's all politics. Each side is damning the other for the thing it would do itself."

3

The most flagrant acts of partisanship have normally come from the members of Congress, at least in the instances just cited. The question naturally arises: how faithfully have these representatives reflected the desires of the Republican and Democratic voters?

No positive answer can be given for the remote past, but for more recent years, when dozens of public opinion polls were taken, a clear pattern emerges. From 1939 to 1941, when the Democratic administration of Franklin Roosevelt took an interventionist stand in behalf of the embattled democracies, notably in connection with lifting the arms embargo, the partisan prejudices of the opposition were as plain as a pikestaff. The great mass of Republican voters was consistently less favorable than the Democrats to every interventionist or cooperationist proposal of the administration, and to every similar proposal suggested by the public opinion polls. This is not to say that a majority of the Republicans opposed all these schemes; in fact a majority of the Republicans usually went along with a somewhat larger majority of Democrats. But the Republican majority was consistently less favorable than the Democrats, even though at times by only one or two percentage points.

During these years before Pearl Harbor the Republicans were less favorable than the Democrats to preparedness and conscription, but after the fall of France they were less well satisfied with Roosevelt's defense measures than their opponents. The same negative attitude toward intervention in World War II carried over to measures for international cooperation. The Republicans were less favorable to the old League of Nations (carrying on the anti-Wilson tradition); they were somewhat less favorable to a new League (partly no doubt for the same reason); and they were more inclined to deplore our participation in World War I (which was Wilson-led). The

Republicans were likewise less favorable to an alliance with Britain, China, and Russia after Pearl Harbor; less favorable to an international police force; less favorable to working for an international organization before the war was over; less favorable to cooperation with Russia; and less favorable to the loan of 1946 to Great Britain.

4

Certain basic explanations are necessary. During the period of World War II the Republicans had long been the party of the "outs," and they were bitterly if impotently opposed to the continued "reign" of "that man" Roosevelt. If he led the nation into war, he would have to be reelected in 1944; if he won the glory of fashioning a durable peace, he would have to be reelected in 1948 in order to carry it out. One of the bitterest complaints of the Republicans is that their opponents have managed our two greatest wars; and as the Republicans opposed Wilson for political reasons, so they had to oppose Roosevelt. The Yalta agreement, one of Roosevelt's last important international acts, was much more coldly received by the Republicans than by the Democrats. Before and during the war, any Roosevelt proposal that had any possible political implications could not be enthusiastically welcomed by the opposition.

The Republicans have traditionally supported big business and a high protective tariff. As the party of conservative businessmen, they could be expected to view the Russian experiment with more distrust than the Democrats; as the party of protection, they could be expected to register strong opposition to the piecemeal leveling of the Smoot-Hawley tariff wall by the reciprocal trade agreements. As the party of big bankers and retrenchers, they could be expected to oppose the Bretton Woods proposals and government loans to foreigners.

The "outs" must not only tarnish the glory of the "ins," but they must fight any scheme designed to increase the influence and power of their opponents. The Republicans should be just as much interested in national defense as anyone else, but they were reluctant to trust the Roosevelt administration with huge expenditures. These would mean more jobs for "deserving Democrats" and more political influence. The Republicans no doubt had such considerations in mind when they were cold to the calling of a world disarmament conference in the 1930's (it would mean more glory for Roosevelt), and when in 1946 they were less enthusiastic than the Democrats for setting up a new government agency to send propaganda abroad.

Anything that will reduce the power of the "ins" is consistently applauded by the "outs," who shortsightedly fail to see that when they regain the seats of the mighty these restrictions will bear just as heavily on them. The Republicans were more favorable to the Ludlow Amendment,* no doubt because

---

* Requiring a nation-wide referendum on a declaration of war, except cases of actual invasion.

it would reduce the war-precipitating power of Roosevelt and the war-declaring power of the Democratic Congress. For the same reason they were less well disposed toward a peace negotiated by Roosevelt and his Cabinet, rather than one against which their minority in the Senate could get in its licks. When Secretary Hull arranged in 1944 for a bipartisan Senate committee to cooperate with the State Department in planning for peace, the Republicans were considerably more enthusiastic than their Democratic brethren. They would now have a voice where they had not enjoyed one before, with a consequent watering down of the influence of the administration.

After Pearl Harbor the Republicans were less sure than their opponents that the Roosevelt administration was doing all it could to win the war. One must never admit any virtue in the opposition. The Republicans were likewise avid for anything that would blacken the New Deal, and Senator Butler's viciously unfair attack on the costliness of the Good Neighbor policy (1943) was grist for the party mill. When the war was over and Roosevelt lay in his grave, the Republicans were eager for the Pearl Harbor probe, and earnestly delved for muck with which to besmirch their opponents. Yet in cases where national defense could not be identified with any specific administration program, the Republicans lost their partisanship and became good Americans. They were no less determined than the Democrats to defend Canada, the Caribbean, and South America against the Hitlerian menace.

In fairness to the Republicans one must refer to the geographical distribution of partisan sentiment. The Solid South was overwhelmingly Democratic, and partly out of loyalty to Roosevelt it was far more interventionist than any other section during the pre-Pearl Harbor era. The Middle West at the same time was not only preponderantly Republican but conspicuously isolationist, in large part because of geographical introversion and the large German-American population. Hence in the national opinion polls for these years the Republicans, even disregarding partisan attachment, were bound to appear less cooperative and interventionist.

5

Rabid partisans are seldom distinguished by a devotion to consistency. Artemus Ward speaks of a politician whose principles were of an "exceedin' accommodatin' character"; and there is an American proverb: "In politics a man must learn to rise above principle."

Political somersaults without number may be attributed to plain partisanship. The Federalists when in power under Washington and Adams consistently opposed the desires of the West; when out of power they posed as champions of the West in seeking to force the Jeffersonian Republicans to secure the mouth of the Mississippi. Before the Civil War the Democrats established a remarkable record as expansionists; about two thirds of our present continental domain was added by them or by the party from which they evolved. The Republicans, while in power after the Civil War, became the party of expansion (reversing their previous stand), and the Democrats became the party of nonexpansion (reversing their previous stand).

The Republicans in the days of Secretary Blaine—the 1880's and early 1890's—worked up considerable enthusiasm for commercial reciprocity. When the Democrats under Franklin Roosevelt revived the same principle in the Hull reciprocal trade agreements, the Republicans, refusing to recognize their own baby in Democratic diapers, turned sharply against it. A few of them complained that the Blaine baby had been kidnapped.

Senator Henry Cabot Lodge and his fellow Republicans denounced the League of Nations as a dangerous foreign entanglement. Then the Democrats were thrown out of power, the Republicans came in, and the Harding administration, with Lodge as a sponsor, drew up the entangling Four-Power Treaty for the Pacific. Lodge fought for it in the Senate as effectively as he had fought against the unreserved Wilson League a few months earlier, and when Senator Borah accused him of inconsistency, the latter replied with a resigned wave of his hands: "What are you going to do? It is an Administration measure." The Democratic Brooklyn *Eagle* hit the nail squarely on the head when it remarked: "One great difference between the Four-Power Treaty and the League Covenant is that one was of Republican and the other of Democratic origin."

The handsome young Franklin Roosevelt, vice-presidential candidate of the Democrats in 1920, was an ardent champion of the League of Nations and internationalism. But the mood of the country changed in the 1920's, and rather than be burdened any longer with the corpse of the League, Roosevelt cast it completely aside in 1932. Upon becoming President, he generally pursued the same policy as his Republican predecessors in regard to debts, the League, isolationism, and economic nationalism, including the spectacular torpedoing of the London Economic Conference. If Roosevelt had not trimmed his sails to catch the gusts of popular opinion, he almost certainly would not have been elected president, and hence would not have been able to carry through his program of reform at home and subsequent intervention abroad. James Russell Lowell caused Hosea Biglow to remark:

> A ginooine statesman should be on his guard,
> Ef he *must* hev beliefs, nut to b'lieve 'em tu hard.

6

The party out of power tries to make political capital out of foreign affairs, but the party in power is no less guilty of the same sin, though it is generally less conspicuous. Whatever the administration achieves it can point to with pride in a political platform, and it often espouses programs with the intention of making capital for the next election, as was partly true of Taft's Canadian reciprocity fiasco in 1911. Thus partisanship often promenades in the toga of statesmanship. When the administration comes forward with a presumably constructive program for the good of the country (and party), the party sponsoring such a scheme appears to be much less partisan than those who oppose it, even though both sides may be equally motivated by politics.

The prize example is provided by the League fight of 1919-1920. Even before the Treaty of Versailles was presented to the Senate, the party lines were tightly drawn. The Republican centers of the North and West were skeptical if not downright hostile. As the *Ohio State Journal* put it: "The attitude of most of us thoughtful Republicans seems to be that we're unalterably opposed to Article X [of the League], whether we know what's in it or not." The Democrats, notably those of the Solid South, were solidly behind the program of their distinguished President, whether they knew what was in it or not, and they complained bitterly about the partisan obstruction of the Republicans. In a good-humored vein one South Carolina newspaper wrote: "The South is heart and soul for the Treaty. It hasn't read it, but it has read some of the speeches of them darned Republicans."

Must one assume that there is something about the magnolia-scented atmosphere or the corn-pone diet of the South that predisposes its inhabitants to leagues of nations, and something about the frigid climate and beef diet of the North that turns its people the other way? No, the Democrats were as keenly aware of the partisan advantage that would accrue to them from a successful League as the Republicans were of the partisan credit that would accrue to them by reserving and otherwise "Americanizing" the League. Much if not most of the struggle was a partisan contest for credit in getting the treaty through. The "ins" are normally determined to score a glorious diplomatic triumph, while the "outs" are no less predetermined to brand whatever is proposed as a base betrayal of American rights.

The State Department and the foreign service have often been used as a football field by an administration seeking to score touchdowns in the political game. James Monroe was sent to France as a special envoy in 1803, not because our minister in Paris needed any help in purchasing Louisiana, but because the West needed quieting. William H. Harrison of Ohio was appointed minister to Colombia, not because he was fitted for the diplomatic service, but because an election was imminent and some concession had to be made to the doubtful West. Secretary Seward purchased Alaska in 1867, not because we then needed Alaska, but partly because the administration of Andrew Johnson needed rehabilitation. President McKinley, against his better judgment, yielded to the clamor of the masses for war, partly because he feared that if he did not the opposition party would ride into power with "Free Cuba" and "Free Silver" emblazoned on its banners. Theodore Roosevelt's unfortunate precipitancy in "taking" Panama was due partly to a burning desire to be elected "in his own right" in 1904.

Franklin Roosevelt handled the Mexican seizure of American oil property with velvet gloves, partly, it was assumed, because he did not want to alienate the American labor vote. The able Sumner Welles rather than the aging Cordell Hull was forced out of the State Department in 1943, presumably because Roosevelt dared not alienate the Southern conservatives on the eve of the fourth-term campaign of 1944. Hull stayed on as a venerable façade until the election was won, and then resigned before the month was out. His successor, Edward R. Stettinius, Jr., was kicked upstairs in 1945 to make room for Secretary Byrnes, largely because a figure of greater political prominence was needed as a potential successor to President Truman.

More offensive to outside countries is what may be called "stump-speech diplomacy," or the practice of addressing a resounding statement to some foreign government for home consumption, and then publishing it. In 1850 Secretary Webster, hoping to unite a country badly torn by the slavery controversy, seized an opportunity to send a note to the Austrian envoy, declaring that compared with the rich and fertile domain of the United States the possessions of Austria "are but as a patch on the earth's surface." The enthusiastic response of the American people was highly gratifying, at least to Webster. A half century later, in 1904, the Republican national convention, meeting in Chicago to nominate Theodore Roosevelt, was displaying disconcerting lethargy. Roosevelt brought it to life by having Secretary Hay send his famous telegram to Morocco, demanding the release of a Graeco-American citizen, Ion Perdicaris, from the clutches of the "bandit" Raisuli. "Perdicaris alive or Raisuli dead" was the pulse-stirring ultimatum. Arrangements had already been made for the release of Perdicaris, and at the time there was serious doubt as to his American citizenship. But there was no doubt whatever as to the political value of the manifesto.

A more defensible practice is that of publishing diplomatic correspondence on the eve of an election, with the intent of harvesting votes. During the heated Wilson-Hughes presidential campaign of 1916, the British proclaimed a blacklist of German-tainted American firms. They had a perfect legal right to do this (we followed their example in two wars), but the move was highly unpopular in America, and the State Department not only drafted a strong protest but promptly published it in the press.

Foreign envoys in America have at times been made the whipping boys of partisanship. In 1856 the British minister in Washington, John Crampton, was hastily dismissed for recruiting activity, and the news was promptly wired by the newly perfected telegraph to Cincinnati, where the Democratic national convention was debating whether or not to renominate President Pierce. In 1888 the British minister in Washington, Lord Sackville-West, blundered stupidly when he wrote a private letter advising in effect that a vote for the Democratic President Cleveland was a vote for England. When the Republicans gleefully published this indiscretion, Cleveland had to bundle the noble Briton off home before the Irish vote had completely slipped away. The Republican New York *Tribune* published a jingle in which Cleveland addressed John Bull:

> Believe me that I made him go
> For nothing that he wrote,
> But just because, as well you know,
> I feared the Irish vote!

Thus friendly relations with foreign countries have repeatedly had to take a back seat when some partisan advantage was to be gained.

7

Foreign governments recognize to some extent how largely politics enter into American foreign policy, and consequently make some allowance for them. The British lion was keenly aware of the Irish problem in the United States, and learned to brace its tail for the quadrennial twisting. In 1926, when Secretary of Commerce Herbert Hoover sought to break the British rubber monopoly in the interest of American tire-users, certain British critics branded his efforts as a "political stunt" which merely proved that he was "grooming himself for the Presidential fight in 1928." In 1932, six days after his renomination for the presidency, Hoover came out with a sensational proposal to limit existing armaments by one third. Whatever the truth, this bold stroke was widely regarded, as is any similar move during a political campaign, as inspired at least in part by a desire to win votes.

The indiscreet letter-writing of Minister Sackville-West taught the British in particular and foreign governments in general the folly of meddling in American elections. In 1940 and 1944 the British overwhelmingly favored the reelection of Roosevelt; he had abundantly proved his sympathy for them; he was a known quality; his opponents had yet to prove themselves. But rather than defeat their favorite candidate by too open an espousal, the British press kept itself under wraps until the results of the elections were known. The British showed similar restraint in 1941 when the momentous Lend-Lease bill was being debated by Congress; they did not want to ruin its chances by betraying too great enthusiasm. Less wise in the ways of the world, the Russian radio and press came out in 1946 for Democratic Congressional candidates, and this kiss of death undoubtedly contributed to the subsequent Republican landslide.

Preelection paralysis, whether in domestic or foreign affairs, is a familiar American phenomenon. Emerson wrote in 1851 that "every election is a revolution," and in a larger sense he was correct. The paralysis is discernible every two years, when the Congressional elections come; it is acute every four years, when the presidential election is superimposed upon that for members of Congress. Most Americans have heard the airy explanation of why something is not done: "Oh! This is an election year." The paralysis is most pronounced when issues are involved in which the hyphenates are interested.

In 1940 the bomb-battered British were in a critical plight, but pending the outcome of our election Roosevelt had to hold back any all-out program of assistance. Three days after his reelection he announced a larger allocation of aid for Britain, and shortly thereafter he got behind the Lend-Lease program, which he could not have unveiled earlier. After we entered the war in 1941, the long shadow of the coming Congressional election of 1942 (in which the Republicans scored important gains) either slowed up or postponed necessary action on rationing, price control, and the drafting of teen-agers. One wit noted that we did not get into the war on December 7, 1941 (Pearl Harbor day), but on November 4, 1942 (election day).

8

One of the hoariest myths in American history is that our great presidential election lotteries have been and can be mandates on questions of foreign policy.

The fact is that we have never had a mandate in this country on an issue involving foreign affairs, although such issues have figured prominently in a number of our most important campaigns. The only way to have a mandate is to have a mandate; that is, to conduct a true referendum vote, as the Swiss did in 1920 on the question of joining the League of Nations. We simply do not have the machinery for such a test, although we could easily set it up.

In 1844 the Democrats under the leadership of Polk shouted for "Fifty-four forty or fight," "All of Oregon or none," and the "Reoccupation of Oregon and the reannexation of Texas." The Democrats won, by the narrowest of margins and partly because the Liberty party in New York, which was opposed to taking Texas, seduced enough voters from the Whig camp to throw the election to Polk. There was much additional confusion. The tariff issue loomed large, and the Democrats were divided on expansion, with the Southerners generally favoring Texas but opposing Oregon, and with the Northerners generally opposing Texas but favoring Oregon. Yet in spite of this confusion, and in spite of the fact that Polk owed his victory to the Liberty party, which was anti-Texas, the triumphant Democrats claimed a mandate to take all of Oregon and Texas, and forthwith annexed the Lone-Star Republic.

The election of 1900 is alleged to have been a mandate on the question of retaining the Philippines—that is, imperialism. But by 1900 the issue of imperialism was stale, and no matter how the election came out we were going to keep the Islands for a while anyhow. The voter was further perplexed by some sixty issues and ten tickets, only two of which were major. The Republican candidate, William McKinley, was distrusted because of his presumed lack of backbone, and the Democratic aspirant, William Jennings Bryan, was feared because of his financial heresies. "It is a choice between evils," wrote one disgusted voter, "and I am going to shut my eyes, hold my nose, vote, go home and disinfect myself." The Democrats insisted that imperialism was the paramount issue, and the Republicans insisted that Bryanism was the paramount issue, and when the Republicans won they loudly announced that they had received a mandate to keep the Philippines. Yet about all that can be said with certainty is that McKinley polled more votes than Bryan. It is entirely probable that if the single issue of keeping or not keeping the Philippines had been submitted to the voter in a national referendum, unconfused by candidates and irrelevant issues, a majority of the people would have voted to turn the Islands loose, at least ultimately.

In 1916 the most effective Democratic slogan in behalf of Wilson was: "He kept us out of war," and this undoubtedly won much support. The narrow victory for Wilson was widely interpreted as a mandate from the people to keep out of the conflict, and some of the members of Congress who voted against the war resolution in 1917 claimed that they were bound by the clear results of the election. But were the results clear? Many issues were involved, such as the railroads and the tariff and Mexico, and the election was extraordinarily close. If the Republican candidate, Charles Evans Hughes, had only managed to shake hands in California with Republican Senator Hiram W. Johnson, Hughes would almost certainly have carried the state and the nation, and if this had happened what would the result have been a mandate on? To take the nation into war?

The outcome of the Harding-Cox election of 1920 was hailed as a mandate to keep out of the League of Nations, for Woodrow Wilson had appealed for a "great and solemn referendum" and Cox, his standard bearer, had lost. In general there were four positions to take on the Treaty of Versailles, of which the League Covenant was an integral part: (1) rejection, (2) unconditional ratification, (3) ratification with mild reservations, (4) ratification with strong reservations. How could the voter express his stand on four different propositions by voting for one of two candidates, both of whom took an ambiguous stand on the League? Besides, there were scores of other issues, ranging from the Armenian mandate to the tariff on California lemons. Harding polled some 16,000,000 votes and won by a plurality of over 7,000,000, a percentage of the popular vote not even equaled by Franklin Roosevelt in any of his four successive landslides. Before long the Republican leaders were claiming that every single one of the 16,000,000 citizens voted with the firm intention of turning down the League and foreign entanglements. On the contrary, the evidence indicates that the people by a substantial majority then favored entering the League of Nations outright or at least with safeguarding reservations.

The defeated Democrats knew that there had been no mandate, as did every other discerning person not blinded by partisanship, and in their platform of 1924 they asked that there be a true national referendum, in which the people could vote on the single issue of the League, as Switzerland had done. But the Republicans hooted them out of court; the Democrats had had their mandate. The winner in politics never wants the race rerun; he might lose the second time.

9

Why can a national election never be a true referendum on an issue of foreign affairs, or possibly on any other issue?

A presidential election is primarily a domestic affair, a struggle between two great parties to determine which shall control the government of the United States for the next four years. Foreign policy must in the nature of things play second fiddle.

The sovereign voter pays relatively little attention to the issues, whether domestic or foreign. Public opinion polls merely confirm what everyone knows; namely, that the average voter does not read the platforms of either party, and that if he does he is realistic enough to know that politicians have little intention of carrying out their promises. After generations of betrayal, the citizen has learned his lesson well. His few remaining illusions were somewhat shaken when so high-minded a presidential candidate as Wendell Willkie, testifying before a Senate committee in reference to his charge that a Roosevelt victory in 1940 would mean war by April 1, could dismiss his alarmist statement as "a bit of campaign oratory."

Many voters choose between the personalities of the nominees, rather than the alleged issues. Is Wilson a better man than Hughes; is Roosevelt a better man than Dewey? Some of the personal issues are trivial if not frivolous, ranging from the illegitimate child of one candidate to the mustache of another. Several minor-party aspirants are usually in the race, and the citizen can always register a protest by "throwing away" his vote on them. The public opinion polls reveal a widespread conviction that the candidates are the choices of the politicians rather than of the people themselves, and many earnest citizens vote negatively rather than positively. "Thousands of voters seem unable to make up their minds which candidate to vote against," observed the Philadelphia *North American* in 1916.

There are always scores of issues, whether major or minor, national or local, impersonal or personal. All that the citizen has to do is to pick his issue, cafeteria style, vote his "mandate" on that particular one, and rest content.

Then there is the "congenital" voter. In every national election there are millions of regular Republicans and Democrats—estimated at about three fourths of the total—who within limits will vote the straight party ticket, regardless of the issues and the candidates. Most of these people were born with their beliefs, and they may be confidently counted on, particularly in the Solid South, to vote the way their fathers shot. The "dry" and Protestant Solid South made a wry face in 1928 when presented with the bitter brew of a "wet" and Catholic candidate from the sidewalks of New York, but millions of Southerners loyally gagged it down. "Some men never change their opinion," said an Ohio newspaper in 1930, "because it's been in the family for generations."

To assert that a clear referendum can emerge from the confused and dust-filled arena of a national election is to fly in the face of reason. Yet the leather-lunged politician, after he has won, claims a mandate on everything in sight. Sometimes he claims a mandate on issues that were mentioned only incidentally, or that were not even mentioned at all.° Oftentimes his interpretation of the election is exactly the opposite from that placed upon it by intelligent and unprejudiced students. But he can invariably outshout the defeated, for the defeated like the absent are always wrong.

We continue to operate under a crazy system. We hold elections, and then try to guess what they mean, which is a thoroughly unscientific procedure. Until such time as we are willing to have true referenda on specific issues, we shall have to seek the truth not in official election returns but in unofficial public opinion polls. While the latter admittedly have their limitations, they are applied science in its purest form when compared with the present kind of guesswork.

10

The true politician is loath to confess that he plays politics with foreign affairs: he invariably is working for the good of the country, which in his eyes is synonymous with the good of the party. Wicked partisans are always on the other side. Yet the naked truth is that making a political football of foreign policy, with a consequent weakening of our position abroad, is a species of treason. The Republican Round Robin of 1919 is a case in point.

As long as we have a democracy, we shall have politics, and as long as we have foreign affairs, we shall have politicians using them for partisan advantage. This is one of the prices that we have to pay for governing ourselves. There was no opposition party in Hitler's Germany or Mussolini's Italy.

Fortunately we are getting more sophisticated, although it took the fiery furnace of a second world war to bring a sharp improvement. In the autumn of 1941 as many as three fourths of those citizens with opinions favored the foreign policy of Roosevelt, which was a far heavier majority than ever supported the New Deal. By common consent, issues regarding foreign affairs were subordinated in the Roosevelt-Willkie election of 1940 and the Roosevelt-Dewey election of 1944. After the campaign of 1944, sixteen newly elected senators of both parties pledged their support to the President, and when Roosevelt died in 1945, forty Republican senators came forth with an unprecedented pledge of loyalty to Truman, quite in contrast with the Round Robin of 1919. The United Nations Charter was promptly approved by the Senate, 89 to 2, quite in contrast with the prolonged negation of 1919–1920. All these forward steps were taken while a sense of crisis overshadowed the world, and although partisanship will undoubtedly invade foreign affairs during the years that lie ahead, the American people are clearly becoming more adult about their responsibilities.

° In 1930 the New York *Sun* claimed that in 1920 our "people rejected, by a majority of 7,000,000, the proposal to enter the League Court [World Court]."

One of our greatest needs is to educate the average citizen to the dangers of injecting politics into foreign affairs. When we have succeeded in doing this, the demagogue will be loath to whip up antiforeign prejudices, partly because his appeals will fall on sterile ground, and partly because they will boomerang against him.

No less imperative is the necessity of electing men who are statesmanlike enough to eschew cheap electioneering tricks. "A politician thinks of the next election," wrote James Freeman Clarke; "a statesman, of the next generation." Yet many of our ablest men shun public office as they would leprosy. A public-opinion poll taken in 1944 showed that nearly seven persons out of ten did not want their sons to go into politics. "To let politics become a cesspool," observed Howard Crosby, "and then avoid it because it is a cesspool, is a double crime."

The American public is itself to blame for driving the ablest men to the sanctuary of a private business or profession. If they offer themselves as candidates, we invade their privacy, shower them with abuse, and "smear" them with scandalous falsehoods.° If they run this gauntlet successfully, we pay them inadequately in money and appreciation, but richly in criticism, and then cast them aside like last-year's garment. Members of Congress, who on the whole are earnest and hard-working but who are damned by the antics of a few bigots and buffoons, have been generously berated. "Reader, suppose you were an idiot," wrote Mark Twain, "and suppose you were a member of Congress. But I repeat myself."

A democracy cannot work without politics, and politics cannot work without politicians. Since we are going to have politicians, our nation would fare better, both at home and abroad, if we sought men to match our mountains. Such men might consent to be public servants if we were to show more appreciation of genuine public service.

° A case in point was the abusive and prolonged partisan struggle in the Senate to prevent the confirmation in 1947 of so able a man as David E. Lilienthal as chairman of the Atomic Energy Commission.

CHAPTER NINE

DIFFERENT MEN IN DIFFERENT SECTIONS

"We know no North nor South, East nor West."

—THEODORE ROOSEVELT, 1896

1

THE UNITED STATES is a nation of sections, sprawling from Maine to Miami, from the Golden Gate to Hell Gate. The crowds on Hollywood Boulevard in California, on Peachtree Street in Atlanta, on Fifth Avenue in New York, and on Beacon Street in Boston may have diametrically different points of view on the same national questions. This is one of the prices we pay for spreading over a huge area: the orange growers of California have little in common with the fishermen of Maine.

In 1938 a Gallup poll found that the most interesting news stories of the year were: (1) the Czech-Munich crisis, (2) the Nazi persecutions of the Jews, (3) Republican gains in the recent Congressional elections, (4) Corrigan's wrong-way flight to Ireland, (5) the wages and hours bill, (6) the great New England hurricane. The sectional breakdown is most revealing:

New England	South	Middle West	West
1. Hurricane	Munich	Munich	Munich
2. Munich	Nazi persecutions	Republican gains	Nazi persecutions
3. Republican gains	Wages and hours bill	Nazi persecutions	Sino-Japanese War

One is immediately struck with the purely local interest in the New England hurricane; with the jubilation of the Republican sections over their recent gains at the polls; with the concern of the South (then in the throes of industrialization) over the wages and hours bill; and with the anxiety of the West regarding the Sino-Japanese war, which did not even appear among the first six events in the national reckoning.

This poll accentuates a profound truth. The more sections there are, and the more diversified their interests, the more difficult it is for the national government to settle upon a policy which will command the support of the entire country. This is true of foreign affairs, but it is even more true of domestic affairs, which often shade into foreign affairs. All too often a foreign policy is a patchwork compromise among the clashing views of the sections, and the result, frequently arrived at after prolonged and even dangerous indecision, is not completely satisfactory to the sections, to the national government, or to the foreign nation involved.

Sectionalism and partisanship are so closely interwoven that they often cannot be disentangled. The Solid South may be relied upon to lend powerful support to the foreign policy of a Democratic administration, not because southerly latitudes predispose one to support Democratic principles, but because a preponderance of Democrats happens to live in that section. The trans-Mississippi Middle West may be relied upon to be unenthusiastic about the foreign policy of a Democratic administration, not because landlocked areas are inherently prejudiced against Democratic principles, but because a preponderance of Republicans happens to live in this area. Reverse the political complexion of the Washington government, and these attitudes will normally be reversed.

In the pre-Gallup era Ph.D. candidates and others used to study American opinion (and some still do) by scanning the editorial pages of a few Eastern newspapers, predominantly those of New York City. Such a practice is open to serious criticism on several counts, including the assumption that New York is America. Actually the Manhattan metropolis is in many ways the most non-American part of America. While New York is a leading cultural center, and publishes most of the books and some of the best newspapers, it is often not representative of the United States. Some of the more important editorial offices in New York could well be set down in Kansas City for a while to find out what the American people are thinking. "Things get very lonely in Washington sometimes," Woodrow Wilson told a St. Louis audience in 1919. "The real voice of the great people of America sometimes sounds faint and distant in that strange city." The grass roots often speak a different language from that of Brooklyn, and with a different accent. The English critic D. W. Brogan has aptly said: "Great areas may be thinking nothing; great areas may be thinking totally different things."

America has no Paris. It has no provinces subserviently following the lead of some political or intellectual center. It is a nation of semisovereign states and contending sections.

2

Many of our most significant manifestations of sectionalism, from the earliest days to the present, have been the direct result of economic forces.

Long before 1776 the fisheries of Newfoundland had been the "gold mines of New England," and doughty John Adams, a New Englander representing the United States at the peace parley with Great Britain in 1782, threatened to wreck the negotiations rather than yield our codfish lode to the British. Adams carried the day when he won for America (and New England) some ambiguous and precarious concessions. The two-thirds rule on the approval of treaties by the Senate was forced into the Constitution in 1787 as a result of sectional pressure. New England wanted to block any pact that would surrender fishing rights, and the South and West wanted to block any attempt by the East to surrender the mouth of the Mississippi to a foreign power or otherwise stifle Western economic life.

The British again sought to snatch away the fisheries when they offered us peace terms near the close of the War of 1812. Again an Adams rushed to the rescue. The doughty son of doughty John Adams fought the British (and his colleague Henry Clay) for the fishing interests of the United States (and New England). Clay, a true Westerner, was quite willing to yield the "stinking codfish," if he could only persuade the British to concede navigational rights on the Mississippi to the United States (and the West).

The controversy with England over fish persisted for more than a century, and bobbed up dangerously at most embarrassing times. Although fishing became relatively less important to an industrialized New England, the representatives of that section continued to bait their political hook with appeals to their sea-going constituents. In 1887 the Canadians seized several American fishing boats, and the rising young Congressman Henry Cabot Lodge declaimed: "Whenever the American flag on an American fishing smack is touched by a foreigner, the great American heart is touched."

If the Pacific Coast could shed no tears for New England codfish, it could emit loud outcries when its own fishing interest was affected. This was true in the 1890's, when the fur seals were threatened with extermination by Canadian (and later by Japanese) poachers. It was no less true in the 1930's, when the menace to the Alaska salmon by Japanese floating canneries elicited strong protests from the Pacific Northwest and an official protest from the State Department.

The cane-sugar senators of Louisiana fought commercial reciprocity with Hawaii from the 1850's on, and naturally were hostile to the annexation of both Hawaii and the Philippines. Together with the beet-sugar growers of the rest of the United States, particularly in the Western states, they rallied behind the movement to give the competing Philippine Islands their independence in the 1930's.

The powerful silver bloc from the thinly populated Rocky Mountain area has been a potent force not only in domestic but in foreign policies. Joining with sugar blocs and other special interest groups, the fourteen or so silver senators from these "acreage states" have been able to exert pressure grossly disproportionate to the population they represent, which is much less than that of the single state of New York, with its two senators. Near the turn of the century the silverites were outstanding Anglophobes, largely because England was then the leading champion of the gold standard, and senators from the silver-producing states took a prominent part in defeating the general arbitration treaty of 1897 with Britain.° In 1934 the silver bloc forced upon the Washington government a silver purchase plan which further undermined the shaky Chinese currency, and in this way contributed to the demoralization of a friendly power which we were hoping to bolster as a

---

° The soft-money West long distrusted the sound-money, British-connected Wall Street interests. In 1944 the appointment of Secretary of State Stettinius was criticized by Senators Langer of North Dakota and Johnson of California on the grounds of the Wall Street, House of Morgan association.

counterweight to Japanese imperialism. Here we witness shortsighted and penny-grabbing sectionalism at its worst.

The Great Galilean once remarked that where the treasure is there the heart is also. Man being an acquisitive, self-seeking, and often greedy animal, narrow economic considerations have all too often proved decisive. From 1915 to 1917, the East was far more eager for war with Germany than the Middle West or the Far West. There were many reasons for this enthusiasm, but one cardinal fact is that by 1917 the East had invested such an enormous sum in the success of the Allied cause, through loans and otherwise, that it simply could not afford to see the Allies collapse.

3

The attitude of the various sections toward territorial expansion often revealed economic motives of a broader sort.

The West in American history was chronically expansionist; the East was generally antiexpansionist. The opening of new lands meant the draining off of underpaid "factory fodder," the depreciation of local land values, and the admission of new states which would ultimately outvote the thirteen charter members.

The "men of the western waters" were willing to fight both Spain and France in 1803, rather than permit the mouth of the Mississippi to be shut, while the New Englanders were vehemently opposed to the acquisition of Louisiana. The South craved Texas and California and other Mexican territory in the 1830's and 1840's, while the New England Whigs bitterly condemned the war with Mexico, which they alleged was fought for "bigger slave pens." As late as the end of the century the West, which faced the Pacific, was more zealous than the East for securing the Philippines, with their promise of a foothold in the rich markets of Asia.

The money centers of the country usually do not want war; it unsettles the financial marts and accelerates unhealthy trends. Steady profits are preferable to a feast-or-famine diet. The concentration of banking centers in the East has given that section an additional motive for opposing wars of expansion. The West, on the other hand, has had more to gain in lands and less to lose in financial derangement than the East, and this explains in part why the West has been more expansionist, more nationalistic, and (at times) more sensitive to insults than the East. The landlocked West in 1812 demanded a war for a free sea, and when the maritime East resisted such a gift, the "War Hawks" accused the New Englanders of permitting their patriotic impulses to be atrophied by the narrow calculations of the counting house. Where commerce waxes, patriotism wanes.

In 1846 the West and Southwest favored war with Mexico, while the East grew increasingly hostile to it. In 1898 the Eastern money centers vigorously opposed a clash with Spain. The bellicose Theodore Roosevelt shook his fist at Mark Hanna and other "patriots of the ticker," and proclaimed that the country was going to have war in spite of Mark Hanna, Big Business, Wall Street, and the banking fraternity. He was right.

In 1917 and 1941 the situation was radically different, and the financial centers of the East were more actively in favor of intervention and war. By 1917, as just noted, they had a tremendous financial stake in the risky Allied cause; by 1941 they not only had a loan and investment stake, but they realized that if Britain toppled and Hitler came, they and their fat coffers would be plundered as ruthlessly as Pizarro had plundered Atahualpa.

4

Proximity to a bone of contention or to a particular foreign nation has often accounted for our sectional vagaries.

During the French and Indian wars of the colonial era, New England provided substantial assistance in men and money, while the South, which was hundreds of miles from the bloodshed, betrayed an astonishing indifference. The Westerners of 1812, whose brothers and sons were being butchered on the frontier by red men, were far more anxious to wipe out their assailants than were the secure, dollar-grubbing merchants of New England. In 1837, when the Canadian insurrection broke out, the farther south one traveled from the American border, the less enthusiasm one found for the rebels.

Chinese and Japanese coolies began to come to the Pacific Coast in alarming numbers during the years after the Civil War, and this thinly populated land, facing the human rookeries of the Orient, found itself holding the dike against an Oriental inundation. But the good people of Boston, separated by some three thousand miles from the yellow menace and worried about the prolific Irish, were slow to see the danger. The South was more sympathetic toward the Pacific Coast, presumably because the Southerners already had an overshadowing race problem of their own, and did not welcome the appearance of another. The Californians, in order to prod Eastern congressmen into action, were forced to resort to extreme measures, against both Chinese and Japanese, which no decent American today can view with pride.

The first Japanese-American crisis was precipitated in 1906, when San Francisco forbade Japanese children to attend the same public schools with whites. President Theodore Roosevelt worked out a compromise solution, and then fearing that the Japanese thought him afraid of them, sent the entire American battleship fleet on a spectacular cruise around the world. Many Easterners objected violently to stripping the East coast of its naval protection. If the fleet should be sunk by Japanese mines in the Strait of Magellan, what would prevent the German Navy from descending upon the defenseless cities of our Eastern seaboard? Senator Hale of Maine, Chairman of the Committee on Naval Affairs, told Roosevelt flatly that Congress would not provide the money for the contemplated world cruise. Roosevelt replied that he had on hand enough funds to send the fleet to the Pacific Coast, and that if the Eastern senators did not want to vote the funds to bring it back, it could remain there. The battleships went and returned.

The Californians continued restive as the Japanese infiltrated into agriculture, but President Taft helped head off discriminatory legislation by urging in 1911 that San Francisco rather than New Orleans be chosen as the site for the great Panama-Pacific International Exposition of 1915. Thus, as Taft put it, California was "under bonds to keep the peace." The scheme may have had some effect for a while, but in 1913 California precipitated another major crisis when the Sacramento legislature passed an antialien land ownership law, obviously aimed at the Japanese. At times the Golden State seemed bent on provoking a war which the other forty-seven states did not want but which they would have to fight. "Of the two it might be cheaper to go to war with California than with Japan," remarked the Hartford (Connecticut) *Times*. The federal officials attempted to mediate between California and Japan, and at one stage the quarrel seemed to be not between the United States and Japan but between California on one side and Japan, Washington, and the forty-seven states on the other. The national government is theoretically sovereign in foreign affairs; yet it is not sovereign when the states take the bit in their teeth regarding incidents that are primarily under state jurisdiction. Foreigners have not been able to comprehend this overlapping authority, and they have thought us insincere when we have undertaken to explain to them how a sovereign may not be a sovereign.

5

A highly interesting object lesson in propinquity is provided by World War I. The East was the section most eager for intervention, and it was also nearest the conflict. The *Lusitania* sailed from New York in 1915 with many socially prominent New Yorkers aboard—the Vanderbilts and Frohmans— and it never came back. The transatlantic shipping lanes of the East were threatened, and during two successive days in October, 1916, the German submarine U-53 sank nine foreign merchantmen off Nantucket Island, Massachusetts. The belief was widespread in 1917, as in 1941, that if the Allies collapsed, the East would have to bear the brunt of the German assault.

The Middle West, with its concentration of German immigrants, was far removed from the fury of battle, and hence less excitable. It was less in favor of preparedness, more in favor of an embargo on arms for the Allies (which were used to kill Germans), and more in favor of barring American citizens from Allied ships. The West was also indifferent. The *Lusitania* tragedy shocked the entire nation, but it aroused the East far more than the West. Secretary of Agriculture Houston, then in California, found the people much more interested in citrus fruits than in the sunken Cunarder. The next month ex-Secretary of State Bryan congratulated the people of Lincoln, Nebraska, on their good fortune in living thirty-six hours from New York. The Allegheny Mountains were the salvation of the rest of the country, he said, because "they serve as a dike to keep the prejudice, the venom, the insolence, and the ignorance of the New York press from inundating the Mississippi Valley."

The German declaration in 1917 of unrestricted submarine warfare, which was in effect a declaration of war on the United States, did not immediately stir the West and Southwest nearly as much as the far less important Zimmermann note. This fantastic document revealed that the Berlin Foreign Office was plotting to turn Texas back to the Mexicans and was hoping to detach Japan from the Allies and induce her to enter the war on the side of Germany. The publication of the note in America brought immediate and violent reactions. The submarine warfare might be far away, but no self-respecting Texan was going to give his Lone-Star State back to the "greasers," and no self-respecting Californian was going to turn his Bear-Flag State over to the slant-eyed Orientals. Distant dangers, no matter how serious, usually seem less menacing than those close at hand.

From 1937 to 1941 the Eastern seaboard, which was within theoretical bombing range of German aircraft, showed greater concern about the Hitlerian menace than did the Pacific Coast, which was more worried about the Japanese menace. After Pearl Harbor, much of the agitation for making Hirohito rather than Hitler the Number One enemy was centered on the Pacific Coast, in contrast with the East, which was more eager to dispose of the Nazis first. *Fortune* observed in 1942 that many irate citizens in the West were eager to blast those "little yellow devils" out of the Pacific, and "the hell with what happens in Europe."

6

The Middle West for many years has been the backbone of American isolationism. Geographical remoteness from the broils of Europe has been a major factor in molding the Middle Western mentality; and, as earlier indicated, the strongest opposition to "a navy second to none" has come from the interior areas. The Middle West is also the stamping ground of the great bulk of German-American immigrants, and since our two great foreign wars have been fought with Germany, we could hardly have expected any enthusiasm on the part of our German citizens to rush over and kill their kinsmen across the ocean.

The Middle West for decades has also been the stronghold of Republicanism: Iowa is just about as solidly Republican as Louisiana is Democratic. The Democrats were in power when the events unfolded that led to our two all-out wars, and the Middle West could therefore be counted on to oppose administration measures looking toward intervention—or peacetime administration measures looking in almost any direction.

Middle Western isolationists have wielded unusual influence because of several favorable circumstances. They were able to produce colorful leaders like Lindbergh, the La Follettes, and Senator Gerald P. Nye. Chicago was long an isolationist citadel, largely by reason of its hives of hyphenates, and this huge concentration of isolationism was able to exert disproportionate political power. The Chicago *Tribune,* self-elected "The World's Greatest Newspaper," has long enjoyed the rather dubious distinction of being the most influential isolationist newspaper in America, and its prosperity has been insured by a large and sympathetic clientele.

A recent writer has attempted to prove the proposition that Middle Western isolationism is all a myth. He maintains that on national issues the Middle West presents no marked difference from other sections of the country. This was generally true after Pearl Harbor, when we were all in the same leaky boat together, but it certainly was not true before. From 1935, when the neutrality issue became acute, to the day of Pearl Harbor, the Middle West or large parts of the Middle West were consistently more isolationist than any other section on every question regarding neutrality and intervention on which public opinion polls were taken. Scores of such polls are available, and while only one or two percentage points often separated the Middle West from the rest of the country, the consistency with which the Valley of Isolation led all other sections is highly impressive. This is not to say that a majority of Middle Westerners opposed every move toward preparedness or intervention. The Middle West was usually found voting with the rest of the nation, but almost invariably behind the national average.*

Before Pearl Harbor the Middle West was by far the most certain that we had made a grave mistake by entering World War I, and that we had been wise to avoid entrapment in the old League of Nations. After Pearl Harbor and the demise of America Firstism, these sectional differences tended to flatten out or disappear. In 1943 the Middle West was only slightly less trustful of Russian cooperation, slightly less enthusiastic about a new League of Nations, and slightly less favorable to an international police force. By 1944 the Middle West was at one with the rest of the country in wanting to take an active part in the new world organization.

7

The South reveals some of the most significant manifestations of sectionalism in American foreign affairs.

The Southerners have long been under the shadow of their all-pervading Negro problem, and they are ever sensitive to the possible undermining of white supremacy. The South was reluctant to send American delegates to the Panama Congress of 1826, partly because white men would have to sit

---

* From 1939 to 1941, on the nine major bills concerning foreign policy and preparedness, the members of Congress from the Middle West voted 97 per cent against administration measures. But this was more a manifestation of Republican partisanship than Middle Western isolationism.

at the same table with Latin-American Negroes. The recognition of the black Republic of Haiti was opposed and long delayed by Southerners; no true gentleman from the South cared to see ebony-hued diplomats putting on airs in the national capital. In 1919 Senator Reed of Missouri (a border state) appealed to Southern prejudices when he condemned the League of Nations on the ground that "dark" peoples would outnumber whites in the ratio of three to one. Senator Cole Blease of South Carolina, a fanatical Negro-baiter, assailed the World Court in 1926:

> I call attention of Senators from the South . . . to the fact that they are voting for a court where we are to sit side by side with a full-blooded "nigger." . . . The Southern Senators are voting to throw the destinies of Southern women and Southern men into the lap of a black man.

As late as 1943 some of the Southern congressmen opposed the admission of Chinese on a quota basis. Let the Oriental get his foot in the door and the superiority of the Occidental would be threatened.

The race problem figured most ominously in the controversies over abolition and expansion before the Civil War. When the European revolutions broke out in 1848, many Northerners urged intervention on behalf of the embattled liberals, but the Southerners, not wishing to set a precedent for abolitionist interference, hung back. The insistence of the South on more slave territory had much to do with our acquisition of the Mexican Cession and our unabashed lust for Cuba. The Southern drive for the "Pearl of the Antilles"developed great momentum in the 1850's, but by this time the nation had become riven over slavery. The North would not let the South take Cuba, and the South would not let the North take Canada, so neither got either.

The burning desire in the South for more territory died with slavery, and this prostrate section was little heard from regarding foreign affairs during the decades that followed. Woodrow Wilson was a Southerner and a Democrat, and the Democratic Solid South gave strong support to his war program and his peace vision, especially the League of Nations. But such enthusiasm was as much partisan loyalty as a predilection for international cooperation. The same in general was true of the Democratic Franklin Roosevelt, who by his personal association with the paralytic center at Warm Springs, Georgia, was something of a Southerner by adoption, although many of his New Deal policies were anathema to Jeffersonians of the mint-julep school.

The most striking revelation of Southern sectionalism in recent times came during the period from 1938 to 1945. Prior to the Munich capitulation of 1938, the South was not markedly out of line with other sections on questions like preparedness and neutrality. In some respects, and quite in contrast with its later bellicosity, it was behind the rest of the country, particularly in ranking neutrality as more important than unemployment, and in its desire to withdraw our troops from the Far East, rather than become involved with Japan.

But the shock of Hitler's bloodless victory at Munich wrought a tremendous transformation. In practically every national poll thereafter that had to do with American rights, defense, intervention, aid to Britain, or war with Hitler, the South was not only ahead of the rest of the country but was ahead by an extraordinarily wide margin. A majority of Southerners did not favor all of these proposals, but even the minority was invariably more interventionist and more belligerent than the corresponding groups in other sections. One must not forget that even on the day before Pearl Harbor a majority in no section was willing to fight the Axis at once.

The picture that emerges from the South in the years before Pearl Harbor is one of grave concern over the Hitler menace, a determination to prepare for armed eventualities, a willingness to bolster the British at all costs, and a desire, more than in any other section, to get into the war, both in Europe and the Far East. Many Southern boys volunteered for service with the Allies, and the Royal Canadian Air Force was jokingly referred to as the Royal Texas Airforce. One true Texan is said to have remarked that Texas would be in the war before the United States was.* In 1942, when there was some talk of a negotiated settlement with Hitler, a large San Antonio newspaper for some time carried the slogan on its masthead: "Texas will never declare a separate peace."

8

Why was the area below the Mason and Dixon line so outstandingly interventionist and bellicose during the months before Pearl Harbor?

A belligerent tradition, one must note at the outset, is a distinguishing feature of the South. The Southerners were conspicuous in agitating for the War of 1812, the Mexican War, the Spanish-American War, and the two wars with Germany. The ante-bellum slave owners were accustomed to command and to bear arms, and arms-owning and arms-bearing are still common in this section. The duel persisted in the South long after it had died out or had been outlawed in other sections. Oscar S. Straus, who spent his boyhood years in Georgia, concluded that Southern boys were soft-spoken because loud and offensive talk often led to serious consequences.

With the Lost Cause as their inspiration, the Southerners have elevated a preponderance of military heroes to their pantheon: men like Robert E. Lee, and "Stonewall" Jackson. They hold in hallowed memory the triumphs of Bull Run, Chancellorsville, and Fredericksburg.

The military tradition persists even in the schools. The South has a disproportionately large number of high-grade military academies, including the Virginia Military Institute, where "Stonewall" Jackson taught and where General George C. Marshall was trained. An appointment to Annapolis and West Point is highly prized in the South, and the Southern graduates of these institutions are strongly disposed to remain in the service. The martial tradition and social prestige are not alone responsible for this attachment;

* Texan nationalism is distinctive, and derives in part from the glorious Alamo tradition and the unique experience of having been an independent republic for nine years.

the more limited economic opportunities in the South add attractiveness to the security of a commission in the armed forces.

Economic insecurity on a broader scale also enters into the picture, and no one will deny that the South, which ranks at the very bottom in national wealth, has plenty of that. Where unemployment and poverty are oppressive, the feeling may take root that war is a blessing which may bring jobs and higher wages. What can the worker lose? One national poll late in 1939 revealed that, taking the entire country into account, the highest vote for an immediate declaration of war against the Axis came from the unemployed.

The Negroes of the South were conspicuously bellicose in the opinion polls, and this may be attributed in part to their economic and social insecurity. Knowing full well the treatment that had been accorded to them in the Land of the Free, they could hardly expect favored treatment under the Hitlerian gangsters who made no bones about the Herrenvolk idea. But probably only a few Negroes looked that far ahead.* A great many no doubt were attracted by the money, glamor, and social prestige resulting from membership in the armed forces.

The South during these years seems to have felt less secure physically than any of the other sections, and this probably accounts in part for its willingness to fight. The Negroes and the poor whites combine to give the South our highest rate of illiteracy, and just as children are more afraid of the dark than adults, so the ignorant are prone to read into an international menace a greater threat than often exists, although many of them go to the other extreme.

Yet physical insecurity was not just an under-the-bed bogey to many of the most literate Southerners. In 1939 those sections on the periphery of the United States, including the South, were most favorable to fighting for the Monroe Doctrine. If Hitler had overcome the British, he presumably would have sought to attack the United States not by direct assault but indirectly from South America, in which case the South would have been the first to feel the weight of his onslaught. The Southerners, with the memory of Sherman's march still vivid, preferred to fight the Battle of the Bulge in Belgium rather than in Georgia. They knew that war could settle things, and settle them the wrong way; it had for them. They were much less worried about the Japanese than the Germans; let the Pacific Coast concern itself with that phase of the fight.

One cannot credit the South with having been more far-visioned than the rest of the United States. If it arrived at a far-visioned result, it did so by rather narrow-visioned methods. By every test of literacy and education, the South ranks lowest in the sectional scale. The Southerners during the anxious days before Pearl Harbor were comparatively less favorable to participation in an international organization for peace than they were for outright participation in the war. More than any other section, they were anxious to

* A sprinkling of the more radical Negroes in fact said: "What can we lose? How can we possibly be worse off under Hitler?"

forsake tradition and form a permanent military alliance with both Russia and Britain, especially Britain. The Southerners were not too proud to fight; in a very real sense they were too apprehensive to stay out of the fight.

9

Anglo-Saxonism has frequently been cited as the primary reason for interventionist sentiment in the South prior to 1942. There is some basis in fact for such a theory. Excluding the Afro-Americans, who are not Anglo-Saxons but who generally have Anglo-Saxon names, this section is by blood the most English part of the United States. For various reasons, economic and otherwise, the great bulk of our foreign immigrants sought the cities and prairies of the East and Middle West. The original Anglo-Saxon stock was consequently less diluted, and since blood is thicker than water, the Southerners can cultivate whatever pro-British predisposition they may have without a contradictory clamor from a huge body of hyphenates.

Another aspect of Anglo-Saxonism goes back to the Civil War. The South feels sympathetic toward England, it is alleged, because during the conflict the British government and ruling class displayed warm friendliness toward the South and almost intervened in its behalf.

What is the truth? Before the Civil War there was clearly a close affinity between the aristocracy of England and the aristocracy of the South, bolstered by a strong Southern attachment to the romantic novels of Sir Walter Scott. Perhaps the lingering chivalry of the South was touched in 1939 by the cowardice of permitting the British to fight our battles while the American Ivanhoes refused to enter the lists. At all events, cultured Southerners felt much sympathy for England, and regarded her as the bastion of our civilization.

As for the alleged Civil War assistance of Britain, one finds it hard to believe that such a tradition persists in any strength among the masses. This presupposes a highly literate South and an awareness of history which one does not ordinarily find elsewhere in the United States. The British government in fact was technically neutral, and when it failed to intervene and break the Northern blockade, it aroused a good deal of resentment in the South. The theory of Anglophilism is hard hit by a national opinion poll, published two months after Hitler's invasion of Poland, which showed that the Southerners, even more than the rest of the country, believed that Germans made better citizens than the British.

But one aspect of the Anglo-Saxon argument is undoubtedly valid. For considerably more than a century the South has been heavily dependent on the British textile mills as a market for cotton, and the British mills have been no less dependent on the South for raw fiber. The Southerners have long sent their staples, including tobacco, to other foreign consumers, and reliance on a world market promotes international-mindedness. When the guns began booming in 1914, the Galveston *News* remarked: "Here in the South our chief fear now is that the European savages will quit wearing clothes." When Hitler ascended to power, the Southern producers of staples could not afford to see the Nazis overrun Europe and set up systems of barter and blocked exchanges inimical to Southern exports. The Hitlerian threat to the South was economic as well as physical.

10

The smaller a nation, the less likelihood of sectional differences; the larger a nation, the more likelihood of sectional differences. Sweden can present to the world a unified foreign policy; the United States has more difficulty. The successive defeats of the St. Lawrence waterway-and-power project in the Senate are instructive examples of the pulling and hauling among the sections, complicated by the pressures of the railroad, power, and other lobbies.

The London *Statist* in 1926 published a striking commentary on the United States:

America is not a homogeneous political organism. The prairies of the Middle West and New York are as far apart in political thought as Albania and Amsterdam. The West is intolerant of European perplexities; the East, less remote, is more sympathetic toward Europe's difficulties. Thus it comes that Washington, the capital of a Great Power, is occasionally forced to behave as the head of a petty state.

This picture is less accurate now than it was in 1926. Sectional differences in recent years have actually been far less crippling than political or racial differences. Sectionalism has been discernible, at times significant, but usually of relatively minor importance. In any nation-wide poll on foreign affairs, the various sections are usually separated by only a few points. The Middle West was generally more isolationist than the rest of the country from 1939 to 1941, but not seriously so; the South by a wider margin was more interventionist during the same years, but not by enough to affect the final result.

Sectionalism, like hyphenism, is gradually breaking down. The Spanish War of 1898 helped close the bloody chasm between North and South,* and World War I also helped. "One of the sad things about this war," lamented a Florida newspaper in 1918, "is the fact that after it is over all Americans will be called Yankees." The shuttling of draftees all over the country to training camps during World War II was a great fusing experience. The South and the Pacific Coast are becoming industrialized, and one can no longer speak accurately of the industrialized North and the agricultural South. Greater ease of travel, whether by train or highway or airway, is encouraging intersectional visits, and great folk movements, like the migration of the "Okies" and "Arkies" to California during the dust-bowl 1930's, are

---

* In 1898 the Detroit *News-Tribune* said: "Nothing short of an archeological society will be able to locate Mason and Dixon's line after this."

contributing substantially to the erasing of sectional lines. The radio and the cinema are forcing us to listen to the same performances, and dialectical differences are fading. We are increasingly, and at the risk of monotony, wearing the same clothes, eating the same breakfasts, smoking the same cigarettes, drinking the same beverages, and riding in the same automobiles.

One day we shall be a nation instead of a bundle of sections, and then we shall be able to present to the rest of the world a more definitely united front.

CHAPTER TEN

THE PERILS OF APATHY

"The tyranny of a prince in an oligarchy is not so dangerous to the
public welfare as the apathy of a citizen in a democracy."
                                        —CHARLES MONTESQUIEU, 1748

1

A P A T H Y is perhaps the greatest single barrier in a democracy to the conduct of an intelligent foreign policy. Ignorance is no less important, but
apathy is either the mother or the daughter of ignorance. One may go even
further and say that indifference is the greatest single barrier to the successful
operation of a democratic government.

If it is true that eternal vigilance is the price we must pay for liberty, it is
no less true that eternal vigilance is the price that we must pay for a successful
democracy. More than a century ago the penetrating young French observer,
Alexis de Tocqueville, recorded after visiting America that democracies are
incompetent to manage their foreign affairs wisely, because those who manage them are ignorant of them, and they are ignorant mainly because they
lack interest in them. Apathy slays republics. It is the sole epitaph that need
be written over dozens of republican corpses in the political graveyard.

Indifference is not a failing peculiarly American. Other democracies have
it as well, and in some cases to an even greater degree. England, though close
to the rising fury of Hitler, slumbered under Baldwin about as peacefully as
we did under Roosevelt.

Nor is indifference to be found only in foreign affairs. At times it is even
more pronounced in our domestic affairs, and with much less excuse. One
can understand why the American people could sleep in the 1930's, separated
as they were from Hitler by three thousand miles of billowing ocean, but they
sleep no less soundly while a stench arises from the city hall under their very
noses. The Teapot Dome and other scandals that oozed from the Harding
administration should have turned a vigilant and liberty-loving people
against the party in power, yet Coolidge and the Republicans were triumphantly reelected by a thumping majority. The nation was mentally and
morally dulled by prosperity.

The stay-at-home voter—the citizen who votes with his feet—has long
bedeviled American politics. We have suffered and continue to suffer from
government by the "Don't Cares"—government by default. Normally only
about half of the eligible voters cast their ballots, and in some Congressional
elections as few as one tenth have straggled to the polls. In 1946 critics noted
that the American turnout was behind that of every other large democracy
that had recently voted: Australia, France, England, Canada, and even

Italy.* Someone has cleverly said: "Bad officials are elected by good citizens who do not vote." Yet nothing real is gained by lashing the apathetic and ill-informed American to the polling booth with the threat of a fine, as is done in Australia. The incentive to vote must lie deeper. If the Man in the Street is not vitally enough interested in his government to spare a few minutes at the polls, he will not cast a very thoughtful or intelligent ballot. Democracy cannot long endure on the foundations of a galley-slave vote.

A Gallup poll in 1940 revealed that not three in ten had read even a part of the current Republican platform. In 1944 the question was repeated, and the percentage arose to almost four in ten. Yet in the same election, when international collaboration was a vital issue, only one in ten knew what the Republican platform had to say about the role of the United States in postwar world affairs. One is torn between condemning the apathy of the American people and applauding their realism. The average voter has long perceived that the teeter-totter known as a political platform is built not to stand on but to get in on, and he is perhaps to be commended for confining his reading of fiction to accounts which are clearly labeled such.

The dozing American citizen is often urged by pressure groups to communicate with his congressman. A nation-wide poll in 1946 indicated that not two adults in ten had ever sent letters or telegrams to their representatives in Congress. A preponderance of those who had done so were business or professional people, among whom the largest percentage of college graduates may be found, and most of them had expressed their views on domestic rather than foreign issues.

One obstacle to putting pressure on congressmen is that a disquieting number of voters do not know their names. When in 1935 the radio priest, Father Coughlin, delivered an impassioned tirade against the World Court and urged his malleable listeners to wire their senators, the Cleveland *Plain Dealer* was overwhelmed with telephone calls from aroused citizens wanting to know who their senators were. In 1942 only half of the American voters could name the congressman from their district, and only 65 per cent of this select group knew his attitude before Pearl Harbor on the vitally important issue of staying out of war. In 1944 only three in ten could name both senators from their state, and four in ten confessed that they paid no attention to the record of either senator. Little wonder that the senator, barricaded behind the six-year term and shielded by public apathy, can often defy what appears to be the majority opinion of the nation.

If the American citizen is not vitally interested in foreign affairs, or in the record of his representatives regarding them, one should not be surprised to find the representatives themselves showing little interest. Often there is a shockingly sparse attendance at debates in Congress, and this was notably

* Australia has compulsory voting; England, France, and Italy no doubt were aroused by the novelty of general elections. The vote is also kept down in America by the repressed Negro, the poll tax, the Southern primary, and lack of permanent registration in some states.

true during the discussion of the proposed loan to Britain in 1946, when many members were away patching up political fences. "One explanation of rotten politics," remarked a newspaper in 1920, "is that the people don't know what they want and the politicians do."

2

A primary reason for our indifference to foreign policy is that our own personal affairs seem to us more pressing. David Hume wrote in 1739: " 'Tis not contrary to reason to prefer the destruction of the whole world to the scratching of my finger." We are interested first in ourselves and our immediate family, then in our near neighbors, then in our distant neighbors, and then, both last and least, in foreigners far across the seas.

In all our history there have been only a few times when the sense of outside danger became so acute that foreign affairs were comparable in importance with domestic affairs. One was the period of the French Revolution and the Napoleonic wars, from 1793 to 1815; another was the menace of the Kaiser, in World War I; another was the menace of Hitler, in World War II. Yet after the shooting had informally started in the autumn of 1941, and the Senate had repealed the restrictions of the Neutrality Act, the House, dissatisfied with the failure of the administration to press antistrike legislation, reluctantly followed suit with a distressingly close vote. Many members were saying, "Get John L. Lewis first—then Hitler."

The decade of the 1930's presents an illuminating case study. The year 1937 was critical; preliminaries of World War II were being waged both in China and in Spain. Yet the American public listed as the ten "most interesting" news stories of the year the following in the order given:

1. The Ohio floods.
2. The Sino-Japanese War.
3. The Supreme Court "packing" fight.
4. The Edward and Wally marriage.
5. Amelia Earhart's last flight.
6. The business slump.
7. The Texas school explosion.
8. Justice Black and the Klan.
9. The General Motors strike.
10. The Supreme Court decisions on the New Deal.

The Sino-Japanese War, surprisingly enough, rated second, but no other foreign embroilment won a place, unless one excepts our romantic interest in King Edward's surrender of his crown for a wedding ring. Yet this was the year of the Brussels Conference, the Spanish Civil War, the fantastic Soviet purge trials, none of which placed among the first ten. The entire list is further proof of local or sectional interest, which was previously discussed in connection with the "most interesting" news stories of 1938 (p. 102).

The line-up for 1939, the first year of World War II, is no less striking:

1. The declarations of war on Germany by Britain and France.
2. The lifting of the arms embargo.
3. The attempt on Hitler's life at Munich.
4. The scuttling of the German pocket battleship *Graf Spee*.
5. The German Blitzkrieg into Poland.
6. The visit of the King and Queen of Britain to America.
7. The Russian invasion of Finland.
8. The German seizure of Bohemia and Moravia.
9. Roosevelt's New Deal Thanksgiving date.
10. The Russo-German treaty of friendship.

In these two polls, 1937 and 1939, the women voted much more heavily than the men for the Edward-Wally marriage, Amelia Earhart, the Texas school explosion (where about 300 children lost their lives), and the visit of the British King and Queen to America. Here we see the feminine interest in fellow women, in children, in marriage, and in high society. The visit of the King and Queen rated fourth place with women, eleventh with the men.°

In all fairness it must be emphasized that the voter was asked to give the "most interesting" rather than the most significant news story of the year. Even so, something was wrong when the American people in 1938 ranked the World Series above the Sino-Japanese conflict, from which evolved the assault on Pearl Harbor; and when in 1939 they ranked the unorthodox New Deal Thanksgiving holiday above the Russo-German pact, which gave Hitler the green light for starting World War II in Poland.

3

Fortunately, interesting evidence exists as to what the American people regarded as the most significant issues, as contrasted with the most interesting ones.

During the early 1930's the overshadowing and oppressive problem was unemployment. In 1935, the year of the first Neutrality Act growing out of the Ethiopian crisis, Dr. Gallup found that the three top issues were unemployment, economy, and neutrality. (One respondent, presumably a Notre Dame football fan still mourning the untimely demise of the coach, replied: "The issue is—Where can we find another Knute Rockne?") In 1936 the three outstanding problems were rated as unemployment, New Deal spending, and neutrality. In 1937, with the Spanish Civil War and the China "incident" going full blast, neutrality climbed to second place, behind unemployment but ahead of Social Security. In May of 1939, on the eve of World War II, neutrality rose to a first place tie with unemployment, and in December of

---

° The polls have consistently shown that the men are markedly more interested than the women in public affairs, whether national or international. The old German ideal that the woman's place is with the church, the kitchen, and the children has a certain universality.

1939, following Hitler's devastating assault upon Poland, neutrality shot ahead of unemployment and business recovery.

After the shock of Pearl Harbor, winning the war was the number one issue, and this was taken for granted. But from 1943 to 1945 unemployment rated higher in the public mind than working for an enduring peace. During the presidential campaign of 1944, one poll discovered that unemployment ranked above world affairs in the selection of presidential candidates. Such results did not lead to undue optimism among those who realized that a vitally interested public opinion was essential for the fashioning of an enduring peace.

In 1944, a month before the second front was opened in France, a Gallup poll inquired if it was true, as the soldiers were saying, that the home front was not taking the war seriously enough. Nearly seven out of ten confessed that we were not. The next year Dr. Gallup asked the people if they had made any real sacrifice. More than six out of ten admitted they had not, though one waitress in Dayton, Ohio, complained: "All my boy friends have gone overseas; so I can't get married"; and a stenographer in Detroit lamented: "I've had to get along without nylons!" If the American people by their own admission cannot take a desperate war for survival seriously when they are deeply involved in it, one could hardly expect them to take foreign affairs too seriously when they are distracted by strikes, unemployment, elections, and other domestic crises.

Then came the end of the war, and the rank and file, as was usual and natural, slipped back into preoccupation with their domestic problems. In 1946, a year after the shooting stopped, Dr. Gallup found that concern about inflation and various shortages, including food, outranked at least two to one our interest in the maintenance of peace and the conduct of foreign affairs.

4

It would be erroneous to assume that only in recent years have the American people displayed indifference to foreign developments.

The opening of Japan by Commodore Perry was one of the red-letter dates in the history of the world, but it passed almost unnoticed in the United States. Even though the real significance of the event did not become fully apparent until much later, President Pierce did not reveal unusual prescience when he gave the dramatic episode only two sentences in his twenty-one-page annual message to Congress. Secretary Seward tried arduously to pick up real estate bargains for the United States in the years after the Civil War, and although he stumbled upon Alaska, he encountered so much preoccupation with domestic difficulties that he was sorrowfully forced to conclude that we had come to "value dollars more and dominion less." The colorful Secretary ("Jingo Jim") Blaine, with all his theatrical talents, encountered great apathy in working up even lukewarm interest for his Pan-American ideal.

"Dollar diplomacy" during the Taft and Wilson era, though an important prop of our national security and foreign policy, was viewed with indifference if not opposition by the bankers who controlled the dollars.

The outbreak of war in 1914 was regarded with "curiosity rather than concern," as Senator George Norris put it. The assassination of the Archduke Francis Ferdinand made the headlines for a few days, and then the whole affair sank out of sight for a few weeks, until the shooting had virtually started.° Then our general attitude was that Europe could stew in her own juice, and three cheers to Columbus for having discovered America. The year after the *Lusitania* tragedy, and while the U-boat warfare was still being actively waged, an inquiry among twenty-three hundred Chicago businessmen elicited the incredible admission that fewer than 10 per cent of them were interested in foreign affairs. We approached the brink of war in 1917 with scant enthusiasm; we waited almost literally for Germany to kick us in.

When Wilson brought back the League of Nations Covenant from Europe, the memory of the recent war was still fresh and there was strong popular support for the proposed new order. The strategy of the "irreconcilable" senators was to stall for time, introduce irrelevancies and further confusion into the debate, and wait for strikes and other disorders to distract the American people so completely that they would permit the League to die a quiet death. The scheme worked to perfection. Senator George H. Moses later testified that if prompt consideration of the treaty could have been secured, approval would have been a certainty. But the strikes spread, the World Series came, only to be followed by the reverberating Black Sox scandal, and the League of Nations issue grew stale. A few dull-pated citizens believed that it was a new baseball league, which gives point to Norman Angell's remark that the American people are not interested in foreign affairs at all but in the World Series.

5

After we had turned our backs on Europe, and began to revel in the mad prosperity of the 1920's, our indifference to the outside world was almost beyond belief. "We never knew that China had a cabinet until it resigned," remarked a South Carolina newspaper in 1922. The normal bickering with Mexico was intensified in 1926, and after it had been smoothed out a Washington dispatch reported that we were back on good terms with our southern neighbor. "This will come as a shock to a lot of us who don't even know we were mad at them," commented a Buffalo newspaper. The Los Angeleans could boast through their leading newspaper in 1927: "A change of Ministers

° One reason for our unconcern was that the "Wolf! Wolf!" talk of a great European war had been going on for the better part of two decades. As early as 1901, the Baltimore *American* wrote: "That great European war that is to start in the Balkans is again to the front, threatening as ever, but with its edges slightly frayed."

in France is of less importance to the residents of Los Angeles than a change of grade on an important thoroughfare."

In 1932, after Japan had sowed the dragon's teeth of another world war on the wind-swept plains of Manchuria, a Philadelphia newspaper truthfully observed: "The American people don't give a hoot in a rainbarrel who controls North China." After the Chinese powder keg blew up in 1937, the significant thing was not that an overwhelming majority of Americans *with opinions* favored China, but that more than half of our citizens favored neither side. The percentage of "Don't Knows" declined as the issues sharpened, but even the *Panay* outrage of 1937 failed to arouse the nation to a fighting pitch. The opinion polls showed that while a majority supported a boycott of Japanese goods and an embargo on arms shipments, a clear majority favored pulling our troops out of China and not defending the Philippines at all, even if the Japanese should seize them. Not until August, 1941, five months before Pearl Harbor, was a slight majority of the people willing to stop Japan even at the risk of war.

Other threats appeared, but the American people wrapped the mantle of their neutrality about them, and lay down to a quiet sleep. When Franco raised the standard of revolt in 1936, with the openly "secret" assistance of Hitler and Mussolini, we denied arms to the Loyalist government. Roosevelt vainly tried to arouse the somnolent citizenry from their slumbers when in 1937 he delivered his Quarantine speech, but a surly growl from the slumbering giant forced him to take a less forthright tack. Munich jarred us from our fool's paradise, but even then we focused our eyes on Europe and not on the Far East. We continued to think of China as far away and of minor importance, a nation at the back door of the world, as though the world were not spherical and as though it had a front and a back door. We failed to see that there was not a German question or a Chinese question but that there were world aspects of German and Chinese questions.

In 1941, after Japan had elbowed her way into French Indo-China and had concluded a triple alliance with Germany and Italy, our people were asked by Dr. Gallup if American interests would be threatened by a Japanese occupation of Singapore and the Dutch East Indies. The surprising total of four out of ten replied "no" or "undecided." For a nation that ate out of tin cans and rode on rubber tires, from the maternity ward to the cemetery, these results are almost incredible. The explanation is that a vast number did not know where their rubber and tin came from, and did not seem to care. The snapping of our rubber life line after Pearl Harbor was hardly less serious than the sinking of our battleships, and we quickly learned a great deal about rubber and tin. If we had only known these things before we were taught them in the school of hard knocks, we no doubt would have amassed the necessary stockpiles. We also would have supported the President more actively in his Far Eastern policy, and would have given him a Big Stick with which to back it up. Theodore Roosevelt, the original brandisher of the Big Stick, said in 1917: "Nine tenths of wisdom consists in being wise in time."

6

American indifference and preoccupation are due largely to the absence of any feeling of imminent peril. Only when a threat to our security plainly emerges do we concern ourselves vitally with foreign affairs, as was notably true when France collapsed in 1940 and Britain was left to struggle on alone. Then and only then did we become aroused, and even then it was almost too late.

The people of England, whose economic lifeblood pulsates through imperial life lines, do not have to be urged to resist a threat to their trade arteries. The Belgians, who are crowded into the cockpit of Europe, do not have to be implored to interest themselves in foreign affairs. Even well armed nations, like France in the 1930's, which was menaced by a renascent and vengeful neighbor, show a vital concern about the outside world. But over the years we have been too big, too powerful, too rich, too fat, too complacent. We have reveled in the false security of our two mighty oceans and our two weak neighbors.

We escaped much too easily from the fiery furnace of World War II. Our mainland soil was not violated, except for a few aimless shells lobbed over by Japanese submarines in the hectic days just after Pearl Harbor. None of our cities received the semblance of a bombing, and our enviable fortune merely confirmed the conviction of the isolationists that our oceans and our neighbors still confer a mystic immunity. The soldiers who served overseas saw the frightfulness of war at first hand, but they are only a small segment of the population, and the horrors through which they passed tend to fade into blessed forgetfulness. The terrible actualities and potentialities of the atomic bomb kept the American people from sliding back too rapidly into their post-1919 somnolence, but even though we saw pictures of pulverized Hiroshima, the new weapon seemed too unreal and too horrible ever to be used against us, and besides we had the "secret." "How worried are you about the atomic bomb?" queried one national poll after the Bikini tests. Fifty per cent replied, "Not at all." The human animal finds it hard to keep uppermost in mind what he regards as a theoretical menace.

The traditional indifference of the American people to foreign affairs may also be explained by their unique experience. They had a continent to conquer, and they did it with a speed and efficiency and rapacity unparalleled in the annals of mankind. While felling trees and Indians, while constructing canals and railroads, they were torn with controversies over States' rights and slavery, and finally were convulsed by Civil War. Then for the next decades their abounding energy was absorbed by reconstruction, industrialization, reform, and World War I. The feverish prosperity of the 1920's was diverting, and the economic depression of the 1930's was debilitating. The harassed American had neither the time nor the taste for foreign adventures.

A German proverb tells us that in the United States the hour is only forty minutes long. After working at high tension all day, after battling his way through crowded subways at nightfall, the weary citizen has no urge to delve deeply into learned tomes on world affairs and don the mantle of a states- man.° He much prefers his old dressing gown and slippers. He would much rather escape from this overburdened world to the dream world of *Superman,* or enjoy the mental narcotic of a detective story or a homicidal radio program. Joseph P. Kennedy, then United States ambassador at the Court of St. James's, remarked in 1938 on the eve of Munich: "Right now the average American is more interested in how he's going to eat and whether his insurance is good than in foreign policies." In 1946 the ordinary citizen was more interested in Social Security than in the Security Council.

The Man in the Street has only time and energy for those things that rather directly touch his everyday life—the meat-and-potato problems. Democracy comes close to being a full-time job, and since we are able and willing to give it only the tag end of the day, the wonder is that our failures are not more disastrous. The barber and the farmer cannot be successful spare-time statesmen.

7

The complexity of foreign relations is enough to discourage the ordinary citizen. In the oxcart days of Thomas Jefferson, the farmer could discuss the outside world in a leisurely fashion over the corner cracker barrel; in the days of atomic terror, international problems have become so confused as to demand the full time of a Philadelphia lawyer. "The Chinese question would be difficult enough," remarked the Indianapolis *Star* in 1921, "if the Chinese themselves would agree upon what it is." The perplexed American is apt to throw up his hands in despair. He is urged to inform himself, and an avalanche of literature and radio programs descends upon him. What is fact and what is propaganda? How much of the government handouts can he believe?

The American people are not stupid; their mass intelligence is at least comparable with that of any other great nation. Lord Bryce long ago ob- served that we are well enough educated relatively, but not well enough educated for the tremendous burden of self-government that we are attempt- ing to shoulder. In England the average person is more willing to delegate responsibility, and let the trained diplomats of Downing Street conduct for- eign affairs. In the United States the ideal course would be for public opinion to indicate the general lines of policy, and then permit the Washington offi- cials to select the ways and means of carrying it out. An analogy would be the back-seat rider who tells the chauffeur where he wants to go but does not sit over his shoulder and advise him exactly how to avoid every bump in the road. The American people, when they are articulate at all, not only

---

° The Treaty of Versailles was 268 quarto pages long. "Nobody is competent to discuss the Versailles Treaty until he has read it," remarked the Peoria *Transcript,* "and nobody who would take the time to read it would be competent to discuss it."

tell their officials where they want to go, which is sometimes in the wrong direction or over the wrong road, but they frequently joggle the driver's elbow as he tries to dodge the ruts.

Another difficulty with the conduct of democratic foreign policy is that the people become bored with the old issues. We were tired of hearing about imperialism by 1900, and voted for McKinley; we were tired of hearing about the League by 1920, and voted for Harding and "normalcy"—anything for a change. The Socialist New York *Call* in 1920 thought the League issue "as vital as a dead cat in a gutter." After World War II and Hiroshima, we began to weary of discussing the atomic bomb.

The American people are to an unusual degree sensation-hungry, not so much because they differ from other human beings,° but partly because, through their newspapers and other agencies, they have been encouraged to expect and savor successive sensations, particularly regarding their neighbors. "A dog fight at home is more important than a civil war in China" has long been a newspaper axiom. Our vampire press has pandered to the public taste for the scandalous, with the result that this perverted appetite has grown with eating. Oscar Wilde once observed: "The public have an insatiable curiosity to know everything, except what is worth knowing."

Problems in the foreign field are often complex and dull; problems regarding one's neighbors or prominent personages may be treated simply, interestingly, and perhaps scandalously. The actress Gloria Swanson fell ill in Paris during 1925, and her name was in the front-page headlines for three days, while a German mine disaster which killed five hundred laborers received scant inside paragraphs. The Massie rape-lynching scandal in Hawaii in 1932 crowded the Far Eastern crisis off the front pages. Late in July, 1936 the Spanish Civil War broke into the headlines, and then it was submerged by the election and King Edward's sensational abdication.

8

There is further evidence that our people not only tire of old sensations but that they can sustain only one big sensation at a time. In 1896 the Cuban crisis was much in the public eye, but it was obscured by the heated free-silver campaign, only to emerge later. Foreign offices are well aware of this American weakness, and during the *Lusitania* negotiations of 1915 our ambassador in Berlin wrote that the Germans hoped to keep matters "jollied along" until our people got excited about baseball or a new scandal. In 1922, when the League issue was slowly dying and spring was in the offing, a South Carolina newspaper remarked: "Soon we shall forget this trivial dis-

° Edmund Burke said in 1774 that a remarkable highway robbery at Hounslow-Heath in England would make more conversation than all the prerevolutionary disturbances in America. The sex-murder trial of handsome Neville Heath in England during 1946 detracted interest from the current peace negotiations.

cussion of empires and turn again to the more vital matter of umpires." The World Series of 1942 largely overshadowed interest in Hitler's most important speech of the year, and the World Series of 1946 did much the same for the Paris peace negotiations.

This accentuation of the trivial has trained Americans to mistake the individual waves for the rise and fall of the tide, and to emphasize the sensational rather than the significant. The *Lusitania*, a British ship flying the British flag, was sunk by a German submarine in 1915, with a loss of 1198 lives, 128 of them Americans. The nation was profoundly shocked. Seven days earlier, the *Gulflight*, an American tanker flying the American flag was torpedoed with a loss of three American citizens. The attack on an American ship was technically more serious to us than the one on a British ship, but the mass slaughter blinded our eyes to these realities. We are interested in sensational incidents which plunge us into war, like the sinking of the *Maine*, but are much less interested in the long series of underlying causes which fundamentally are more dangerous.

The American flair for sensationalism may sometimes be turned to good account, as when Secretary of State Hughes launched the Washington Disarmament Conference in 1921 with tremendous momentum by verbally sinking more battleships than had ever been sunk before in the history of the world. The public imagination was captured, and the success of the conference seemed assured.

Sensationalism may also be turned to bad account, as when Senator Gerald P. Nye of North Dakota conducted his munitions investigation in 1934-1936. The popular mood was antibanker, antimunitions manufacturer, and antiwar; and by stressing the scandalous the investigators succeeded in stirring up a maximum of publicity with a modicum of significant new facts. The public became aroused over the wrong things, and this state of mind contributed powerfully to the passage of the head-in-the-sands neutrality legislation of the 1930's.

9

The people of the United States are notoriously provincial. They have traveled little, except perhaps to see America first, and they are little interested in their neighbors, whether transborder or transoceanic. Some years ago a Haitian visited the United States thinking that our entire nation was bent on devouring his tiny country. His fear quickly gave way to resentment, and upon his return he complained bitterly: "Why, they don't even know where Haiti is!"

Much of our unconcern grows out of a feeling that foreign affairs can be sharply separated from domestic preoccupations. Many earnest citizens are convinced that domestic policy can be put into one container and foreign policy into another, like sugar and flour. What we do at home is domestic; what we do abroad is foreign.

Lord Curzon in 1922 underscored a profound truth when he said that foreign affairs are not only domestic affairs, but "the most domestic of all our affairs." They affect "the life, the interest, and the pocket" of every citizen, for the proper conduct of foreign relations may secure "immunity from war, relief from the heavy burden of taxation, prosperity of trade and industry." International affairs are often but the projection of domestic affairs into a larger theater. The very term "*foreign* affairs" bespeaks provincialism; "international relations" is a much more meaningful phrase.

A grave danger results from compartmenting domestic and foreign affairs, at least in our thinking. The Man in the Street is apt to feel that whatever we do here at home cannot possibly have any important diplomatic repercussions. Nothing would seem to be more domestic than a presidential campaign, but the election of 1916, with the "He kept us out of war" slogan, encouraged the Berlin government to believe that it could treat the United States as a kind of doormat. Nothing would seem to be more domestic than the raising of revenue and the protection of our own industries through import duties, but the Smoot-Hawley tariff of 1930 brought remonstrances from more than a score of foreign governments, and started a tariff war which recoiled disastrously upon American economy. Nothing would seem to be more domestic than the right to select those immigrants, if any, whom we wish to invite from foreign lands, yet when in 1924 we slammed the immigration gates in the faces of the Japanese we aroused bitterness that found only partial solace in the attack on Pearl Harbor and in the subsequent torture of American prisoners. Yet a few years prior to the fateful act of 1924 the St. Louis *Republic* observed: "It is hard to understand how anything as dull as the American-Japanese correspondence in relation to immigration could ever be an international danger."

The American voter will take a more active and intelligent interest in international relations when he perceives that so-called domestic measures may invite serious foreign reprisals, and when he realizes that seemingly remote incidents, such as the Japanese invasion of Manchuria in 1931 and the subsequent breakdown of the League, may profoundly affect his life and that of his children's children.

10

The ordinary citizen is not apt to be aroused from his apathy by theoretical arguments. Quarts of ink were spilled during the nineteenth century over the necessity of constructing an isthmian canal for defensive and commercial purposes. If pens had been shovels the waterway would have been dug long before 1914. But the American people, immersed in their daily doings, turned a deaf ear, and by 1898 the canal seemed as far from reality as ever.

Then came the approach of the Spanish-American War. The battleship

Oregon, refitting in Puget Sound, was ordered to proceed under forced draft around South America to join naval units in Cuban waters. As the American people mentally pushed the *Oregon* with tantalizing slowness around the southern continent, they learned an unforgettable lesson. Suppose the *Oregon* were wrecked in the Strait of Magellan; suppose it did not reach Cuba in time, and because of its absence the American fleet were wiped out. All these fears finally proved groundless, but for the first time we saw the necessity of having a canal to shuttle our navy back and forth. Within a few years after that "the dirt began to fly." The practical-minded American is educated quickly by events, slowly by arguments. The smashing assault on Pearl Harbor was the strongest argument ever delivered against isolation.

The people of the United States are now less indifferent to foreign affairs than they were twenty-five or even five years ago. More extensive press coverage by abler foreign correspondents attests to this increased interest, but we still have a long way to go. If our interest has increased substantially, the complexity of foreign affairs has increased immeasurably.

In the days of Franklin and Washington, when we were struggling for our very lives, we recognized the supreme importance of foreign affairs, and we drafted our ablest diplomats: the Franklins and the Adamses and the Jays. With the passing of time our position became more secure, and we were content to send abroad broken-down politicians and inexperienced second-raters. We paid them a pittance, and then begrudged them that. With fearsome supersonic weapons in the making, and with the safety of our very homes more seriously menaced than in the days of Washington, we shall do well to return to the earlier practice of drafting our ablest men. We ought no longer to be content with party hacks in high places.

Above all we need to develop a keen sense of responsibility. Foreign affairs are not the job of Ivan Ivanovitch of Leningrad: they are handled for him by the Kremlin and if the Kremlin makes bad moves, one cannot blame Ivan. But foreign affairs are the direct concern of Mr. Joseph Doakes of Sioux City, Iowa. He has taken on that task by accepting his citizenship under our democracy, and until such time as he is willing to sublet more authority to his officials, he should be doing a more alert job.

"They also serve who only stand and wait," wrote the blind Milton. This may be true in certain situations, but in regard to foreign affairs the citizen who passively stands by may be a traitor to his responsibility. In some crises doing nothing at all—floating along with the tide—is an act of criminality.

Somnambulistic drifting plays into the hands of the aggressive, well organized minority bloc, with a consequent defeat of majority rule. "In a free country more especially," wrote Lord Bryce, "ten men who care are a match for a hundred who do not." The American Revolution, in Lecky's famous passage, was foisted upon an apathetic or unwilling majority by a militant minority. "It is not the neutrals or the lukewarms who make history," screamed Adolf Hitler in 1933, and then proceeded to prove his theory.

The lethargic majority suffers from one fatal defect. It seems to feel that it is going to prevail through sheer weight of numbers. But numbers without intensity of feeling or skill of organization may be completely ineffective. The great weakness of public opinion, someone has noted, is that so many people express it privately. The voice of the people is very much in need of a megaphone.

If the ordinary American citizen can only work himself up to a point where he is as deeply interested in the outer world—in the fate of his country, his civilization, and his planet—as he is in the doings of his next-door neighbor and his favorite comic-strip character, then we shall make greater progress toward a successful democratic foreign policy.

CHAPTER ELEVEN

THE INCUBUS OF IGNORANCE

"No nation is permitted to live in ignorance with impunity."

—THOMAS JEFFERSON, 1821

1

AN APPALLING IGNORANCE of foreign affairs is one of the most striking and dangerous defects of American public opinion. This is not to say that we are thick-witted; there is a world of difference between a stupid person and an uninformed one. Even the most brilliant scholars must necessarily be ignorant of a vast body of knowledge.

The American people have informed themselves very creditably on a number of complex questions, *once their interest was aroused.* The heated nation-wide debates on imperialism in the 1890's, on the League of Nations in 1919-1920, on the neutrality issues of the 1930's, on the repeal of the arms embargo in 1939, and on Lend-Lease in 1941, while bringing out specious as well as valid arguments, on the whole gave encouragement to those who have faith in the democratic ideal. But we seldom become aroused to this high pitch, and largely because we are uninterested we lack information. The journalist Raymond Clapper used to say: "Never over-estimate the people's knowledge, nor underestimate their intelligence."

As a nation we may be reasonably well informed, yet we are not well enough informed to exercise understandingly our present direct and hence dangerous control of foreign affairs. For many years the average citizen has passed judgment on, and exercised pressure regarding, knotty problems of international law upon which not even the ablest international lawyers could agree. Questions of blockade and maritime rights, which figured so prominently in our history during the nineteenth century, baffled both the jurists of that time and the historians of a later generation. But this did not prevent the layman from expressing his judgment with great vigor, often substituting emotion for reason. A true patriot has been aptly defined as one who is unable to wait for the facts. Sanity indeed receives a setback when interpretations of treaty obligations and international law fall into the hands of the mob.

The same danger is no less evident in international trade and finance. Even if the average citizen had the incentive to make a profound study of these subjects, his intellectual capacity and training are not equal to mastering the intricacies of international exchange, international banking,* international debts, international reparations, and reciprocal trade agree-

---

* In 1946 Mr. Jesse Jones, with long experience as head of the Reconstruction Finance Corporation, criticized the loan to Britain of $3,750,000,000 on the ground that there was not adequate "collateral," as though an international loan and a domestic loan operated on precisely the same basis.

ments. We are largely and perhaps inevitably a nation of economic illiterates. When the proposed bank for international loans was being discussed in 1944 at Bretton Woods, New Hampshire, one interested citizen wrote an academic economist inquiring: "What is this *Barton* Woods bank, and how do I go about borrowing money from it?" Other unenlightened persons thought that Mr. Bretton Woods had something to do with the whole scheme. Yet the American people were by far the largest shareholders (totaling $5,925,000,000) in the international loan fund and the world bank growing out of the Bretton Woods plan.

Lord Bryce, who was as sympathetic a critic of American democracy as one could hope to find among foreigners, wrote regarding control of foreign policy: "Not one in a thousand of the citizens, not one in ten of the representatives, may have enough knowledge to enable him to form a sound opinion." If this was true in the horse-and-buggy era, it is even more true today. In the nineteenth century, when the Atlantic was a tremendous barrier, the American people could better afford the luxury of being ignorant or apathetic or wrong or late, but even then they had some narrow escapes. Those happy days of blessed ignorance are gone forever; we shall continue in some degree to be ignorant, but in a perilous rather than in a blissful state. Facts cannot be ignored out of existence.

The average American is a self-reliant individual; his forefathers rolled back a wilderness with their own muscular arms and backs. He is too prone to rely on himself for an opinion, whether he is in possession of the facts or not—a not uncommon failing. "Nothing is so firmly believed as that which we least know," wrote the French philosopher Montaigne in the sixteenth century. The ordinary citizen is also inclined to believe most readily that which he hopes for most earnestly, and he is all too often most easily persuaded by arguments which he cannot understand. All these human shortcomings are to be found in a despotism, but in a democracy they are more dangerous, for a democracy is the one system in which the ignorant have the most influence and where they are listened to with the most respect.

2

In the midst of the Roosevelt-Dewey campaign of 1944, one opinion poll revealed that 14 per cent of the people did not know the name of the Republican candidate then running (Dewey), though many of this group no doubt were going to vote for him. If the American citizen is not better informed than this about political campaigns being waged under his very window, how can he be well informed about controversies on the other side of two wide oceans? The answer is that he is not.

The opinion polls from 1940 to 1945 turned up some almost incredible information as to our general ignorance.

In 1940, when the debate over renewing the Reciprocal Trade Agreements Act was at its height, only one voter in ten understood what the law was designed to accomplish. The informed one tenth were overwhelmingly favorable to renewal.

In 1941, when the Good Neighbor Policy was being actively pushed, nearly two in ten did not know that Latin America is rich in natural resources. Such ignorance of foreign countries is more or less typical of Americans.

In 1942, several months after the Atlantic Charter had been dramatically drawn up by Roosevelt and Churchill, and the results had been heralded in the headlines, nearly eight in ten admitted that they had neither read nor heard about the Charter.

In 1942, when the Four Freedoms were presumably on every tongue, only one citizen in ten could name them, and a tremendous number had never heard of them.

In 1943, slightly more than half of our people thought we were getting something in return for Lend-Lease, and a majority of these believed that our repayment was good will and cooperation rather than the substantial amount of reverse Lend-Lease then being received.

In 1944, when "unconditional surrender" was a vital part of our military policy, only half of our citizens could give a reasonably satisfactory explanation of the term.

In 1944, when there was strong popular agitation to amend the Constitution so as to deprive the Senate of the one-third veto voice on treaties, nearly seven Americans in ten did not even know that the Senate has to approve treaties by a two-thirds vote. This explains in a nutshell why the Constitution was not amended. Nothing short of a veritable tidal wave of public sentiment can drive an amendment through two thirds of both Houses of Congress and through three fourths of the states, and no such tidal wave arises from an ocean of ignorance and apathy.

In 1944, when a new League of Nations was being widely discussed, more than half of our citizens did not know that we had never joined the old League of Nations. Perhaps some of the ill-informed were suffering from a guilt complex growing out of the breakdown of the League and the coming of World War II, and they were wishfully thinking that we had joined.

In 1945, when a homeland for the Jews in Palestine was being hotly debated, fewer than one third of the American people were aware that Palestine was a British mandate.

In 1945, when delegates from the United Nations were assembling in San Francisco to frame a world charter, only two voters in three had ever heard of the conference, and most of these had either no ideas or erroneous ideas as to why it was meeting.

In 1945, when Japan was collapsing and our future security depended on the fate of her government, only slightly more than half of our citizens could name the Japanese emperor (Hirohito). Some guesses were as far afield as Tito, Yokohama, Fujiyama, and Hara-Kiri.

3

The American people became allies of Russia after Pearl Harbor, or, more correctly, we found ourselves fighting on the same side as the Soviets. Co-operation between the U.S.S.R. and the U.S.A. was seldom friendly and never wholehearted, partly because the Russians remembered that from the outset in 1917 we had been hostile to their experiment, and that we had attempted to thwart it by various means, ranging from armed intervention to delayed recognition. Yet in 1945 an American opinion poll showed that more than seven out of ten citizens could not think of a single thing we had done since 1917 to cause Russia to distrust us.

The Russian masses, blindfolded by an ideological blackout, cloistered behind an iron curtain, and nurtured by propaganda releases from the Kremlin, developed completely false ideas regarding American capitalism and the American way of life. But our people, living behind their self-created iron curtain of ignorance and apathy, also developed false ideas about the Soviet Union which in no way smoothed the path for cordial re-lations. The opinion polls during the period of World War II showed that our citizens were entertaining mental images regarding Bolshevism, com-munism, the church, private property, and the "nationalization of women" which were much more applicable to Russia of the early 1920's than to Russia of the 1940's.

The average American did not know that the Greek Orthodox Church had to a considerable extent been rehabilitated. Not even one third of our people were aware that Ivan Ivanovitch could own private property, and only slightly more knew that he might receive a higher wage than his fellows. The American voter widely believed that most Russians were mem-bers of the Communist party,° and he was generally unaware that the Rus-sian economic system had attained socialism but had not yet attained com-munism. Four Americans in ten did not even know what type of government Russia had. Only about one in ten realized that it was an avowed purpose of Moscow to spread communism throughout the world. Fewer than two in ten were aware that Soviet sympathies had been with Czechoslovakia when that ill-starred republic was betrayed to Hitler in 1938 by its western allies. The conclusion of these surveys was that only one American in ten was even reasonably well informed about the Soviet Union.

American ignorance of Russia was evidently much less than Russian ignorance of America, and if this be true the picture is a dismal one indeed. Even if the two peoples had known each other like an open book, relations between the two governments would undoubtedly have deteriorated after World War II, as is invariably true of wartime associates. Assuming that we are well intentioned toward the Soviets and fully informed about them, and assuming on the other hand that Moscow does not want our friend-ship and deliberately poisons its people against us, there can be no real

° In 1946 about 5,500,000 out of some 190,000,000 were party members.

cordiality. The proverb to the contrary, it does not take two to pick a quarrel, only one; but it takes two to make friends.

"Ignorance never settled a question," Disraeli once remarked. In international relations the flow of information and good will must proceed over a two-lane highway. The Russian lane may not be unblocked in our time, but both lanes will never be unblocked unless we unblock ours.

4

The following table, taken from the census of 1940, tells its own shocking story:

Persons in the U.S. 25 years of age or over	74,775,836
Persons who never completed one school year	2,799,923
Persons who completed grades 1 to 4	7,304,689
Persons who completed grades 5 to 6	8,515,111
Persons who completed grades 7 to 8	25,897,953
Persons who completed high schools years 1 to 3	11,181,995
Persons who completed 4th year of high school	10,551,680
Persons who completed 1 to 3 years of college	4,075,184
Persons who completed 4 or more years of college	3,407,331
Not reported	1,041,970
Median school years completed	8.4

About six adult Americans in ten—hereafter referred to as "graders"—have never gone beyond the eighth grade. Hundreds of thousands have never attended school at all, and several million are completely illiterate. This huge mass of the educationally underprivileged is a great abscess on our body politic.

An analysis of the opinion polls from about 1937 to 1946 reveals some startling conditions. On a question of purely factual information, such as the capital of Iceland, the grader invariably ranked below the high school and the college group. This is precisely what one would expect. But for present purposes, opinions and attitudes are much more significant than the "Information Please" type of inquiry.

The more ignorant the citizen, the more bellicose and jingoistic he was, the more certain that we could knock the stuffings out of any or all other nations. After Pearl Harbor the uninformed group was most confident that we would whip the Japanese in short order.

The grader was by far the most chauvinistic and imperialistic. He was much more willing than his less ignorant fellows to take on the task of running the world alone, and more inclined to say that we should grab all the new territory we could get, not merely island bases for military purposes. He was the most reluctant to turn American conquests over to a trusteeship of the United Nations; he was most favorable to starting an atomic war against Russia on mere suspicion.

The poorly educated citizen was the most militaristic of all, possibly because he felt the most insecure. He was more disposed to spend money for armaments rather than for education, and he was more willing to rely upon a powerful United States Army than on any international police force. He was also more favorable to conscripting young men for the army in time of peace.

The grader operated on the principle of "our country right or wrong," but our country has never been wrong. Of all groups he was the most favorable to highly nationalistic textbooks, and he was the least willing to have them examined and revised by an outside agency in the interests of balance and fairness. Naturally he was attached to the sacred cow of sovereignty, and he was not at all enthusiastic about giving up the control of anything to foreigners, whom he distrusted on general principles, especially Japanese, Russians, Germans, and British imperialists.

The grader was the most provincial, the least interested in other countries, and the most preoccupied with local trivia and the comic-strip doings of Dick Tracy and Orphan Annie. He was the least concerned about the opinions of the outside world regarding us, and he was the least favorable to broadcasting informational programs to foreign lands. He was the least farsighted, and the most eager to grasp the present short-run gain to the exclusion of the more important long-run advantage.

Rather than undergo the mental sweat of thinking complex issues through, the grader much preferred to personalize foreign affairs. He was inclined to blame World War I on the Kaiser, and our participation in it on J. P. Morgan and the Du Ponts. He was disposed to attribute World War II solely to Hitler, and commonly believed that the deranged housepainter had ordered the Japanese to attack Pearl Harbor.

Prejudice is the child of ignorance. The grader betrayed the largest amount of anti-Semitism, and during the war he was the most bitter against the Japanese, who had not only humbled his pride but had done so by delivering a sneak punch below the belt. He approved less humane treatment of the Germans than did his better educated brothers, and he was the most favorable to using poison gas on the Japanese. He most begrudged relief for our devastated Allies, and he was the least willing to rehabilitate the prostrate nations of Europe.

Generally more gullible, the grader group was the most satisfied with the war news printed in the press, and the least critical of information received over the radio. More than his fellows the ill-educated citizen was stampeded by Orson Welles's realistic broadcast in 1938 of the invasion from Mars. Ignorance has a numerous brood, but one of her least lovely sucklings is mass hysteria.

5

In certain other categories the grader sticks out like a sore thumb. He was the most opposed to reciprocal trade agreements, though generally he did not know what they meant. He showed the least enthusiasm for the proposition that we must buy abroad in order to sell. He was the most favorable to tariff walls and other weapons of economic noncollaboration, presumably because he was a laboring man who had suffered from unemployment and hence was easily swayed by the argument about cheap coolie labor.

During World War II the grader was the least aware that Britain was giving us reverse Lend Lease, and he was the least willing to say that Britain's assistance in the war was repayment enough. Despite our unhappy experience with debts and reparations after World War I (of which he was generally unaware), he favored harsh terms for our international debtors, and was determined to extract the full pound of flesh from recent Allies. He was desirous of getting reparations from both Germany and Japan, and particularly anxious to secure reparations *in money* from Japan, notwithstanding the obvious difficulties involved.

The grader was the backbone of American isolationism. He was the most hostile in 1939 to lifting the arms embargo in favor of the Allies, and he was the least willing to send aid to Britain in 1940. Throughout 1941 he was most determined not to risk war in helping England, even though she was in danger of sinking. He was the least worried about Hitler's winning, and to the very end was the least favorable to declaring war on the Axis, though no group was prepared to do so.

After Pearl Harbor the grader was the least agreeable to ties of close alliance with other nations, and he was the most disposed to say that it was not our job to help keep world peace. He was the least concerned about war prevention, the most reluctant to begin peace planning in the midst of the war, and the most fatalistic about the coming of future conflicts. He was the least clear as to why he was fighting, and the most antagonistic to even an embryonic world government in which foreigners might outvote the United States. He was the least enthusiastic about a new League of Nations; he was more favorable to American control of the new world organization than equal control with other nations; he was less willing that we should share the costs of the new organization; and he was the most unfriendly to a powerful world government, especially one commanding military forces. Yet when the United Nations was actually started, the graders were more complacently pleased with its halting progress than any other group.

The most poorly educated citizens were the least happy about a united military command in 1945, and more inclined to be satisfied with our war effort. They were also more inclined to believe that the "secret" of the atomic bomb could be kept, and that foreign observers should be barred from the Bikini atom bomb tests.

6

The attitude of the grader toward specific outside nations was most revealing.

He was the backbone of Anglophobia and xenophobia. He was more predisposed to annex Canada than other groups, and most hostile to world union with Britain and Russia. He was the least favorable to the British loan of 1946, presumably because he felt that "the slick British diplomats" would cheat us out of our money, as they had allegedly done after World War I.

Regarding Germany, the grader was inclined to believe that we had not treated the Reich too harshly in the past, and that we were in no way responsible for the conditions that spawned Naziism. He was the most certain that the Germans would always want war, and he was all for knocking them down and stamping on them so hard that they would never want to fight again. He was the most eager to punish Germany by dividing her into small states and by reducing her to a potato patch through the destruction of her industry. Yet after having ruined her economically, he was the most anxious to drain heavy reparations from her, as though one could get both milk and beefsteak from the same cow.

The prejudices against Russia, discussed earlier in this chapter, were most deeply rooted in the lowest educational group. If you scratched an ignoramus you often found not only an isolationist but an Anglophobe and an anti-communist as well. Curiously enough, the poorer classes in America, to whom communism is supposed to appeal, were much more distrustful of Russia than the more well-to-do classes, which are supposed to be in mortal fear of a communistic redistribution of their wealth. The basic answer appears to be that the American masses, which are relatively poor and ignorant, were still being frightened by the Bolshevist bogies of the 1920's, while the wealthier and hence better informed classes were able to discount some of these exaggerations.*

Specifically, the grader was more disposed to resent Russia's delay in getting into the war against Japan, and to say that Russia owed it to the United States to enter the Far Eastern conflict. (This feeling was no doubt bottomed on ignorance of what Russia had done and was doing for the common cause.) Yet the poorly informed Americans were less willing to see Russia join equally in making the peace. They were also the most unfavorable to a proposed six-billion-dollar loan to Moscow, though no group in America supported it. Russia was not regarded as a good risk.

The Roman Catholic Church is understandably hostile to the Soviet Union, and Catholics in America reflect the stand taken by their spiritual guardians. The great mass of South European immigrants that arrived near the turn of the century were Catholics. They were generally poor; and poverty and ignorance are common bedfellows. They were without much school-

---

* The predisposition of certain intellectuals to foreign ideologies led to the quip that communism is the opiate of the intelligentsia.

ing, and hence more ignorant than the old-stock Americans. The net result was a relatively high incidence of Catholicism among the educationally backward. What conclusions may be drawn?

The Catholics constitute about one sixth of our population, and while they are generously represented among the graders, they do not come anywhere near a majority. Ignorance rather than religious affiliation is the more serious barrier to a clearer understanding of the Soviet Union. If and when the Russian iron curtain is lifted, and we have a truer picture of what is going on in the Soviet Union, we may not trust Russia any more, but at least we shall have a more intelligent basis for our distrust.

7

Glancing backward at this disquieting picture, the reader cannot escape one fundamental conclusion. On practically every public question where the respondents were classified by education, the lowest bracket revealed itself to be the most narrow, short-sighted, and unenlightened.

Yet one highly important qualification must be made. A *majority* of the graders *with opinions* were not to be found in these illiberal camps on every public question. If a strong majority were consistently there, our democracy would have cut its own throat long ago. *On most public issues the grader was on the same side as the high school and college groups, but almost invariably by a smaller percentage,* ranging from a negligible figure to a substantial one. On practically every question the strongest trend toward unenlightenment came from the graders, and this is a fact of disturbing significance.

The educationally underprivileged constitute the largest single group in the United States. They are prone to think with their emotions rather than their brains, especially in a crisis, or not to think at all, which may be almost as bad. The distressingly large number of "Don't knows" or "Undecideds" or "No opinions" in the various polls is concentrated in this group. The graders are apt to have the wrong opinion or the myopic opinion on problems of grave public import. Sometimes it is a confused opinion, as when an earnest citizen, possibly suffering from back trouble, wrote his congressman at the time of the repeal of the arms embargo in 1939: "Keep the lumbargo."

A critic would be presumptuous indeed to make up a list of public questions, indicate the right and wrong side, and then condemn more than half of one's fellow citizens because they did not happen to be bracketed with the angels. Who shall say that the graders, on certain broad questions here discussed, were not right? They were most inclined to overrate the destructiveness of the atomic bomb, to show less optimism about the ability of the United Nations to avert a future war, and to reveal deep distrust for the Soviet Union. Time may prove that they were nearer right than their college-bred compeers. Yet even here one warning must be posted. Our distrust of

Russia may cause (in fact has caused) the Kremlin to take countermeasures which may seem to prove, in an ever widening vicious circle, that our distrust was fully justified in the first instance.

Another encouraging note is that the grader lined up fairly well with the rest of the country on such critically important issues as preparedness, security, a greater air force, distrust of Hitler, and Lend-Lease. The explanation seems to be that there is a good deal of native shrewdness among the poorly educated, to say nothing of a vast amount of untutored intelligence, and that these people operate best when broad and rather simple issues are placed before them.

Some little comfort may also be derived from the fact that most of the nonvoters in our elections are to be found in the lowest educational bracket. This means that the ignorant are strongly disposed to leave the control and management of public affairs to their better informed brothers, who as a result exert disproportionate influence. Except during those infrequent occasions when mob hysteria breaks loose, the graders bring far less pressure to bear on their government than their numbers would indicate.

Yet this group is nothing to be proud of, for it contains the most unpredictable and explosive elements. It is the great dragging anchor of the ship of state, whether in domestic or foreign affairs. Its very existence advertises one of the most conspicuous failures of our democracy.

CHAPTER TWELVE

THE HARVEST OF IGNORANCE

"Do not be too severe upon the errors of the people, but reclaim them by enlightening them."—THOMAS JEFFERSON, 1787

1

IT WILL BE instructive, even though depressing, to turn from the ignorance of our least favored group to the danger growing out of ignorance on the part of the American people generally. A lack of information on foreign affairs is not confined solely to the sub-eighth graders.

The unenlightened populace is the dupe of demagogues. Father Coughlin, the microphone messiah of the 1930's, had a listening audience of nearly four million, most of whom were drawn from the more ignorant lower-income group. His violent anti-British and proisolationist fulminations contributed to the final defeat of the World Court in 1935 and to the purblind neutrality legislation of the late 1930's.

Suspender-snapping politicians, like Governor Talmadge of Georgia, batten on the ignorant mob. "The man with the hoe is too prone to follow the politician with the hokum," observed the *Wall Street Journal* in 1926. Someone has said that if the politician will but fashion a better claptrap, the vulgar herd will beat a path to his door. The demagogue succeeds in America because too many of the ignorant want to be led by the nose, and because in this uncertain world they demand certainties. These he provides, and he is on his way to position and power.

The vast majority of the American people want to spare themselves the pain of heavy thinking, and they demand simple solutions. Some years ago a professor of economics delivered a scholarly address to a popular audience on economic problems and foreign affairs. The applause that rewarded his discourse was anemic but respectful. The next speaker rose and said: "Professor Dry-as-Dust has given us a learned address, but I think he missed the essential point—what the world wants is brotherly love." The applause was deafening. Emerson was not far from the mark when he observed: "The great majority of men seem to be minors." Yet these minors, who are perpetually minors, are called upon to exercise the responsibilities of adults.

The ill-informed masses are also dupes of the sloganeer. The slogan in a democracy is a treacherous device not only because it makes for herd thinking but because it is a substitute for hard thinking. Smooth, alliterative slogans, like "Fifty-four forty or fight," are shouted most loudly by those with the biggest mouths and the smallest brains. We tend to think that by shouting a slogan we solve the problems that gave rise to it; we have the pleasant feeling of generating a maximum of statesmanship with a minimum of mental effort.

140

The ignorant are also the dupes of the propagandist. The Bryce Report of 1915, bearing the name of the beloved commentator on American democracy, was loosed upon a public that was still reeling from the *Lusitania* tragedy, and it contained versions of German atrocities in Belgium that were a travesty on the truth. Yet this official document was widely accepted as gospel, even by a considerable number of college-trained people who should have been less gullible. Senator Nye, as chairman of the Senate Munitions Investigating Committee in the 1930's, built up the legend among the uninformed that we entered the war in 1917 not to make the world safe for democracy but to make it safe for the Du Ponts. The Negroes are our least literate group, and significantly they were twice as ready as anyone else in America to swallow Hitler's propaganda to the effect that mistreatment of Germans in Czechoslovakia had brought on the Munich crisis.

The poorly informed citizen is apt to become the dupe of a prominent figure who, having made his reputation in some other field, such as the movie industry, sets himself up as an authority on international relations. Henry Ford, who had amassed a tremendous fortune by building cheap automobiles, was listened to with worshipful respect when he exposed his ignorance on various subjects, including history, which he branded as "bunk." Charles A. Lindbergh, who became a national hero by his solo conquest of the Atlantic in 1927, made many isolationist speeches from 1940 to 1941, and until Pearl Harbor was the idol of millions of America Firsters.* Even Albert Einstein, a scientist so distinguished as to be recognized as a genius while still living, had a wide audience when he spoke on foreign affairs, although specialists who have devoted a lifetime to the subject are largely brushed aside. The public demands not only simplified certainties but also big names.

Politicians have long since learned that they ignore the multitude at their peril if they want to get into office and stay there. The caustic English critic, Sydney Smith, expressed astonishment in 1837 that the British ministers neglected the simple precaution of a "foolometer." He meant "the acquaintance and society of three or four regular British fools as a test of public opinion."

2

The difficulties resulting from an ill-informed public opinion are often of a more positive sort. Ignorant clamor is liable to hamper the progress of delicate diplomatic negotiations.

In 1818 unthinking agitation in the United States for a prompt recognition of the Latin-American republics offended Spain and threatened to dis-

---

* Lindbergh guessed badly when in 1941 he said that it was "physically impossible" to base enough aircraft in the British Isles to gain air mastery over the Germans. He was an acknowledged authority on airplanes, and if he could be this far wrong in his specialty, what about questions to which he had given much less study?

rupt Secretary Adams's ticklish discussions regarding the acquisition of Florida. During the Civil War, a demand from the populace for drastic action against the French intruders in Mexico embarrassed Secretary Seward, whose policy was to negotiate patiently until our hands were freed by the Confederate collapse. During World War II the well known Catholic layman and historian, Dr. Carlton J. H. Hayes, was made ambassador to Spain with the specific object of keeping Franco from entering the war at the side of Hitler and thus jeopardizing Allied plans for the invasion of Fortress Europa. The American envoy naturally found it necessary to "appease" Franco to some extent, and he was rewarded by caustic criticism from ignorant or designing groups at home, who were not fully aware of his instructions and who at times seemed more eager to fight Franco than Hitler. The Spanish Foreign Office was keenly aware of the uproar in a section of the American press, and Ambassador Hayes was consequently placed in an even more awkward position.

The American people during World War II showed similar impatience and lack of understanding in regard to Washington's dealings with Pétain of Vichy France, with Darlan and Giraud in Morocco, and with Badoglio in Italy. While such goings on were certainly not above criticism, their basic purpose was to win the war, and this salient fact seems never to have dawned on some of our more vocal citizens.

Ill-advised pressure from the masses also interfered with military operations. When General MacArthur was beleaguered at Bataan in 1942, a cry arose from the most ignorant quarters that we send aid to him in nonexistent ships convoyed by nonexistent battleships. But the painful realities of the situation were so clear to our more intelligent citizens that the administration could safely ignore such pressure. Much more formidable was the popular demand to "get Hirohito first." "We should take care of the Japs first and then take on the Germans," Sergeant Alvin C. York was quoted as saying in his Tennessee mountain home. Sergeant York had singlehandedly captured a group of 132 Germans in World War I, and this naturally qualified him as an authority on the grand strategy of World War II.

The confusion was thickened by the globe-girdling flight in 1943 of five United States senators, among whom was Senator "Happy" Chandler of Kentucky, soon to be named "baseball Czar." The solons had made a quick trip to the Far Eastern and other combat theaters, and had returned military experts. Senator Chandler had the effrontery to tell the Senate that the basic military strategy of the Allied command should be changed, and that Japan should be made the top priority. He further declared that when the European phase of the war ended, the British would leave their American ally in the lurch, a charge which Prime Minister Churchill ringingly rebutted in an address before Congress. The New York *Herald Tribune*, referring to Senator Chandler, prayed to be "spared the braying of this long eared legislator."

Early in 1942, in the aftermath of Pearl Harbor, six out of ten citizens were for concentrating our main effort or all our efforts against Japan. This sentiment weakened as the memory of Pearl Harbor receded, but it was dangerous. The administration was able to ignore it, partly because it lacked great intensity, but primarily because, as earlier noted, public opinion may be defied in wartime with greater impunity.

3

Much more ominous was the agitation in America for opening a second front. The problem was both a military and a diplomatic one, because it was intimately connected with the improvement of relations between Russia and the other United Nations.

The demands for action came dangerously to a head in the United States during the summer of 1942, when the Soviets were reeling under the Nazi sledge hammer. The fear was prevalent that unless a diversionary threat could be promptly launched, the Soviets would be knocked out of the war, and Britain and America would have to face the fury of Hitler alone. Few spokesmen in the Allied camp were openly disputing the desirability of establishing a second front, provided it could be done with a reasonable prospect of success, but a premature attack would only invite another Dunkirk. Failure would further depress the Russians, divide the Allies, inspirit the Nazis, and postpone the day when a successful front could be opened.

The average American had no more than a faint appreciation of the technical problems involved. He suffered from the vague, Bryanesque notion that somehow armies would spring forth when a buzzer was pressed, and that huge fleets of ships could be conjured out of thin air by a magic wand. In 1942, when clamor for a second front was reaching a crescendo, the United States was virtually powerless to defend its own coasts against U-boats, or to dislodge the Japanese from its Aleutian Islands, or to extricate itself from the slough of steel priorities.*

The second front, which finally opened some two years after the agitation had started in earnest, was perhaps the most complex large-scale operation ever undertaken by man. It involved problems of specially trained troops, of specially designed boats, of naval screens and aerial umbrellas, of underwater oil supply lines, of tremendous floating harbors that could be towed across the English Channel. The military leaders also had to worry about such questions as meteorology, terrain, logistics, the attitude of civilian populations, the jealousies of the Allies and their commanders, synchronization with the Russians, and other equally vexatious questions. Yet in spite of the unprecedented preparations, and in spite of the prolonged delay, the fighting was touch-and-go for a protracted period, and the whole

* In 1942 the Citizens for Victory in California published a large advertisement in the San Francisco *Chronicle* urging an immediate second front. By unfortunate timing it appeared on the very day that Tobruk fell to Rommel during his terrifying drive toward El Alamein..

operation came close to complete disaster. Probably it would have failed if we had not learned valuable lessons from the earlier invasion of French Morocco.

In the late summer of 1942, when the agitation was at its height, the United States *News* wired a group of nine leading citizens asking whether we should open a second front at once, "regardless of our present preparedness." Only one of the respondents, a distinguished professor of political science, declared that the attack should be launched at once, even if it should fail, because the Soviets needed the moral if not the physical support of a diversion. The other eight men replied in effect that the second front was not a matter of maudlin sentiment or brilliant improvisation, and that the decision as to time, place, and tools should be left to the military leaders who were giving it their prolonged professional study. Such study would in fact be more intelligent if not distracted by ignorant clamor. The President of Earlham College quoted Kenesaw Mountain Landis: "This is the time for all those not clothed with authority to keep their shirts on."

In July, 1942, Dr. Gallup discovered that nearly five out of ten Americans wanted a second front "in the near future," while the remainder were undecided or preferred to wait until we were stronger. Those well-meaning but naïve citizens who demanded an immediate invasion were not numerous enough or intense enough to force their will, and consequently the military leaders were able to avoid being stampeded. The alarming fact is that if this group had been somewhat larger and somewhat more zealous, it probably could not have been ignored, in which case the outcome almost certainly would have been disaster. The episode further demonstrated that there is a distressing tendency for the most ill-informed to be the most vocal.

4

The Man in the Street is not aware that statesmanship is the science of alternatives, and that his leaders must choose, not between the good and the bad, but all too frequently between the bad and the less bad. He is not properly aware, as earlier indicated, of the necessity of give and take—of the *quid pro quo*—in diplomatic negotiations. He fails to perceive that an international conference in peacetime is a place where nations both give up and get things.

The Washington Disarmament Conference of 1921-1922 is a case in point. The Japanese demanded naval parity, but finally accepted the short end of a 5-5-3 ratio in battleship strength. In return for this crucial concession, we agreed not to build additional fortifications on our Pacific outposts beyond Hawaii. To get naval limitation at all we further agreed to scrap a considerable number of new warships then under construction and nearing completion.

American public opinion *at the time* was generally satisfied with the bargain. Japanese opinion definitely was not: Japan had lost face; she had suffered a severe naval defeat. Some of the delegates, upon their return home, were presented with hara-kiri daggers, with which to commit honorable suicide.

When naval limitation broke down in the 1930's, and war with Japan loomed, we discovered that we were without enough modern battleships and without adequate defenses on our Pacific outposts. The legend took deeper root that we had been cheated at the Washington Conference. We had scrapped battleships while our adversaries had scrapped blueprints; we had foolishly agreed to a scheme by which Japan would be impregnable in the Far East. We completely forgot that if we had not given up the right to fortify, the Japanese almost certainly would not have accepted the small end of 5-5-3, which, as their ambassador later said, sounded like Rolls Royce-Rolls Royce-Ford. We forgot all about the *quid* we had received in our anger over the *quo* we had given up. Again we were unwilling to recognize that one cannot eat one's cake and have it too.*

Ignorance may take yet another unpleasant form. The workaday American is not only inclined to get excited, but to get excited about the wrong things. One of the least wise moves that Wilson made at Paris, in 1919, was to appeal over the heads of the Italian negotiators to their constituents on the Fiume issue. Yet this dramatic blunder was the one act of Wilson which was most loudly applauded at home.

Ignorance and imprudence are unlovely Siamese twins, and we Americans have repeatedly indulged in jingoistic orgies, with complete ignorance of the odds we were up against, and with complete indifference to the consequences of our rashness. As earlier noted, the mob took us into war in 1812 and 1898, and almost did so again on a number of other occasions.

The self-confident citizen is hampered, although he may not realize it, by his ignorance of foreign countries. He does not know for sure who will be elected the next mayor of his own town, but he is prone to have convictions as to what Germany will be doing after he is dead. Not realizing that the Spaniards are a proud people, he did not see why they could not be bundled out of Cuba in 1898 without loss of dignity. Not realizing that the Japanese are a proud and sensitive people, deeply concerned about "face," he did not foresee that they would react violently to the affront conveyed by the Immigration Act of 1924. Even if he had, he probably would not have responded differently. No little yellow men were going to threaten us with "grave consequences," or tell us how to control such "purely domestic" matters as immigration gates.

The American citizen is ignorant of his history, although it has been glorious and is studied repeatedly if sketchily in our schools. "We can not escape history," as Lincoln said, but we can escape a knowledge of it, and have succeeded pretty well in doing so. If we could only project ourselves

* The London Naval Treaty of 1930 was under fire in the capitals of the three major participating powers, which indicated that each delegation had outtraded the others.

back into our past, we could learn to deal more wisely and tolerantly with foreign nations, and we would see more clearly the implications of power politics and the relation of military preparedness to them.

We are not only ignorant of our own past, but we are even more ill-informed as to that of other peoples. If we knew more Russian history, we would recognize that the Russians have long been a suspicious and secretive people, as is natural for a nation which lacks strong natural barriers, and which as a consequence has been repeatedly overrun by invaders. If we were more familiar with Russia's background, we would not join our favorite news commentator or columnist in believing that Soviet interest in the Dardanelles was recently cooked up in the Kremlin. The driving impulse for a warm-water port is one of the oldest motifs in Russian history. An American diplomat from Moscow recently remarked that the more he read about Russia's past the less he found new in her present.

5

For more than a century our leaders have come from the common people, with a few exceptions like the two Roosevelts, and men of humble origins naturally share many of the prejudices and misconceptions of the masses. This is notably true regarding foreign affairs. The President is commander-in-chief of the army and navy, but he is usually not a military man; he is commander-in-chief of our foreign service, but he is seldom a trained diplomat.

In the period before Andrew Jackson, our Presidents were distinguished leaders, experienced in statecraft, both at home and abroad, and not identified with the untutored crowd. Our secretaries of state were generally men of high caliber, the ablest of whom had served as diplomats in foreign lands.

Then came Jacksonian democracy, with its emphasis on the worth and dignity and sovereignty of the common folk. The one-suspender man had at last attained the seats of the mighty. From that day to this our Presidents and secretaries of state were almost invariably without active experience in foreign affairs before taking office, although they later learned a good deal at public expense and on a trial-and-error basis. Such mistakes were not ruinously costly in the last three fourths of the nineteenth century, partly because Europe was at peace or preoccupied elsewhere.

The fiery Andrew Jackson was an ordinary citizen in his knowledge of international relations, although not an ordinary citizen otherwise; and when he pushed the French into a corner over unpaid claims, he caused the dogs of war to bark ominously. If Jackson had been more familiar with domestic conditions in France, and had known that the situation was so delicate that the French could not be hurried, he might have moderated his bull-in-the-china-shop tactics.

President Grant was an ordinary citizen as far as foreign relations were concerned, possibly below average, and he did not know when he took the oath that the Senate rather than Congress consents to the ratification of treaties. He learned the hard and humiliating way when he tried to railroad through the Senate a pact for the annexation of the sugar-rich but bankrupt Republic of Santo Domingo.

President McKinley was a reasonably well informed man, but after Commodore Dewey's smashing victory in the Philippines he confessed that he could not have told "where those darned islands were within 2000 miles!" Probably not one American in ten thousand could have done better.

Woodrow Wilson was a highly intelligent man, a profound student of our government, and well equipped to deal with domestic problems. But as fate would have it, he was soon overwhelmed with foreign complexities. He applied himself to his task with assiduity and he learned a great deal in his eight years, but he almost certainly would have moved more sure-footedly, at Paris and elsewhere, if he had been better informed at the outset.

Senator William E. Borah, by virtue of seniority, became chairman of the powerful Senate Committee on Foreign Relations in 1924, and served in that capacity during the nine critical years that followed. He was a leading isolationist, and his outlook was somewhat neolithic, in certain respects not markedly higher than that of the average citizen from his sheep-and-potato State of Idaho. Yet on the interventionist question in 1934 he was convinced that he was right, and he annoyed President Roosevelt by insisting that his private sources of information were more reliable than those of the State Department. Emerson wrote in 1857:

Because our education is defective, because we are superficial and ill-read, we are forced to make the most of that position, of ignorance. Hence America is a vast know-nothing party, and we disparage books, and cry up intuition.

Harry S. Truman, the ex-haberdasher, was a small-town citizen, the product of a Missouri political machine, without college education, and without experience in foreign affairs. When Roosevelt suddenly died, Truman could not journey out to California to open the San Francisco Conference because, as was explained in the press, he had to stay home and study his foreign-relations homework. At Fulton, Missouri, in 1946, he sat on the platform while Winston Churchill delivered a speech which launched a thousand protests, and which was a turning point in the deterioration of postwar relations with Russia. Through the White House press secretary, Truman apologized by saying that he had not known in advance what Churchill was going to say. If he had, he did not tell the truth. If he had not, he was incredibly naïve. By his very presence he appeared to be approving commitments of an incalculably serious nature. This was but one of several costly blunders.

Few sane Americans would entrust a banking business to a person totally without knowledge of finance, yet we continue to elect men to the presidency without much regard for their ability to handle foreign relations. We need statesmen, not politicians picked from the ruck of the masses—politicians who, in the Jacksonian tradition, sneer at "career men" or anyone else who is specially trained to do his job. Much of the education that our people receive in foreign affairs comes from agitators who do not themselves know what they are talking about. If the ignorant lead the ignorant, who shall be wise?

6

The theory behind democracy is that collective wisdom can arise from the masses, or to put it more brutally, that sound judgment may be distilled from ignorance and inexperience.

The Man in the Street knows zero about international bimetallism, but if one multiplies that zero by fifty-million voters one gets sound policy—at least theoretically. Unhappily this conclusion flies in the face of both arithmetic and logic. "Ten million ignorances do not constitute one knowledge," said Metternich, the archpriest of reaction in post-1815 Europe.

Even when the citizen possesses some knowledge it is apt to be limited, one-sided, and otherwise out of focus. The three blind men felt different parts of the elephant, and one pronounced it a rope, another a post, and the third a house. Each was correct within his limited field of perception.

Yet, as Aristotle noted, a person does not have to be a cook to determine whether the food tastes good, nor a carpenter to judge whether a house is desirable. The American citizen is relatively intelligent, and he possesses an uncommon amount of common sense. Hence on simple and basic issues, such as those involving security or defense, he often appears to good advantage.

Some years ago the present writer, traveling incognito, met a man in the smoking car who said emphatically that he would trust the judgment any day of one-hundred average citizens against that of "one damned college professor." This was when a handful of academic economists in the Roosevelt Brain Trust had not succeeded in pulling the nation out of its economic tail spin.* The man in the smoking car was probably right, at least with regard to nontechnical problems that demand a maximum of good sense, for the "one damned college professor" might happen to be an erratic soul, whereas the percentage of erratic persons in one hundred representative citizens would be relatively small.

Earlier in this chapter reference was made to the nine prominent persons who were polled on the question of opening a second front in 1942. The only respondent who favored immediate attack was a professor of political science, and he was the one most palpably wrong. If he had been in the

---

* Gallup pollees in 1935 said: "Rid the government of bookworms and put in level-headed businessmen." "Put men at the head of the government that have at least a child's mind."

seat of power, and had launched the assault, the unfortunate effects no doubt would be felt for a long time to come. (In fairness to his breed, one must add that he almost certainly did not represent majority opinion among academicians.)

Not only does government by the elite open the door to ill-balanced judgment, but, as Lord Bryce long since observed, rule by aristocracy is subject to all the limitations of class blindness and bias. The British statesman Gladstone, noting that most of the desirable social reform had come from the common people, said: "I painfully reflect that in almost every political controversy of the last fifty years, the *leisured classes*, the *titled* classes have been in the wrong."

The decisions of the American voter have often been wrong or faulty, but on the other hand they have more often been basically sound. Although one must agree in part with John Dryden that the judgment of the crowd is a "mere lottery," one must also conclude that on the whole the American people have done better than a dictatorship or an aristocracy could have done for them, and they have done much better than the logician had any right to expect.

7

Demagogues and statesmen without number have paid tribute to the collective wisdom of the crowd, some no doubt sincerely, and others to curry favor with the voters. Thomas Jefferson, Martin Van Buren, Theodore Roosevelt, and Woodrow Wilson have all joined in the chorus of commendation. Abraham Lincoln, who was a master at assessing and directing popular currents, is alleged to have said: "You can fool some of the people all of the time, and all of the people some of the time, but you cannot fool all of the people all the time."

This famous statement merits analysis, for it is often used to justify inertia and ignorance. In the first place, one does not have to fool *all of the people* in a democracy. All one has to do is to fool a simple majority, or in some cases a plurality, and one may attain the office from which to direct the destinies of the nation. Hitler, be it remembered, received only a plurality in Germany's last free election, that of 1932.

Secondly, the demagogue who attains office by a bare majority or by a plurality can do a vast amount of damage before his term expires, or before a majority of the masses get unfooled and throw him out. Hitler fooled the people of the democracies for a protracted period, and disaster almost overtook us before our eyes were unglued. "The species is wise," said Edmund Burke in 1782, "and when time is given to it, as a species it always acts right." But the atomic age has now burst upon us, and the opportunity may not always be given us to awaken from our slumbers and rectify our errors.

The time has come to dissect some popular presuppositions. We are prone to assume that the majority is right simply because it is a majority, and we bow down and worship the golden calf of numbers. But every majority was once a minority, and every minority movement, to paraphase Emerson, was once an idea in one man's mind. The size of the majority favoring a given cause does not necessarily bear a proportional relationship to its essential wisdom.

The masses, though often right, have often been demonstrably wrong. Henry Maine observed in 1885 that universal suffrage would have blocked the spinning jenny and the power loom, the threshing machine, the Gregorian calendar, and many other steps in human progress. Norman Angell, with undue cynicism, has written more recently: "The hope of democracy lies in fully realizing the truth that the voice of the people is usually the voice of Satan."

Such accusations have been written with domestic affairs primarily in mind. If they are true or partially true with reference to things that the people know at first hand, how much more damning is the indictment with reference to things beyond their vision. Aesop, in one of the earliest recorded instances of popular misjudgment, tells of a man who imitated a pig so successfully that the crowd enthusiastically voted his imitation more realistic than the squeal of a real pig which his competitor had concealed beneath his shirt.

The masses are disquieting enough when merely ignorant and inert; they are downright dangerous when ignorant and on the loose. The mob feels but does not see; it has many heads but no brains; it rejects all counsel of moderation. At the time of the clamor for war with England in 1895 over the Venezuelan boundary, one could well believe with Lord Halifax that "the angry buzz of the multitude is one of the bloodiest noises in the world."

8

The common people, for all their shortcomings, fortunately can be taught when their interest is aroused. When Secretary Seward agreed to buy Alaska in 1867, his treaty was almost hooted out of court, but after he had discreetly spread information regarding the great natural resources of the territory, much of the opposition faded away. In 1946 public opinion poll takers found strong opposition to the proposed loan to Britain, but once its general purposes were explained, disapproval often gave way to approval.

The multitude is more inclined than the intelligentsia to brush aside legal obstacles and move straight ahead, once they can see in what direction their interests lie. When the treaty for the purchase of Louisiana reached President Jefferson in 1803, he dilly-dallied with the idea of a constitutional amendment to legalize this tremendous transaction. Yet the mass of the people, who were fully capable of recognizing a magnificent bargain when they saw one, were impatient of delay, and Jefferson reluctantly swallowed his reverence for constitutionalism and completed the purchase.

The populace is also endowed with the valor of ignorance. As Francis Bacon observed: "In counsel it is good to see dangers; but in execution, not to see them unless they be very great." The American people are stronger in execution than they are at the council table, but this is not always a liability. As previously noted, men will cheerfully tackle problems from which they would recoil if they were not ignorant of what they were up against.

One other point must be stressed. In dealing with democratic public opinion the important thing is not what is so but what the people think is so. A state of mind, even though based on falsehoods rather than facts, is nevertheless in itself a fact—a fact sometimes as formidable as a fortress. In 1863 the people of the North were immensely cheered when the Russians sent two fleets to the United States, presumably to help us against England and France should these powers intervene in our Civil War. The warships actually were dispatched so that they might strengthen Russia in her diplomatic clash with England and France, and not out of love for the United States. An American historian exhumed the evidence in 1915, more than a half century after the event, and long after popular interest had disappeared. In this case by far the more significant thing was not the truth, but what the Northerners had assumed was the truth. Upon such an illusory foundation was based a rather substantial Russo-American friendship, which later influenced our action, notably in purchasing Alaska.

Bad as ignorance is, it is not so bad as error. "Ignorance," wrote Thomas Jefferson in 1782, "is preferable to error; and he is less remote from the truth who believes nothing than he who believes what is wrong." It is easier to chisel the truth upon a blank stone than to chisel away the false inscription and then record the truth.

9

As long as we have a democracy, the ignorance of the people will control affairs if their enlightenment does not. After the great Reform Bill of 1867 had enfranchised the masses of England, the aristocratic Dr. Robert Lowe said resignedly: "Now we must educate our masters." If the people—uninformed, misinformed, ill-informed, or half informed—do as well as they do in their collective judgment, how much better ought they to do when proper information is placed before them. Education is our major hope.

But we need vastly more than mere literacy. The Japanese before Pearl Harbor boasted one of the highest literacy rates in the world, and the Chinese had one of the lowest. Yet what shall it profit a nation if it teaches the people to read and they read and believe only government propaganda? The United States has a relatively high literacy rate, but what shall it profit a nation if great numbers of its literate illiterates scan only the sports page and the funny sheet? Or if they read the rest of the paper gullibly?

The voter needs to have sound information when the sky is blue so that when the clouds of international crisis roll up, and tempers are heated, he will have the background against which to form wise judgments, as well as a shield against false prophets. Educational institutions should present not only information but significant information. No particular harm is done if the people believe, as Norman Angell has pointed out, that the world is flat. The schools actually do an excellent job of teaching the sphericity of the globe. But incalculable harm may be done if we teach or even tolerate unsound ideas about tariff fences and foreign psychologies. Our schools and colleges and universities need to offer more and better work in foreign languages, history, geography, foreign affairs, comparative government, international economics, international law, and international organization. There is no royal road to international understanding, and it would be folly to encourage the idea that the voting booth is a cathedral which endows the ballot stamper with heavenly wisdom.

The little red school house—no longer little and red—is the sword and buckler of our democracy. Taxation for education is the cheapest kind of premium to pay for international life insurance, because a well informed citizenry is as important as battleships. Yet when depressions come, one of the first things we do is to scrimp and starve the schools. The salaries of school teachers in certain areas have fallen below the wages of janitors or the allotments of unemployed persons on relief. Tens of thousands of teachers have been driven into more profitable employment, and hundreds of thousands of our best minds, who would like to teach and should be teaching, are repelled by the prospect of a coolie wage. We are willing to pay liberally for well trained lawyers and doctors and veterinarians, yet we turn over our children during their most impressionable years to poorly paid people, some of whom we would not entrust with our personal affairs.

If our government cannot operate successfully without an educated citizenry—and this is acknowledged—then the strangulation of the schools is the perfect example of democracy slowly committing suicide. More than that, it is self-cannibalism of the most appalling sort, for it works in a vicious circle. The greater the illiteracy, the less willing the taxpayers are to support the schools. To their eternal shame the American people in 1947 were spending three times as much for cosmetics and two-and-one-half times as much for liquor as for the education of their children.

10

The Herculean task of lifting the intellectual horizon of the whole people, whether through the schools or the press or the forum or the radio, is at best slow, almost glacial. But we must grapple with the problem of the mentally unfit, the illiterates, the unassimilated immigrants, the underprivileged Negroes and whites. The greatest undeveloped resources of this country, one should repeat, lie not in its mountains or prairies but in its people.

A partial solution may be to stress education for statesmanship as well as for citizenship. Let us give our ablest youths the finest kind of university training, at public expense if necessary; send them abroad for first-hand observation and experience;* keep them in the public service by high salaries and security of tenure; and delegate to them a higher degree of responsibility in the conduct of foreign affairs.

We must at the same time educate our people for tolerance. Little is gained by elevating able men to public office, and then overbearing them with mob pressure. We cannot teach every citizen to be a statesman, but we can teach him that in delicate international negotiations there is always more than meets the eye, and that he should temper his criticism while seeking the facts. Water can rise no higher than its source, and the level of American foreign policy can rise no higher than our people will permit. It will not rise high enough unless we can plug the leaks of ignorance, misinformation, and prejudice.

The American citizen would do well to ponder the implications of John Erskine's title, *The Moral Obligation to Be Intelligent.* If he has a responsibility which can be discharged only by informing himself, and fails to inform himself, then he is in a measure guilty of the disaster that his neglect brings. To reverse the adage, what we do not know may hurt us a great deal; it may bring catastrophe. The American Republic cannot endure forever nine-tenths ignorant and one-tenth informed.

* "We don't go about it right," wrote the inexperienced Ambassador Walter Hines Page shortly after reaching London in 1913. "If we did, we shouldn't pick up a green fellow from the plains of Long Island and send him here; we'd train the most capable male babies we have from the cradle."

SELFISHNESS AND SHORTSIGHTEDNESS

"One of the weaknesses of a democracy . . . is that until it is right up against it, it will never face the truth."—STANLEY BALDWIN, 1935

1

THE IRON LAW of national interest or self-interest governs the foreign affairs of all powers, great or small. In this respect we are probably no better and no worse than other peoples. We may not have pursued our national interest with as much success as other countries, but no one can accuse us of not having tried.

One qualification must be entered. The Man in the Street aims at what he conceives to be the best interests of his country, but often his judgment is faulty. The neutrality legislation of the 1930's, which gave substantial aid and comfort to the rising Hitler and Mussolini, was enacted in response to what the American people thought was to their advantage, but with the wisdom of hindsight we may conclude that storm-cellar neutrality was shortsighted folly.

Another qualification must be made. In pursuit of national interest we sometimes bark up the wrong tree. The German declaration of unrestricted submarine warfare in 1917 was of epochal significance, but at first certain sections of the country were more deeply aroused over the rather ridiculous Zimmermann note. Walter Lippmann has observed that the true interests of the people are not always the things that interest the people most.

The good Christian is no doubt shocked to hear that our national policy is, has been, and must be conceived in selfishness. Recent events provide ample proof of the tendency in international relations for moral standards to be dragged down to the level of the lowest. Before Pearl Harbor we were horrified to learn that merchantmen were being sunk by submarines without warning and without regard for the lives of innocent noncombatants. We declared war on the Germans in 1917, among other reasons, for starting and persisting in this inhumane practice. Yet after Pearl Harbor we were faced with the necessity of fighting the devil with fire, and rather than lose the war we torpedoed scores of Japanese ships without warning, and within a few years were dumping atomic bombs on Hiroshima and Nagasaki. If a statesman insisted on pursuing in undiluted form the ethics of Jesus, if he turned the other cheek and refused to match the weapons of his adversary, he would not only have to abandon the aspirations of his nation, but he might even sacrifice the nation itself, in which case he would go down in history as a simpleton rather than as a statesman. These unfortunately are the realities of international life, and will continue to be until a better day dawns.

National leaders must devote themselves to selfish aims, because this is what their people demand of them, and this is why they are put into office. If elected officials insisted upon kicking over the traces and pursuing in public life the philosophy of Christ, they would probably be thrown out of office and given ample time to continue their devotions privately. The millionaire and philanthropist, Andrew Carnegie, could spend a fortune establishing public libraries and pensions for college professors, because the money was his to disburse, and he had to account to no one except his Maker, who no doubt approved. But if the board of directors of the United States Steel Corporation were to give away one hundred million dollars to establish a peace foundation, they would undoubtedly be faced with a revolt among the stockholders and possible criminal prosecution.

Government officials are agents, not principals. They are expected to discharge their duties with due regard for the desires and interests of the people. Sentiment and philanthropy seldom square with those desires and interests, and when they do not they are tossed out of the window. Otherwise the stockholders—the American people—would take prompt and vigorous action.

2

The illusion persists that it is wholly bad to base a nation's foreign policy on the bedrock of national interest. But the fact is that self-interest is about the only predictable certainty in the vast maze of international uncertainties.

Diplomacy is a deadly game, played for incalculably high stakes. The statesman is like a chess player, and he makes a certain move in his own interest with the expectation that his opponent will make countermoves on the same principle. Sometimes a given move is so clearly to the advantage of one of the contestants that it may be predicted with certainty. The various maneuvers on the international chessboard are often hard enough to anticipate when national interest is plainly in view; the confusion would be confounded if sentiment and self-interest were combined.

In 1898, when we decided to fight Spain for the freedom of Cuba, our motives were both selfish and humanitarian, though primarily humanitarian. Yet it was impossible to convince Europeans that we were fighting to free and not to keep Cuba. Our explanations did not make sense, for they squared with neither history nor human nature.

Mutual self-interest is the only effective cement for alliances, and when it dissolves the alliance falls to pieces.* This was notably true of our compact with France, from 1778 to 1800. Self-interest caused us to sympathize with Finland against Russia, during 1939–1940; against Finland and with Russia, during 1940–1945. The nexus of a common cause bound the Soviet

* Thomas More wrote (1516) that the Utopians never made alliances; if common ties did not knit men together, then written promises would have no binding effect on them.

Union and the United Nations together in a crude fashion until 1945, when the Axis was defeated and the erstwhile Allies began to drift apart.

The United Nations Organization was forged in 1945, not because of sentiment but because of grinding necessity. The atomic fireworks at Hiroshima demonstrated, as had already been apparent, that if the nations of the world could not come together around one table, they almost certainly would destroy each other and their civilization. Even Russia, the most suspicious of the great powers, joined the others, not because she felt at ease in their company but clearly because the United Nations could be used for her own ends.

The principle of self-interest—of bargaining a *quid* for a *quo,* of giving nothing away without an equivalent, and of expecting nothing without an equivalent—is so firmly established in diplomatic intercourse that any departure from it is noteworthy. The Trojans, as legend has it, stupidly accepted a handsome wooden horse from enemies whom they had been fighting for ten years, when they should have known that one must beware of Greeks bearing gifts. During World War II Uncle Sam was so generous in giving certain supplies outright to his hard-pressed Russian ally as to arouse suspicion in the Kremlin as to the existence of some hidden motive.

3

Sentiment is not only a dangerous foundation upon which to base a foreign policy but it is also a shifting foundation. Friendships fluctuate; interests remain fairly constant. There are no enduring friendships; only enduring interests. Our passion for security—one of the basic principles of the Monroe Doctrine—has remained vigorous for well over the century and a half of our national existence, but during that time we have been the enemies of old friends (France) and the friends of old enemies (Britain). The enemies of today are the friends of tomorrow, and the friends of today the enemies of tomorrow. In the eighteenth century England sent gold to Prussia so that Prussia could fight France, and in the twentieth century she twice sent troops to France so that she could fight Germany. In World War I, Japan and Italy fought on our side; in World War II, they fought on the other side.

Friendships may fluctuate suddenly, but fundamental interests, although they do on occasion change, are apt to do so more slowly. We passed the neutrality legislation of the 1930's in what we conceived to be our national interest. But when we discovered that it got in the way of helping our fellow democracies, we first ignored it, then evaded it, then openly violated it, and finally discarded it, at least the most shackling part of it.

The narrow pursuit of self-interest may in fact have certain altruistic by-products, and this is one reason why nations are sometimes supposed to act from sentimental motives. The Monroe Doctrine was enunciated primarily to protect our own skins, but the "chivalrous" Uncle Sam has received considerable credit (in the United States especially) for his presumably unselfish defense of Latin America.

Pure selfishness must sometimes be invoked to seduce the people into following what their leaders regard as the nation's long-range interests. When Lend-Lease was proposed in 1941, a considerable minority of Americans believed that England was fighting our fight, that we should get into the war on her side, and that in the meantime we should send her such weapons as she needed. The vast majority of our people did not want Britain to perish, but they were even more resolved to stay out of the conflict. So the advocates of Lend-Lease were forced to sweeten the pill of intervention with the syrup of self-defense. The scheme was urged by administration sponsors, not on the ground that Britain was deserving of our help, but on the purely selfish ground that if we sent arms to England, the British would keep the war going, and we would not have to get into it. We would let Britain fight (with our weapons) to the last Englishman, while we remained fat and neutral. In 1945, when the shooting stopped and our safety was assured, we ended Lend-Lease with indecent haste. Many an American feels that the British are not grateful enough; they have a most unmannerly way of reminding us, as Lord Halifax did in Boston during 1944, that the Lend-Lease Act, according to its official title, was designed not to help England but to defend America.

Sentiment likewise had to be soft-pedaled when, in 1946, the British sought a loan of $3,750,000,000. On moral grounds they were entitled to a prompt and generous subvention—perhaps even a gift. They had held back the "Hun" for more than two years before Pearl Harbor; they had suffered frightful damages through bombing; they had lost vital shipping, foreign trade, and foreign investments; they had been compelled to reduce their food rations after victory; they had emerged from the war bruised and dazed, while we were experiencing the greatest boom in all history. But the American friends of the loan, aware of our latent anti-British prejudice and our general ignorance of Britain's plight, knew that they would be beaten if they relied on moral argument. They would have to appeal to unadulterated selfishness—to the long-run advantages that would accrue to our industry through the revival of world trade. The average American is not noted for his perception of distant goals, but this argument probably was decisive in insuring the passing of the loan.

4

Self-interest is not necessarily bad, but shortsighted selfishness is, for it defeats the aims of genuine long-range interest. Selfishness and self-interest daily lock horns, and selfishness wins a disquieting number of the encounters. How fortunate it is, some wit has remarked, that diplomats have long noses, because they usually cannot see beyond the ends of them. The same may be said of Mr. Average Citizen; only he does not have a very long nose.

The existence of public shortsightedness, combined with acute astigmatism, is especially dangerous in a democracy like the United States. Adolf Hitler could confidently lay plans for a thousand-year empire, and while he fell short of his goal by some 990 years, we shudder to think how close he came to it and how completely justified he was in planning for it. The President of the United States can be sure of no more than four years in office, and he cannot be sure of Congressional support for more than two years, even assuming that he had it to begin with. Under such conditions a long-range program in foreign affairs has a discouraging sense of unreality.

The American masses have repeatedly been called upon to exercise their limited gifts for longsightedness, and their record is conspicuously poor. Countless thousands of our countrymen still think that the sun rises over Farmer Green's barn and sets over Widow Smith's haystack. To expect the apathetic and ill-informed masses to discern long-run dangers, or to perceive the long-run consequences of a short-range act, is to expect every voter to be a statesman with an extremely long nose.

The busy American gives little thought to the possible international repercussions of "purely domestic" activity. In political campaigns he delights in lambasting foreign nations, and then he wonders why they are suspicious of us and unwilling to extend cordial cooperation. The people of Chicago, many of whom supported the violently anti-British mayoralty campaigns of "Big Bill" Thompson, did not seem to realize that goods bearing Chicago trademarks would thereafter be less than welcome in the undarkened domain of the British empire. There was in fact a substantial cancellation of orders.

The tariff is another "purely domestic" problem. But every single one of our protective barriers has provided a wailing wall for those foreign exporters whose trade was dislocated. Although no sensible person would argue that our domestic policies should be guided primarily by the wishes of foreigners, we should at least count the cost, but usually we do not have even the vaguest idea of the cost. The Morrill Protective Tariff of 1861 antagonized influential manufacturing interests in England on the eve of the Civil War, and at a time when English sympathy for the North was of extreme importance. The McKinley Tariff of 1890 was a direct cause of the Hawaiian Revolution of 1893, and the Wilson-Gorman Tariff of 1894 was similarly related to the Cuban Revolution of 1895. The Armistice of 1918 ended military warfare but not economic warfare: the Fordney-McCumber Tariff of 1922 in certain categories built up our tariff fences to a new high. It was followed in 1930 by the towering Smoot-Hawley Tariff, which brought retaliation abroad and industrial colic at home. A foreign diplomat was asked when he reached New York: "What do you think of our skyscrapers?" He replied:

"They make me think of your tariff."

Other "purely domestic" issues have embroiled our relations with foreign countries. The results of the slap in the face delivered to the Japanese by the Immigration Act of 1924 are familiar, but less well known is the crippling commercial boycott instituted by the Chinese in 1905 as a protest against our policy of racial discrimination. President Theodore Roosevelt was so thoroughly aroused that he seriously contemplated sending an army to China by way of the Philippines.

Even a "purely domestic" campaign for military and naval preparedness may be started at the wrong time and consequently stir up trouble. In 1898, when President McKinley was negotiating for peace with Spain, Congress suddenly passed an appropriation of $50,000,000 for military purposes, a gesture which raised doubts in Madrid as to America's pacific intentions, and encouraged the Cubans to keep up their resistance pending our intervention. The Bikini atom bomb test of 1946, though no doubt desirable from the standpoint of improving naval architecture, could better have been held with less ballyhoo, for this vulgar flexing of our atomic muscles did nothing to quiet the fears of the Soviets and others who had told themselves that Uncle Sam was up to no good. A postponement of the first test was followed by a noticeable easing of the international tension, and a cancellation of the third had a similar effect.

The self-centered American is prone to forget that he lives in a glass house, and that others can hear and see what he says and does. In 1946, when we were giving moral support to the British-succored Greek conservatives against the Russian-backed Greek leftists, considerable criticism was voiced among left-wingers, at home and abroad, to the proposed sending of United States battleship and carrier units to the eastern Mediterranean. Many red-blooded Americans applauded Admiral Halsey's forthright retort: "It's nobody's damn business where we go." From our point of view perhaps it should not be, but the fact is that other peoples make it their business. Some of them also wear their honor on their sleeves, and we ought to act with our eyes open and not register too much surprise when foreigners flare up in ways inimical to our own interests.

5

The American people are also prone to take on, blithely and shortsightedly, dangerous new commitments, like the Philippine Islands, without any serious thought as to how to defend them.° In the case of the Philippines, we lightheartedly gave a hostage to Japan for our good behavior, a hostage which she could have seized at any time, and this incubus weakened us both defensively and diplomatically. The islands, in the belated judgment of Theodore Roosevelt, who impulsively had a good deal to do with acquiring

° The Philadelphia *Ledger* in 1898 asked why Uncle Sam was like a woman throwing a stone. The answer was: "Because he aimed at Cuba, in the West, and hit the Philippines, in the East."

them, were a veritable "heel of Achilles." The events of 1941–1942 proved him right.

We have repeatedly taken a position in world affairs, to our subsequent embarrassment, which we were unable to back up by force. This was notably true of the Far East before 1941: when we were expected either "to put up or shut up," we were unwilling or unable to do either. The volcano erupted in our faces at the time of Pearl Harbor, when we clearly did not have the strength to do more than bluff, and the Japanese knew it. We have at times reversed the famed axiom of Theodore Roosevelt to read: "Scream loudly and carry a toothpick." In 1946 the faster we demobilized our tremendous engine of victory, the "tougher" we talked to Russia.

We have habitually cooled off too rapidly when the shooting ceased. After keying ourselves up in 1917–1918 to a spirit of sacrifice, idealism, and world cooperation, we quickly wearied of well-doing, and lapsed back into the cares of our everyday existence. "A lot of people will pick up their 1913–1914 thoughts right where they laid them down," remarked the New York *Evening Sun* after the Armistice in 1918, and it was right. The resulting reaction was then known as the "slump in idealism," and the same thing occurred in some degree after World War II, only then we did not have so much idealism to lose.

We have been less successful in making peace than in waging war, primarily because war is a tangible, short-range problem with a definite goal and one that can be attained primarily by brute force. But the goddess of peace is much more delicate than the god of war, and the strong-arm embrace of the caveman does not suffice. Peace is a long-range problem, calling for intelligence and vision rather than for courage and strength, and here we have fallen down badly. We fail to realize that great modern wars have two phases: the fighting duration and the peace duration. The intangibles and complexities of the peace duration we cannot grasp in sinewy hands; they baffle and discourage us, and bring a sense of disgust and disillusionment.

We fought the Civil War with an exhibition of raw courage and devotion to idealism on both sides seldom paralleled, yet we botched reconstruction horribly. We fought the Spanish-American War with great dash, but shortsightedly got ourselves involved in Puerto Rico and the Philippines. We fought World War I, though handicapped by "broomstick-gun unpreparedness," with tremendous élan, but we speedily became discouraged over the delays in peacemaking. The net result was that we abandoned the League, born of war's agony and Wilson's sponsorship, leaving it an orphaned waif on the doorstep of its reluctant European foster parents. Refusing to ratify the Treaty of Versailles, we made a separate peace with our fallen foe, despite a moral obligation not to do so, and in this way claimed all the advantages accruing to the victor under that selfsame treaty which we had declined to approve. We found ourselves in the essentially immoral position of demanding equal rights and opportunities but not equal responsibilities.

We wanted peace without having to pay for it; we wanted to go swimming without getting wet; and our enthusiasm for international collaboration cooled when we found that we would have to purchase it with some of our precious sovereignty. The good things of life may be free, but peace is not one of them, and although it is vastly cheaper than war, it still has its price.*
Yet we wanted something for nothing.

What have we learned from these experiences? In 1938, the year of the Munich surrender, fewer than two out of ten Americans believed that America's failure to join the League had been even partly responsible for Europe's troubles. After World War II started, a strong majority held that Germany should be dealt with more severely next time, even to the extent of paying for the cost of the war. As late as 1944 fewer than 5 per cent of the American people were willing to confess that the failure of the United States to "accept a fair share of the responsibility for maintaining a peaceful world" had contributed to the debacle of 1939–1945.

6

In economics, as well as in politics, the preoccupied American betrayed a costly shortsightedness during the years after World War I. Prior to that conflict we had been an international debtor; we emerged the world's creditor. We greedily tried to play both ends against the middle, with the objective of enjoying all the advantages of both a debtor and a creditor, without any of the disadvantages of either. We demanded the money from our European debtors, though they had borrowed goods rather than money. And even though they could pay us back only in goods, we stupidly erected high tariff dikes over which their merchandise could not flow. Then we lambasted the defaulters because they were dishonest and would not remit. We further declined to acknowledge that there was the remotest connection between our demands upon the Allies, and the Allied demands upon Germany for reparations.

Our narrow and shortvisioned attitude on debts and reparations retarded the economic rehabilitation of Europe, gave ammunition to Hitler in his meteoric rise, and was not unrelated to the coming of the war which cost us some $350,000,000,000 in treasure, to say nothing of blood and continuing expenses. Hitler might have risen anyhow, but in a valiant effort to collect $10,000,000,000—less than one thirtieth of the final cost—we embarked upon a course that played directly into his hands.

The shortsightedness of the Smoot-Hawley Tariff, passed under Republican auspices, has already been mentioned. Yet when Cordell Hull sought to whittle down this barrier by the Reciprocal Trade Agreements Act, he

* Many wealthy citizens of Westchester County, New York, fearing for real-estate values, bitterly protested in 1946 against the proposal to locate the United Nations there. Posters were put up showing minute men ready to repel the foreign invader, in the spirit of 1776.

was opposed by a substantial block of Republican votes in Congress, and this was true of every subsequent renewal.* The urge to sell everything to foreigners and buy nothing from them is hard to kill. The Bourbon kings of France learned nothing and forgot nothing, and certain shortsighted Republican politicians still fail to recognize that the first commandment of international trade is: "As ye sell, so also must ye buy." We Americans have perceived only dimly that trade is a two-way street, that tariff fences not only keep foreign goods out but American goods in; that the corollary of "Buy American" is "Sell only in America." We have realized only imperfectly that trade restrictions are a game at which two can play. When we employ them, they are "protection"; when foreigners use them it is a "tariff war." We believed during World War II, and no doubt still believe, that it is better to suffer the deprivations of complete economic self-sufficiency than to risk the hazards of completely free trade.

We wonder why we have not got along better in recent years with Argentina. A basic reason has been our tariff and quarantine restrictions on Argentine beef, which in the judgment of connoisseurs is the most succulent in the world. The Argentinians resent the implication that all their beef is diseased, just as we resented similar charges against American pork by European countries in the 1880's. The government of Argentina concedes that the dread hoof-and-mouth disease is endemic in certain areas, but insists that there is little danger, under proper inspection, from beef raised in the non-infected areas, and none whatever from canned beef. But thanks to the cattle lobby in Washington, the meat-hungry American people went without beef during World War II, while tremendous supplies were available in the Argentine.

It is perhaps unfair to single out the cattle growers for special censure. Every American economic interest that is adversely affected by foreign imports emits loud squawks, and if it is noisy enough and well organized enough it gets results in the form of tariff protection. The time may come when we shall lower our barriers and cushion the blow to domestic producers by granting them a government subvention. Such a subsidy, which has ample precedent at home, might be a cheap price to pay for friendly relations abroad.

The shortvisioned citizen does not perceive that prosperous neighbors and a prosperous world are essential for our own prosperity. We cannot become economic cannibals and live upon ourselves alone, except at a ruinously high cost. Depressions are bacilli that leap lightly over international boundaries, like other bacilli. If a farmer or manufacturer loses his market through world economic dislocations, he is apt to blame the bank, or the railroad, or the New Deal, or the local congressman, or something else near at home that he can see with his own eyes. He must learn to raise his sights.

* In 1946 the rank and file of Republicans, in contrast to their politically conscious congressmen, were only slightly less favorable to reciprocity than the Democrats.

7

Shortsightedness sometimes becomes so acute as to verge on blindness in the face of dangers that should be perfectly plain to any reasonably alert person. We are not unique in this, for even after the terrible preview of Hitler's smash into Poland, the British and the French, with their Maginot-line mentalities, continued largely with a business-as-usual program.

We were blind for a long time to the dangers of an independent Texas; we were blind to the danger that Hawaii might fall into the hands of Japan. We were blind to the possibility of involvement in World War I, even after the German U-boat had been unveiled; and we did not really begin to see the hazards clearly until some weeks after we had actually been plunged into war. We were blind to the implications of the "phoney war" in Europe from 1939 to 1940, and only with the fall of France and the near black-out of democracy did we begin to see. We were blind to the results of Japanese aggression in the Far East even down to 1940 and 1941. We failed to build up stock piles of rubber, tin, and quinine, though fatally dependent on the Far East for them. Our government (though the public lukewarmly disapproved) permitted the export of oil, scrap, and other sinews of war to the Japanese military machine, partly because of diplomatic reasons, and partly because of wishful thinking. Early in 1942 American officials estimated that 60 per cent of the war materials that Japan was using in her unprecedented conquest of the Pacific had come from us, and they were being returned with compound interest.

On the eve of Pearl Harbor, Congress extended conscription with only one vote to spare, and by this narrow margin we escaped crippling our military establishment at a time when anyone with postadolescent acumen could recognize that we were being sucked into the vortex of war. Even after we had slithered over the edge, and had practically lost the conflict in 1942, we refused to become unduly concerned, proceeding on the Pollyanna formula that we had never lost a war and that everything would work out all right.

"The public is a bad guesser," wrote Thomas De Quincey, and while he may not have been thinking of the American people, he might well have been. When war broke out in 1939, approximately one half of those with opinions thought it would be over in one year or less. The more ignorant a citizen was of the tremendous problems to be solved, the more confident he was that the whole conflagration would end speedily. The month before Mussolini stabbed France in the back, nearly half of our citizens with opinions believed that he would enter the war *on France's side*. After Pearl Harbor there were many wild guesses as to the duration of the conflict, with the preponderance of optimism among the more ignorant voters.

8

National shortsightedness as to our aims in World War II will ever be a source of amazement. Even the troops in the combat zones had no clear idea about their long-range objectives. A communications officer in the South Pacific wrote: "Actually nobody is fighting for any ideal at all. . . . They're fighting for their lives and to get this damn mess over with so they can go back home and forget about the rest of the world." This was the natural but not too intelligent reaction of a good many of the draftees. We won the war not because we had any long-range vision, but because we were big and strong and we had a job to do.

In time of peace one should prepare for war; in time of war one should also prepare for peace. The complexities of peacemaking are today so overwhelming that one cannot begin thinking about them too soon. During 1943 and 1944 the question was raised as to whether it was wise to divert time and energy from the war effort so as to plan for peace. While a majority of citizens with opinions thought we should do so, as many as three or four out of ten thought that we should win the war first and then begin to think about the peace.

The lack of vision on the part of both soldiers and civilians was noteworthy after the Armistice of 1918. The boys wanted to get back to their native hearths as soon as possible, and their families were hardly less eager to have them back. Few Americans on either side of the Atlantic were able to understand why the troops should linger, once the shooting had stopped and the job was done. Scarcely anyone seemed to realize that the most delicate task of all lay ahead.

The impulse to "wanna go home" before the fire is completely out was seen again in 1945, both in the European and Pacific theaters, when to the astonishment of the conquered peoples our troops engaged in spirited demonstrations against further detention. The United States Army in Germany was disbanded with such indecent haste, in response to pressure from both the soldiers and their families, that it was necessary to use beardless boys and Polish mercenaries to help man the breach.° Evidently the army had not undertaken a successful campaign of educating soldier opinion, assuming of course that even the most determined efforts would have met with success. The men in uniform should have learned that it was dangerous to go home while the embers were still glowing; that if we withdrew our troops before we had built up a liberal and enlightened Germany, we would almost certainly guarantee a resurrected and unrepentant Germany; and that in this case we probably would have to come back for a third time, and perhaps under less pleasant circumstances.

But one should not blame the battle-worn and homesick soldier. Early in 1945 one in five adult civilians back home thought that one year of policing

---

° In Berlin in 1947 the present writer saw ex-German soldiers being employed as civilian guards of United States Army property.

Germany would be enough. Yet in the fall of 1946, after tension with Russia had increased, eight out of ten voters favored keeping the boys in Europe, and even those who had a member of the family in the services were generally of the same opinion. We had evidently grown more worldly-wise in twenty years, but how long this feeling would continue in the face of an expensive and prolonged occupation of Germany, no one could say.

Elsewhere we have shown singular blindness regarding future combustibles. Japan is notoriously overpopulated, and conditions have grown more congested since the war. Here is a situation of almost certain explosiveness, for one cannot tie down the safety valves and not expect some kind of explosion. Yet late in 1945 a strong majority of our citizens were not willing that the Japanese should ever have an additional acre; let them get along with what they had.

The American people, like others, largely ignore the lessons of their own history, and even the lessons to be drawn from the experience of their own generation. The horrors of war fade as its glories take on a brighter hue. We have excellent memories for the things that we should forget, such as uncollectible war debts; and excellent "forgetters" for the things we should remember, such as the follies of unpreparedness.

9

A basic reason for national shortsightedness is the lamentable tendency to look upon international complexities from the personal point of view. Or, in the immortal words of a Tammany politician: "What's in it for Mrs. Murphy and the children?" Even the American sponsors of the United Nations Organization deemed it necessary to dangle the bait of increased world trade before the American people, as though world peace in itself were not reward enough.

We tend to live just for the moment, or at least between elections. We often cannot agree what our vital interests are, and the resulting babel of tongues confuses the government, which has a right to expect some guidance from the citizens whom it is serving.

A favorite preoccupation of the ordinary voter is to criticize the State Department for not having a foreign policy—or for having a no-policy policy.* Our government has certain basic principles, like the Monroe Doctrine and the Open Door, which it has pursued with rare consistency over long periods of time. But we are woefully deficient in farvisioned, positive policies, designed to use the power of the United States to shape events in our own interests. A dictatorship, like that of Hitler, can project centuries-long programs. Even a business corporation, like the Standard Oil Company, can make long-range plans to develop the oil of the Middle East. But the State

* In 1920 the Washington *Post* wrote: "Paris is puzzled about the stand of the United States in world affairs, and so is the United States."

Department either cannot do so at all, or cannot do so as easily. Why? The answer is that a shortsighted public will not let it.

American statesmen, to their dismay, have long since learned that instead of spending all their energy on some constructive policy, they must devote much of their attention to the sheer negativism of neutralizing the ill effects of popular ignorance and prejudice. They have long since learned that if they wish to keep out of hot water, especially when they make public speeches, they had better not elaborate any dynamic policy but strike off the conventional platitudes about home, mother, and the flag. As long as President Wilson spoke in vague terms about a league of nations, he found general acquiescence, but as soon as he came out with a specific League of Nations, with vulnerable Articles X and XVI, he gave critics something tangible into which to sink their teeth.

The State Department actually does work on long-range policies, but generally it does not dare announce them to the public. If it did, dissentient groups all over the country would join in the cry that the scheme was too reactionary or too liberal or too narrow or too visionary or too halting or too daring or too inadequate or too costly or too something else. It is much easier—and much safer from a political point of view—to keep policy on a twenty-four-hour basis and hence be able to catch the shifting gusts of popular opinion. Statesmen have learned from cruel experience that they had better not seek brilliant solutions but continue on the day-by-day basis of simply avoiding mistakes. This is, of course, not a policy but a predicament. Yet it is about the best we can hope for as long as an ignorant electorate will not tolerate a great deal more.

Again one gets back to the principle that water can rise no higher than its source. The State Department can not, in fact dares not, fashion a policy that is too far in advance of what public opinion will permit. If it does, the administration will be thrown out of office, and the ranking officials with it. President Hoover, and his predecessors and successors, must have known that there was a vital connection between reparations and war debts, but they could not admit it publicly, because such an announcement would have been unpopular and hence politically harmful. But saying that there is no connection between the moon and the tides, for the purpose of placating the voter, does not remove that connection. So the State Department has to limp along with the ball and chain of an ignorant, apathetic, and shortsighted public, and it will continue to limp until there is a greater delegation of responsibility, or until the public is better educated to its responsibilities, or both.

CHAPTER FOURTEEN

THE CURSE OF CAPRICE

"When public opinion changes, it is with the rapidity of thought."
—THOMAS JEFFERSON, 1816

1

FICKLENESS—or, perhaps better, changefulness—is a distinguishing trait of American public opinion, although our critics cannot say that we are mercurial, like some Latin peoples. The instability of our moods is puzzling to those foreign countries that try to do diplomatic business with us, let alone understand us.

In France of the eighteenth century things were much simpler. The foreign envoy first had to discover the king's taste in mistresses, which was usually not difficult, then ascertain her taste in bonbons, and then get her ear. She would get the king's ear, and the desired course of action might be effected.

The process today is infinitely more complicated. Capricious though females are, public opinion in a democracy may be even more capricious. There are so many different ears to be reached, male and female, there are such varying tastes in bonbons and other goodies, that the foreign envoy who would influence governmental action by manipulating public opinion has before him a task of immense difficulty.

Lord Bryce long ago observed that Americans have what chemists call a "low specific heat." They are apt to warm up suddenly and cool off quickly. At the time of the *Trent* affair in 1861, when a Union commander seized two Confederate envoys from a British mail steamer, the North burst into a delirium of rejoicing. But more sober heads quickly perceived that the two prisoners were white elephants, and that to retain them would prod the British into war. Public excitement gradually waned, and the two unwilling guests were eventually released.

The news of the *Trent* affair arrived in England by steamer eleven days after it had reached Washington, and the British outburst of indignation matched the Northern outburst of rejoicing. If the then dead Atlantic cable had been working, and the Americans had learned promptly how bitter the British were, and the British had learned promptly how overjoyed the Americans were, the public in both countries probably would have demanded uncompromising courses from which there could have been no graceful retreat. As it was, the necessary delay in transmission gave passions on both sides a chance to subside, and war was avoided.

The mass mood, when it fluctuates violently, is more likely to do so regarding foreign affairs than domestic affairs. Problems like currency regulation and housing touch our daily lives and consequently hold our sustained attention. But in regard to faraway foreign affairs, we are usually less keenly

167

or protractedly interested, and less able to see how a proposed move is going to affect us directly. We are also less well informed, and hence more liable to be led astray by a propagandist, who knows that we have little or no firsthand evidence against which to check his story.

2

The hurried American is traditionally more changeful than his European counterpart. "Progress crawls in Europe, but gallops in America," noted one early British traveler in the United States.

The explanation is obvious. In Europe the masses were not going anywhere: they and their ancestors had dwelt for centuries on the same piece of land, every rock of which has a history. In America the masses were going somewhere; there was a vast amount of cream to be skimmed before someone else did the skimming. Edward Eggleston had one of his characters say, "git a plenty while you're agittin." To the astonishment of foreign visitors we moved our homes easily and often, and still do, sometimes in the typically American auto trailer. There are areas in the United States today, particularly in California, where it is rather unusual to find an adult who was born in that locality.

We early showed ourselves to be a nervous-breakdown people, and to a great extent still are. We have traditionally put speed above safety, and to a considerable degree still do. From the days when steamboat boilers burst under too much steam, to the days when airplanes crash into the sides of mountains, we have been in a hurry. We are impatient of long-view projects, whether at home or abroad; and we are impatient of protracted diplomacy to gain specific ends. When the time came to build an Isthmian canal, and Theodore Roosevelt decided to dig it across Panama, the dirt began to fly—various kinds of dirt in fact—despite diplomatic delays and international decency. The Big Stick tactics of Roosevelt were his own, not those of his people. But he knew his constituents well enough to realize that they would support vigorous, direct American tactics—and on the whole they did.

"A foolish consistency is the hobgoblin of little minds," wrote Emerson in one of his more famous essays. If this test is accepted, the American people at times in their history have had capacious intellects. Our population is relatively intelligent, and when the brutal facts convince us that a certain course is unwise, we toss it out the window. Before the Munich crisis of 1938 we were strongly opposed to selling arms to the democracies; after the outbreak of war in 1939 we reversed ourselves and lifted the embargo.

The avidity of the American masses for new sensations is notorious. They quickly grow tired of current issues, like the League or imperialism, and seek change for change's sake.* When Jacksonian democracy was rampant,

---

* The same is to some extent true of certain public figures, like Admiral George Dewey. "Every hero becomes a bore at last," observed Emerson.

the ideal of rotation in office was regarded as thoroughly American, and Lincoln ran against the incumbent congressman on the issue, "a turn about's fair play." In the campaign of 1944, when Roosevelt was seeking his fourth term, the most effective Republican slogan was: "That's why it's time for a change." Twelve years were long enough for any one President, so his opponents argued, even though there was a war on.

The masses of the United States have habituated themselves to alternate periods of repose and excitement. Every four years we enter upon the bitterness of a presidential campaign, and wage it with intensity and heat. Within a few days after the balloting, the fever dies away almost completely, to the astonishment of foreign observers, and we settle back into four more years of relative calm. The counting of the ballots in America ends the revolution; it does not signal the beginning of one, as in certain Latin countries. If issues do not exist when the Congressional or Presidential elections are in the offing, we must make some out of whole cloth, or puff up small ones into big ones, and we must do this every two years. Such a procedure not only makes for changefulness but for changefulness of an artificial sort. The unfortunate system of working by the calendar rather than by the crisis has probably affected to some extent our attitude toward foreign affairs. At times we have been indifferent when we should have been excited, and excited when we should have been indifferent.

3

Mr. Joseph Doakes can hardly be blamed for changing his mind overnight about foreign policy when his own government in Washington has sometimes set him a bad example by doing the same thing. One may say "bad example," because caprice in a foreign office is as damaging as caprice in an investment house. The confidence of the depositors will be shaken if the bank announces one policy today and another tomorrow. In 1919 Woodrow Wilson, as our head banker, gave the European statesmen assurances that we would join the League of Nations and cooperate in the postwar reconstruction of Europe. They invested their future security in Wilson, but the Harding administration repudiated him and reversed his policy. The net result was that the European nations felt toward us much as a depositor would feel toward a bank which, with bulging vaults, refused to honor its promises.

Someone has said that a "permanent tariff" is one that is drafted to last until the next election. The machinery of our national government is unfortunately geared to encourage impermanence. The members of the House of Representatives are sure of only two years; the President of only four; and the senators of only six. When the Democrats go out of office and the Republicans come in, we may expect a house cleaning and reversals of existing policy, either of a minor or a major nature. When the Democratic Cleveland succeeded the Republican Harrison in 1893, he promptly withdrew from the Senate a Republican treaty for the annexation of Hawaii.

Even when the same party remains in power and a new Secretary of State takes the oath, he may announce a sharp change in policy or perhaps a reversal. When Secretary Blaine left the cabinet following the assassination of President Garfield in 1881, his successor, though also a Republican, rescinded the invitations which had recently been issued for the first Pan-American Conference. The idea lay dormant until Blaine returned to the department some seven years later, and the call again went forth.

Sometimes there are attempts at reversal within the same administration. In 1946 Secretary of State Byrnes made a sensational speech in Stuttgart, Germany, proclaiming a "get-tough-with-Russia" policy. A few days later Secretary of Commerce Wallace, speaking in Madison Square Garden, New York, proclaimed a "go-easy-on-Russia" policy. President Truman told the newsmen that he not only approved Secretary Wallace's right to speak freely, but that he had previously approved the entire speech as completely in line with that of the Secretary of State. Secretary Byrnes, who was then engaged in delicate peace negotiations in Paris, was placed in a humiliating position, whereupon the President, in an unprecedented exhibition of double talk and confusion, retracted his approval of Wallace and forced him from the cabinet. As a Republican spokesman put it, we can follow only one Secretary of State at a time. Little wonder that the average citizen is confused and inconstant when this sort of thing can happen at the highest levels.

There are also times when, under the stress of military necessity, reversals seem imperative. During our first seventy-five or so years, we upheld freedom of the seas against the overweening naval might of England. During th Civil War, when the Union was in travail, the Washington government, in order to blockade the South more effectively, turned its back upon its historic position and created precedents which were later cited against us by the British when we were neutral from 1914 to 1917. During World War II, in connection with Pétain's France, Franco's Spain, Badoglio's Italy, and Darlan's North Africa, we departed from our anti-Fascist policy, or modified it sharply, in the interests of winning the war.

Overnight fluctuations of policy have become less common in recent years, partly because of the prolonged tenure of the Democrats after 1933, and partly because our growing maturity has to some extent counteracted the impulse to sudden change. Franklin Roosevelt undertook no major scrapping of the Hoover foreign policy, except perhaps in launching the reciprocal trade agreements program, and Hoover's outgoing Secretary of State, Henry L. Stimson, conferred at length with both the incoming President Roosevelt and Secretary Hull regarding continuity in the Far Eastern arena.

To reverse foreign policy with every new administration is to proclaim the absurdity that our fundamental interests shift with cyclical certainty every four or eight or twelve years. Nothing could be more fatuous. Our fundamental interests are based upon solid political, economic, geographical, and other factors, and they ordinarily change not with cataclysmic suddenness but with glacial slowness.

On occasion our Presidents have sought to reverse our foreign policy in a manner contrary to the national interest, and they have been hurled back after running headlong into the rock of public opinion. When Thomas Jefferson took office in 1801, he was anti-British and pro-French, opposed to "entangling alliances," favorable to "peace at any price," and hostile to the expansion of the navy. The inexorable impact of national need, far from permitting him to reverse his predecessors, actually forced him to reverse himself. When the Democratic Woodrow Wilson came to the White House in 1913, he was an avowed foe of dollar diplomacy, and with dramatic suddenness he undertook to withdraw support from American investors in the Far East and Latin America. Like Jefferson, he ran headlong into a stone wall of national interest. Instead of reversing the policy of his Republican predecessors, he was forced by circumstances to reverse himself, and before very long his critics charged that he was making Republican dollar diplomacy look like ten-cent diplomacy.

4

Propagandists, aided and abetted by the turn of events, may bring about misleading or dangerous changes in the public mind.

In 1917 we declared war on Germany because she was sinking our merchant ships and jeopardizing both our fundamental rights and our security. We were convinced at the time that we had a just and righteous cause—the cause of a free people taking up the sword in self-defense.

But the American nation could not key itself up to a spirit of high sacrifice by merely proclaiming that it was fighting to make the world safe *against* the submarine. We had to be fighting *for* something. Wilson sensed this, and in a series of inspiring addresses declared that we were out to make the world safe for democracy and to end wars. In the heat of conflict we accepted this theology so wholeheartedly that we began to project our newly born conviction back into the days before April, 1917, and to believe that we had plunged into the holocaust, not to battle for our basic rights, but to make the world safe for democracy.

Then came the bungling of the peace. The world was less safe for democracy than it had been before 1914, and wars were raging in the four corners of the globe. The disillusioned Americans slammed the door on Europe and sank back into a cynical stupor, convinced that they had gained nothing from the conflict except casualty lists, influenza, near-beer, prohibition, high prices, heavy taxes, bad debts, and ungrateful Allies.

Then came the Great Depression, with a further dose of disillusionment, and the American people were in a mood to seek whipping boys. Into this favorable atmosphere stepped Senator Nye of North Dakota, a brash young legislator in need of something that would bring him before the public eye. His investigation of the pre-1917 period, while exhuming nothing essential that the historians had not known for a decade or so, seemed to prove to his satisfaction, and to that of a host of gullible admirers, that we had been drawn into the war by the machinations of the sloganeers, the profiteers, the munitioneers, the propagandists, and the bankers. In April, 1937, the twentieth anniversary of Wilson's appearance before Congress with his war message, Dr. Gallup published the results of an inquiry as to whether it had been a mistake to fight Germany. A heavy majority of 64 per cent believed that it had been; 28 per cent thought that it had not been, while 8 per cent were undecided. The question was in some measure misleading: "Do you think it was a mistake for the United States to enter the last World War?" The implication is that by March and April of 1917 we had a choice. Actually, by March, 1917, Germany was making war on us by sinking our ships on the high seas.

In December, 1939, several months after Hitler had attacked Poland, Dr. Gallup asked why we had entered the conflict in 1917 with Germany. The results deserve full quotation.

1. America was the victim of propaganda and selfish interests   34%
2. America had a just and unselfish cause   26
3. America entered the war for its own safety   18
4. Other reasons   8
5. No opinion and undecided   14

These figures are eloquent testimony of our basic disillusionment, buttressed by Senator Nye's overemphasis on the influence of designing schemers. Instead of being dragged into the war of 1917 by propagandists, we were dragged into a false interpretation of our entry by antiwar propagandists.

5

The American public, as already observed, is more speedily influenced by events than by abstract arguments or propaganda. Events are the great persuaders.

No one will deny that there was a good deal of Allied propaganda in the United States before 1917, but no one can deny that events played into the hands of Allied agents. The invasion of Belgium by the Germans, the torpedoing of the *Lusitania,* and the execution of Nurse Edith Cavell were all facts. From the point of view of the Germans there was complete justification for these deeds, but we in America did not hear the German defense, and in any case would not have accepted it. The sheer brutality of these outrages shouted down all justification. And while Allied propaganda exaggerated and colored them, the events by themselves prejudiced the American people against the German war lords and their cohorts. It would be impossible to prove that the circumstances which caused Germany to make war on the United States would have been substantially changed if there had been no Allied propaganda whatever in this country, and if the facts of German aggression had been presented without bias in the American press. But it would also be impossible to prove the opposite.

The earth-shaking events of World War II completely overturned the opinions of the American people. In 1944, as in 1937, we were asked whether we had made a mistake in entering World War I. The results are striking:

	Yes	No	No opinion
1937	64%	28%	8%
1944	18	61	21

Within the span of seven years the original "Yes" had become about as emphatic a "No."

What had happened during this troubled era to bring about a complete reversal of opinion? Had the essential facts of 1917 changed? Had historians uncovered sensational new evidence or propounded challenging new interpretations of the essential facts? The answer in each case is "No." Facts are facts and do not change. Additional evidence may be unearthed, and new interpretations may be given to them and to the old evidence, but the most scholarly book published during these years helped support the Nye "devil theory" of war. The American people are not history-minded, and they pay little or no attention to the researches of professional historians. The brilliantly unsound *Road to War*, written by the journalist Walter Millis, played in with the false slant of Senator Nye and was given wide distribution by the Book-of-the-Month Club. But not even it could work much change. The explanation must be sought elsewhere than in perverted history.

In 1944 we were again fighting Germany, our foe of 1917, on the side of Britain and France, our two closest associates in 1917. We had gone to war in 1941, following German U-boat attacks on our shipping, much as we had in 1917. We were about to open the second front in France, and American boys were preparing to fight over some of the same terrain, albeit in jeeps and tanks, that their fathers had inched their way over in 1918. There were many other parallels between the two wars, and to assert that in 1917 we had been lured into the conflict by selfish interests was to suggest that in 1944 we were again fighting an unrighteous war at the behest of selfish interests. Such a conclusion was utterly unpalatable.

So it was that our views regarding a purely historical problem were radically changed, not by the historians or even by the journalists, but by current events and by the desirability of viewing the existing clash in a highly patriotic light. The facts had not changed, but our mood had.

6

World War II was a peculiarly potent persuader in still other ways. Prior to 1939 the proposal to conscript able-bodied men for a year of army service met powerful opposition. But in 1940, after the collapse of France, the popular demand for strengthening the armed forces became so irresistible that Congress could safely pass the Selective Service Act. Public support for defending any South-American country was lukewarm before Munich; overwhelming after the fall of France. Sentiment for Finland was almost unanimous when she was resisting Russian invasion in 1939–1940; woefully weak when she was invading our Russian Ally from 1941 on. In March, 1940, during the period of the "phoney war," Dr. Gallup asked the American people if they would be personally affected should England succumb to Germany. A substantial minority thought not, but after the fall of France the minority became a powerful majority.

No less revolutionary was the shift in opinion regarding the League of Nations.

Following the Harding landslide of 1920, the American people, though probably favoring the League in some form, lapsed back into an isolationist dream world. Old Guard Republicans sneered at the League's successes and jeered at its failures—failures that were probably attributable in some measure to the defection of the United States. In 1941, before Pearl Harbor, Dr. Gallup asked whether we should have joined the League of Nations; in 1944, after the second front was opened in France, he repeated the same question. The "deadly parallel" is again most revealing:

	Yes	No	No opinion
1941	37%	37%	26%
1944	53	20	27

The change in attitude, though marked, is not as striking as one might expect. The basic explanation seems to be that the old League (unlike the war-declaration "mistake" issue) had been a partisan football, kicked back and forth by the Republicans and Democrats for more than a decade. The Democrats, out of loyalty to the memory of Wilson, had to say that not joining was a blunder; the Republicans, out of loyalty to the policy of their leaders or perhaps in response to troubled consciences, had to say that not joining had made no difference—or a difference that was advantageous to the United States.

During the period of World War II the idea of a non-Wilsonian league of nations could be discussed without the same partisan bitterness, although there no doubt was some carry-over. The results of the Gallup polls on the question of a new world organization are significant:

	Yes	No	No opinion
1937	26%	52%	22%
1944	72	13	15

In 1941 a majority could not be mustered for the proposition that we had made a mistake in shunning the League; three years later, a majority could. What had happened in the meantime? Had any essential data come to light regarding the wisdom or unwisdom of joining the League in 1919? Had any important new facts turned up regarding our policy from 1919 to 1939, the twenty years between wars? The answer in both cases is "No."

By 1944 we were deep in the morass of World War II. After almost losing the conflict, we had pulled ourselves together and were preparing, with a heavy expenditure of treasure and blood, for a fight to the finish. The conviction grew that if this conflagration could have been prevented by the League, and that if our participation could have strengthened the League, then we should have joined. But we were not of this mind until the losses of World War II had hit us directly, and the dimly remembered sacrifices of the Meuse-Argonne in 1918 were revived.

7

It would be grossly unfair to overstress our changefulness as a people. We are not unique in having national moods, whether of exaltation or of depression. We have been guilty of acts of inconsistency or volatility, but for practically all of these the student could find some kind of parallel in the record of other democracies.

The danger of moving too impulsively may on occasion be less serious than the danger of not moving at all. At times we have clung to certain basic principles with a consistency and persistency that have jeopardized our own welfare. We have been tenacious in our devotion to the Monroe Doctrine, although in its extreme version it has created much Yankeephobia and cost us much good will. We have been tenacious in our devotion to the ideal of no entangling alliances, although at times our national needs would have been well served by such pacts. Does anyone suppose that Hitler would have kicked over the applecart in 1939 if the abortive Anglo-French-American alliance of 1919 had been approved by the United States Senate and ratified by its signatories?

Our blind worship of isolation has on occasion brought us to the very brink of disaster. Before 1939 our people demanded a course of shortsighted neutrality at the expense of national dignity and honored tradition. Then war broke out in Europe, and a majority perceived that our interests required succoring the beleaguered democracies, even at the risk of involvement. A tremendous ideological battle raged in America between those who wanted to help our overseas brothers, and the strong minority who wanted to continue with igloo isolationism. We resolved this painful dilemma by trying to ride tandem the mismated horses of intervention and nonintervention, with resulting inconsistencies and anomalies.

Some weeks after our unofficial declaration of war on the Axis in 1941 through the Lend-Lease Act, a strong majority of Americans with opinions agreed that for all practical purposes we were in the conflict. Yet on the very day of Pearl Harbor eight out of ten persons were for staying out of hostilities. They wanted to eat the cake of neutrality, while enjoying the unneutrality of aiding England, and all the while praying that war would not come from their flagrantly unneutral acts.

Such illogical compromises are perhaps preferable to the perils of moving too conservatively when we ought to move speedily, or moving too speedily when we ought to move conservatively. As Montesquieu observed in 1748, public affairs ought to have a certain steady progress, neither too fast nor too slow. "But," he added, "the people have always too much action or too little. Sometimes, with 100,000 arms, they overturn everything; at other times, with 100,000 feet, they crawl like insects."

Fickleness is dangerous, but changing one's mind in the light of changing conditions is evidence of alertness and intellectual growth. Blind adamancy is also dangerous. But at least it provides a dependable factor which other nations may take into account when framing their policy toward the United States. The ideal practice is a happy medium between the two. We should be willing to change, but not too suddenly. We may not be farvisioned as a people, but we instinctively recognize that our basic interests do not fluctuate from day to day.

CHAPTER FIFTEEN

THE SUCKER TRADITION

"A sucker is born every minute."—American proverb, commonly attributed to P. T. BARNUM

1

THE AMERICANS, with their Puritanical heritage, are prone to preen themselves on their superior national morality, and their politicians long ago learned that it is profitable to harp on this theme. Huntington Wilson, a career diplomat of the Taft period, used to speak of "the national foible for grandiloquent sentimentality." Nor are other countries immune from such an affliction. Macaulay's observation in 1831 has become a classic: "We know no spectacle so ridiculous as the British public in one of its periodical fits of morality."

The superficial student of American history would not expect to find any trace of sentimental softness in our national character. We emerged from a primitive struggle for existence, in which no holds were barred and in which the principle of the survival of the fittest worked in its crudest form. One cannot agree with the quipster who said that the Pilgrim Fathers first fell on their knees, and then fell on the aborigines, but there can be no doubt that we pushed aside, despoiled, or destroyed the Indians in a ruthless campaign that continued almost without interruption for nearly three centuries. We evicted the redman as thoroughly and as methodically as we exterminated the passenger pigeon and the buffalo. The Indian gave us many things, including corn and tobacco, but above all he gave us a toughness of fiber that contributed powerfully to making us great.

Our centuries-long battle with the elements and with the natives developed within us a certain callousness to human suffering. Just as omelettes are not made without breaking eggs, wildernesses are not conquered without breaking necks, and in our haste to get on with the job we developed an extraordinary indifference to life and limb.

Like other peoples, and particularly in recent years, we have also developed a marked callousness toward wartime atrocities. In 1914 we were scandalized when the Germans goose-stepped into Belgium, and in 1915 we were horrified when they torpedoed the *Lusitania*. We were aroused over the bombing of Shanghai by the Japanese in 1932, and we developed considerable sentiment for boycotting Japanese goods, with a consequent falling off in the sale of Woolworth knickknacks. We were distressed by the poison-gas attacks of the Italians on the Ethiopians, and by the brutal bombing of Barcelona by Franco. But we were becoming less distressed, and gradually we came to accept these things as a part of what is known as "civilized" warfare. The destruction of Warsaw by the Germans in 1939, and of Rotterdam in 1940, were so much more diabolical than the invasion of Belgium and the sinking of the *Lusitania* that if we had still retained our 1914–1915 standards we might have gone into the war relatively soon. But it took a good deal more than that, plus a direct assault on us, before we were willing to join the blood bath.

We have to some extent been held back from idealistic crusades abroad by a traditional Yankee hardheadedness and shrewdness in business. David Harum, the canny horse trader, has come to be something of a folk hero. Early British travelers in America noted that "cuteness" or "acuteness" in driving a bargain was greatly admired. It was "slick" to outdo the other fellow, and the Golden Rule was somewhat modified to read that one should do unto the other fellow what he would do unto you, but "do him fust." The story is familiar of the Yankee storekeeper who shouted down the stairs to the hired hand, instructing him to sand the sugar, chalk the flour, and water the vinegar before coming up for prayers. Even to this day there is something of a fear in America that the outside world may regard us as soft-headed idealists.

2

The Man in the Street, perhaps more than men in foreign streets, dislikes being "played for a sucker." Few people enjoy being duped, especially if they are citizens of a nation that has developed a world-wide reputation for canniness. The night-club hostess, "Texas" Guinan, made considerable money and some little reputation by working on the principle: "Never give a sucker an even break." The great showman P. T. Barnum amassed a fortune and also attained a dubious immortality by cashing in on the principle: "A sucker is born every minute," although he may have underestimated the birth rate. But these two entertainers were artists in the "Yankee slicker" tradition, and the profitable result no doubt flowed in part from admiration for fellow artists and for the egregiousness of the imposture. (As Hitler discovered, the bigger the lie the bigger the result.) Also, "Texas" Guinan and P. T. Barnum were Americans, and we take more kindly to being gulled by Americans than by foreigners.

Uncle Sam's great experience as a sucker, and one from which he has not yet completely recovered, was his crusade in World War I. Swallowing Allied-sponsored atrocity stories, he plunged into the conflict with tremendous enthusiasm for Wilsonian idealism. But when the smoke cleared away, all his fine hopes lay in dust and ashes. The world apparently had been made safe for only the unspeakable Turk and other aggressors.

The experiences of our doughboys in France had not been altogether happy, what with manure piles near the cottages, overcharging by French shopkeepers (as though Americans never overcharged *), and the canard

---

* Nathan and Mencken recorded it as a part of the American credo in 1921: "As soon as the American Army landed in France half of the men in each French company were allowed to go home to help the wives swindle the Americans."

that we were forced to pay rent for the trenches in which we fought for French liberties (and incidentally our own). The boys had gone abroad thinking that the French wore wings and the Germans horns. After seeing the clean cities of the German Rhineland, and after fraternizing with the friendly *Fräuleins,* who resembled typical American blondes at home, the lads in khaki were not so sure they had fought on the right side. (And some were saying the same thing again after World War II.)

We at least had the hollow satisfaction of knowing that we had won the war. Yet within a short time the British Marshal Haig was saying in England (for home consumption) that the British would have muddled through all right without our intervention. "Gosh!" exclaimed the New York *Sun.* "How we wish they had!"

We wanted nothing from the peace conference but peace, and the world was not given that. We got a treaty which we would not ratify, a League which we would not join, debts which we could not collect, and dictators more menacing than the Kaiser. We asked for no territory except the six feet of ground in which each of our dead soldiers slept his last sleep, and we did not even own that. Yet our Allies made off with oil-rich prizes in the guise of mandates, while they sought to saddle us with trouble-rich liabilities like Armenia. "Unto the victors belong the oils," remarked one South Carolina newspaper. We asked for no reparations (except later for the cost of maintaining our Rhineland army of occupation), although we did not seem to realize that the devastated countries of Europe really needed them. "About all that America got out of Europe," remarked another Southern journal, "was its army."

3

Not content with having been "slickered" by his friends, Uncle Sam was gullible enough to be suckered by his old enemies. He and the Allies confiscated Germany's merchant fleet, which meant that the Germans were forced to build speedy new ships that could successfully compete with anything afloat. In 1921 the Berlin government inflated its currency, and the gambling-minded Yankee, not unwilling to turn an unearned penny, lost millions of dollars by buying depreciated marks which were rapidly forced into astronomical worthlessness.

During the feverish 1920's American banking houses, for profitable commissions and without too scrupulous a regard for security, invested in Germany hundreds of millions of dollars entrusted to their care. The Germans used the money in part to pay reparations to the Allies, and the Allies in turn used our money to pay their war-debt installments to us—a robbing-Peter-to-pay-Paul process which lasted until the financial crash of 1929 dried up even Uncle Sam's fabulous coffers. Then the merry-go-round jolted to a complete stop. But more important, huge American private loans to our former enemy enabled her to rebuild, modernize, and perfect the vast industrial machine with which Hitler rode roughshod over Europe and came within a hair's breadth of extinguishing the lights of western civilization.

At least we had the satisfaction in 1917–1918 of knowing that we had gone into the conflict to curb an atrocity-mad monster, who had deliberately provoked the war for diabolical purposes, and who was determined to enslave us. Gradually, through firsthand observation and otherwise, it dawned on us that the German atrocities had been greatly exaggerated. Arthur Ponsonby and others demolished the myths of the crucified Canadian and of the Belgian babes with their hands cut off, to single out two of the better known horror tales. Actually, without prompt and expert medical attention, such treatment would have caused the babies to bleed to death. Then we realized how completely we had been taken into camp by Lord Bryce and others who had lied dutifully and patriotically for flag and country.

In the 1920's a group of historical scholars, of whom Harry Elmer Barnes was a leading spirit, began to demonstrate from the documents that Germany was not solely responsible for the coming of the war, whatever her degree of "guilt" might have been.

Long before the decade ended it was clear that Uncle Sam, the proverbially shrewd horse trader, had been played for a sucker by both his associates and his enemies. The Nye investigation of the 1930's merely sowed seeds of doubt on a field well fertilized with disillusionment. We had been gulled once; we would not be gulled again.

Then came the Hitlerian beast. When farsighted observers raised the cry of "Wolf!" the American people responded by burying their heads deeper in the sands. We had heard that alarm once before in connection with the Kaiser. We had become overdisillusioned to such an extent that we swung the pendulum too far in the other direction. As late as 1944, when we had invaded Germany and secured ample photographic evidence of the horror camps at Buchenwald and Belsen, only three fourths of the American people were willing to accept these reports as true. On the whole, the atrocities of World War II were probably underplayed rather than overplayed.

4

Uncle Sam was annoyed but not deeply concerned by getting nothing out of the peace conference; he was disturbed but not profoundly distressed when at the Washington Conference of 1921–1922 he agreed to scrap splendid new battleships nearing completion so that the world (and we) might have a disarmament that never came. To some extent he was reconciled to the not altogether flattering conclusion, usually attributed to the cowboy humorist-philosopher Will Rogers: "This country has won every war, but lost every conference."

But the thing that really rankled with Americans was having been defrauded of some $10,000,000,000 in war loans by their friends. The average citizen is inclined to concede that in international diplomacy he is something of an innocent abroad, but when it comes to money matters he is a pretty sharp fellow. He prides himself on his ability to spurn a bargain in a gilded brick or the Brooklyn Bridge.

The mental picture that we have regarding the debts, in so far as we have any clear picture at all, is something like this. After we "rushed" into World War I to save the skins of the quarrelsome Allies (and our own), we found that our new comrades-in-arms needed cash. So we shoveled some $10,000,-000,000 worth of gold dollars into barrels, rolled them down gangplanks, and shipped them across to France, England, Italy, and other bankrupt associates. (Actually, about one fourth of the sum was for post-Armistice reconstruction, and much of this went to countries other than former Allies.)

When the guns grew cold, our erstwhile friends, instead of returning the barrels full of dollars, began to spend a large share of their income on armaments which, we felt, would only lead to another war that we would be called upon to finance and fight. "European nations could make more progress in paying for the last war," remarked the Washington *Post* in 1923, "if they would stop spending for the next one."

Anyhow, we were sure that we had been cheated out of our loan by a designing and dishonest coterie of defaulters. Fifteen years after the Armistice one South Carolina newspaper said: "George Washington's feat of throwing a dollar across the Potomac River isn't so hot to a generation that threw twenty billions across the Atlantic Ocean." Calvin Coolidge's tight-fisted remark: "They hired the money, didn't they?" was reechoed by Senator Vic Donahey of Ohio in 1935: "We went across, but they won't come across."

5

The true picture briefly is this. We declared war in 1917, but had no formidable army. While we were raising one, the only way we could help hold the common enemy back was by dispatching munitions and other supplies of war. We did not send great quantities of gold at all; the French could not shoot the Germans with gold dollars. We advanced huge credits to the Allied purchasing agents, and they in turn bought the essential supplies. While our army was being cumbersomely drafted and trained (it took more than a year), the French gave their lives (with American arms) in holding back the foe; we for the most part gave our dollars, or rather extended the credits.

When the shooting ceased, we stubbornly refused to forgive the Allies their debt if the Allies would forgive the Germans a substantial part of the desired reparations. We insisted that our erstwhile associates not only pay us back, but pay us back the principal in full, although we were willing to adjust interest charges to presumed capacity to pay. This amounted in all cases to a large reduction of what we were entitled to claim at the original

5 per cent interest. For example, 60.3 per cent of the entire French obligation was wiped out when the interest rate was set at 1.6 per cent.

Britain was the first of the great powers to come to terms, in 1923; France the last, in 1926. The French did not sign the agreement until Washington had brought various types of pressure to bear on them, including an official frowning on private loans from the United States. The reluctance of the French evoked caustic criticism from the American press. "When we helped France in the war," said Hearst's New York *American,* "she said she owed us a debt which she could never repay. It begins to look as if she meant it." The final approval of the debt-funding agreement by France was accompanied by many demonstrations of bitterness, including a parade of crippled war veterans and economic discrimination against the United States. "The French have reluctantly ratified the debt agreement," reported the *New Yorker.* "This does not mean, however, that they will ever forgive us for lending them the money."

Several years later, in 1932, when the depression had struck, and the United States had declined to reduce the war debts, a Parisian daily sneered: "Americans are the only race which passed directly from barbarism to decadence without knowing civilization." Before the year was out, France and five other debtor nations defaulted outright. The American humor magazine *Judge* paraphrased a popular song: "Fifty million Frenchman can't be wrung!"

The point of view of the French was not understood or appreciated in America. When the war ended, the French did not ask for the blood of their young manhood back, and they felt that Uncle Sam should not ask for his money back—money that they had never received, money that had been spent in America to fatten American war profiteers, money that had swelled the United States Treasury (in excess profits taxes), and money that had enriched the American people generally. Yet America counted her lost dollars, while France counted her dead. The Allies had borrowed not gold but goods, goods that had been shot off at a common enemy. Repayment was possible only in services and merchandise (there was not enough gold available in Europe), yet Uncle Sam in the 1920's and 1930's erected ruinously high tariff barriers. He could not see that the French had a strong moral position; they had been devastated and decimated in holding back the German foe for three years in a war which we finally recognized was ours all along.

As for spending money on armaments, the French had a powerful case. Wilson had promised them security, but the Senate had repudiated his commitments and left France naked to a vengeful "Hun." She had no recourse but to spend her money on armament. Does anyone expect a city to give up its police department so that it can make payments on defaulted bonds?

But whatever the moral issues, the American voter was intelligent enough to recognize that if his government cancelled the outstanding debts, he would have to dig down into his dungarees and come up with the equivalent to reimburse the Treasury. One newspaper realistically urged all citizens who favored cancellation to mail in their Liberty Bonds. We felt that we had been big enough suckers already without throwing away all hope of repayment, and our government in Washington could not do other than obey the will of the people.

Not even one citizen in ten approved outright cancellation in 1937, and late in 1938 nearly five in ten favored collection in full. On the eve of Hitler's invasion of Poland, only three voters in ten would support loans to our fellow democracies, Britain and France. We feared that the money would never be repaid, and that it would only draw us into a new conflict. "We gave them gold in the last war and got brickbats in return," said an Indiana coaldealer. "Why lend them money again when they would only drag us into a fight?"

6

The amount of ill will stirred up by the debt imbroglio is simply incalculable. We may not have rolled barrels of dollars down the wharves, but we did receive back hogsheads of hate. The Europeans called us names, and we called them names in return, with the name-calling mounting to a crescendo. By one of the ironies of history we began to feel much more kindly toward our fallen foe than toward our contentious associates. The debt controversy probably did more than anything else in the 1920's to condition our minds for the ostrich isolationism of the 1930's.

In the eyes of Europeans, Uncle Sam the savior became Uncle Shylock, and he was repeatedly bracketed with Shakespeare's pound-of-flesh Jewish money lender. In America the rejoinder was that Shylock did not get his money either; he was talked out of his loan, both principal and interest, by a tricky lawyer. In 1933 a Georgia newspaper urged that when Europe came over again with tin cup outstretched we should be Shy enough to Lock the Treasury. And when during the Great Depression we forced the debtors to default, another Southern newspaper said: "Old Uncle Sam would rather be regarded as a Shylock than a busted Santa Claus." This at least was more in accord with American tradition.

The debt embroilment also aroused distrust as to the future designs of the European countries on the United States Treasury. American newspapers said in 1921 that the only American book "supremely popular" in Europe was "Uncle Sam's pocketbook"; in 1923, that we had become a leading member of the "League of Donations"; in 1928, that Europe counted too much on being "Yank-ed out of economic difficulties"; in 1932, that our being expected to "succor" Europe suggested too strongly "sucker"; in 1933, that whenever an international conference met "to get at the bottom of things, one of the things is Uncle Sam's pocket."

The conviction gradually took root that we had fought not in our own interests but had been "used" to pull Europe's chestnuts out of the fire; and this general state of mind did not promote a healthy internationalism. In 1926 an Iowa newspaper declared: "All efforts of Europe to make us believe it was our war and they came in to help us out will prove unavailing." In the same vein a Pittsburgh journal opined: "We used to brag that we won the World War for Europe. It now develops that's whom we did win it for, but we no longer brag about it."

The American taxpayer cannot be blamed for wanting to collect all or a substantial part of the sums advanced; any other people would have taken the same stand. But we put ourselves in a bad light when we erected tariff walls to keep out goods, while demanding payment in unavailable gold, of which we already possessed most of the world's supply.*

Another unhappy by-product was that Europe began to blame the United States for many of her troubles. There can be no doubt that our narrow economic nationalism contributed to the continuing distress of Europe, and hence indirectly to the rise of Hitler. But there can also be no doubt that Europe would have gone about the task of reconstruction with more energy and persistence if she had not had such a convenient scapegoat in Uncle Shylock. In 1925 one American newspaper concluded that the nearest Europe had yet come to agreement was "to blame everything on the United States."

Another by-product of the debt misunderstanding was the feeling among many of the more ignorant Americans that since Europe had fought World War I with our money she would not be able to fight World War II (and drag us into it) if we withheld our money. The isolationists naturally united to support the Johnson Act of 1934, which forbade loans to governments in default to the United States. Even after Hitler had crushed Poland, nearly seven Americans in ten were opposed to repealing this somewhat spiteful restriction.

Late in 1939, after the outbreak of World War II, the proposal was made in Congress that we accept the West Indian islands of Britain and France in lieu of the clearly uncollectible debts. The isolationist Senator Lundeen of Minnesota even came forward with the sporting proposition that we take advantage of the preoccupations of our former Allies and seize the islands outright. Such strong-arm suggestions received scant public support, but nearly seven out of ten Americans favored the islands-for-debts scheme, not so much because we wanted more Caribbean liabilities, as because we believed that otherwise we would never get anything. At the same time isolationist Senator Clark of Missouri proposed that June 15, when the debt installments were due, be set aside as "Keep-Us-out-of-War Day," which would be devoted to national meditation and prayer regarding the unpaid debts and kindred matters. The lessons of the debts were clearly in view when Franklin Roosevelt sought to eliminate the dollar sign from the Lend-

---

* Mussolini in his speech declaring war on the democracies, June 10, 1940, referred bitterly to the nation which had a "monopoly" on "all the gold on earth." This jealousy was a strong ingredient in European hatred of the United States.

Lease Act of 1941. We accepted reverse Lend-Lease, and otherwise wrote off a part of the obligation. But while we were avoiding some of the absurdities of the debt imbroglio, we still clung in some measure to the Coolidgean grocery-store idea that international loans are just a matter of "hiring money."

7

The canny American is most apt to be a sucker regarding conditions in overseas lands beyond his ken. We have shown the Englishman's penchant for meddling with abuses abroad, from Ireland to India to China, and we are prone to sympathize with the underdog in all foreign places. Distance and ignorance seem to lend a large amount of enchantment. "Our national policy of aloofness from Europe," wrote an Ohio newspaper in 1923, "is the harder to understand on account of our national policy of butting in on everything else."

Civilized nations have been defined as those that simply cannot endure wrongs or injustices except at home, which is another way of putting the Chinese proverb: "The path of duty lies in what is near, but men seek it in what is remote." We have frequently raised our bejeweled hands in horror at conditions abroad, while completely unable to see our own sharecroppers and slums.* The heart of Andrew Carnegie bled for the poor downtrodden Filipinos, while he seems not to have felt similar pangs for the ignorant South European immigrants who sweated for a twelve-hour day in the blast furnaces of Pittsburgh.

Little harm is ordinarily done by our sentimental attachment to the cause of the downtrodden abroad, or by our uncritical acceptance of their story. But sometimes the reverse has been true. To choose only a few examples, our devotion to the cause of Ireland embroiled relations with England for well over a century; our championing the underdog cause of Venezuela in her dispute with Britain in 1895 almost resulted in conflict; our building up of China during World War II as a great democracy merely paved the way for saddening disillusionment; and our interference in the insoluble problem of India during the same years only strained relations with our wartime British ally.

Suckers may do damage in two ways. They can rush into things they ought to stay out of, and they can stay out of things they ought to rush into, for fear they might be deceived. The whole problem is linked with ignorance, for the more ignorant a man is the more apt he is to be the dupe of the propagandist, the more sure he is of his ability to solve the difficulties of others, and the less able he is to see the viewpoint of other nations.

* In 1929 a newspaper published in Peking, China, said: "Fifty million Americans who heartily approve of Jim Crow laws are shocked at tales of caste distinctions in India."

CHAPTER SIXTEEN

DOLLARS AND IDEALISM

"Civilization and profits go hand in hand."—CALVIN COOLIDGE, 1920

———

1

SHORTLY BEFORE the middle of the nineteenth century, the British philosopher and economist, John Stuart Mill, referred unpleasantly to the United States as a land where "the life of one sex is devoted to dollar hunting, and of the other to the breeding of dollar hunters." The pursuit of the almighty dollar has long been something of an obsession, partly because in America there were more dollars to be pursued—and the race was to the swift. The American also worships the goddess Success, and money is unquestioned proof of his devotion. We are in fact quick to admit this failing, if it is a failing. Mr. Dooley (Finley Peter Dunne), in describing the patriotism of the people of the sixth ward, once remarked: "They love th' eagle on the back iv a dollar."

We may have a reputation for money-grubbing, but despite a certain congenital callousness, we are not the most indifferent of peoples to the sufferings of our neighbors. In any cross section of any population one will find the greedy and the selfish, the generous and the unselfish. The humanitarian standards of a nation cannot be expected to rise above the level of its melting pot, but in some measure we have defied the laws of physics.

The truth is that our national conduct, with a few notable lapses, has on the whole been honorable, at least on a relative basis. The infant United States started with a clean slate in 1776, and was not bound by the precedents of deviousness that had so long characterized monarchical courts. No other major power publishes its diplomatic documents so completely and recently, and no other great foreign office permits scholars such unrestricted access to relatively current archives. Partly because of our democratic professions, the world has come to expect a higher standard of conduct in Washington than elsewhere. A thinly disguised coup like Theodore Roosevelt's "taking" of Panama, which would have passed almost unnoticed among European imperialists at the turn of the century, was received with raised eyebrows in foreign capitals. Most right-thinking Americans were aware of this at the time, and were distressed that the good name of their country should have been blackened with the brush of Old World intrigue.

2

If it is true that we have an international conscience more sensitive than that of some other nations, what is the explanation?

First of all, many of the early settlers in America, especially those who came to Massachusetts, were idealists and reformers, willing to risk their lives in the New World wilderness for their religious convictions. Other pioneers came in response to economic motives, or a commingling of economic and other-worldly motives, but there was undeniably a strong idealistic leaven which in some degree has persisted to the present.

Secondly, there was the frontier tradition of logrolling, which in its original sense meant helping one's neighbor to roll his logs into place for his cabin. The pioneer was a bootstrap-pulling individualist, but in tasks clearly beyond his strength he turned to neighborhood cooperation. A British traveler in the 1830's was impressed when two American passers-by stopped to help extricate a wagon from the mud, and on departing refused to accept any pay for their backbreaking services.

Thirdly, the absence of powerful enemies on our borders enabled us to expand without the apprehensions and hates which for centuries have blighted the more crowded peoples of Europe. Not having been tutored in the harsh school of experience, we were inclined to think well of other nations until the contrary was proved, sometimes under disagreeable if not highly dangerous circumstances. Having been blessed with the birthright of an empty continent, and not having felt either the propulsive pressure of population or the compulsive pull of raw materials, we developed a live-and-let-live philosophy which was not commonly found in less favored places.

Fourthly, our huge hyphenate population has retained a strong sympathy for the welfare of the Old Country, and this group alone has kept alive an unusual responsiveness to the sufferings of overseas lands.

Fifthly, by the accident of birth we were endowed with vastly more material wealth than other peoples, and as a consequence we could give without hurting ourselves. Not only is it easier for the rich to be generous, but wealth, as Woodrow Wilson pointed out, conferred upon us fortunate Americans a special obligation to help others. Yet the ideal of *richesse oblige* or *noblesse oblige* did not take deep root in America of the 1920's.

Sixthly, especially in the nineteenth century we were young in heart and so ignorant of world conditions as to find it difficult to resist idealistic impulses. Lord Bryce observed that the tired and cynical Frenchman or Britisher responded much less quickly to a noble or pathetic cause than his transatlantic kinsfolk. The undisillusioned American, not appreciating the cost, was more eager to make over the world along decent, American lines. His reforming zeal may in part have come also from colonial New England, which was settled in considerable measure by protesting Puritans. We lost many of our illusions and much of our naïveté after the experience of World War I, and to some extent after World War II, but there is still a substantial residuum of idealism left.

Finally, we enjoy a larger degree of popular control over foreign affairs than any other great power, and for this reason our idealistic impulses have been allowed freer rein.

3

American history may be written largely in terms of crusades, both at home and abroad. The United States in fact is a crusade, a centuries-old crusade for democracy and the freedom of the individual.

The Civil War was largely the result of prolonged antislavery agitation, and was itself a campaign for the Union on the one hand, and for Southern self-determination on the other. It was a singing war, with the mighty "Battle Hymn of the Republic" leading the list, and with God on the side having the better songs. The inspired struggle finally bogged down in the bungling, brutality, and boodle of Reconstruction.

The brush with Spain in 1898—John Hay's "splendid little war"—was also a crusade, this time to free Cuba, and also a singing war, with "There'll Be a Hot Time in the Old Town Tonight" leading the popularity parade. Before fighting began, the Cuban propagandists in the United States opposed the efforts of President McKinley to secure relief for suffering Cuba; they were counting on continuing misery to stir the well known humanitarian impulses of the American people into a war of intervention. The slump came when we wound up some 10,000 miles away shooting Filipinos, administering the water cure to them, and putting them in concentration camps that strongly resembled those of the Spaniard "Butcher" Weyler in Cuba. In 1902 the Chicago *Record-Herald* jibed: "The war in the Philippines has cost the United States over $170,000,000 thus far. But think of the glory!"

The struggle against imperialism at the turn of the century was a crusade, albeit a fruitless one. How could self-abnegation and idealism win in a contest with imperial glory and the wealth of the Far East. Many of the antiimperialists were heirs of the abolitionists—Old Guard Republicans who had voted for Lincoln in the days of their youth and who believed that they were holding aloft the ancient antislavery banner. Some of the imperialists regretted that Congress, in the flush of idealism, had proclaimed to the world that Cuba would be given her freedom; now we would have to honor the bond. "What a pity we did not keep Cuba and let the Philippines find another owner," remarked a Southern newspaper several years later.

World War I, though a bit slow in gathering momentum, was a tremendous crusade, and it produced great songs, with "Over There" the most pulse-tingling. Nothing could be more glorious than a war to end war and to make the world safe for democracy. In the months that followed the Armistice, our doubts increased as to what the world had been made safe for, and the whole crusade degenerated into the confusion, double talk, cowardice, and scandals of the Harding administration. There seems to be a kind of political law of gravitation: the higher the idealism the greater the subsequent disillusionment. There is a corollary law: a nation is able to key itself up to a high pitch for only a relatively short time, and then reaction sets in. "One characteristic of American idealism," sadly remarked the Berlin *Zeit* in 1922, "is the fact that it often fails to function over long periods."

4

World War II was in no sense a gigantic crusade, at least as compared with World War I. No truly great song came out of this earth-girdling conflict, although the somewhat silly "Praise the Lord and Pass the Ammunition" had a brief vogue. We did not whip ourselves into a blind fury, but did our killing methodically, scientifically, and cold-bloodedly.

Unpalatable though the thought may be, the misled Nazis developed much more fanatical enthusiasm than the Americans. We might have been able to work ourselves up to a mild frenzy, or at least to a real spirit of self-sacrifice (which was notoriously weak), if we had not been so thoroughly in the grip of the sucker complex that developed after World War I. We almost certainly would have gone at the task with more zeal if we had only had a clear idea of what we were fighting for rather than against. Many Americans were the slaves of sheer negativism: they were fighting to get it over with; to turn back the hands of the clock to 1939, as though the past were not dead beyond all hope of resurrection. Others were waging war purely in defense of their liberties. At best, they were fighting not so much to make the world safe for democracy as to make it safe against dictatorship.

Franklin Roosevelt was aware of this weakness, and sought suggestions more inspiring than "World War II" or the "Second World War," both of which were numerical, mechanical, and much too suggestive of the disillusionment and betrayal of Number One. He himself favored "Survival War," although one anti-New Deal journalist cynically suggested "My War."

Dr. Gallup, taking the cue from Roosevelt, asked the American people in April, 1942, what they would suggest, aside from "Second World War" or World War II." The results are further proof of negativism and confusion.

War of World Freedom	26%
War of Freedom	14
War of Liberty	13
Anti-Dictator War	11
War for Humanity	9
Survival War	7
The People's War	6
Anti-Nazi War	5
Total War	5
War of Liberation	4

None of these suggestions took hold, and we continued with unimaginative and uninspiring number two.

If we had fought World War II with more idealism and dynamism, we might have displayed more dash but less efficiency. Blind devotion or rage may in the long run prove disastrous; modern conflicts have to be waged with unclouded vision. It is perhaps better to have fewer ideals than to key one's self up for unattainable ideals. War has two phases: the fighting duration and the peace duration, and we must "pace" ourselves so as to take both in stride. If we key ourselves up too fanatically for the first, we may suffer a corresponding let down as we approach the second, with consequent harm to enduring peacemaking.

In World War I we overdid idealism; in World War II we underdid idealism. In 1941 we were much more sophisticated and cynical than in 1917. Even so, we were somewhat disillusioned, although we did not have so far to slump as in 1919–1920.Our faith in Chinese "democracy" suffered a severe jolt before the bombing stopped, and our somewhat synthetic faith in Russia's willingness to cooperate was still harder hit. Even before the war jolted to an end, the belief was strong that there would be another gigantic conflict in twenty-five or fifty years. Perhaps it is better to prepare for a holocaust that never comes, than to wish away one that is coming.

5

The wealthy American has often responded commendably to the needs of suffering and stricken people all over the world. To some few of us the mental picture of a child starving in China is about as vivid as a child starving before our eyes. But the great mass of us have less active imaginations, and ten Americans killed in a railroad wreck seem more important than ten thousand Chinese dying seven thousand miles away.

A partial list of noteworthy American relief activities would include Hoover's work in Belgium during World War I; the $100,000,000 voted by Congress in 1919 for the aid of needy Europeans; and the famine relief for Russia from 1921 to 1923. American conservatives could feel little real enthusiasm for succoring starving Bolsheviks, and one Dallas newspaper spoke sneeringly of "soup to nuts." The Tokyo Earthquake of 1923 was the greatest God-made disaster in history, and although some of our jingoes expressed satisfaction at the weakening of a potential foe, the response of the United States was prompt and generous. The American quota was oversubscribed by three million dollars, and this surplus was used to build and endow a hospital in Tokyo. The building was dedicated with an inscription that made strange reading after Pearl Harbor.

In recent years we had relief drives for the Spanish Loyalists; bowls-of-rice campaigns for the Chinese; Bundles for Britain; and the preponderant share of responsibility for UNRRA during and following World War II. American bumper grain crops in 1945–1947 saved countless hundreds of thousands of lives, and Herbert Hoover, the famed humanitarian of two wars, was again drafted into service.

Even though our record in relief enterprises has been noteworthy, it is not as good as it might have been, or as befitted our wealth and bulging storehouses. The widow who gave her mite was judged not by what she gave but by what she had left. In the autumn of 1942, four Americans in ten thought that at the end of the war there would be a "moral responsibility" on the United States to see to it that every person in the world was well fed. Considering the "whole world" inclusiveness of this question, the response seems astonishingly good. But we must remember that we were then in the midst of war; that we had Allies and some pleasant illusions regarding them; and that public opinion pollees often want to appear in the best possible light.

Our humanitarian impulses have been chilled on occasion by the ingratitude of our beneficiaries. We forget that unalloyed and lasting gratitude is a rare thing in international relations. Nations are individuals in the mass, and we ought to know enough about human nature to realize that few individuals feel altogether happy as the objects of charity. No one is going to shoot Santa Claus, as Al Smith once said, but the recipients of presents from Uncle Sam's capacious pack are apt to have mixed emotions.

We heard the customary complaints in connection with the relief that we supplied to a starving world in 1945–1947. We did not send enough, we did not send it soon enough, we should have sent more (we are the most notoriously overstuffed people in the world), we should have sent food of a different kind, and we gave it under the wrong conditions. (Moscow was displeased when we sought to force Soviet-controlled areas to admit American observers, so that we could determine whether the supplies were being used to promote Russian ideology.) Finally, the rich and grasping Americans were regarded as Shylocks if they expected anything in return, even gratitude. The ultimate came in 1946 when the Communist press of Czechoslovakia was inveighing against American dollar imperialism at the same time that the Czechoslovakian government was seeking to negotiate a large loan from the United States. The officials in Washington were human enough to bring an abrupt halt to the discussions. "General dislike for America," noted the Washington *Post* some years earlier, "doesn't prevent the other nations from coming around at feeding-time."

Actually, we have never given "until it hurt." We waste enough food annually to feed tens of thousands of starving people, and our charity consists of only a relatively small part of our overflow. Yet even on this scale we weary of well-doing, and on the whole we do not give at all if our donations inconvenience us too much, or cost too much, or run afoul of our prejudices. We are so well fed that we simply cannot conceive of starvation. This is perfectly natural, and there is no reason to believe that if we were hungry and the Europeans were well fed their attitude would be markedly different from ours. The parable of the Good Samaritan is noteworthy because the Samaritan went above and beyond the simple call of humanity; too many people are prone to pass by on the other side.

6

We have often wavered between a humanitarian impulse to be helpful and a hardheaded instinct to count the cost.

Before 1919 we were outraged by the repeated massacres of Christian Armenians at the hands of the "unspeakable" Turks, and we made various attempts to aid the victims of Moslem brutality. But when Wilson urged the Senate to accept a League of Nations mandate for Armenia, we would have none of it. Such a responsibility would involve millions of dollars, tens of thousands of homesick soldiers, embroilment with the European powers, and a departure from our isolationist tradition. We would support a few missionaries in Armenia, dole out some bread and old clothes, and ship over cartloads of sympathy. We felt kindly toward the Armenians, but at long range. We suspected also that the late Allies were handing us the dirty end of the stick: they had made off with oil-rich mandates in the Near East, leaving us with devastated Armenia. One Chicago newspaper was sure that Armenia would not find a desirable foster parent "until she discovers oil or something." Whether or not we should have shouldered the mandate is here irrelevant: the point is that when real cost and trouble enter into the humanitarian picture, our people instinctively tend to draw back. Many of us prefer a preach-and-run policy.°

In 1940, when it was proposed to evacuate large numbers of children from the beleaguered British islands, Dr. Gallup found that about six in ten Americans were willing to allow British and French women and children to find a haven in America until the war was over. When the pollees were asked whether they would take one or more of these refugees into their homes for the duration, the six in ten dropped at once to fewer than three in ten. The figure probably would have fallen even lower if the theoretical situation had become a practical one, for we would have been confronted at once with such questions as personal income, overcrowding, and the character of the children.

The Jewish problem over the years has presented similar difficulties. We have traditionally protested against anti-Semitic persecutions abroad, and we were scandalized by the Nazi excesses of the 1930's. We urged strong diplomatic action by Washington, but we were much less favorable to a proposed boycott of German goods. Boycotts are two-edged swords, and they hurt business. During the period of World War II, we were unwilling

° When we abandoned Europe after World War I, a British cartoon showed rich Uncle Sam urging tattered Europa to try harder. "Giving Europe moral support," said the Sioux City *Journal* in 1922, "is much like standing on the bank and cheering the fellow who is yelling for a rope."

to admit hordes of refugee Jews and other displaced persons, even on a temporary basis: they would aggravate problems of unemployment, housing, and public support. Let Canada or Australia or South America shoulder the burden. We are human enough to prefer long-range and piecemeal charity—piety without responsibility.

7

The attitude of the nation toward Nazi Germany and Japan during the period of World War II provides a revealing commentary on our humanity.

In the early stages of the fighting a majority of Americans were not willing to crush Germany, just Naziism; and in 1944, when we were deep in the conflict, a substantial majority favored a reasonably humane treatment of Germany, even to the extent of helping her get her industries going.

In 1943 our people were asked their preferences regarding food shipments if the Germans were starving at the end of the conflict. Only 16 per cent opposed selling, exchanging, or giving supplies of foodstuffs, and a surprising total of 39 per cent favored outright gifts if necessary. We felt a good deal more bitter toward the almond-eyed Japanese, our presumed racial inferiors, whose sneak attack at Pearl Harbor had humiliated us, and whose atrocities against Americans had been widely publicized. Three out of ten would send no food at all, while at the opposite extreme the same number would give it outright if the Japanese had no money. Even discounting the disposition of the pollee to appear moral, and taking into consideration the current war hatreds, these figures spoke well for our humanitarian impulses.

In 1943 eight out of ten Americans favored local food rationing at home for five years more in order to help the hungry peoples of other countries, which included enemy as well as occupied nations. Yet the Truman administration, when the war ended, took hasty steps to end rationing, while much of the rest of the world began to slide toward the abyss of starvation. The war-weary citizen no doubt wanted a removal of the restrictions on food, but on the other hand he was not so lacking in sensibility as to be willing to wax fat while millions of people died. Yet once rationing was lifted, the administration perceived that a return to food controls would be both awkward and politically inexpedient. Presidential leadership of the highest type might have caused the people to measure up to their responsibilities in a more becoming manner.

No less significant was the attitude of the voter toward poison gas and the atomic bomb.

In 1944 Dr. Gallup asked if the American people would approve showering poison gas on civilian centers if such attacks would shorten hostilities. A surprising total of 76 per cent disapproved using it on the Germans; 71 per cent on the Japanese. The question was more heavily weighted in 1945 when the respondents were asked how they would vote if resorting to poison gas would reduce casualties among American troops. Five out of ten were still unfavorable. We not only regarded gas as inhuman, but we were aware that the enemy had large supplies and would no doubt reply in kind.

The atomic bomb was inconceivably more destructive and perhaps more inhumane in its lingering effects than any known poison gas, and since we alone had it there was apparently no possibility of reprisals. Besides, our forces had dropped it not on the Germans but on the Japanese, whom we then regarded as only a little higher than the apes. After the initial explosion at Hiroshima, Dr. Gallup found that 85 per cent of our people—a tremendous majority for any question—favored the use of the new bomb on other Japanese cities. A few weeks later a poll under different auspices showed the following results: °

1. I would have refused to use it on their cities at all.   4%
2. I would have first shown how powerful it was by dropping it where there were no people so Japanese leaders could have watched it from a distance, and then used it on their cities if they didn't surrender.   27
3. I would have used it on one city at a time until they surrendered.   43
4. I would have tried to wipe out as many cities as possible before they had a chance to surrender.   24
5. Undecided.   2

The American people are not so brutal as this table indicates. They did not then understand the aftereffects of the bomb; they had been embittered by Japanese atrocities; and they were anxious to bring the war to a speedy end (a war which they believed had been forced upon them) without the further loss of American boys.

8

The Washington government has on occasion done some self-denying or even altruistic deeds. Most of them can be explained on the basis of self-interest, but this is not true in all cases.

In the roaring, mid-century days of Manifest Destiny we might have seized much more territory than we did, but failed to do so, partly because we had some regard for international decency, and partly because we did not want to aggravate the slavery controversy. In 1846–1848, after Mexico was unwilling to accept $25,000,000 for California and intermediate territory, we provoked her into attacking us, beat her to her knees after a series of costly campaigns, and then handed her $18,250,000 for the lands that we annexed. For the victor to pay the vanquished an indemnity is perhaps unique in the annals of nations. Some have called it the American spirit of fair play; others have branded it a guilty conscience.

In 1864 we joined in a multipower naval demonstration against the obstreperous feudal lord at Shimonoseki Strait, Japan, but we returned our

° National Opinion Research Center, *Opinion News*, Nov. 27, 1945.

share of the indemnity when we found it grossly in excess of our losses. In 1867 we took Alaska off Russia's hands for $7,200,000, not so much because we wanted it as because we felt under some obligation to the Tsar for his friendly attitude during the Civil War. In 1898 we administered a crushing defeat to Spain, but having captured Manila a few hours after the armistice was formally signed, we felt under a strong obligation to award her $20,000,000 before taking the Philippine Islands. A less scrupulous power could undoubtedly have arranged to shoulder this insular liability without having to pay handsomely for the privilege of doing so. We remitted a substantial part of the Boxer indemnity from China, growing out of the disturbances of 1900, and this generous gesture paid rich dividends in good will when the Peking government used the funds to educate Chinese students in America.

All this does not mean that other nations have never done honorable things. It does not mean that our purposes were in all cases purely or even primarily altruistic, although they may have appeared to be. Human motives seldom come unmixed, and the course of our government is generally shaped by realism, sometimes seasoned with a dash of idealism.

9

Other decisions taken in Washington have been cloaked in a mantle of helpfulness or disinterestedness, but actually they have often been motivated largely, if not primarily, by selfish considerations. Genuine self-interest is generally not reprehensible, as long as it is not gilded with hypocrisy.

The Monroe Doctrine of 1823, which ostensibly was proclaimed to save the Latin-American republics from the Holy Alliance, was actually designed to save ourselves, plus the Spanish-American markets. The seizing of the Mexican Cession territory, which we justified in part by our alleged civilizing mission, appeared to the outside world like a brazen example of Yankee land-grabbing. We declared war on Spain in 1898 primarily to free Cuba, but not without an eye to our investments, trade, health, and military security.

After the battle of Manila Bay in 1898, our first impulse was to drop the Philippines as soon as convenient, and Admiral Dewey reported that the Filipinos were more capable of self-government than the Cubans. But as the rich and undeveloped resources of the archipelago became more apparent, the capacity of the Filipinos for self-government became less evident. "The Filipino is treacherous and deceitful," observed the St. Louis *Post-Dispatch*. "Besides, we want his country." Cheered on by Kipling's "White Man's Burden," we decided to stay, though a simple promise to get out at some definite time in the near future almost certainly would have forestalled the bloody insurrection. McKinley's message to Congress has been paraphrased to read: "God direct us; perhaps it will pay." But the wealth of the Philippines did not materialize, and we found the Islands not only an expensive white elephant but a source of economic vexation during the Great Depression. As a consequence we agreed to cut them loose under terms not altogether generous to our unwanted wards. Conceived in commercial greed, our ill-begotten offspring was abandoned in commercial fear.

The so-called Open Door of John Hay, though apparently enunciated out of concern for the poor heathen Chinese, was prompted largely by solicitude for American trade. Our merchants did not want to be elbowed out of the foreign leaseholds in China. We shipped enormous quantities of munitions to the Allies in 1914–1917, and practically none to the Germans, who did not control the sea. An embargo on all arms exports was strongly urged by many humanitarian-minded Americans, vociferously seconded by the German-Americans. But all attempts in that direction failed. We were more sympathetic with the Allies than with the Germans; international law did not forbid the sale of arms—and besides the business paid handsomely. We entered the conflict in 1917, not so much to rescue the Allies as to fight for our own rights and security. Even in 1939, after war had broken out in Europe, a sizeable minority of Americans were willing to sell arms to Hitler as well as to the democracies if the embargo should be lifted.

In 1903 Theodore Roosevelt did Colombia a grave wrong by acting as a midwife in the Caesarian seizure of the Canal Zone, but we resisted all efforts to solace her with pecuniary balm. For more than fifteen years the ex-Rough Rider loudly asserted that Colombia had been a bandit blocking the highway of civilization, and that any indemnity would be paid over his dead body, which is almost literally what happened. After he was laid to his well earned rest, we began to see a new light. Oil was gushing from the soil of Colombia, and the more the oil gushed, the more tears of remorse gushed from the eyes of American oil promoters, whose reception in Colombia was definitely chilly. Congress in 1921 voted a gift of $25,000,000, without a definite expression of regret, but that much money is an eloquent apology in any language.

The list could be lengthened, but our generous actions have often been generously diluted with selfish motives. We are likely to be less idealistic when the pocket nerve is directly touched, and the "Christ and petroleum" motif has repeatedly protruded. Someone has said: "We are an idealistic people and we'll make any sacrifice for a cause that won't hurt business."

10

The golden rule should theoretically be as applicable to international as to personal dealings, but actually it is not. More than two thousand years ago Plato in the *Republic* suggested that the rulers of a state ought to be the only ones privileged to lie. With perhaps undue cynicism Thorstein Veblen declared in 1923 that since a nation is "in effect a licensed predatory concern," it is "not bound by the decencies of that code of law and morals that governs private conduct. To lie, to cheat, and to steal is immoral in private life but statesmanship in public life." The great Italian unifier Cavour said: "What scoundrels we would be, if we did for ourselves what we are ready to do for Italy."

Softheadedness in international dealings can well be a source of weakness rather than of strength. Champions of public morality, whether they be prohibitionists or collegiate deans, have a thankless task, and their zeal sometimes causes them to make a burning issue of a sleeping one. There is so much wickedness in the world that the longheaded statesman is often well advised to turn a blind eye toward some of it. Woodrow Wilson was the slave of his Presbyterian upbringing, and his efforts to eliminate disorder and murder from Latin-American governments degenerated into moral meddling, without wholly satisfactory results.

The conscience of the American people has to a considerable extent been in the keeping of a small but influential group of liberals, some of them professionals of the New York *Nation* or *New Republic* type. In World War I they urged the welcoming of revolution-torn Russia into the family of nations, and they cheered Wilson's Fourteen Points as the foundation stone of a fair peace. Being idealists, and seeking perfection in an imperfect world, they are generally unwilling to compromise with a half loaf, and when the Treaty of Versailles betrayed their expectations, they turned against it and found themselves bedfellows of the most reactionary groups. (An idea is not responsible for all those who embrace it.) During the 1920's the liberals sought to use the influence of American Democracy to halt Fascist aggression, and many of them were among the leaders of intervention. After Pearl Harbor, blind to the dictates of military necessity, they bitterly critized our temporary and unhappy marriages of convenience with Fascist elements. Yet in spite of their dogmatism and impracticality, the liberals have brought a strong and healthful dose of idealism to an otherwise inert body politic.

Our sentimentality in dealing with foreign peoples depends largely on our firsthand knowledge. During World War II we regarded the Japanese as much more brutal than the Germans, and their leaders much more deserving of the hemp.* Most Americans had probably never seen a real Japanese, although they had seen many Germans; and this preference for the Germans continued even after Hitler's wholesale horrors were proved to be worse than anything conjured up by the Oriental mind. Our feeling toward Nippon was affected by the race problem and the sneak attack, but one must note that the Pacific Coast, which could not be accused of loving the Japanese but which knew them as neighbors, was inclined to think better of them as human beings than the rest of the country.

* There are always some sadists in any population, and it is not surprising that late in 1944 Dr. Gallup found that 13 per cent of the people favored killing all the Japanese, adding such comments as "Sink the whole damned island." "We don't want any rising sun left to set."

We need ideals and idealism in international relations as much as bread and bases, but we must not let them run away with us. Wilson was accused of being an idealist, and he pleaded guilty. But much of his so-called idealism was farvisioned realism. The shortsighted politician who barters away a long-range advantage for a smaller shortrange gain is praised as practical, while his longer-visioned opponent is hooted out of court as a hopeless visionary. This does much to explain the tragedy of Woodrow Wilson.

CHAPTER SEVENTEEN

THE ROLE OF RELIGION

"Render to Cæsar the things that are Cæsar's, and to God the things that are God's."—MARK 12:17

1

RELIGION has always played a profoundly important part in American life. Our devotion to things of the spirit has become less intense over the years, and even though many of us are only Easter Day churchgoers, about three fourths of us belong to some denomination. Franklin Roosevelt included freedom of religion among his famed four freedoms, and in October, 1941, when seeking to arouse our people to the Nazi peril, he referred with sure instinct to a secret document which revealed that Hitler planned "to abolish existing religions."

If religion is important to us, and if foreign policy is also important to us, each is bound to have some influence on the other, for the two cannot be compartmented in our thinking. This has been true from the earliest days of the Republic. The irreligion of the French Revolution, with its obeisance to the Goddess of Reason, scandalized devout American Christians, especially those of the pro-British Federalist party, and they sought to orient our foreign policy behind the British and against the atheistical French.

A solicitor for missionary funds once asked the irascible Horace Greeley for a contribution to save millions of his "fellow creatures from going to hell." His memorable snort was: "I won't give you a damned cent. There don't half enough of them go there now." Yet this irreverent reply was not representative of our better self. The American people, with more than ordinary reforming zeal, have long interested themselves in salvation abroad. For well over a century the activities of the church in foreign fields have been of vital importance in partially offsetting our isolationist introspection, and consequently in altering the course of American diplomatic history. A few noteworthy examples will illustrate the point.

In 1820 the first contingent of New England missionaries arrived in the Polynesian paradise of Hawaii. They saved the souls of the natives from perdition by teaching them the Christian faith, and their loins from shame by clothing them with calico, which incidentally benefited the New England textile factories. Some cynic has remarked that the missionaries went out to Hawaii to do good—and did well. There is a measure of truth in this witticism, but it would be fairer to say that their sons did well. In any event the missionary enterprise flourished, aroused much interest in the Sandwich Islands (Hawaii) at home, and played a vital part in the Americanization of the archipelago. This in turn meant that eventual annexation was facili-

199

tated, and that the Paradise of the Pacific was saved from British and Japanese designs.

The activities of American missionaries in Oregon during the 1830's and 1840's, among whom Marcus Whitman is the best known, were vitally important in awakening an acquisitive interest in this far and fair land. Hundreds of pioneers poured out over the Oregon Trail to the fertile Willamette Valley, and their very presence helped persuade the British to yield the vast area south of the present Canadian border.

2

In the Far East, particularly in China, the missionaries did more to shape our basic attitudes toward foreign policy than anywhere else. China is a land of strange sights, sounds, and smells, and it is so inaccessible to the great body of Americans that our impressions regarding it are neither clear nor accurate. Much of what we learned about the Far East during the nineteenth century was brought to us by missionaries or by missionary contacts. Letters from the laborers in the vineyard, which were often widely circulated through church journals, made a deep impression, and the most reliable books on China, although revealing a natural pro-Christian bias, flowed from the pens of missionaries.

A subtle but effective form of propaganda is to induce people to contribute to a particular cause.* Where the treasure is, there the heart is also, and Americans who invested their money in Chinese missionary enterprises could not help becoming in some degree pro-Chinese.

In the 1880's, when the white people of the Pacific Coast, fearing an Oriental inundation, sought to bar their gates against Chinese coolies, many of the missionary groups took sides against their own race. The unchristianlike mass lynchings of pig-tailed Chinamen by alleged Christians in the Western states lent a certain unreality to the teachings of our earnest missionaries in China.

At the turn of the century the predatory powers of Europe were tearing leaseholds from the side of helpless China like huge hunks of blubber from a stranded whale. The missionary groups in America, which feared for their vested interest in souls, teamed up in somewhat unholy alliance with certain commercial groups, which feared for their vested interest in trade, and brought pressure upon John Hay to enunciate his famous, if somewhat futile, Open Door policy.

The soul-savers in China not only struck heavy blows at Satan, but they also struck heavy blows at a more mundane Satan—Karl Marx and his economic interpretation of history. What are the facts?

The Japanese, during the decades before Pearl Harbor, ranked near the

---

* The Americans who gave liberally to Belgian relief during World War I tended to become more pro-Ally and anti-German.

top among our import-export customers, and the Chinese near the bottom. The statement was commonly heard that America and Japan would never fight each other because their trade was reciprocally of such vital importance. Nipponese propagandists harped ceaselessly on the string that Japan's New Order would end China's disorder, and that our share of the Japanese-sponsored trade would far exceed any business we were then doing on the battlefields of China's Civil War.

On the narrow, shopkeeping basis of trade profits—at least short-run profits—we should have fought with the Japanese against the Chinese. Yet in the 1930's the Nipponese militarists ran amok in China, destroying American missions, debauching the inhabitants, and undoing the endeavors of generations. The church people in the United States, whose money and hearts had long been with the Chinese, were more influential in shaping opinion and policy against Tokyo than the relatively few American commercial houses doing business with Japan. The State Department could therefore confidently decree that international law, morality, and orderly change were paramount to mere huckstering considerations.

3

Another unholy combination of pressure groups got behind the drive to retain the Philippines in 1898, and not the least among them were the church and missionary people.

The Protestant Church almost unanimously endorsed the humanitarian war to free Cuba, and it was hardly less enthusiastic in seeking to retain the Philippines for missionary purposes. The American, with his usual ignorance of conditions in foreign lands, did not realize that, except for a relatively few Mohammedan Moros and wild tribesmen, the Filipinos had long been converted to Catholicism. The Islands were in fact the most flourishing outpost of Christianity in the Far East—actually in some ways the only flourishing outpost. But to a huge number of Protestant Americans, conversion to Catholicism was not conversion at all. The vineyard had to be recultivated under Protestant auspices, a conclusion which Catholic Americans were less willing to accept.

The clamor of the clergymen, church organizations, and church journals for potential "missionary fodder" in the Philippines was not lost on President McKinley. As a devout Methodist he was sensitive to things of the spirit; as a skillful politician he was sensitive to the rumblings of public opinion. His invalid wife, for whom he revealed a Christlike solicitude, was deeply concerned about the heathen of the Philippines. She spoke earnestly to a White House visitor about "converting the Igorrotes," and besought prayer for these naked, perdition-doomed wretches. She was probably not without influence on her tenderhearted husband.

McKinley was profoundly troubled by the whole problem, and, as he told a group of his Methodist brethren some months later, on more than one night he went down on his knees "and prayed Almighty God for light and guidance." Late one night the guidance came, presumably from God, although the clamor of the masses may have distorted the message. If one agrees with the proverb that the voice of the people is the voice of God (*vox populi, vox dei*), then it was all the same thing. McKinley, so it seems, was advised from on high that for reasons of national honor, commercial advantage, and the well-being of the Filipino people, there was no alternative but "to take them all, and educate the Filipinos, and uplift and civilize and Christianize them, and by God's grace do the very best we could for them, as our fellow men for whom Christ also died." Then McKinley went to bed and slept soundly, apparently not realizing that God is without nationality, and that He had allegedly touched upon the three main strings of the harp of imperialism.

The sacrilegious combination of Christianity and commercialism won for us the entire archipelago. Mark Hanna, the prototype of big business in politics, burst out that if to want this magnificent opportunity was commercialism, then "for God's sake let us have commercialism." Religious motives were also strong, and although they may not have predominated, the story might well have been different if we had been completely unconcerned about the fate of the Igorrotes.

4

The role of clergymen in promoting war, and in stirring their congregations to warlike impulses, is a fascinating story. With the conspicuous exception of the Quakers and perhaps the Unitarians, the ministers of the gospel, despite the turn-the-other-cheek philosophy of their great exemplar, have generally been content to go along with the popular tide, and in a number of conspicuous instances, which should not be overstressed, they have been in advance of it.

One basic reason for the bellicosity of preachers is that those of the evangelical type are professional emotionalists who have been trained to accept on faith what cannot be seen. In times of stress, when we need calmness and stability, some pulpiteers unfortunately give us hysteria and gullibility. Where human suffering abounds, and atrocity tales proliferate, as in Cuba of 1898 and Belgium of 1914, the more excitable men of the cloth, permitting the heart to rule the head, fall prey to propaganda and cry out for a righteous war.

Some of these traits appeared at an early date. During the colonial wars against the French, our Protestant clergymen stressed the defensive nature of the conflict, played up atrocity stories, emphasized the holy nature of the crusade (Protestants versus Catholics), and showed that God would not condemn Englishmen for dying in so glorious a cause. Samuel Davies, one of these impassioned divines, was regarded as the best recruiting agent in Virginia during the 1750's.

The Congregational and Presbyterian churches of New England were among the mainstays of the revolutionary movement against George III, and the pastors cried out for resistance and finally freedom. They were rather generally opposed by the Anglican (later Episcopal) clerics of the more southerly colonies. The ecclesiastics of Federalist New England thundered against President Madison's efforts in 1812 to take the nation into war against England, on the side of Napoleon, the anti-Christ. The Congregational and Unitarian churches of antislavery New England developed strong hostility to the Mexican War, while the churches of the proslavery and expansionist Southwest largely favored it.

The burning question of slavery, during the years before the Civil War, caused the congregations of both North and South to develop flexible consciences. Many Northern churches condemned the "peculiar institution" on biblical grounds, while those of the South (Garrison's "synagogues of Satan") defended it no less vehemently by appealing to the word of God. The explanation is not difficult. Congregations were (and are) bodies of people who both made and represented local opinion, and on the issue of slavery the clergyman conformed to that opinion, or refrained from antagonizing it, or preached the gospel somewhere else, or left the service of the Lord altogether. Worshipers want to hear what they want to hear.

The clergy behaved relatively well at the time of the British-Venezuela boundary crisis in 1895. Britain was a civilized nation; nothing humanitarian was involved; a war would be bloody and of uncertain outcome; and the Episcopal Church, closely related to the Church of England, could not welcome a fratricidal clash.° One exception was the chaplain of the House of Representatives, who prayed: "Heavenly Father, let peace reign throughout our borders. Yet may we be quick to resent anything like an insult to this our nation." But the Episcopal Bishop Henry C. Potter of New York condemned the jingoes as "pinchbeck patriots," and a convocation of Baptist ministers declared that the United States might better go to war to save the Christian Armenians from the infidel Turks.

The servants of God reacted with less restraint during the Cuban crisis at the end of the century. Both the Spaniards and the insurrectionists were guilty of barbarities, but we heard only the bad things about the Spaniards, whose reconcentration camps were made to order for the yellow journalists. The clergy, along with their parishioners, swallowed these lurid and exaggerated atrocity stories; and the Baptist Rev. Thomas Dixon elicited cheers from his audience when early in 1898 he sermonized against "hesitation, delay, diplomacy and idle talk." After the mysterious destruction of the

---

° Senator Walsh of Massachusetts (Catholic, Irish, and Anglophobe) attacked President Franklin Roosevelt's membership in the Episcopal Church, and when King George VI visited America in 1939, Roosevelt was criticized for worshiping with him while an Episcopal minister prayed for the king.

Maine, one Methodist minister felt it "in his bones" that the explosion was not accidental. Only the Quakers and the Unitarians opposed the war, and the Catholic Church, while not actually in opposition, was less enthusiastic than the Protestant denominations, partly because the latter made no secret of their desire to rid Catholic Cuba of the papal-monarchical influence. One Presbyterian journal declared: "And if it be the will of Almighty God, that by war the last trace of this inhumanity of man to man shall be swept away from this Western hemisphere, let it come!" The pastor of the Church of the Redeemer in Germantown (Pennsylvania) cried out that war against Spain was even more righteous than that for American independence or for Union in 1861, "because in this war we are fighting for the freedom of those who are bound to us by no other ties than those of common humanity. God bless our soldiers! God bless our sailors!"

The ministers of the gospel, no less than the rank and file, were swept off their feet by the smashing victory of Commodore Dewey at Manila Bay on May 1, 1898. On the Sunday following the glorious news, one properly patriotic preacher entitled his sermon: "The Dewey Days of May."

5

The war of 1914–1918 was a delectable dish for the professional emotionalist. The Germans violated a solemn pledge to respect the neutrality of Belgium (which they cynically called a "scrap of paper"); they marched over their helpless victims with (allegedly) a babe fixed to each bayonet; they (allegedly) mutilated children, violated women, crucified men, and used the bodies of their victims for soap; they ruined the priceless Cathedral at Rheims (which was believed to have been used by Allied military observers); they shot Nurse Edith Cavell and they sank the *Lusitania.* If ever one side had a complete monopoly on righteousness and morality, that was the side on which the Allies were fighting. Many earnest clergymen swallowed these atrocity stories uncritically, thumped the pulpit in behalf of the Allies, and thus made more palatable our final descent into the abyss.

Once we were at grips with the Kaiser and his underlings, restraint was largely thrown out the window. The clerics were not slow to call the conflict a "Holy War." The Rev. Dr. Newell Dwight Hillis, a Brooklyn Congregationalist preacher, lectured widely on German atrocities. One of his most sensational questions was: "Why do the German soldiers cut off the breasts of French and Belgian girls?" The answer was that the Hunnish satyr, after abusing the women, took this means of warning his undiseased comrades that she was now infected with syphilis. In fairness to other clergymen, it must be pointed out that Dr. Hillis was an extreme case.

The acrobatic evangelist Billy Sunday, who had forsaken the dusty paths of baseball for the sawdust trail of evangelism, screamed during 1917–1918: "If you turn hell upside down, you will find 'Made in Germany' stamped on the bottom." His "Who's Who of Hell" included Jezebel, Voltaire, Tolstoy, and the "Kaiser and his ilk."

Bracketing the Kaiser with Beelzebub was a popular pastime among even less sensational exhorters. "If the Kaiser is a Christian then the devil in hell is a Christian," and "I am an atheist" proclaimed the Rev. Cortland R. Myers, of the Baptist Temple, Brooklyn. Another minister announced that in comparison with the Kaiser, "Nero was a sanctified angel." The Rev. W. W. Bustard, pastor of John D. Rockefeller's church, said simply: "To hell with the Kaiser." In Harrisburg, Pennsylvania, according to one witness, a giant skull of the German emperor was set up and clergymen in ministerial garb outbid one another for the privilege of driving a nail into it. These men must have worshiped a wrathful Jehovah, the God of Battles, rather than the humble Galilean who was nailed to the cross.

Lyman Abbott, himself a Congregational pastor, but perhaps better known as editor of the *Outlook*, declined to pray for the Predatory Potsdam Gang: "Father, forgive them for they know not what they do." They did know what they were doing. "I hate it [Potsdam Gang] because it is a robber, a murderer, a destroyer of homes, a pillager of churches, a violater of women. I do well to hate it."

Such expressions as these, while not representative of the more sober clergymen, nevertheless expressed a typical sentiment.* One of the more restrained ministers defined the issue as "the demolition of deviltry and the dominance of democracy." But the moderates were drowned out in a tidal wave of emotionalism. Some of the more courageous clerics had the hardihood to point out that vengeance was not the spirit of Christianity, that war was organized murder, and that even our boys when in enemy country had not always behaved like Sunday School pupils on a picnic. Such sentiment might be tolerated before we actually got into the fighting, but not after. A New Jersey Unitarian-Universalist pastor, saying that he "would rather be right with Jesus Christ than with Woodrow Wilson," resigned rather than be dismissed. The rough-riding apostle of Mars, Theodore Roosevelt, struck a popular note when he cried: "The clergyman who does not put the flag above the church had better close his church and keep it closed."

6

World War I was no doubt the high-water mark in ecclesiastical extravagance regarding foreign affairs. In the cold gray dawn the clergy and the church may have felt somewhat shamefaced for their lack of balance, and in any event they shared the "slump in idealism" which swept the entire country.

* In a New England meeting, held under the auspices of the church, the speaker demanded that the Kaiser be boiled in oil when captured, whereupon the entire audience stood on chairs and screamed approval.

The League of Nations and the World Court were rather actively supported by Protestant groups, although the Catholics, with a strong German and Irish coloration, were less enthusiastic. The membership of the church contains a preponderance of the "best" and "right-thinking" people, and enjoys the leadership of the most active moralists, with the result that it has been rather more friendly to pacifism, arbitration, and internationalism than the nonreligious groups.

When Hitler unleashed the dogs of war in 1939, the clergymen and their churches refused to cut loose from their intellectual moorings, as they had done before. The Kaiser was but a pale imitation of anti-Christ when compared with Hitler, who not only encouraged wholesale barbarities against the Jews, but who also viciously attacked the church in Germany. Among American denominatioris and congregations, with some notable exceptions, there was a strong isolationist and noninterventionist undercurrent, and some of the leading religious journals were prepared to let England collapse rather than intervene. On the eve of Pearl Harbor, only 34 per cent of the entire population was willing that the ministers should discuss American participation, pro or con, from the pulpit. Church members were somewhat more favorable, and Catholics slightly less so than Protestants.

The church was merely reflecting the confused, disillusioned, and isolationist mood of the country. There was a general feeling that we had been gulled by the glorious but fruitless crusade of 1917-1918; we were afflicted by the neutrality neurosis of the 1930's; we were hoping to cherish the flame of democracy so that if the light failed in Europe it might be relighted in America. The confusion thickened when Hitler furiously attacked the "Mongol half-wits" of Russia in June, 1941. A great majority of Americans were afraid that Stalin might lose; a substantial number, chiefly Catholics, were afraid that he might win. "I have no more confidence in Stalin," declared Archbishop Curley of Baltimore, "than I have in Hitler." Dr. Gallup found that 74 per cent of the Protestants wanted the Soviets to triumph, as compared with 65 per cent of the Catholics.

After the Pearl Harbor debacle, religious groups generally took the view that the only way out was forward, but the zeal of 1917–1918 was conspicuously lacking. Six out of ten clergymen (Catholic and Protestant) agreed in 1942 that the church should actively support the war. Others felt that it should build morale and not be used as a recruiting station or a bond mart; and still others looked upon the temple of the Lord as the hope of a lasting peace. Right-thinking churchmen threw themselves behind the drive to fashion a new world organization, and their influence was potent in sweeping away such opposition as developed in the Senate. But generally the church reflected the doubt and cynicism of the masses regarding a complete elimination of the man-made curse of war.

7

The Catholic Church, as previously noted, did not become a real power in American foreign affairs until the number of its communicants was enormously increased by the South European immigration near the end of the nineteenth century. Before this time Roman Catholicism had been largely identified with immigrants from Ireland, and to a lesser extent with non-Lutheran Germans. It had also become identified with the Democratic party, which, as the antiaristocratic champion of the forgotten man, not only rolled out the welcome mat for the lowly immigrant, but solicited his vote. Nothing hurts like the truth, and the Rev. Dr. Burchard spoke more wisely than he knew when, in his immortal blunder of 1884, he repeated the accusation that the Democratic party was the party of "rum, Romanism, and rebellion." It was undeniably the party of rebellion, for the Republicans had preserved the Union against the Democrats of the South and the Copperhead Democrats of the North. It was the party of Romanism, for the great body of Irish-Catholics sought sanctuary in its fold. It was the party of rum, for the maladjusted Irish immigrants of those years were notorious for their addiction to the bottle.

The Irish-Catholics for more than a century deliberately embroiled our relations with England, but this was a manifestation of hyphenism rather than of religion. The Irish caused trouble not so much because they were devout Catholics as because they were frustrated nationalists.

The Catholic Church in America was less ardent for the Spanish-American War of 1898 than the Protestants, partly because Spain was a Catholic monarchy and Protestants made no bones about disapproving of Catholicism in Cuba. The Catholics over the years have pursued a policy of less active participation in political questions than the Protestants,* and during World War I the priesthood in America stuck to its ecclesiastical knitting more faithfully than colleagues of other faiths, thus avoiding ridiculous and unchristian excesses. The Catholic Church has made its influence felt in various other ways, notably in connection with the attacks of the reformist Mexican government on the church in 1935–1936. The Knights of Columbus, the Catholic Daughters of America, and the Ancient Order of Hibernians were among those groups that besought the Washington government to interfere.

In the closing agonies of World War I, when the Bolsheviks despoiled the reactionary Greek (Catholic) Orthodox Church, the Catholic Church in America bitterly and quite understandably assailed the new regime, and in so doing departed conspicuously from its general policy of avoiding politics. The Catholics were active among the great pressure groups in America that opposed the recognition of Russia, and they contributed to postponing such

* A notable exception was Father Coughlin, the radio priest of the 1930's, who had a tremendous following, chiefly isolationist and Catholic. The church denied that he spoke for it, and he was finally silenced.

action until 1933. The American Catholics denounced in 1939 the Stalin-Hitler pact, which opened the door to World War II, and they likewise assailed the Soviet assault on Finland later in the year, although many Protestant groups were hardly less hostile.

After Pearl Harbor the undisguised distaste of the Catholics for Communism was one of the major barriers in the path of desperately needed cooperation with Russia. In 1944 a Polish-Catholic priest from New England by the name of Stanislaus Orlemanski, whose sympathies were with the Russian-sponsored Polish regime, journeyed to Moscow and there conferred with Stalin. When he reported to the press that Stalin was not such a bad fellow after all, and indicated that there was hope of cooperation with Russia, he was promptly disciplined and relegated to the obscurity and silence from which he had skyrocketed. In 1945, when the Moscow *Pravda* singled out two American journals, the *Commonweal* and the *Catholic World*, as outstanding examples of "the war-mongering Catholic press," the Catholic Boston *Pilot* replied bitterly that this distinction was worth "more than five years of Pulitzer awards."

The Catholics were strongly sympathetic with Franco in his war against the Spanish Loyalists, for the latter had undermined the privileged position of the church. The great body of Americans were apathetic, and as a consequence the zealous pro-Franco Catholic group was able to make its weight felt disproportionately in what was openly referred to as a holy war. The burning question of the hour was whether to lift the embargo on munitions so that help could be sent to the anti-Franco Loyalists, in accordance with previous practice and the prodemocratic American tradition. A hot debate was waged between the ardent Protestant repealists and the Catholic retainists, although the more liberal Catholics were somewhat divided on the issue. Protestants flooded Congress with letters and telegrams; and following an impassioned radio appeal by the Catholic Father Coughlin, an estimated 100,000 messages urging retention descended upon Congress. There can be no doubt that pressure from such individuals, to say nothing of that from organizations like the Knights of Columbus and the National Council of Catholic Men, had some influence in retaining the embargo.

8

During World War II the Catholics in America, aside from expressing profound distaste for the enforced partnership with Russians, made their influence felt in various ways.

Catholic Irish were markedly less favorable than their Protestant neighbors to proposals for forcing neutral and Catholic Eire to cooperate actively with the Allies.

Italy and the Vatican also entered into the picture. In May of 1943, before the Allied invasion of the peninsula, Dr. Gallup asked whether Allied air forces should bomb Rome, the "ancient center of Catholic culture." The percentages are highly revealing:

	Yes	No	No opinion
Catholics	24	67	9
Protestants	86	52	12
Nonchurch	47	40	13
Over-all vote	87	51	21

In April, 1944, when American boys were dying in Italy, many of them the sons of Catholics, the picture was roughly reversed. Dr. Gallup asked: "If military leaders believed it necessary to bomb historic religious buildings and shrines in Europe [Rome was not specifically mentioned], would you approve?"

	Yes	No	No opinion
Catholics	63	28	9
Protestants	75	19	6
Nonchurch	78	15	7
Over-all vote	74	19	7

The common opinion was: "Lives are more important than a few relics."

When the invasion of Italy was finally launched, President Roosevelt was at pains to assure Pope Pius XII, no doubt with an eye to the American Catholic vote, that so far as possible churches and religious institutions would be respected. The necessity of bombing communications in Rome, and more particularly the destruction of the German-fortified Monte Cassino Abbey, dampened the cordiality of relations between the Vatican and Washington.

When the fighting ended, the Catholics in America abated not one whit their distrust of the Soviets, whose postwar antics both confirmed and inflamed current suspicions. American Catholics continued to condemn attempts by the Kremlin to deal harshly with Franco's Spain, and when in 1946 the Russians induced the Security Council of the United Nations to vote condemnation of the Spanish regime, the Catholic Knights of Columbus published large advertisements criticizing this kind of "Kangaroo Court" procedure.

The appointment of Myron C. Taylor in 1939 as Roosevelt's personal representative to the Pope aroused much criticism among American Protestants. The Vatican is a spiritual more than a temporal state, and this species of recognition was condemned as violating the century-old American principle of the separation of church and state. Perhaps a more potent reason for opposition was the persistence in America of a large amount of anti-Catholic animus.

Protestants often ask why there have been so many Catholics in the Department of State and in the foreign service, notably such men as Ambassador Joseph Patrick Kennedy in London (1937–1941) and Ambassador

Carlton J. H. Hayes in Madrid (1942–1945). The answer is that Catholic communicants represent about one sixth of our entire population, and it would be both undemocratic and discriminatory if there were not considerable numbers of Catholics in all branches of the public service. It would also be impossible, even if it were desirable, to preserve exact religious proportions on a merit basis or even on a political basis.

Catholic immigrants, as earlier explained, have been more welcome in the Democratic than in the Republican fold, and hence there are more Democratic Catholics than Republican Catholics. The Democrats were continuously in power from 1933 to well past the close of World War II, and one should not be surprised to find that there were more Catholics in high places during these years than under a Republican regime. Franklin Roosevelt's three Postmasters General were all prominent Catholics—James A. Farley, Frank C. Walker, and Robert E. Hannegan. Since the Catholics are preponderately Democratic voters, and since the Democratic party is anxious to retain their support, they are naturally listened to with a good deal more respect by a Democratic administration than they would be if they were clamoring in the opposition camp. This is but one of the many facets of hyphenism in our melting-pot democracy.

Catholicism in America, while at times injecting discordant notes into the symphony of our foreign policy, has nevertheless been an important force in promoting international-mindedness and hence breaking down the dikes of isolationism. For nearly two thousand years the Catholic Church has been *the* single continuous international organization, transcending national boundaries, and the Catholics in America are naturally heirs to this attachment. Yet nativists and other bigots in the United States resent even a nominal or spiritual allegiance to a foreign potentate. When the League of Nations was before the Senate in 1919, Senator Sherman of Illinois appealed strongly to religious prejudice when he declared that twenty-four of the forty Christian nations in the League would be under the domination of the Vatican.

9

A few final observations on the role of religion in American foreign policy.

Much as we may applaud the devotion and selflessness of missionaries, the fact is inescapable that they have embroiled our foreign relations. The proselyting zeal of the Salvation Army,° the Mormons, and the Christian Scientists, among others, has involved our government in a good deal of diplomatic controversy. In recent years the determination of evangelical Protestants to convert the Catholics of Latin America from the presumed error of their ways has been a substantial barrier in the path of Good Neigh-

---

° The Salvation Army encountered the disapproval of both Tsars and Soviets. The latter in 1947 accused it of being a quasi-military organization because its members wore uniforms and had military titles.

borism. The missionaries in China have not only done much to develop a pro-Chinese bias, but in the days before Pearl Harbor, by understandably refusing to leave the field of their labors in spite of stern warnings from Washington, they exposed themselves to mistreatment which visibly affected American public opinion.

Narrow and fanatical religionists have not been without influence in helping to promote an isolationist or otherwise unrealistic foreign policy. In Denver, Colorado, in the hours following the Japanese assault on Pearl Harbor, one irate listener telephoned a local radio station, wanting to know why the Lutheran hour had been cancelled. When told that the schedule had been upset by the Nipponese attack, he snorted: "Do you think the war news is more important than the gospel?" A clergyman or other moralist occasionally blossoms forth with a statement that international discord would be ended if the diplomatists did not befuddle their brains with alcoholic liquors. Fortunately such zealots are more noisy than numerous.

One great step forward would be for the various denominations to raise the educational standards of their clergy. The record reveals that in time of crisis the better educated ministers, like the Unitarians and the Episcopalians, keep their heads much better than the poorly educated exhorters of the evangelical groups, who tend to bring the entire church into disrepute. At the same time we must raise the educational standards of the people, for poorly educated congregations are not disposed to welcome pastors who refuse to give them a maximum of emotionalism.

The church, as such, has not been as influential a factor in foreign affairs as one would suspect from the importance of religion in our daily lives. One basic reason is that other factors like security, traditionalism, and economic gain crowd in ahead of spiritual motives. Another reason is that while the church is a gigantic pressure group, the various denominations are often at cross-purposes, and tend to offset each other. This was notably true in the Catholic-Protestant controversy over Franco's Spain.

Religion is also intimately tied in with hyphenism, as earlier indicated. Among Jewish-Americans and Catholic-Americans, race and religion and national background all tend to shade into one another. These two groups are either racial or religious minorities in a land whose tolerance leaves something to be desired, and as a consequence they have been forced to unite more effectively than the apathetic Protestant majority. In this respect it is true that the non-Protestant minorities exercise an influence out of proportion to their numbers. If the intolerant majority deplore this result, they must remember that their intolerance has in considerable measure brought it upon themselves.

CHAPTER EIGHTEEN

XENOPHOBES AND XENOPHOBIA

"We can hardly hate anyone that we know."—WILLIAM HAZLITT

1

THE MAN IN THE STREET, like men in foreign streets, has developed curious infatuations for other nations, and equally curious antipathies against them. Both impulses are dangerous, as George Washington indicated in his Farewell Address, for emotions swerve us from the true track of national interest. Emotions all too often arise from surface information or erroneous conceptions, and as a consequence make for irrationality in a world where sanity is urgently needed.

Mankind in general seems to have an instinctive dislike for the foreigner. The Greeks divided their tiny world into two parts: Greeks and the others, whom they termed barbarians. "Everyone is ready to speak evil of a stranger," wrote the great Greek tragedian, Aeschylus. Bret Harte referred to the "defective moral quality of being a foreigner," and the alleged remark of a cockney Englishman has become classic: "There goes a stranger; 'eave 'arf a brick at 'im.'

A Dictionary of International Slurs was published in 1944 by A. A. Roback, and it is to be warmly recommended to those naïve souls who are wondering why we do not make haste to beat our atomic bombs into power stations. In France syphilis is called the Italian disease, and in Italy the French disease, and so on. The amiable Dr. Samuel Johnson expressed a not uncommon British view when he dismissed foreigners as "mostly fools," but he did not go so far as an English lady in the Rhineland who, on hearing a German speak of her party as foreigners, exclaimed: "No, we are not foreigners; we are English; it is you that are foreigners."

Today some nations still regard themselves, even the backward ones, as islands of enlightenment in a sea of barbarism, and Americans have sinned worse than many. Our textbooks, especially the earlier versions, have given the impression that all history dates from Plymouth Rock, that the wilderness drama of America held the center of the world stage from the beginning, and that what happened in Europe and elsewhere was but a dim and unimportant rumbling in the wings.

The average American, being no less human than the various peoples from whom he sprang, is inclined to suspect and even hate the "furriner." The British traveler Buckingham was impressed in the 1830's with our strong prejudice against all foreigners, especially the British, who were infuriatingly contemptuous of our backwoods experiment.

As late as 1919 the more unenlightened Americans viewed the League of Nations with deep suspicion; it would be controlled by foreigners of all races and climes, who would outvote us. In 1925, when the debate waxed hot over the World Court, Senator Fernald of Maine cried out against being hailed before a court of eleven judges, ten of whose names no American could pronounce, as though foreigners could not understand jurisprudence, and as though Legnano, Suárez, Gentili, Grotius, Van Bynkershoek, Pufendorf, Thomasius, Barbeyrac, and a host of others had not been formulating international law long before we proclaimed our Declaration of Independence. The rabble-rousing Senator Reed of Missouri, during the 1925–1926 debate on the World Court, appealed to baser emotions when he asked how the American people would like to have decisions on American questions handed down by Dionisco Anzilotti or Antonio Sánchez de Bustamente; and to cap his argument he read pages of the foreign names of League of Nations delegates, as though one would expect only Anglo-Saxon names in a genuine world assembly. In the 1935 debate on the World Court, the blind Senator Schall of Minnesota—blind in more ways than one—summed it all up simply and succinctly: "To hell with Europe and the rest of those nations!"

Our suspicion of foreigners stems partly from the feeling that they are scheming to use us for their advantage, and this distrust was given a tremendous boost by the Uncle Shylock experience after World War I. "The chief argument in favor of American isolation," declared a California newspaper in 1921, "is the fact that Europe thinks it a very narrow and dangerous policy." During the period of World War II, a common expression encountered by poll takers was: "We can't trust them foreigners."

2

Why do we have this xenophobic complex, and why do we dislike certain nations more than others?

First of all, we harbor an instinctive and entirely natural antipathy for our hereditary enemies. Until the American Revolution the traditional foes were Catholic Spain and Catholic France, both of which instigated and led Indian attacks on our wavering but advancing frontier. The bloody French-Indian raids on Deerfield and Schenectady have faded from memory but not from the pages of history books. For decades New England mothers hushed their crying children with the warning that if they did not keep quiet the Frenchmen would hear them. When the French entered the Revolutionary War on our side, but primarily for their own purposes, we rather suspiciously clasped their bloodstained hands in alliance, and the myth of French love for America was born. But we never did become even partially reconciled to the proud and perfidious Spanish Don, and we rejoiced at his going from the Western Hemisphere in 1898, and sped the day of his exit.

From the Revolutionary War down to about 1898, and to a considerable extent beyond that, the traditional foe was Great Britain, especially among the Irish-Americans. Family quarrels are notoriously bitter, and ours of 1776 with the Mother Country was no exception. The killing of brother by brother, aided and abetted by Hessian hirelings and Indian hatchet men, left a century-old legacy of hate. When peace came, the problems of breaking up housekeeping, such as joint custody of the fisheries, continued for well over a century to vex relations between the mother and her giant daughter in the west.

The embers of the War for Independence had scarcely cooled, when the War of 1812, with its antecedent grievances, came to stir them anew. The British invader put the torch to the Capitol building, and one congressman proposed that the ruins be encircled with an iron balustrade bearing the inscription: "Americans! This is the effect of British barbarism!" A biographer of Townsend Harris, our first permanent diplomatic agent in Japan, records that his hero was brought up to say his prayers, fear God, and hate the British.

Until about 1898 the ancient grudge was kept green by patriotic societies, nationalistic textbooks, and other agencies. Near the end of the century Downing Street, finding that its "splendid isolation" was becoming dangerous rather than splendid, and casting about for lusty allies, inaugurated an era of "patting the eagle's head." The British were especially friendly to us during the Spanish-American War, in glaring contrast to some of the European powers, and they were happy to claim the victorious Admiral Dewey as a worthy scion of Lord Nelson.

A good many Americans could not adjust themselves to the sudden purring of the British lion, after more than a century of supercilious criticism. The Detroit *Journal* in 1898 devised a fable:

> Once upon a time, a lion, attacked by all the other beasts, and being in sore straits, chanced to raise his eyes and beheld an eagle, soaring aloft and contemplating the strife with indifference.
> "My long-lost daughter!" cried out the lion, in a loud voice. "Don't you know your mamma?"
> What this fable teaches is still uncertain at the moment of going to press, the eagle not having made up his mind as yet.

At the same time another Detroit newspaper, the *Tribune*, expressed a not uncommon sentiment: "It might have been better if Great Britain's friendship for the United States were less intense and had been stretched over a long period of time."

The era of the Spanish-American War inaugurated a sharp cooling of Anglophobia, and from then on, especially when we were partners in two great world wars, the relations between the mother and daughter nations were marred by only rather minor friction. The notable exception was our neutrality period during World War I, when we again ran afoul of British blockade practices. In 1915, when the British were about to seize an American ship, the *Dacia*, laden with cotton for Germany, our pro-British Ambassador Page in London advised Downing Street to let the French do it, for they were our traditional friends, and there would be no serious uproar. His prognosis was completely correct.

3

We dislike those nations that seek to block our national ambitions. In our formative years we distrusted Spain because she tried to coop us up east of the Alleghenies, tried to close the mouth of the Mississippi, tried to keep us from buying Louisiana, and tried to get it away from us after we acquired it. We distrusted the British, and to some extent the French, because they schemed to prevent us from annexing Texas, Cuba, and other meat for the maw of Manifest Destiny. (Japan later reacted similarly toward those powers that tried to thwart what she regarded as her imperial destiny in the Far East.)

We turn against those countries whose policies conflict with ours. For much more than a century we were a small-navy power with a large merchant marine, striving to do business as usual with all potential customers, in war as well as in peace. Britain was a big-navy power, and while employing her fleet as her most potent offensive weapon, she trod on the toes of the United States and other weak neutrals. We championed a liberal interpretation of freedom of the seas; Britain championed an illiberal interpretation. The resulting bitterness was acute in the pre-1812 days, and somewhat less so in the pre-1917 days, but all this disappeared in 1917 when we entered the conflict on the side of Britannia and became a partner in upholding her narrow concepts. Great Britain is the only major power with which our relations on the whole have steadily improved over the past fifty years. One basic reason is that during this era we also became a big-navy nation, and much of our policy ran parallel to hers, whereas formerly it had clashed.

During the nineteenth century we were a debtor nation, and we were human enough to detest our creditors. The farmer who toils from sunrise to sunset to pay off both the principal and interest of his mortgage has no love for the glassy-eyed and tightfisted banker who dwells opulently on the crest of the hill. We borrowed huge sums from English and other foreign investors to construct canals, railroads, and other improvements. The man behind the plow, who congenitally hated Great Britain anyhow, resented his subserviency to overseas "money power," and the epithet "bloated British bondholder" rolled bitterly from many an American tongue. While the hardy American pioneer battled with the wilderness, in imminent danger of being scalped, the gouty English lord clipped coupons in the security of his ancestral castle. During World War I we abruptly lost our position as a debtor and became the world's creditor, and the epithet "Uncle Shylock" rolled bitterly from many a European tongue. Despite our long generations of experience as a debtor, we were totally unable to understand why we should be regarded with the same lack of affection that we had long displayed toward John Bull.

4

We dislike arrogant nations, and did so most intensely during the years when we were weakest and poorest. The aristocrats of England long looked down upon their transatlantic stepcousins as "peasants," and as the scum and offscourings of Europe.* "They are a race of convicts," remarked Dr. Samuel Johnson in 1775, "and ought to be thankful for anything we allow them short of hanging." This infuriating attitude of condescension was painfully noticeable in the early criticisms of British lecturers and authors, who generally came over to prove their prejudices, and who rather uniformly discovered that the only thing about America that did not disappoint them was the gleaming curtain of Niagara Falls. Britain's overweening naval power in the nineteenth century, which was reflected in the cock-of-the-walk attitude of her officers and seamen, merely rubbed salt into old sores.

The British have long suffered from a disagreeable if well-founded superiority complex. Emerson in 1868 spoke of the Briton's faith in the Fortieth Article; "namely, that he shall not find his superiors elsewhere." Joseph C. Grew, our last pre-Pearl Harbor ambassador in Japan, refers to a rather high and mighty English lady who was passing through Japan, and who on landing said to her host: "Ah, so this is Kobe. Tell me, who is our Governor General here?" The Americans also suffer from a superiority complex which in the nineteenth century was less well founded than that of the British, and which as a consequence was more than ordinarily irritating. After we tipped the scales in World War I, and "won the war for the Allies," there was no living with us. Superiority complexes as overdeveloped as those of both the British and the Americans cannot live together comfortably at close quarters. There is much point in the witticism that an Englishman walks into a room as though he owned it, and an American walks in as though he didn't give a damn who owned it.

The bumptiousness of nations on the make, with which we were generously endowed in the nineteenth century, was particularly offensive to us when exhibited by Germany during the era of Theodore Roosevelt. The swaggering Prussian militarists and imperialists, and above all the swashbuckling and theatrical Kaiser Wilhelm, helped turn us against Germany even before the 1914 invasion of Belgium. As early as 1899, a poem "Hoch der Kaiser," recited by a naval officer at a dinner in New York, stirred up something of an international incident. It began:

* We still react against British class distinctions and noble birth. In 1942, following the disaster at Tobruk, Dr. Gallup asked why the British were not winning. Among the answers were these: "Too much wine, chess games and noble blood in the leadership." "Too much tea-drinking and not enough fighting—not among the men but among the officers." "The British should take more generals from the ranks and fewer from the ruling classes."

Der Kaiser auf der Faterland
Und Gott on high all dings gommand,
Ve two, ach! don'd you understandt?
Meinself—und Gott.

The Kaiser was keenly aware of the disfavor into which he had fallen, and he launched an active campaign to ingratiate himself with the American public. His most conspicuous gesture was the sending of his brother, Prince Henry of Prussia, on a good-will tour. The distinguished visitor dispensed gifts with such lavish hand that the Chicago *News* could inquire generically: "Is your Prince Henry decoration on straight?" But such clumsy courtship was of little avail.

5

We have long cherished a powerful democratic and liberal tradition, and we dislike those nations that represent aristocracy, illiberalism, and repression, whether of Communism or Fascism. Late in 1945 informed opinion in America was overwhelmingly against admitting Franco's dictatorship to the United Nations. We distrust monarchy, autocracy, and dictatorship, whether of king or commissar. During the nineteenth century we got along reasonably well with Russia, but we did not like the absolutism of the Tsar and the exploitation of millions of sodden serfs. (We had Negro slaves, but here again we could see things clearer at a distance.) We did not applaud the Tsar's part in stamping out the Hungarian rebellion of 1848, nor his brutal crushing of the Polish rebellions of 1830 and 1861–1864. Near the end of the century we were distressed by the attempts to Russify Finland; by the banishment of liberals to bleak Siberian dungeons; and above all by the bloody anti-Jewish pogroms.

Then came the Russian revolution of 1917, and we promptly recognized the new "democratic" government. It is a curious fact that throughout the century and three quarters since our independence we have enjoyed a degree of ideological affinity with Russia only during those few months in 1917. Then came the red specter of Bolshevism, and Hearst's Baltimore *American* could refer to Lenin and Trotsky as "filthy pocket-pickers and despicable degenerates of lucre." Then came the bloody purges, the dread N.K.V.D., and other evidences of cruel repression. We cared even less for the dictatorship of Stalin than for that of Nicholas II.

We instinctively feel unfriendly toward "imperialistic" nations, blissfully overlooking the fact that we embarked upon an imperialistic adventure of our own at the turn of the century. We got into the game with a small ante, and crawled out of it as gracefully as we could when we found that it did not pay, so we cannot count that. But "perfidious Albion" is an imperialistic power whose holdings no night could darken, and this concept has been driven home by the schoolbook practice of coloring the British empire in great gobs of red, as though there were something malevolent about the whole business. Not being crowded together on a small island, we have never been able to see any justification for imperialism. American isolationists in 1939, during the debate over lifting the arms embargo, naturally concentrated their attack on Britain. Senator Holt of West Virginia desired neither British imperialism nor German Naziism; and Senator Clark of Idaho declared that the British empire had been built on only two things: "blood and treachery." Clark condemned the British more savagely for not having helped Poland than he did the Germans for having attacked her.

Many Americans still think of the British empire as a single entity rather than as a group of self-governing commonwealths. Secretary of Commerce Henry A. Wallace pained his British cousins in 1946 when, in his sensational Madison Square Garden speech, he referred unfavorably to "British imperialism." At about the same time Henry L. Mencken objected to our being a "bottleholder" for Great Britain, and to our "pulling ashore the corpse of the British empire."

We regarded Britain as the only incorrigible "colony snatcher" until the end of the nineteenth century, when fellow "felons" entered the game. Germany stuck her thumb into the Chinese pie and came up with the prize plum of Shantung. The pretext was the murder of a couple of German missionaries, whose value came high when spheres of influence rather than souls were at stake. A wave of resentment swept America, and the Springfield (Massachusetts) *Republican* queried: "If the lives of two German missionaries are worth Kiao-Chou bay for a period of ninety-nine-years, what are the lives of four German sailors worth?" At the same time "the bear that walks like a man" was lumbering toward ice-free ports in Manchuria, and American businessmen feared that the Open Door would be clawed shut. All this crass imperialism did much to prejudice the American mind against both Germany and Russia during the years preceding World War I.

6

We distrust rivals for a place in the sun. For many decades after 1854 we took a motherly pride in the emergence of Japan from her medieval cocoon. But after she proved that she was a great civilized nation by efficiently killing tens of thousands of Russians in the war of 1904-1905, we began to entertain doubts. By one of the accidents of history we both burst upon the same stage as a major Far Eastern power at about the same time, and as a consequence we began to look upon each other as rivals. The ancient friendship was replaced by suspicion, not unmingled with fear; Uncle Sam could no longer pat the little fellow on the head and show him off.

Germany also emerged as a world power late in the nineteenth century, and finding herself a latecomer in the scramble for colonial spoils, she sought frantically to scrape up some of the crumbs that had fallen from the banquet table of those who had already dined. Revealing the haughtiness of the newly arrived (which we dislike in others), and the greed of the frustrated, she ran afoul of the United States in Samoa, where in 1889 we both had covetous eyes on the same prize. War might have come then and there if a terrifying hurricane had not wrecked both the German and the American fleets before their guns could go off. Less serious trouble developed a decade later, when we both betrayed a lively interest in the fate of the Philippine Islands.

We suspect and fear those nations that threaten our security. We turned vigorously against the French and Napoleon III when in the 1860's they sought to build a Europeanized puppet monarchy on the ruins of the Mexican Republic. We mistrusted the Germans at the turn of the century because of their obvious desire to challenge the Monroe Doctrine in Latin America. We fought them with great spirit in 1917–1918 because we regarded them as both an actual and potential menace to our physical security.

The foreign threat may be ideological rather than physical, and this accounts in large part for our apprehension regarding the Soviet Union. After Communist fellow travelers and fifth columnists have bored from within long enough, we fear that we may fall easy prey to attack from the outside. But apart from actual conquest, we dislike those nations with an ideology which may bring about undesirable changes in our social or economic structure, whether it be French syndicalism or Russian Communism, whether it be the state socialism of a Bismarck or the labor-socialism of an Attlee. The British loan of 1946 was attacked in Congress on the ground that we were being put in the position of subsidizing the unpleasant specter of socialism. "Too damned much socialism; too damned much imperialism," cried one ardent Anglophobe.

7

We feel less kindly toward those nations whose products—whether of forest, field, or factory—compete with and beat down the prices of our own. For many decades our relations with Brazil have been the most friendly of those with any South American republic, largely because she is our coffee bag, and we do not raise coffee in quantity. In recent years our relations with Argentina have been the least amicable of those with any South American republic, largely because the land of the Gaucho and tango grows great quantities of grain and beef, just as we do. The producers of American competitive products naturally lobbied for and secured tariff barriers and quarantine restrictions. The Argentinians, as the aggrieved parties, naturally feel more bitter toward us than we do toward them, but bitterness begets bitterness in an ever widening vicious circle.

Germany, in the latter part of the nineteenth century, shot to the fore as a great economic power. In the interests of her own farmers, she excluded American pork as diseased, and we arose angrily and patriotically in defense of the native hog. In the interests of her own manufacturers, she erected tariff barriers (which we abhor elsewhere), and she edged us out of foreign markets by trade practices which we regarded as unfair. From the commercial standpoint the trademark, "Made in Germany," was more to be dreaded than the dreadnaughts being built for the German Navy.

Russia and the United States have not got along well since 1917, but not because of competitive economies. At one time there was some little outcry in America against Russian "dumping," but on the whole our trade with Russia has been small, and mainly in items like furs and manganese ore, which we do not produce in sufficient quantity. We actually developed some resentment against the Russians because they did not show more interest in buying our machine tools, automobiles, and other goods. "A dangerous Red" was defined by a Texas newspaper in 1930 as "any Russian who appears in America without placing an order for machinery." The recognition of Russia by the United States was delayed until 1933, and was baited with the prospect of a huge trade which never developed. We were then trying to pull ourselves out of the Great Depression, and in these circumstances business proved to be more potent than Bolshevism.

The existence of competing rather than complementary economies does not necessarily spell bad relations. Canada and the United States produce much the same sort of thing, except for such items as pulp and nickel, yet they have developed the most profitable and voluminous two-way trade in history. This happy result has come about in spite of, rather than as a result of, competing products and tariff walls.

8

We instinctively turn against nations that do not pay their debts. Several of our states in the period before the Civil War, notably Pennsylvania, defaulted on their obligations to British creditors, but we conveniently forget this, although the British do not. The poet Wordsworth, whose family had lost heavily in American bonds, in 1845 wrote an uncomplimentary sonnet, "To the Pennsylvanians."

The Bolshevist ideology would have been distasteful to us in any event, but nonrecognition of Moscow was made easier because the new government refused to honor the debts contracted by its predecessor, and continues to do so. All of our major Allies of World War I finally defaulted on their war debts, but France during the 1920's incurred the most unpopularity in America because of her extreme reluctance to agree to any terms. Britain, with the largest borrowings of all, was the first major power to step up and arrange to shoulder the burden. She got rather ungenerous terms for her promptness, at least as compared with the others, but we praised her honesty and manliness. Yet when all the debtors were forced to default in the 1930's, much of our hereditary anti-British feeling reasserted itself. During the 1939 arms-embargo debate in Congress, Britain rather than France was assailed for her dishonesty; her debt default was ranked just below imperialism as her worst crime.

We draw apart from those nations that too obviously try to use us for their own ends. The honeymoon period of the Franco-American alliance of 1778 passed away, and we became very unwilling partners when we perceived that France planned to exploit us for her selfish purposes. The isolationists of 1941 bitterly accused Britain of scheming to drag us into the conflict for the purpose of salvaging her ill-gotten empire. A booing Detroit crowd threw rotten eggs and ripe tomatoes at the British Ambassador, Lord Halifax, who nonchalantly remarked, so the report went, that we were fortunate to have food for such purposes.*

We have traditionally abhorred militarism. During the years before World War I, we resented the militarism and chauvinism of the strutting German war lords. The historian Albert Bushnell Hart later testified that his antipathy for Germany dated back to his student days, when he was offended by the cut of the trousers worn by Prussian officers. In 1914 Lieutenant Forstner, of the German Army, was acquitted after having wounded a lame cobbler with his sword in Alsace-Lorraine. The shoemaker had allegedly not shown proper respect. The American public was shocked, and the Cleveland *Leader* observed: "Science quails before the thought of what would happen if an irresistible force encountered a German colonel."

We have never felt kindly toward naval rivals, partly because the navy rather than the army has traditionally been regarded as our first line of defense. Germany was a serious competitor prior to 1914, as was Japan after World War I, and it is more than coincidental that we fought Germany twice, and Japan once. Russia, for all of her distastefulness to us in other ways, has not yet sought to challenge us on the high seas. Competition in merchant shipping, which is an auxiliary of naval power, has also colored our thinking, especially toward Britain in the nineteenth century and Germany in the early twentieth. We were deeply angered during the Civil War when Confederate raiders, built by our British rivals and cheered on by them, ravaged our merchant marine. A picture of the notorious *Alabama,* which was widely purchased in the North, bore the inscription: "Built of English oak, in an English yard, armed with English guns, manned by an English crew, and sunk in the English Channel."

We feel no real cordiality toward those nations that are openly irreligious, or who ardently champion a faith incompatible with our prevailing Protestantism. We were shocked by the atheism of both the French and the Russians during their great revolutions. We likewise deplored Hitler's attempts to introduce the pagan worship of Woden, and thus revive a Teutonic religion

* Some twenty-five women in the crowd bore placards proclaiming: "Remember the burning of the Capitol in the War of 1812."

untainted by Judaism. The French and Spaniards of our colonial era were no less hated because they were Catholics, and even to this day Protestant America finds Catholicism in foreign lands something of a barrier to the most cordial intercourse.

We respond unfavorably to any nation that mistreats the subjects under its jurisdiction, particularly if they are the cousins of large hyphenate groups in America. The Irish and the Jews have already been discussed in this connection.

9

An abiding unfriendliness toward other nations is often based upon fugitive impressions. Our shirt is burned or lost by a Chinese laundryman, or we get an acute attack of indigestion at a chop-suey house, and we develop antipathy for the Chinese. A Greek candy merchant short-weights us, or an Italian fruit peddler palms off some rotten bananas on us, and we think less kindly of Greece and Italy.

This sort of thing is unavoidable. The Man in the Street is asked to form judgments about people whom he has never seen, who live in lands he will never visit, at distances he is powerless to comprehend. He therefore grasps at the few Chinese or Greeks or Italians who swim within his limited ken. The unfortunate but natural practice of judging all by an unrepresentative few is not confined to international relations.

We are instinctively repelled by those who differ from us in habits and folkways. We feel (with Mark Twain) that the Germans are queer because they put verbs at the ends of their sentences, and that the Chinese were perverse because they shaved their heads rather than their chins. Turgenev observed that man is capable of understanding how the ether vibrates, but he cannot understand how some other man can blow his nose differently from him. The American Army and Navy authorities in World War II, realizing that our service personnel in foreign lands would be offended by strange customs, issued an admirable series of little handbooks warning them that things would be different: in France, men would kiss one another on the cheek; in China, they would put food instead of flowers on graves, though the deceased could neither eat nor smell. These customs had come into existence centuries before the United States was ever heard of, and the troops were warned that they would get into trouble if they disregarded them, argued with the natives about them, or sought to force conformity to American ways. The extent to which we are intolerant of the customs of others is the measure of our own provincialism.

Much of our hatred of foreigners springs from a lack of information. The more ignorant an American, the more apt he is to be antiforeign; scratch an ignoramus and you often find a nativist. Logic would seem to indicate that the more we read about foreign peoples, and the more we travel in their countries and come into intimate contact with them, the more we shall like them. As already observed, those Americans who have lived among German or Japanese immigrants in the United States are more likely to believe that there are "good" Germans and "good" Japanese.

But distance is "a great promoter of admiration," as Diderot once remarked, and foreign travel often has an effect opposite from that intended. God's-country American tourists who misbehave in other lands create bad feeling, and they are sometimes treated with a contempt that merely confirms the existing prejudice. Most of our Main Streeters go abroad without any real appreciation of the language or historical background of the countries they are visiting, and the trip does not prove very enlightening. "If an ass goes traveling he'll not come home a horse," remarked Thomas Fuller. He is in fact likely to come home a bigger ass. The Spanish proverb puts it more delicately: "He who would bring home the wealth of the Indies, must carry the wealth of the Indies with him."

A large proportion of American "tourists" of the past quarter century were soldiers who traveled, not because they wanted to travel, but because they got "greetings" from the President, and they did their sightseeing under highly unfavorable conditions. We idealized and to some extent idolized the land of Lafayette until in 1917–1918 some two million doughboys got there, only to be disenchanted. The American boys who fought in the China–Burma theater went over with naïve ideas about the Chinese "democrats," but they were rudely disillusioned when the ragged and lousy Chinese troops stole their jeeps, and when the Chinese peasants, not knowing what side they were supposed to be fighting on, hacked holes in the pipe lines so as to steal the precious gasoline. The homesick GI's repeatedly vowed that when they got home they never wanted to hear of a foreign country again. Significantly, the veterans were markedly less favorable to the loan to Britain in 1946 than the rank and file.

Firsthand contact may not cause us to *like* a people any better, but it will help us to *understand* them better. We can at least discover what their prejudices are, and make some attempt to reconcile divergent points of view. After doing all this, we may still dislike a foreign nation intensely, but we shall have a more rational basis upon which to base our dislike. And even this is a move in the direction of a more intelligent foreign policy.

CHAPTER NINETEEN

XENOPHILES AND XENOPHILISM

"I do not know the method of drawing up an indictment against a whole people."—EDMUND BURKE, 1775

1

A MORE PLEASANT TASK than analyzing international hates is exploring the reasons why we get along reasonably well with certain of our global neighbors.

In 1937 and again in 1938 and 1939 Dr. Gallup asked the American people to rate their favorite European country. The results are highly interesting:

	1937 (April)	1938 (November)	1939 (July)
England	55%	48%	43%
France	11	12	11
Germany	8	4	3
Finland	4	5	4
Ireland	4	4	3
Italy	3	3	2
Switzerland	3	6	4
Sweden	2	5	4
U.S.S.R.	1	2	1
Netherlands	1	2	—

What does all this add up to? First, there was a vast amount of indifference. In 1937 *Fortune* concluded: "The United States is definitely not international-minded. It regards foreigners as people whose business is their own, and to hell with them anyway." Secondly, of all the nations in the world we like ourselves by far the best. A common answer was: "America's the only country I like."

As for individual nations, England overshadowed all others, although her popularity waned after the Munich deal. Here one sees in convincing form the blood-is-thicker-than-water attachment. We may not get along too well with Englishmen when we are thrown closely in contact with them, but we like them in the abstract because we fancy that they are the most like us.

France ranked uniformly high, obviously because of the Lafayette tradition, and although she was involved in Munich with Britain, perfidious Albion took the lion's share of the blame. The Catholics in America showed a slight leaning toward Catholic countries like France, Italy and Eire.

Germany ranked third until Munich, when Hitler's ambitions were laid naked. We thought well of the clean, industrious Germans whom we had come to know so well as fellow citizens, although we could not say the same of their government. German-Americans in the United States registered a noticeable preference for their ancestral land.

Finland, with her debt-paying proclivities, a democratic tradition, and a good press in America, ranked uniformly high. The same was generally true of the Scandinavian countries.

Eire showed up fairly well, largely because of our racial and cultural heritage from the Emerald Isle. Irish-Americans and Catholics in general registered a marked partiality for Ireland.

The picture changed rather sharply in some respects after we were plunged into war at Pearl Harbor. A national survey in 1942 asked the American people to rate seventeen nationalities in comparison with themselves. Only five of the group were singled out by a majority as being "as good as we are in all important respects." They were, in order: the Canadians, the English, the Dutch, the Scandinavians, (despite the thickskulled Swede tradition), and the Irish. The remaining twelve nationalities were rated as "not quite as good as we are in major respects," or "definitely inferior," and the list tapered off in this order: French, Germans, Greeks, South-Americans, Jewish refugees, Poles, Russians, Chinese, Spaniards, Italians, Mexicans, Japanese. The fact that we were then at war with Germany, Italy, and Japan no doubt had some influence on the listings, particularly as regards the Germans, who in 1939 were rated ahead of the English as making the best citizens.

These figures merely confirm what any observant American could independently determine. We prefer Anglo-Saxon peoples or north European Nordics, from whom we have drawn the bulk of our racial stock. We are predisposed toward Protestant nations, with France and Ireland obvious exceptions. We show a preference for democracies, whether British or Scandinavian. With a natural narcissism, we like those people and those nations that are most like ourselves.

2

It will be interesting to amplify some of the general observations growing out of the ratings just given.

We are naturally attracted to those peoples from whom we have received our cultural heritage, notably the British, though to a lesser extent the German and other immigrant groups. We have inherited the same language as the English (with modifications), the same historical roots, the same ideals of freedom, the same legal system, the same body of literature, and many of the same customs and folkways. We even laugh at the same jokes, although we feel that the British are a bit slow in getting the point.* We were British subjects longer than we have been American citizens, counting the period from Jamestown to the end of the War of Independence, and the

* In 1915 the *Wall Street Journal* suggested "that the Germans paint jokes all over their submarines so the English can't see them."

eighth President of the United States, Martin Van Buren, was the first one not to have been born under the Union Jack. Many of us hardly think of Great Britain as a foreign country, and countless Englishmen can join in the exhortation of Tennyson:

> Be proud of those strong sons of thine
> Who wrenched their rights from thee!

In time of war we like those nations who battle on the side that we favor, or help us in our own struggles, or openly lock shields with us. We appreciated Russia's open (if selfish) friendliness to the Northern cause during the Civil War; we appreciated Britain's open (if selfish) friendliness to the United States during the Spanish-American War. In World War I both Italy and Japan fought on our side, and we felt quite friendly toward them; in World War II they fought on the other side, and we felt bitter toward them, especially Japan. Before America entered both of these conflicts, our sympathies generally went out to England; she was on the side of democracy. The feeling of cordiality thickened after we became associates. We entertained friendly sentiments toward Russia during most of 1917, but when the Bolsheviks took her out of the war, we turned against her. We despised Stalin when he signed the nonaggression pact with Hitler in 1939 and then launched his attack on Finland; we thought better of him after he stood up and struck back at Hitler in 1941; and even better when he was fighting on our side after Pearl Harbor.

3

The Lafayette legend provides a beautiful example of how synthetic friendships are born. France in 1777 was our hereditary enemy; she was Catholic; she was monarchical; she was absolutist; she was Latin. She was anxious to hamstring England during our War of Independence, not for our purposes but for hers; and we were so desperately in need of succor that we rather suspiciously clasped the outstretched hand. The dashing nineteen-year-old boy, Lafayette, loving liberty and leaving behind a beautiful young wife, came over at his own expense, and through his bravery and generosity endeared himself to the American people. Without this romantic personality about which to form a cult, the myth of Franco-American love almost certainly would not have persisted with such vigor.*

After we won our independence (with French help), we perceived that our powerful yokefellow was determined to use us for her own ends, and we fought an undeclared war with her for over two years. Considering the opportunities for friction, our relations with France over the decades have been about as unfriendly as those with any other great power. We hated the French before 1776; suspiciously welcomed them during the

---

* Lafayette returned for an unprecedented triumphal tour in 1824; and eventually some forty places in America were named after him.

Revolution; broke with them after achieving independence; fought on the same side with them against the British during the Napoleonic wars; turned against them under Jackson during the days of an early debt controversy; bitterly resented their sympathy with the Confederacy during our Civil War; and came near fighting them when they invaded Mexico to prop up the puppet Maximilian. The French sympathized with Spain during the Spanish-American War; they did not get along too well with our doughboys in 1917–1918; and after World War I they joined lustily in the transatlantic name-calling against Uncle Shylock.

The French have a tradition of democracy, although they have not been able to keep their democracy too well, and they have a glorious tradition of liberty, dating back to the *"liberté, égalité, fraternité"* of the French Revolution. The Statue of Liberty was completed by the French sculptor Bartholdi in the 1880's, and financed by the sous of French school children and others. But despite our common interest in democracy and liberty, we almost certainly would not have developed a strong sentimental attachment for France if the French had not fought on our side in the days of our youth, and if the gallant Lafayette had not come. As Robert Underwood Johnson put it during World War I:

> Forget us, God, if we forget
> The sacred sword of Lafayette!

The Lafayette Escadrille of aviators was composed of young Americans who volunteered to fight for the French preceding our belligerency, in 1917. When America was finally plunged into war by German U-boats, we accepted the challenge the more willingly because we felt that at last an opportunity had come to repay our debt of gratitude to France. Colonel Charles E. Stanton (not General Pershing) said at the tomb of Lafayette in Paris: "Lafayette, we are here." Then came days of disillusionment and a desire to return home after the Armistice, and American doughboys grumbled: "Lafayette, we are still here." During the second-front days of World War II, the expression was sometimes heard: "Lafayette, we are here again."

We also hold in esteem those who fight our traditional enemies. In the Crimean War of 1854–1856, England and France on the one side tangled with the Tsar on the other. Russia was then a traditional friend (largely because we had seen little of each other), and Britain was the traditional foe. American sentiment turned strongly to the Russians, even though the Tsar's government was a despotism and England was a constitutional monarchy and the custodian of many of our most priceless traditions. Our feeling was doubtless more anti-British than pro-Russian, for we were eager to see our haughty overlord of yesteryear get his comeuppance. The Russian minister in Washington actually received an appeal from three hundred Kentucky riflemen who requested service under the Tsar's banner in the Crimea. The British were annoyed by the reaction of their offspring, and the Tory aristocrats were more inclined than ever to regard as gross hypocrisy all our sniveling about democracy. The Russian writer Tchekhov, though not then born, might well have been thinking of this situation when he said: "Love, friendship, respect, do not unite people as much as a common hatred for something."

4

Some married couples get along best when they see the least of each other. The same thing is generally true of international intercourse, discouraging though such an observation may be. Our relations with Tibet, Liechtenstein, and Outer Mongolia have been generally untroubled because they have been virtually nonexistent. If it is true that the nation which has nothing eventful to record is the happiest, it is no less true that those nations are happiest whose diplomatic files are the thinnest.

The sociologist Pitirim A. Sorokin in 1944 wrote about the "miracle" of unbroken peace between the United States and Russia. There was nothing miraculous about it at all, especially prior to 1917, because neither nation had anything which the other acutely coveted, and the two peoples saw very little of each other. When Russian expansion in the early nineteenth century temporarily encroached on California, which we vaguely regarded as our future preserve, we became concerned, but fortunately this threat passed away. In 1866 the Tsar could remark pleasantly to an American: "The two people have no injuries to remember."

Russia is admittedly the only one of the great powers whom we have not openly fought, yet we were indirectly allied with Napoleon against her in 1812; we battled Russians on Russian soil at Archangel and in Siberia from 1918 to 1920; and we have engaged in ideological warfare with the Russian regime since 1917. When the interests of the two nations come into sharp conflict, as they have in recent years, criminations and recriminations echo and re-echo from the Dnieper to the Chicago drainage canal.

If one were to put a hotblooded youth on a desert island and leave him there for fifty years, one could hardly commend him for his sobriety and chastity. The test of character is temptation, not the absence of it, and the test of international amity is friction, not the absence of it. Quarrels with England loom larger in our annals than those with any other power, but this was not because we are both innately contentious, but because we were in various ways thrown so intimately together. Most of the now unfortified 5,527 mile land-and-water boundary between the United States and Canada was at one time contested between the Americans and the British. The marvel is not that we had a war with England in 1812, but that we had only one war in the decades of tail-twisting and eagle-feather-plucking that followed the struggle for independence.

We are also cordial toward those nations that pursue a policy parallel to our own. During the nineteenth century both Russia and the United States were small-navy powers, upholding a liberal interpretation of freedom of the seas, and naturally driven together by Britain's naval might. We upbraided the Russians in 1939 when they turned aggressor and attacked democratic, debt-paying little Finland, and we cheered them when they resisted the aggression of Hitler and indirectly subserved the cause of democracy. Certain naïve or overzealous Americans acted as though the Russians defended Moscow and Stalingrad primarily because of a desire to help us fight our battles.

Another explanation of the "miracle" of Russian-American amity is that both countries are "have" nations, in the sense of extending over vast areas of undeveloped territory. We have quarreled most bitterly with peoples who wanted something we wanted, or tried to keep us from doing something or getting something we desired. Until recent years Russia and America have seldom collided in these respects. Britain attempted to bar us from Texas and Cuba in the 1840's and 1850's, so there was friction. Japan eyed Hawaii covetously in 1898, so there was suspicion. Germany sought to make a dead letter of the Monroe Doctrine and gain a foothold in South America at the turn of the century, so there was hostility. The Japanese, who have little land, were much more anxious to emigrate to America in the twentieth century than the Russians, who have vast areas, so there was trouble with Tokyo over immigration. Russia's great unrealized territorial ambition is an ice-free corridor to the sea, and fortunately for us no such corridor lies across American territory.

5

With our liberty-loving and democratic tradition, we respond favorably to the sincere flattery of imitation when other nations follow in our steps. We cheered the French Revolution, only to be cooled off by the crashing of the guillotine. We got along better with Britain after she "shot Niagara" and widened her suffrage through the Reform Bill of 1867. We have had a fellow feeling for the European democracies like the Scandinavian countries, Finland, and Switzerland. We rejoiced at the outbreak of the Russian Revolution, only to be repelled by Bolshevist excesses, and we instinctively backed the reactionary White Russians as the hope of democracy.

We feel a natural attraction to nations that we adopt as protégés, such as Liberia and, notably, Japan after the time of Perry. We took great pride in the speed with which the Japanese, whom we had introduced to the world, applied the veneer of western civilization, and "Perry Day" orators without number descanted upon the "ancient friendship." When two of our "ancient" friends, Russia and Japan, clashed on the plains of Manchuria in 1904–1905, our hearts went out to the Japanese. They had yellow skins and a heathen religion, unlike the Russians, but they were the underdogs and they were our wards.* When the Japanese in 1904 engineered a sneak attack at Port Arthur against the Russians, some of our newspapers extravagantly praised the "plucky little Japs" for having caught the stupid Muscovites off guard. Our enthusiasm led us to name several towns after Admiral Togo, and a half-dozen places Tokyo, to our embarrassment after Pearl Harbor.

When Japan emerged from the smoke of the Russo-Japanese War a major power, we were not at all sure that Commodore Perry had not raised up a Frankenstein's monster. As an Indiana newspaper later put it: "The next time an American Admiral finds a backward little nation in the Pacific, he'll let it stay backward." In succeeding years Japan, at least in American eyes, appeared to be getting too big for her kimono, and after her coup of 1931 a New York journal remarked: "Japan's chief trouble seems to be a truck complex on an Austin chassis." Protégés may be all right, but they had better stay protégés. The rise and fall of Japan in American esteem is an instructive commentary on the mutability of international friendship. First we took pride in her, then we suspected her, then we feared her, then we excluded her, then we embargoed her, then we fought her, and then we hated her.

Our sympathies instinctively go out to the underdog, partly because our sporting instinct is aroused when big bullies push little nations around, except when we are doing the pushing, in which case there are always extenuating circumstances. Other countries react not dissimilarly, especially the "sporting" British, and the good wishes of the Tory aristocracy went out to some of our victims, notably the Mexicans in 1846–1848 and the Confederates in 1861–1865. Our concern for the underdog has often been combined or confused with our zeal for revolutionary or prodemocratic movements, as was true of our enthusiasm for the European revolutions of 1830 and 1848, and for the Cuban insurrection which ended in 1898.

We have generally assumed that the top dog was wrong, just because he was top dog, and especially if he happened to be the British bulldog. Our sympathies have rather consistently been with underdog China in her troubles with the Western powers and Japan. We were for the Finns in 1939–1940 against Russia; and for the Greeks in 1940, when their spectacular victories over the loud-mouthed Mussolini brought a revival of the "Greek fever" of the 1820's.

Sentiment for the underdog cannot persist, as Mr. Dooley noted in 1900 when the Boers lost their initial momentum and were being beaten by the British, unless the underdog has a fairly good hold and at least an outside chance of improving it. Our interest rather quickly evaporated when the lost causes of the Boers, the Finns, and the Greeks appeared hopeless. We have also learned that cheering the underdog or helping him may merely

---

* The Russians were displeased when we turned against them and favored the Japanese "monkeys," and they referred to their friendship during the Civil War, particularly the visit of the two Russian fleets, as proof that they were deserving of our support.

bring a new and more menacing top dog, which seemed to be the case when Japan emerged in 1905 and Soviet Russia in 1945. But in the latter instance there seemed to be no choice but to send Lend-Lease help.

6

We like, or at least feel pleasantly indifferent toward, those nations that avoid all the offenses discussed in the previous chapter, such as imperialism and militarism.

We prefer those countries that have stable governments; and during the post-1919 years we were both amused and annoyed by the whirligig frequency with which French cabinets fell. Emerson wrote in 1849 that the "French change their Constitution as often as their shirt," and near the turn of the century Mr. Dooley opined: "The Frrinch are a tumulchuse people . . . not steady ayether in their politics or their morals."

We are human enough to resent criticism, and we are attracted to those nations that say pleasant things about us. We saw no humor in jests about the crudities of Cousin Jonathan or the covetousness of Uncle Shylock. The strictures of British lecturers, as earlier noted, were particularly galling, and a New York newspaper in 1922 complained: "Americans are the only people in the world willing to pay foreigners for the privilege of listening to them tell how uncultured we really are."

We admire those nations that are not bellicose, and that are able to stay out of war, notably Switzerland. We have a conviction that Europe is incorrigibly quarrelsome, for we do not appreciate the age-old stresses and the reservoirs of hatred in the Mother Continent. "It seems that European diplomacy is a poker game," said the Washington *Post* in 1922, "played with chips on the shoulder." We conveniently overlook the fact that even without such provocations we knocked off a few chips on our own account.

As a rule we prefer people who speak our language, such as the Canadians, the Australians, the English. Bismarck was quoted as having said that the most important political fact in the world was that the British and Americans spoke the same tongue. We are somewhat repelled by people who jabber a strange gibberish, gesticulate wildly with their hands, and do such ridiculous things as to say "lo" (*l'eau*) when they mean water. "They spell it Vinci and pronounce it Vinchy," wrote Mark Twain in *Innocents Abroad*; "foreigners always spell better than they pronounce." During the Russo-Japanese War, the Balkan Wars, and World War I, the American press poked a good deal of fun at outlandish foreign place names. "The Germans have seized Przasnysz," said the Boston *Transcript* in 1915, "which is easier done than said." The New York *Evening Post* in 1917 could understand why the German advance in Galicia should slacken as it approached the "line of Okrimovice, Romanouvka, Jerebki, Colodievka, Polnankaletmanska, Eleonorouvka, and Sorokikrogouletz." But one South Carolina newspaper was objective enough to say that if America got into war, "what fun those Russian wags will have with Chillicothe and Punxsutawney."

A common language, while in some respects an insurance of amity, may also be a source of friction. When the British and the Americans say nasty things about each other, as they often do, the sneer can be transmitted directly without being watered down by an interpreter. Perhaps this is what George Bernard Shaw had in mind when he said that the two Anglo-Saxon peoples are separated, not united, by a common tongue. (His own biting sarcasm has contributed appreciably to this barrier.) The Britons have also resented the bastardization of their language by the Americans, and Oscar Wilde skirted near the truth when he remarked that the British have "everything in common with America nowadays, except, of course, language." The same tongue does not guarantee the same interests.

British travelers in the nineteenth century went to France, expecting to find things vastly different, and were agreeably surprised to find much that was familiar. The same travelers came to the United States, expecting to find things as they were in Britain, and were disagreeably surprised to find that there were some differences, including dialectical modifications of the tongue of Shakespeare and Milton.

7

Myths and legends play a powerful part in creating predilections as well as antipathies.

The Lafayette legend that monarchical France intervened in our revolution simply because she loved us and our democratic ideals has been of incalculable importance. When Napoleon sold us Louisiana in 1803 for reasons that were almost purely selfish, he is alleged to have said: "We have helped them to be free, let us help them to be great." This is pure bosh; but if bosh is widely enough believed, it is nevertheless potent bosh.

The myth still persists that the absolutist Russians sent their fleets to America in 1863 simply because they wanted to help us in our Civil War. This too was bosh, but it got us into such a friendly state of mind that we were willing to take the presumed Alaskan liability off the hands of our great and good friend, the Tsar of all the Russias.

The myth that the British spectacularly saved Admiral Dewey from a treacherous German attack at Manila Bay, in August, 1898, was a strong factor in building up pro-British and anti-German feeling at the turn of the century. This pretty story, often repeated with embellishments by journalists and others, was used with good effect in the United States when Britain and Germany went to war in 1914 and again in 1939.

The legend of the "slick" foreign diplomat—particularly the bespatted British—is one of the most enduring. The idea has taken hold—and it is not very flattering to our intelligence—that whenever our Simple Simon diplomats have put their feet under the same green table with white-spatted and monocled Englishmen, we have been "slickered" out of about everything except the Washington Monument. "Every time the American eagle sits in diplomatic conference in Europe," proclaimed Lieutenant Governor Hanley of New York in 1944, "he comes back plucked to the pinfeathers." The fact is that in the only two peace negotiations in which the British and the Americans were adversaries, those of 1783 and 1814, our experienced and astute envoys "hornswoggled" their inexperienced and inept antagonists, and came out much better than they had any right to expect. At the Paris Peace Conference in 1919, at the Washington Disarmament Conference of 1921–1922, and on other occasions we managed to get about as much as we could reasonably expect on a give-and-take basis.

Yet the redcoats-are-coming legend persists. When Prime Minister Lloyd George visited America in 1923, the Paul Reveres of the American press cried out that he had arrived with the intention of persuading us to fight Britain's battles in future wars. The Butte (Montana) *Bulletin* warned:

> Whenever a British statesman visits this country it is well for the people to be on the alert. As Balfour led the American people into war [in 1917] by laying wreaths of flowers on the tombs of men Great Britain wanted to execute 145 years ago . . . so Lloyd George would like to lead America into an alliance with British imperialism.

In 1929, on the eve of Prime Minister Ramsay MacDonald's negotiations with President Hoover regarding naval disarmament, an Albany newspaper neatly paraphrased a popular song of World War I: "He's coming over: Ramsay's coming over, and he won't go back till he's put something over over here." A decade later, on the eve of World War II, the visit of the King and Queen of England, though generally welcomed as a token of friendship, was regarded by a considerable isolationist minority as an attempt to line us up with Britain. On the very day of Pearl Harbor, Senator Nye, introducing variations of the theme that England expected every American to do his duty, shouted: "My friends are betting 20 to 1 that if we don't stop in our tracks now, we'll be in before Great Britain gets in." °

A corollary legend is that our officials are not only outplayed but hypnotized by the British and their insidious "Social Lobby." Representative Tinkham of Massachusetts, who as a Republican was not overfriendly to the Roosevelt administration, declared in 1935: "The President of the United States and the Department of State, his agent, are under the domination and control of the British Foreign Office." The year previous, Representative Britten of Illinois, also a Republican, condemned the large number of American diplomats who wore "a monocle and yellow neckties and blue spats and pink shirts." They did everything in their power "to look and act

---

° In the 1939 arms-embargo debate, Representative Thorkelson claimed that absolute American neutrality would end the war, because the Allies would not fight at all if they had to fight alone. Senator Downey said that "in the last war our American eagle endeavored to mother the British lion; we lost all our tail feathers and almost our wings."

and talk like a Britisher," even to the extent of falling "into the 'hawf' and 'cawf' stuff." Any such nincompoop "ought to be brought home; and if he apes the British again after a stay in America, he should be fired out of the service; because, after all, there is nothing so fine, nothing so strong, nothing so honorable as being a first-class American."

Fortune magazine in 1947 reported the result of a poll on the question as to whether our diplomats "generally get outsmarted." A percentage of 55 thought we held our own; 27 per cent thought we got outsmarted; and the remainder had no opinion. The results were proof to *Fortune* that a "U.S. tradition" has been broken. Yet a great many people still cling to the legend, and curiously enough the college-trained group had the least confidence in our diplomats. This may be because they were less blindly patriotic, more fully aware of the complexity of modern problems, and less complacent about some of our political appointees.

8

The Finnish myth is a prime example of how a gullible and ignorant public may draw completely false conclusions from a presumed set of facts.

Millions of Americans before 1917 had probably never heard of Finland. A few oldsters could remember vaguely that in the dying years of the nineteenth century we had applauded the attempts of the liberty-loving Finns to resist Russification, but that was about all we knew. Finland was off the beaten path of tourists, trade with her was scant, and relatively few of her sons and daughters had come to the United States.

We took a little notice of Finland when in 1918 she won her independence from the Bolsheviks by force of arms and with German help. We naturally commended any nation that would fight Bolshevism, but we were a bit unhappy over the Teutonic connection. "Finland begging America for food must first get rid of the dachshund under the table," advised the New York *World.* Our doubts were partially removed; and under the general relief act of 1919 we forwarded supplies to the Finns which under the final arrangements involved a debt of $8,281,926. This small transaction, only one of a number with various countries, passed unnoticed or virtually unnoticed in our press.

Two developments in 1923–1924 put Finland on the American map. First, her athletes, notably the tireless Paavo Nurmi ("the flying Finn"), stole the limelight in the Paris Olympic Games of 1924. On a per capita basis Finland did about twenty times better than the presumed winner, the United States, and to sports-mad America of the 1920's this achievement was worthy of high acclaim. Second, the year before this, when our Allied war debtors were trying to delay, whittle down, or evade the payment of their obligations, the Finns pluckily stepped forward and were the first to sign an agreement, under the terms of which they were obligated to pay both principal and interest over a period of sixty-two years. The Americans, with their Yankee thrift tradition, were impressed, and Congressman Crisp admiringly said on the floor of Congress: "A little child shall lead them." The terms that we granted Finland were not overgenerous, and if the Finns had pleaded poverty and devastation, which they could truthfully have done, they almost certainly would have won a lower interest rate.

During the ensuing years Finland remitted the installments on her debt with the regularity of Nurmi's pistonlike legs. The Great Depression descended, and the Allies all defaulted, but the Finns, although also hard hit, paid fully and on time. When Finland in 1939 stood up against the demands of Russia for territorial adjustments, and was cast in the role of a democratic David against the aggressive Muscovite Goliath, our enthusiasm for this fearless people reached an all-time high. The Washington government advanced loans, though not for munitions, and countless citizens danced, knitted, orated, bingoed, or banqueted for "brave little Finland," an appellation hitherto reserved for Belgium. Paulette Goddard, the movie actress, went all out for the Finns when she contributed her nightgown to the cause, although she presumably had others left. Congress gallantly offered a postponement of the regular debt payments, and the Finns, although at first declining, ultimately and temporarily took advantage of the respite.

In 1941 Finland was more or less forced into the war against Russia on the side of Hitler. She was keeping bad company, but she was fighting a "Communist" dictator and, caught between two rivals, she was the unfortunate victim of circumstances. Besides, she had paid her debts in the past, and she continued to do so even after Pearl Harbor, to the embarrassment of the so-called "welshers" who were again our Allies. We simply could not bring ourselves to declare war on the brave Finns, to the disgust of Stalin, whose capital they were attacking. We finally and belatedly broke diplomatic relations with them, but our failure to go the whole way was probably an act of mistaken mercy, for we could not become a party to the peace treaty of 1947, which we might otherwise have been able to ameliorate. The British were less squeamish and declared war. Popularity polls in England revealed that the Finns were less extravagantly admired there than in America, partly no doubt because the defaulting British did not relish being compared with upright little Finland. When diplomatic relations were reopened between Washington and Helsinki in 1945, the Finns paid their regular semiannual installment.

The Finns thus won a high place in our esteem, not because they are nationalists who wear no man's collar, not because they had made their democracy work well under adverse conditions, not because they had undertaken commendable social reform, not because they had produced distinguished figures like the composer Sibelius, not because they had worked steadfastly for international organization through leaders like Dr. Rudolf Holsti, but because they paid their debts when the other powers "welshed." It was a man-bites-dog situation, and in the 1920's both the infant radio and the senile vaudeville cracked stock jokes about debt-paying Finland. "The only nation that made any effort to pay its debt to us was Finland," said Henry L. Mencken in 1946, "and we rewarded Finland in 1941 by selling it down the Volga."

9

The truth is that there never was a Finnish *war* debt. The transaction was a purely commercial one in foodstuffs which took place in 1919 after the conflict had ended. Unlike France, Finland did not fight on our side at all; she fought the Bolsheviks with the aid of Germany (our enemy), and she had a volunteer foreign legion battling in the German Army against the Allies. France waged war on our side, and sustained the brunt of the fighting on her pulverized soil. Finland did not. France gave the blood of her sons while we were raising an army. Finland did not. We sent munitions of war to France to be shot away in a common cause; the foodstuffs shipped to Finland went in the cause of humanity, and the Finns recognized the demands of honor. The indebtedness incurred by France was $3,404,818,945; that by Finland, $8,281,926. Although France, devastated and decimated by the war, had a population more than ten times that of Finland (40,000,000 to 3,370,000) her debt to the United States was about 425 times larger. The Finnish debt was so small that Finland, unlike France, could pay her obligation without seriously deranging her currency, or having to clamber over impossible tariff barriers. The Finns paid their installments while the French spent huge sums on armaments; but the French were shell shocked and insecure, owing in large part to their desertion by the United States.

One may conclude that even if the Finns had not had to borrow from the United States, they would have been well advised to do so, if for no other reason than to win American good will by prompt payment. As things turned out, they paid a cheap price for highly favorable public relations. The Finns are a sturdy and honest people who are deserving of our respect and admiration. But it would be more creditable to our intelligence, and more conducive to sound policy, if our attitudes toward them were based on broader considerations than fleet feet and financial fidelity.

10

Likes and dislikes tend to cancel each other out. As a democracy, we should have detested autocratic Russia in the mid-nineteenth century, and to some extent did. But she adopted a policy of attempting to thwart the British, who were our ancient foes, and our resulting satisfaction beclouded our inherent distrust of tyranny. In World War II one soldier declared that he hated the "goddamn" British until he got to France, and then he hated the French so "goddamn" much that he forgot all about the British.

We get along better with some peoples than we do with their governments. During World War II American boys established pleasant relations with individual Russians, on those rare occasions when they were thrown together, but the two capitals were on name-calling terms. We got along reasonably well with Great Britain as a nation, but much less well with individual Englishmen, for reasons that have been indicated. Human beings are prone to be less tolerant of the shortcomings of relatives than of friends, and both peoples have resented the frank criticism of each other. Theodore Roosevelt, who was a thorough cosmopolite, could say that he wished the "average Englishman" well, but he wished him well "at a good distance from me."

The friendship of Americans for other countries has often been one of convenience, and for that reason neither deep-seated nor abiding. This was notably true when we concluded the misalliance with France in our formative years, and when in 1941 we were forced to become political and military bedfellows of the Soviets.

Nations, like dogs and people, usually respond favorably to friendly gestures. Conversely, name-calling begets competitive name-calling, and bitterness mounts in an ever widening vicious circle.

Getting along together in the home, getting along together with business associates, getting along together as states among the forty-eight, getting along together as a nation among the sixty-odd—this is perhaps the most difficult problem of human and international relations. When the peoples of the world learn to think more kindly of one another, there is bound to be an improvement in international amicability. We may not like foreign nations better as we come to know them better, but we cannot avoid approaching common problems with more understanding when we know enough to realize that there are two sides to any complicated dispute.

CHAPTER TWENTY

THE ROOTS OF ISOLATIONISM

"The less we have to do with the amities or enmities of Europe,
the better."—THOMAS JEFFERSON, 1815

1

THE CRITICISM has been common in America for many years that
we have no foreign policy. This complaint was heard less frequently before 1920 than after, for in the period before World War I we were less
seriously involved with overseas affairs. Our subsequent abandonment of
the League of Nations spotlighted the timidity and negation of our tactics,
which were once described as "wallflower diplomacy: we'll sit this one
out."

In the trough of Harding do-nothingism, one newspaper editor observed
that the United States Secret Service might well devote its spare time to
"looking for the American foreign policy," while the New York *Tribune* suggested that the British, instead of sending over statesmen to find out what our
position was, "ought to send men from Scotland Yard." In 1926 the Chicago
Tribune, referring to Secretary of State Kellogg's announcement that there
would be no immediate change of policy toward Mexico, exclaimed: "Ah
ha! Then there is a policy!" In 1946 Republican Senator Wherry of Nebraska, claiming that the senators did not know any more about our
foreign policies than ninety-six men picked at random, undertook to force
the State Department to explain its views until they were well known
"even to the man in the street." Whether the State Department has been
too timid or secretive, or the masses have been too unintelligent or uninterested, the fact is that the average citizen does not have a clear conception of our foreign policies.

Much of the confusion in our thinking grows out of a failure to distinguish between a basic principle and a shorter-range policy designed to
achieve a specific end. For example, a fundamental principle, like the
Good Neighbor, was the broad basis for Roosevelt's policy of nonintervention in Cuba during the disturbances of the early 1930's.

The United States does not lack and never has lacked fundamental
principles or policies, such as isolation and the Monroe Doctrine. They
were foreshadowed, either strongly or faintly, during the long gestative
years of the colonial period, and in a sense our nation came into being
Minerva-like, with a set of basic policies already roughhewn and at hand.
Dr. Gilbert Chinard, a Frenchman by birth, asks in his biography of
Thomas Jefferson what other nation, after outlining fundamental foreign
policies, has adhered to them so closely for over a century and a half.

A short-range policy, like that toward Vichy France in 1942, is apt to be a creation of the State Department; fundamental policies have to be and are creations of public opinion. They have sprung and continue to spring from the soil of our needs and aspirations, and this is what has given them vitality and longevity, as was notably true of the Monroe Doctrine. Policies designed to meet specific situations or to attain immediate goals, such as dollar diplomacy and imperialism, do not often have their roots deep in American tradition, and they wither away once the goal is attained or interest shifts, as was the case with imperialism. Isolation and the Monroe Doctrine have been more fundamental than Pan-Americanism and the Open Door, because the first two are intimately connected with our homeland security, while the last two are more concerned with economic opportunity in distant areas.

2

Our basic principles have been few, simple, and enduring. The historian Ellis P. Oberholtzer, referring to the 1890's, wrote that to the American mind the summation of our foreign policy consisted of little more than two ideas: nonentanglement and the Monroe Doctrine. This was broadly true of any decade between the War of Independence and World War II, although the Monroe Doctrine was not officially launched until 1823.

The sheer negativism of these two basic principles will not escape notice. The emphasis was on the "thou shalt not" rather than on the "thou shalt." Isolation or nonentanglement meant in essence: "Americans, thou shalt not become involved in Europe." The Monroe Doctrine meant in essence: "Europeans, thou shalt not become involved in America." In short, we would stay out of trouble, and expect Europe not to trouble us. The Open Door meant: "Foreign powers, thou shalt not carve up China into special-privilege areas." The nonrecognition doctrine of the Hoover-Stimson period meant: "Aggressors, thou shalt not seize thy neighbors' territory." As a "have" nation from the beginning, and as one that was not going anywhere except on its own or adjoining territory, we became apostles of the *status quo*. One reason perhaps why we hesitate to project clear-cut short-range policies into the future is that we have had generations of training in negativism.*

A half dozen or so fundamental principles have long existed, but they have not always been asserted. Violations of the Monroe Doctrine, particularly in the nineteenth century, were repeatedly ignored if they were far enough away not to pose an immediate threat to our security. Our basic policies have also meant different things in different parts of the world. Until recent times we adopted isolation toward Europe (where we were not strong enough to work our will), intervention in Latin America

---

* Pan-Americanism, which shaded into Good Neighborism, was perhaps our only major "thou shalt" policy, and this may explain in part why it was so slow in taking hold.

(where we were strong enough to work our will), and cooperation with the European powers in the Far East (where we were not strong enough to work our will alone). This further explains some of the contradictions that were discussed in the chapter on caprice.

American foreign policies have also meant different things under different administrations. Taft was for dollar diplomacy in China; Wilson turned sharply against it. Some of our policies, especially the short-range ones, mean different things to the different officials who are formulating and executing them. The present writer heard an officer of the State Department say in 1946 that while the United States did have a policy regarding a certain European country, he did not approve of it, and was doing all he could to change it.

Within the framework of these broad principles, the State Department enjoys considerable latitude in forming short-range policy consonant with popular desires, or in leading public opinion in matters regarding which there is no opinion or a confused opinion. But because the masses are notoriously shortsighted, and because the Department finds it politically inexpedient to "stick its neck out" too far, there cannot be too much imagination, vision, daring, or long-range planning at the higher levels, especially of a kind that can be made public. The Coolidge administration had a policy so intangible that when it failed, said the Baltimore *Sun*, there were no vulnerable points of criticism, and when it succeeded it could claim full credit. Charles Dickens had earlier observed that the British Foreign Office was a "Circumlocution Office," and the State Department has not been immune from such a charge. From the standpoint of domestic politics, excessive caution is no doubt desirable, but from the standpoint of advancing the best interests of the nation, timidity may not be the best policy.

3

The policy of nonentanglement—popularly known as isolation—is perhaps the oldest and certainly one of the most plausible and tenacious of all our fundamental principles. It is grounded solidly in American geography and genius, although the desire to intervene in behalf of democratic uprisings abroad has been a powerful, if less potent, force pulling in the opposite direction.

The term "isolation" has in recent years come to have a sinister connotation, much as a perfectly good word like "appeasement" came to have unfortunate implications from having kept bad company. In certain quarters during the days before Pearl Harbor, one only had to retort "isolationist" to end the argument and heap shame upon one's adversary. But this was not always so.

Only the most ignorant and purblind of our people—and unfortunately their numbers are formidable—believe that we are physically isolated from the rest of the world. The isolationist Senator Hiram W. Johnson of California declared in 1941 that the conflict raging in China and Europe had no conceivable relation to our interests. Such people are true isolationists. They confuse a perfectly legitimate and natural desire to be left alone with a presumed set of facts that does not exist. Although we are separated from Europe and Asia by wide oceans, separation does not spell isolation. The actualities of involvement have often overborne the desire for non-involvement, and the tragedy of Europe has long been one of the vital elements in American life.

The patron saints of the isolationists—Washington and Jefferson—have slept for many years in uneasy graves. Never have the views of thoughtful and farvisioned men been more grossly misrepresented. The Founding Fathers did not take the position that what went on in Europe was no concern of ours; they did not claim that the broad oceans granted us a complete immunity from the combinations and collisions of Europe. Jefferson hoped to draw a line through the middle of the Atlantic that would separate the two hemispheres forever, but he was intelligent enough to see that wishing did not make it so. What the Founding Fathers urged was that, so far as possible, we refrain from getting sucked into the broils of Europe. With this end in view, we would keep out of foreign complications, and expect foreigners to keep their complications out of America.

This was not only good policy but good sense. Minding one's own business, refraining from poking one's nose into all the quarrels of one's neighbors, is regarded as one of the cardinal virtues. We were so weak in those formative years that we would have courted suicide if we had wasted our strength in foreign adventures. Even well established nations, like eighteenth-century England in Hanover and twentieth-century Japan in China, find that ambitious overseas undertakings sap one's strength.

4

The illusion that we are isolated from the rest of the world and hence can pursue a policy of isolation, though an illusion, has nevertheless a substantial if misleading basis in geography.

The United States is separated from (or joined to) Europe and Asia by the two mightiest oceans. Immigrants who in colonial times survived the nightmarish horrors of the crossing knew that the Atlantic was wide, and passed this knowledge on to their children. The maternal grandparents of Woodrow Wilson sailed for America from England as late as 1835. Their ship sighted Newfoundland, was blown back to within sight of Ireland, and finally arrived in the United States, after a voyage lasting over two months.

After independence was won, our people felt reasonably secure for many decades behind their ocean moats, whose width was exaggerated by the spread-out Mercator projection commonly used in school geographies. A geographer has remarked, half in jest, that American foreign policy during the past fifty years would have followed a different course if the personnel of the State Department had not been schooled in the Mercator projection. The waves were our first line of defense, and they cost us nothing in money or effort. "Thank God for two wide oceans," we sighed in 1914, when war burst upon Europe; and two years later a Michigan newspaper observed: "The Atlantic Ocean is America's best liquid asset."

By the advent of World War II, the march of mechanization had narrowed the Atlantic Ocean until it was not much wider than the Dardanelles in the days of Helen of Troy, but it was still a barrier. Hitler halted at the edge of the English Channel and shook his fist impotently at the white cliffs of Dover, on the other side of a twenty-mile-wide tank trap. Even where we commanded the seas, as we did in the closing months of the Pacific war, we found it no easy task to reach Japan's front yard across the broad bosom of the Pacific.

Yet the age of flight has largely cancelled out the magic of the waves. The most electrifying news story of the decade was the conquest of the Atlantic in 1927 by "Lucky Lindy" (Charles A.) Lindbergh. The American people, far from rejoicing that the ocean had now become so narrow, were thrilled that one lone man could fly nonstop across so vast an expanse. The aviator who did this, also paradoxically, later became the Number One hero and spokesman of the isolationists in the months before Pearl Harbor.

The logic of the American land mass has in many ways been a more potent creator of isolationists than the encircling oceans. Most Americans do not travel on the high seas, but they all travel to some extent in the United States, and the vastness of our expanse lends unreality to the faraway embroilments of Europe. Lord Bryce felt this keenly after scaling a mountain in one of our Eastern states. From such an eminence in Scotland he could have seen the North Sea on the east and the Atlantic on the west, but in America he could gaze only sixty miles west and then try to reckon how many equally wide stretches there were to the Mississippi, which is only a third of the way across the continent.

The East, with New England thrust out toward Europe (on a globe), has generally been the section most sensitive to commotions in the Mother Continent; the Pacific Coast, facing the Orient, has been the most responsive to disorders in eastern Asia; the Middle West, regarding itself as America with some fringes about it, has for long periods been the most indifferent to either Europe or Asia. Shortly before World War I, Senator Norris of Nebraska took the lecture platform as an advocate of a league to preserve peace, but, he recorded, "my audiences, with the deep sense of security of the American interior," were more interested in the fight to deprive "Uncle Joe" Cannon of his powers as Speaker of the House of Representatives.

In the spring of 1940, the present writer left Washington, D.C., by automobile for California. Hitler had just launched his Blitzkrieg into the Netherlands, and the Washington bus riders were hunched anxiously over the headlines. But in the vastnesses of Utah, with the blue ramparts of the Rockies towering through the distant haze, with contented cattle grazing between far-flung farmhouses, it seemed incredible that the world was falling to pieces. The collapse of France was like something in a vaguely remembered dream. The United States seemed secure simply because it was so big and so wide.

5

Certain historical developments have contributed to the growth of the isolationist tradition.

In the late eighteenth century, a warm debate was raging in England over the wisdom of continuing the expensive and debilitating foothold on the continent. The arguments against doing so were brought to America by men like Tom Paine and Benjamin Franklin, and were used with some effect against maintaining the connection between America and the Mother Country.

Many of the early immigrants from Europe, especially Germans from the devastated Rhine region, came to America with the specific purpose of fleeing from the hell pits of the continent.° Knowing the miseries of war at first hand, they wished at all cost to stay out of them, and they passed on this conviction from generation to generation. There is much symbolism in the fact that one German pioneer in Missouri cut his first corn with a sword that his brother had used in 1813 against the French. Among the religious sects, the Lutherans were particularly active in preaching abstention from the greedy and imperialistic wars of Europe. They were seconded by refugees from conscription agents, by persecuted Jewish minorities, and by German liberals disillusioned by the collapse of the Revolution of 1848.

Scandinavian elements in the Middle Western melting pot, particularly in Minnesota, have been notoriously isolationist. If Sweden and Switzerland were able to keep out of the wars of the nineteenth and twentieth centuries, why should not powerful and faraway America? Charles A. Lindbergh, Sr., was a Swedish immigrant who bitterly opposed our entry into World War I, and who later published a book, *Why Is Your Country at War?* which was suppressed by government agents. Charles A. Lindbergh, Jr., in his widely acclaimed isolationist speeches of 1940–1941, often referred to his father and to the latter's belief that the United States had a destiny of its own which should be kept independent of foreign intrigue.

With isolationist immigrants forming a large part of our population, and with a tremendous ocean tossing between us and Europe, the idea took root that the Old World had a set of interests radically different from ours, as

---

° The Swedish invaders of the Rhineland during the Thirty Years' War (1618–1648) were alleged to have left behind only the cobblestones, which accounts for the persistence of a German proverb: "Oh, something the Swedes left behind."

indeed she then had. This doctrine of the two hemispheres, sometimes called the two spheres, was a primary factor in building up not only the foundations of nonentanglement but of the Monroe Doctrine as well.

The American experiment in democracy, which was viewed with unconcealed hostility by monarchical Europe, added an ideological barrier to the watery barrier of the Atlantic, especially in the nineteenth century. The idea took hold that an all-wise Providence had set aside this empty continent as a refuge from Europe's century-old hatreds and wars. Timothy Dwight wrote in 1794:

> See this glad world remote from every foe,
> From Europe's mischiefs, and from Europe's woe.

6

There was something about our magnificent forests, our rolling prairies, our lofty peaks, our ribboning rivers, our spacious skies that captured the imaginations of men and gave them a vision of a unique destiny. Our inexhaustible natural resources and multiplying factories, which enabled us to live a semi-Robinson Crusoe existence, implanted in our people a sense of confidence in themselves, and a feeling of seclusion from the rest of the world.

The presence of weak neighbors on either border relieved us of having to seek help from European powers through onerous alliances. Thomas Jefferson, the foe of entanglements, was forced to consider making an alliance with England against France when Napoleon was about to move into Louisiana in 1803, but happily such threats were eliminated by forces over which we had little or no control.

Europe's distresses—her preoccupations, balances of power, and wars—enabled the American people to concentrate on their destiny to a degree that otherwise would have been impossible. "Sir," said the Swedish ambassador in London to Minister John Adams in 1784, "I take it for granted, that you will have sense enough to see us in Europe cut each other's throats with a philosophical tranquility." On the whole we tried to pursue such a policy, and as late as 1941 most Americans would have been happy to see Adolf Hitler and Joseph Stalin slit each other's throats. But when we perceived that Stalin could not do the job without our help, we became increasingly involved. "The trouble seems to be," said a New Jersey newspaper as early as 1923, "that Uncle Sam must go to Europe to mind his own business." Europe's distresses have to an increasing degree become our distresses.

We were so engrossed with the task of civilizing a wilderness that not until the twentieth century did we have time and taste for foreign escapades, and then only on a limited scale. The British, on the contrary, early developed an outer worldliness as a result of their interest in a globe-girdling empire. "Many Americans," noted the Paris *Figaro* in 1921, "have the habit of speaking of Europe and of Paris as if they were places on another planet."

In addition to all these factors, the Man in the Street is a rugged individualist who has learned to hoe his own row without foreign support, who has developed an inherent distrust of foreigners, who has no deep-seated interest in foreign trade, and who, with true Yankee thrift, does not like to squander his money fighting what he conceives to be "other people's wars." Typical isolationist comments in 1940 were: "It isn't our fight." "As long as Germany doesn't bother us, there's no reason to bother her." "At least one nation should be left to pick up the pieces."

7

Bitter experience rather than abstract theory undoubtedly predisposed the American people toward isolationism. A burned child dreads the fire, and British colonials in what is now the United States were sufficiently burned by the European conflagrations to appreciate the wisdom of noninvolvement.

Beginning with 1689, England waged a series of wars with France and Spain, and the American pioneers became involved in every one of these, whether they wanted to or not. We were on occasion but pawns on the European chessboard. If England went to war with Spain, Spanish-incited Indians ravaged the Georgia and Carolina frontier; if England went to war with France, the war whoop of French-led Indians split the night air along the New England and New York frontier. At times it seemed as though the American colonies were but the battleground for Britain's battles. American seamen were captured by the French and imprisoned in the dungeons of the Château at Nantes, on the walls of which one could find carved the names of Nantucket fishermen—mute evidence of early involuntary involvement in Europe's broils. Toward the end of the colonial period, the Americans were willing to fight the French for their own protection, but before this time they resented having to shed their blood when the dynastic and other rivalries of Europe brought travail to the empire of which they were unavoidably a part.

Even before the Revolutionary War the American colonials were hostile to foreign entanglement. But the necessity of first wresting independence from England pointed to the desirability of linking hands with France, despite the anti-French and antialliance prejudices. The American leaders perceived that partnership with the powerful is never safe, and that those who seek protectors will not lack masters. Yet the urgency was great, and the bargain was struck. Among other things the Franco-American Alliance of 1778 was to last "forever" (which is a long time), and the Americans were bound in future wars to defend the French West Indies against the enemies of France.

The alliance worked reasonably well as long as we were fighting for independence, but when the French tried to subordinate our interests to theirs "forever," we sought to cast aside our obligations, and eventually became involved in an undeclared war with France. Napoleon in 1800 finally released us from this unholy marriage of convenience, but not until we agreed to pay alimony of some $20,000,000 to our shippers who had claims against the French.

For well over a century we remembered this unfortunate entanglement whenever the suggestion was made that we contract another, and the burned fingers of an earlier year consistently held us back from what might have been profitable alliances. We entered World War I on the side of the Allies, but not as a formal Ally. Woodrow Wilson, who was well aware of the widespread antipathy to alliances, stoutly insisted that we were an associate of the Allies, though not an Ally; and he sternly rapped the knuckles of subordinates who in unguarded moments referred to the United States (as most Americans were then doing) as one of the Allies. We nevertheless became involved in some expensive entanglements, and solved the whole problem (for the moment) by running out on our associates and leaving them holding the Treaty of Versailles. "Our foreign policy," said an Ohio newspaper, "seems to be that we won't belong to anything but are perfectly willing to butt in."

8

George Washington in 1796 handed down affectionate and mature words of farewell wisdom to the people whom he had so faithfully served, and he included a solemn warning against unnecessary alliances. He had specifically in mind the current difficulties with France over the vexatious treaty of 1778. Contrary to a popular legend, he did not warn against all alliances; he favored temporary alliances for "extraordinary emergencies," but he advised against permanent alliances ("forever") as contrary to our "true policy." In brief, abstention, rather than isolation.

The immortal Farewell Address is one of the least read, most incorrectly quoted, and most widely misunderstood documents in American history. The policy of the Founding Fathers was to make every effort to avoid involvement with the great European powers, for such involvement might destroy the infant Republic. We were simply too small and too weak to play with the big boys. Washington was giving specific advice to a harassed and enfeebled nation in the year of our Lord 1796, and he probably had no intention of attempting to bind the Republic for all time. The day finally came when the United States was so big and rough that the other lads played with us at their peril.

Yet George Washington is such a powerful symbol in American thinking, thanks in part to the Parson Weems cherry-tree-and-hatchet myth, that in some respects his Farewell Address was more potent a century later than when it was born. His sensible words, twisted and misinterpreted by isolationist propagandists, were used with powerful effect to keep us out of the League of Nations and other forward-looking enterprises. As a matter of fact, about two thirds of his address was not even devoted to foreign affairs. There were lengthy and eloquent passages urging the American people to be prepared for war, to avoid bitter partisanship, and to cling to the refuge of religion. The irony is that we have on the whole paid far less heed to these wholly admirable injunctions than we have to his presumed but misquoted remarks about alliances.

We have not only misread Washington's Farewell Address for isolationist ends, but we have misread our history for the same ends. Perusing its pages, we conclude that the encircling seas enabled us to win our independence, strengthen it, and keep out of pre-1917 European clashes. No one will deny that geographical separation was a vital force, but other factors were probably of at least equal importance. We came off well in the War for Independence and the War of 1812 largely because Europe was then preoccupied with other conflicts, and the American theater was a sideshow. We kept out of European clashes from 1814 to 1914, not so much because the oceans were spacious as because there were no general wars in which to become involved. The Atlantic, though rapidly growing narrower by 1914, was still impressively wide, and it did not prevent our participation in World War I, nor for that matter in World War II. The facts of geography have lost much of their former validity, but even to this day vast distances cannot be lightly brushed aside.

One may reasonably conclude that the impulse to isolationism came from a perfectly understandable set of circumstances. Human nature being what it is, any other people similarly situated would almost certainly have developed the same tendency.

THE FRUITS OF ISOLATION

"We are participants, whether we would or not, in the life of the world. The interests of all nations are our own also. We are partners with the rest. What affects mankind is inevitably our affair as well as the affair of Europe and of Asia."—Woodrow Wilson, 1916

1

FROM THE DAYS of the Founding Fathers to the late nineteenth century, the nonentanglement tradition persisted with pristine vigor. The public was so hostile to foreign entanglements that the federal government was even reluctant to become identified with such an innocuous organization as the International Red Cross. The administration of President Arthur was subjected to some little criticism when it recognized the International Association of the Congo, and one cartoonist drew a map of Africa with Uncle Sam sticking his long nose up the Congo Estuary. Until 1884 our government participated formally in only two international conferences. Official intermeddling in Samoa, in Hawaii, in the Philippines, and in China at the time of the Boxer difficulties—all these were condemned as flagrant departures from the precepts of the Fathers.

Theodore Roosevelt, despite his juvenile jingoism, was the first President in modern times with a thoroughly international outlook, and he had a "bully time" brandishing the Big Stick and herding into international conferences the kings and emperors, the tsars and mikados. The Republicans under McKinley and Hay and Roosevelt were not isolationist as a group; they could trust themselves to intermeddle. The Grand Old Party did not become tainted with isolationism until the distrusted Democrats came into power in 1913, and it seemed "good politics" to oppose with every weapon available the Democratic brand of internationalism.

Woodrow Wilson was intelligent enough to perceive that the world had become too small for ivory-tower escapism, but his effort to convert his own people to the League of Nations ran afoul of ignorance, apathy, disillusionment, partisan politics, and the clammy hand of tradition. The abandonment of nonentanglement seemed eminently logical to the quick-witted Wilson, but he made the mistake of assuming similar perception on the part of his less apperceptive countrymen. Believing with Jefferson that "the earth belongs to the living and not to the dead," he tried to go too far and too fast, without first of all undertaking to educate the American people to their new responsibilities. Such a campaign might well have failed had it been launched, but without it failure seems to have been inevitable, either in the short run or the long run. Someone has said that we do not have a democracy but a necrocracy—a government by the graveyards. Dead men actually had a great deal to do with the defeat of the Treaty of Versailles in America, dead men like Washington and Jefferson who could not defend themselves against misquotation and misrepresentation. Another ironical fact is that George Washington could not keep us out of World War I, but he could keep us out of a League designed to prevent World War II.

In the days of George Washington, we had no choice; ours was the isolation of weakness. In the days of Woodrow Wilson, we had a choice; ours was the isolation of power. There was a growing sentiment for abandoning head-in-the-sands isolationism, and the evidence is strong that in 1919 a majority of the American people wanted to enter the League of Nations with some reservations. There was even surprising editorial support, though falling short of a majority, for the abortive defensive alliance with France and Great Britain. We misinterpreted the election of 1920 as a mandate against the League, and the victorious Republicans retreated into a policy of sullen and selfish isolation, refusing to pull their weight in the international boat. While Rome burned, we cooperated in the suppression of narcotics, anthrax, obscene publications, and the traffic in women and children. "Every time Europe looks across the Atlantic to see the American eagle," wrote the British novelist H. G. Wells, "it observes only the rear end of an ostrich."

Even the spineless Four Power Pact of 1921, designed to keep peace in the Pacific, was assailed by Senator Reed of Missouri as "treacherous, treasonable, and damnable." The infantile teeth of the treaty were finally extracted by a reservation. The doings of the League of Nations at Geneva were watched furtively, by "unofficial observers," although one Democratic newspaper in North Carolina would have liked to "see Uncle Sam go in at the front door with shoulders squared, rather than sneak in at the rear entrance like a tramp after a handout." * The war-debts uproar merely confirmed a growing suspicion that we had been "suckers" to depart from the advice of the Fathers and pay for other peoples' wars, let alone fight them. "We positively will not mix in Europe's affairs," jibed a Chicago journal, "except at intervals to settle her disputes."

The Senate declined to join the "death-trap" World Court, although in so doing it clearly defied public opinion. The reservations that it attached were so eviscerating as to prove unacceptable to the other powers. "At the end of a long rope," observed the Chicago *Evening Post*, "the other end of which is held by the Senate, the United States enters the World Court provided with a bottle of disinfectant and a portable fire-escape."

2

When Japan went on the rampage in Manchuria in 1931, Secretary of State Stimson wanted to halt the war-mad Nipponese imperialists. But the

* The Buffalo *Enquirer* said in 1924: "The chief advantage of unofficial observing is that it affords opportunity to claim the credit, and shun the blame."

harassed Americans, then bogged down in the Great Depression, were in no mood to depart from the nonentanglement tradition, and both President Hoover and the British sensed this. Our time-honored policy of mild cooperation in the Far East drifted thereafter toward complete isolationism. Then came the misleading Nye investigation of 1934–1936, which confirmed isolationist suspicions by apparently proving that we had been led into war by the armor-plate patriots, those soulless jackals who fatten on the lifeblood of both sides.

With the munitioneers thus found guilty at the bar of public opinion, and with Europe obviously drifting toward destruction by way of Ethiopia and Spain, the country demanded and got "permanent neutrality legislation." This species of turtle-necked fatalism, with its emphasis on strength through weakness, can be understood only in the light of our isolationist fixation and disillusionment after World War I. President Franklin Roosevelt, frowning upon strait-jacket legislation designed to tie his hands in future contingencies, reluctantly signed the bills, although later publicly regretting his action. He much preferred to have the influence of the United States kept free to shape events so that we would not be left at the mercy of events. But the desire to keep out of war at all costs had become "a national passion," as Dr. Gallup concluded in 1937, and the public regarded Congress as a more satisfactory lightning rod than it did the President.

The time to have joined the League was in 1919, when the League wanted us and needed us. Then we could have entered upon a program of collective security, with somewhat greater prospect of success. But fifteen or so years later the alternatives were not isolation or collective security, but isolation and what was in effect an alliance against the dictators. Our traditions naturally caused us to draw back from the second horrid alternative.

In the late 1930's the Roosevelt administration was repeatedly forced to deny the charge, like John Hay at the end of the century, that the State Department had entered into a secret understanding or alliance with England. Early in 1939, after the tense days of the Munich crisis, Roosevelt was quoted as having said that the frontier of the United States was on the Rhine. The resulting outburst from isolationists was so vehement that the President was forced to declare that some "boob" had invented that "deliberate lie," and that he contemplated no departure from the existing policy of no entanglements. Six years later hundreds of thousands of American boys were on the Rhine.

3

The great debate from 1939 to 1941 between the isolationists and the interventionists was not nearly so clear-cut as one might suppose. There were several rather definitely defined groups.

First, the "insulationists," like Senator Hiram W. Johnson and Colonel Charles A. Lindbergh, who insisted that we had nothing much to worry about, even if the rest of the world was going up in flames. Why, asked Lindbergh, should we defend "the English way of life and the Chinese way of life?"

Secondly, there were the "abstentionists," men like William Allen White, who recognized that the world-wide conflagration was of vital concern to us, but who believed that we should stay out as long as practicable. The Committee to Defend America by Aiding the Allies, which he headed, began to run away with him in 1941, but he insisted that his slogan was: "The Yanks are not coming."

Finally, there were the avowed "interventionists," like Herbert S. Agar, who believed that England was fighting our fight, that if she went under we would have to face the might of Hitler alone, and that as soon as possible we should defend America by fighting the Axis.

Yet the extreme interventionists were to the very end only a small minority. The vast majority wanted to stay out of the conflict, but the outlook was so frightening that they were willing to aid their friends even at the risk of war. The issue finally became: "Can we afford to stay out?" rather than "Can we stay out?"

Pearl Harbor exploded, and in 1942 we subscribed to the Declaration of the United Nations. While this was technically not a treaty of alliance, it was actually our first military compact since the French entanglement of 1778. A year later, in 1943, Dr. Gallup asked whether the United States and Great Britain should make "a permanent military alliance" and agree to come immediately to the defense of each other in the event of attack. The same question was asked regarding Russia and China. The results are illuminating:

	Yes	No	No opinion
England	61 per cent	25 per cent	14 per cent
Russia	39	37	24
China	56	23	21

These figures reveal a marked weakening of the anti-British, antialliance tradition under the spell of a common cause during a global war. But support for military alliances waned when we saw that our hopes for the future were going to be pinned to a United Nations organization. Winston Churchill urged a British-American alliance in his reverberating speech at Fulton, Missouri, in 1946, but the public response was far from favorable, partly because we wanted to give the new United Nations organization a fair trial.

Later that same year Secretary of State Byrnes, then at Paris, offered Russia, Britain, and France a twenty-five-year treaty of alliance to enforce German disarmament. His successor, Secretary Marshall, raised the limit to forty years at Moscow in 1947, but without success. Times had indeed changed when an American statesman could publicly propose such a pact, and when the American people could refrain from emitting an outraged cry of protest. But we were just one war late in our willingness to accept a defensive alliance. The French, in particular, cannot forget that Wilson at Paris had signed a similar pact with France and Britain back in 1919, and that it had never emerged from the Senatorial pigeonhole to be given a loquacious and dignified rejection.

4

The belief that isolation in an extreme form can ever work is a striking example of the triumph of hope over experience.

From 1689 to 1945 there were nine general or world wars.* How many did the American people succeed in staying out of? The answer is none. When the interests of empire demanded it, as in the French and Indian War, or when our national security demanded it, as in 1917 and 1941, we cast aside the ancient fetish and found ourselves fighting.

Ignorance of our history, as earlier indicated, is one of the bulwarks of the rabid isolationist. If we only knew our own history better, if we only were aware of our repeated failures, we would be less inclined to clamor for a policy divorced from reality. We were unable to keep out of general wars when we were sparsely populated colonies, clinging precariously to the eastern fringe of North America; we had even less chance of staying out when we became a great power, with far-flung possessions, with investments in every continent, with citizens in every land, and with ships on every sea. We could not keep out when we were a third-rate debtor nation. How could we hope to escape involvement when, after 1914, we became an international creditor? The world has long since become a bundle of nerves in which a disturbance in one place is immediately reflected all over the globe. Fifty years ago the Dardanelles were a European problem; now they are a world problem.

The blindness of the isolationists has gone even further. They have insisted upon no political entanglements in foreign lands, while at the same time demanding economic entanglements, whether through trade or investment. During the feverish 1920's the Republican politicians ranted against involvement in Europe, and all the while the Republican bankers were pouring hundreds of millions of dollars into Germany, much of which was used to build modern factories. In some respects an economic entanglement is more entangling than a political one. A nation can denounce an alliance or withdraw from a league with relative ease, but it cannot so easily remove a $3,000,000 factory from the heart of Germany.

Commerce makes neighbors of us all, and our exporters, importers, and foreign investors are notoriously more internationally minded than the rank and file. They have generally traveled more extensively than their neighbors, and they recognize that the economy of the various nations is inter-

---

* Excluding localized conflicts like the Crimean War, the Austro-Prussian War, and the Franco-German War. The Austrian War was actually over before our news correspondents could arrive.

twined. We exchange ideas and points of view when we exchange fabrics and wines, and Thomas Jefferson was not far from the mark when he observed: "The merchant has no country."

Another curiosity is presented by the Middle West, which has for protracted periods been the backbone of isolationism, but which on a rational economic basis should not be. The prosperity of this great region has long been dependent upon the price of wheat and other agricultural commodities, and these prices in turn have been dependent on world demand and world production. Disorder or drouth in Russia or in the Argentine or in Australia may mean the difference between profits or indebtedness to the Nebraska farmer, and he, of all persons, should be vitally interested in happenings abroad. He should also be most keenly alive to the expansion of foreign trade. Ex-Governor Lowden of Illinois said in 1923 that we might be able to purchase isolation, but the price would be the reversion of 30 per cent of our wheat fields and 20 per cent of our corn fields back to native prairies, and 50 per cent of our cotton fields back to native forest.

The man behind the plow has long been distressingly impervious to most of these obvious facts. He doggedly tills his corn field and curses the government in Washington for his mortgage. The more shortsighted and ignorant he is, the more likely he is to be an extreme isolationist, and on him the isolationist leaders feed. The less he knows, the more apt he is to feel that we ought to resort to one of two impossible extremes: withdraw from the world entirely or run it by ourselves singlehandedly.

5

The fallacy is common among certain ardent American internationalists that the United States is the only nation that has ever tried to chase the will-o'-the-wisp of isolationism.

The desire to keep out of unnecessary and expensive trouble is so deeply rooted in human nature that countries all over the world have attempted to avoid entanglements when they found it to their interests to do so. A parallel to American isolationism can readily be found in the history of Canada, Australia, South Africa, Argentina, Russia, and other nations. The British were actually forced to forsake their "splendid" but dangerous isolation at the turn of the century in the face of the rising might of Germany. They have for many decades seriously grappled with proposals to construct a tunnel under the English Channel, but a potent objection has been the danger of a surprise invasion from Europe. In the 1920's the British drifted away from their French ally, owing in part to America's refusal to join the League of Nations, and in many respects the post-Versailles isolationism of England was more disastrous than that of the United States.

The skeleton hand of traditionalism has often jerked the United States back from the threshold of courses that would have been advantageous to us. An alliance or even an understanding with England at the time John Hay was trying to prop open the Open Door would have given greater effectiveness to that policy. The rejected Anglo-Franco-American Alliance of 1919 very probably would have prevented World War II, and even in the late 1930's a firm and well publicized understanding with England, instead of our negative neutrality legislation, would almost certainly have acted as a brake on Hitler. World War II was a stiff price to pay for a sacred cow that never did give satisfactory milk. Policies, as earlier observed, should be servants and not masters.

This does not mean that we must go to the trouble and expense of rushing into every political commotion that develops on the face of the earth. Just as the house painter who begins by touching up one panel ends by painting the whole room, so the danger of intervention is to sink deeper and deeper into the international quicksands. There are also serious dangers in ignorant intermeddling. Europe understands its own problems best, and until we are willing to study them and understand them, and until we are willing to stay with the job of reconstruction until it is intelligently done, we had better temper our enthusiasm for foreign adventures. The last two world wars have given the Americans the reputation of being the greatest devastators since Attila the Hun, and Attila was a boy playing with tin soldiers compared with the Americans at Hiroshima. A stock complaint of the Europeans after World War I, especially of the Germans, was that since we intervened and reduced Europe to a shambles, we had some moral responsibility to help pick up the pieces and make sure that they would stay picked up.

Intermeddling may in fact defeat its avowed purposes. Redblooded Americans resented the machinations of French agents in our Philadelphia capital during the 1790's, and the net result was a smarting defeat for French policy. Other peoples also react unfavorably when the shadow of our Big Stick falls on their foreign office. In 1946 the State Department, following the anti-Fascist policy of Ambassador Braden, ill-advisedly interfered in the Argentine general election by publishing a documentary Blue Book. This gesture undoubtedly made votes for dictator Perón, who was triumphantly elected with the aid of the slogan, "Perón or Braden." We should know better than to do this sort of thing clumsily, for the interference of "damnyankees" in Southern politics has long played into the hands of demagogues like Senator Bilbo.

6

The policy of nonentanglement fashioned by Washington and his colleagues was designed for adolescence. But long before Dewey's booming guns heralded the emergence of a new world power in 1898, we had ceased to be the anxious adolescent of Farewell Address days. When a man becomes a man he puts away childish things, or is supposed to. At the close of World War II we had over half the gold, over half the shipping, and over half the industrial capacity of the entire globe. Whether we did something constructively with all this power, or did nothing at all with it, we profoundly affected the fate of the entire world. Do-nothingism may be negative action of a most positive sort.

Narrow isolationism implies cowardice: we are afraid to acquit ourselves like men for fear that we might get ensnared. Narrow isolationism also implies stupidity: we are afraid that, even with all the high cards in our hands, we shall be "outslickered" by suave foreign diplomats. Americans are not cowards, as they proved from Concord to Corregidor, and they are not dolts. But the persistence of the myth that we have never won a conference has tended to give us an inferiority complex, and has made for isolationism. A knowledge of our own past would increase our self-confidence.

The geographical basis of isolationism, though never completely valid, is now much less valid than ever before. In the age of supersonic weapons and atomic bombs, only the most obtuse and dimvisioned can hope to wrap the mantle of their two oceans about them and lie down to quiet sleep. As early as the opening weeks of World War I, a distinguished Englishman referred to the "remoteness" of the United States. "Remote from what?" snorted the American ambassador, Walter Hines Page.

Today we have much less geography, but vastly more power. We have no choice as to participation in world affairs. Destiny and the march of events long ago determined that we should be a great power, and as the greatest of the powers we are inescapably in the center of the maelstrom. The alternatives are not: Shall we withdraw or shall we participate? The alternatives are: Shall we participate shortsightedly and ineptly, or shall we participate intelligently and boldly, striving to control international affairs in our own interest, rather than being tossed about by them like a derelict on a deserted sea? When World War II came to an end, an increasing number of Americans saw these things, but with weariness and disillusionment there was a growing desire for the nostalgic dream world of isolationism. This time there was a tendency to call it by a more seemly name: "nationalism." *

The brutal fact is that we are co-citizens of One World. It is not even One World but One Room. We shall have to dispose of the lunatics, in cooperation with other nations, and learn to live in peace with those who want peace.

* A Roper poll of May, 1945, showed that not 10 per cent were isolationists of the last-ditch variety.

CHAPTER TWENTY-TWO

THE CULT OF MONROEISM

". . . the American continents . . . are henceforth not to be considered as subjects for future colonization by any European powers."—JAMES MONROE, 1823

1

A STORY, probably fictitious but certainly in character, is told of two patriotic Americans who met on the streets of an unnamed town. "What's this I hear about you," demanded one, "that you say you do not believe in the Monroe Doctrine?" The reply was instant and indignant:

"It's a lie. I never said I did not believe in the Monroe Doctrine. I do believe in it. It is the palladium of our liberties. I would die for the Monroe Doctrine. All I said was that I do not know what it means."

The Man in the Street certainly cannot step forward with a clear-cut definition of the Monroe Doctrine. He cannot define an elephant either, but he can recognize one when he sees it, which is more to the point. And even if he cannot define the Monroe Doctrine satisfactorily, he can recognize a situation seriously threatening its basic principles, which also is more to the point.

In the simplest possible terms the Monroe Doctrine means: "America for the Americans." Or, "Europe (and Asia), hands off the Americas." Other powers must not secure any more territory on these continents, because if they do they might use it as a base from which to jeopardize our security, and the security nerve is our most sensitive.

The Monroe Doctrine is now so venerable, and it has commanded so much worshipful respect, that its adulators have formed a kind of cult, as often happens with things but dimly understood. At times the Doctrine has seemed to be not a political issue but an emotional or ethical impulse. John Hay, one of our more flashy secretaries of state, proclaimed in a public address: "The briefest expression of our rule of conduct is, perhaps, *the Monroe Doctrine and the Golden Rule*. With this simple chart we can hardly go far wrong."

Other spokesmen have openly bracketed the ancient altarpiece of the Monroe Doctrine with things spiritual. The founder of Christian Science, Mrs. Mary Baker Eddy, once remarked: "I believe strictly in the Monroe Doctrine, in our Constitution, and in the laws of God." One of her disciples, Mrs. Augusta E. Stetson, published a large advertisement in the New York *Times* in 1923, on the occasion of the one hundredth anniversary of the Doctrine, proclaiming that the sacrosanct shibboleth was "as binding upon America as our God-inspired constitution." An English writer once concluded: "To the Americans, the Monroe Doctrine is like God or religion to a small child—something fearful, something to inspire awe, something, if necessary, to fight for."

The Monroe Doctrine and nonentanglement are so intimately related that, for the nineteenth century at least, they might well have been called Siamese twins. Both policies sprang from the stony soil of our necessities. Nonentanglement meant that we must stay out of Europe because we were weak. The Monroe Doctrine meant that Europe must keep out of America because we were weak. Both principles involved our security, and for that reason commanded strong popular support, which became stronger at those times when our security was threatened.

The Monroe Doctrine has not only been one of the oldest and most enduring of our foreign policies, but on the whole it has been the most popular. Every major declaration of American foreign policy prior to that time had been the subject of violent political contention, but the Monroe Doctrine was applauded by all sections and factions. We have quarreled about isolation, neutrality, the Open Door, Pan-Americanism, freedom of the seas, and other dogmas, although seldom about the original principles of President Monroe. The answer is that policies like the Open Door and Pan-Americanism do not as a rule involve any immediate threat to our continental security, but the lodgment of an unfriendly foreign power in the Americas hits us where we live. The Monroe Doctrine was the only policy for which we would fight at the drop of a hat, because there is simply no quarreling over security.

2

The Monroe Doctrine was in incubation for well over a century. The principle of the two hemispheres, each with different interests, became rooted at an early date in colonial psychology. The Founding Fathers quickly embraced the policy that places like Cuba, on which we cast both apprehensive and covetous eyes, should not be transferred to other European powers. President James Monroe and Secretary John Quincy Adams generally codified existing ideas, and dramatically gave them to the world in the presidential message of 1823.

The Russian bear was presumably lumbering down the west coast of North America from present-day Alaska; the reactionary powers of Europe, popularly known as the Holy Alliance, were presumably preparing to restore the tyranny of the ass-headed Spanish king over his revolted American colonies. Actually, the Russian bear was preparing to *withdraw* up the coast of North America, and the so-called Holy Alliance had no definite plans for reerecting Spanish Bourbonism on the smouldering ruins of nascent Latin-American republicanism. But the contrary belief was popularly held in the United States, and as is so often the case the important thing was not the truth but what the masses believed to be the truth.

The immortal message of Monroe rather incidentally warned Russia in effect that the era of colonization had ended, and that henceforth there would be a closed season on land-grabbing in the Americas. Russia, Britain, Spain, and the others might keep what they had, but they must not seize any more. As for the Holy Alliance, which was then our chief worry, the European powers were emphatically informed that they must not attempt to force their monarchical systems upon the liberty-loving Americas. "Europe," warned Monroe in effect, "you stay on your side of the water, and we'll stay on ours."

The words of Monroe seemed highly audacious, and red-corpuscled Americans instantly expressed warm approval, all the more so because we could thus give vent to our antimonarchical antipathy. It was a first-rate piece of impertinence for a third-rate republic to stand up and tell all the great powers of Europe to mind their own business.

But the challenge was not nearly so bold as one might think. The Holy Alliance then had no definite plans for aggression, and even if it had, the all-powerful British Navy lay athwart its course. The British mercantile interests did not want the Spanish monarchy restored, for in that event the ports which the revolutionists had thrown open to outside trade would be slammed shut. The United States wanted the Holy Alliance to stay out of Latin America primarily for reasons of safety; Great Britain wanted the Holy Alliance to stay out primarily for reasons of trade. The result was a significant parallelism of policy growing out of entirely different objectives. So it was reasonably safe for James Monroe, sheltered behind the stout wooden walls of the British fleet, to blow a republican blast of defiance at all the potentates of Europe.*

The threat passed, and during the next two decades the message of 1823 gathered cobwebs while our people addressed themselves to the task of subduing a half continent. President Polk dramatically resurrected the now sacred principles in 1845, when he reaffirmed them against the British in Oregon and California; and by the 1850's the Doctrine, although associated with the then dominant Democratic party, was being called by its present name, "the *Monroe* Doctrine."

3

The Monroe Doctrine did not really come of age and attain the stature of a national dogma, as distinguished from a Democratic party dogma, until the 1860's. Napoleon III of France, maneuvering behind the smoke screen of our Civil War, attempted to set up the puppet Maximilian in Mexico. This was the most barefaced violation of the Monroe Doctrine ever undertaken: the seizure of a next-door neighbor's territory; the stamping out of

---

* The idea that we then hid behind the buckler of our hereditary foe is offensive to ardent American nationalists. Senator Downey of California jabbed at it during the 1939 debate over lifting the arms embargo for the Allies.

a republican regime; and the propping up of a European-manipulated despotism. Secretary Seward marked time during the all-engrossing Civil War, restraining as best he could the popular outcries against Maximilian. But after General Lee's surrender, and with the authority of a million victorious bayonets, he told Napoleon III to get out, and Napoleon got, taking French leave of his manikin Maximilian, who perished before a Mexican firing squad.

With this threat gone, we laid the Monroe Doctrine on the shelf, and went ahead with our self-appointed task of marching to the Pacific. From time to time a President or secretary of state would add a new interpretation to the Doctrine, but the swashbuckling Theodore Roosevelt in 1904 lifted its entire face. Certain irresponsible Caribbean republics were incurring huge debts, and there was danger that the Germans and other creditors might attempt to collect with armed forces. If they came, they might stay; if they stayed, they would violate the Monroe Doctrine; if they violated the Monroe Doctrine they would present an intolerable threat to our isthmian viscera. The Roosevelt corollary proclaimed a policy of preventive intervention. We would land marines, take over the customhouses, restore order, pay off the debts, and keep inviolate both the Monroe Doctrine and the Panama life line. With reference to the European powers, the St. Louis *Globe-Democrat* summarized our new attitude: "You mind your business, and we'll mind yours."

This was so extreme a stretching of Monrovian principles as to constitute a new doctrine. But our people are somewhat in awe of distinguished names, and there was a much better chance that the new policy would take hold if attached to the time-tried Doctrine of Monroe. So the venerable Virginian was made to say things that he never said or meant.

Under the aegis of the Roosevelt corollary, the marines made many landings on the shores of the Caribbean republics, and the apprehension of our sovereignty-loving victims, whether present or prospective, mounted higher and higher. The idealistic Woodrow Wilson strove earnestly to narrow the interventionist policy of his Big-Sticking predecessor, but he was caught in the web of circumstance. When he brought the first draft of the League of Nations Covenant back from Paris, the American public demanded that a reservation be inserted safeguarding the Monroe Doctrine; and not content with this, the senators added a reservation to the reservation. No foreigners were going to lay unclean hands on our ancient fetish.

The high tide of interventionism in Latin America came in 1927, when President Coolidge found himself waging a "private war" in Nicaragua with some 5,000 men under his orders. But President Hoover adopted a narrow interpretation of the Monroe Doctrine, and President Franklin Roosevelt, in pursuance of the Good Neighbor policy, completely renounced armed intervention in the Americas. Despite persistent provocation he kept this pledge.

4

In times of peace or fancied security, the Monroe Doctrine has gathered dust behind the door. While Mussolini was ravishing Ethiopia in 1936, *Fortune* reported that not two Americans in ten would fight if a Latin-American country were attacked. The urge to defend South American and other outlying areas responded with thermometric precision to the rise in the international temperature before Munich, after Munich, after the invasion of Poland, and after the fall of France.

The figures for the period before the fall of France contrast strikingly with those for the period after. The American people were asked by *Fortune* if they would defend the following places, and the "Yes" percentages are herewith given:

	Jan. 1939 (before France was invaded)	Aug. 1940 (after France was invaded)
Canada	73.1 per cent	87.8 per cent
Mexico	43	76.5
Hawaii		74
Philippines	46.3	65.5
Bermuda	33.9	60.3
Brazil	27.1	54.7
Dutch East Indies	17.1	

The collapse of the Low Countries and France in 1940 aroused fears that Nazi Germany would establish submarine and air bases on the orphaned Dutch and French West Indies, menacingly near our Panamanian nerve center. Congress overwhelmingly passed a no-transfer resolution, in conformity with public opinion and the Monroe Doctrine, but the Nazis created further misgivings when they flatly refused to admit the applicability of Monrovian principles.

Prompted by these perils, representatives of all the American republics assembled at Havana in July, 1940. They formally agreed, subject to ratification by their home governments, that European territory in this hemisphere which was in danger of falling into hostile hands might be taken over by the American republics and administered jointly by them pending a final disposition of the area in question. The principle of joint defense against aggression was confirmed and strengthened at Chapultepec in 1945 and Rio de Janeiro in 1947.

This was an epochal development in the evolution of the Monroe Doctrine. Heretofore it had been the sole property of the United States; hereafter it was to be the joint property of the American republics. Heretofore we had been in the position of opposing both Europe and our twenty neighbors while enforcing the Monroe Doctrine; henceforth we would have their cooperation and active support. A unilateral anachronism had been changed to conform to mutilateral realism. An era had ended.

But all this did not mean that we had renounced the original Monroe Doctrine. If a foreign danger should again arise, and the multilateral machinery should prove too slow or too cumbersome, the United States in its discretion would undoubtedly take prompt, unilateral action, and count upon subsequent endorsement by the Latin American republics. Such a situation was in fact envisaged at the Havana Conference of 1940.

5

Dr. Albert Bushnell Hart once said that much trouble and confusion would have been avoided if Monroe had only had the foresight to take out a copyright on his Doctrine. The misunderstandings that popularly exist may be clarified if one remembers that there have been three Monroe Doctrines, two of them masquerading in the mantle of Monroe. First, the original Monroe Doctrine of James Monroe, which was defensive. Secondly, the Monroe Doctrine of Theodore Roosevelt, which was offensively defensive, or imperialistic. Thirdly, the mutilateralized or continentalized Monroe Doctrine of 1940, which was hemispherically defensive.* One must bear in mind that in most of the present discussion reference is being made to the pre-1940 unilateral version.

The Monroe Doctrine really needs no distinguishing name. It is basically a security or self-defense formula, and in some respects it might just as well be called the "Security Doctrine" or the "Self-Defense Doctrine." The challenge flung down by Maximilian in Mexico was the most flagrant in the long history of the dogma, but, strangely enough, Secretary Seward never once mentioned the Doctrine by name in his numerous diplomatic interchanges with the French, although no one could doubt what he had in mind. He told the French to evacuate because their presence imperiled our security, and this fact was so plain that he did not need to drag James Monroe or George Washington or other dead men into the discussion.

A rose by any other name would be just as thorny, and a Monroe Doctrine by any other name would have just as much potency, for its teeth are the battleships and aircraft and other weapons that can be mobilized by the United States and (latterly) its co-sponsors. During the nineteenth century the dogma was just as strong as the Army and Navy of the United States, and no stronger. In the midst of the Civil War the Monroe Doctrine was impotent to eject the French from Mexico, so it went by default. When the conflict ended, we had ample power, so Napoleon went. We have never had to fight to uphold the Monroe Doctrine, although we have had some close calls. The threat of armed force that lay behind the Doctrine was usually

* Six years later, the Moscow radio was apparently unaware of these developments, for one of its commentators said: "The Monroe Doctrine has become a symbol of economic, military, and political supremacy of the United States." It was "a direct threat to the sovereignty of Latin-American countries."

all that was needed. As the Chicago *Tribune* put it in 1902: "You let the Monroe Doctrine alone, and it will let you alone." In short, if we had the power, we did not need the help of a doctrine; and if we did not have the power, the doctrine did us no good.

Yet, the proverb to the contrary, the Monroe Doctrine by a more prosaic name would have had a somewhat different odor. The "Security Doctrine" or the "Thomas Pownall Doctrine" would not have added much in the way of prestige or longevity. James Monroe was not a giant himself, a fact not generally known, but he walked and talked with the Virginia giants like Washington and Jefferson, and his name gave the Doctrine the aura of venerability and immortality. The American people, as is true of others, like to personalize policies, to attribute guilt to Kaisers and credit to Monroes. A recently published collection of anecdotes enjoyed a phenomenal sale, partly because the compiler was clever enough to hang his hoary jests on Franklin Roosevelt, Charles Chaplin, or some other figure currently or recently in the public eye, and preferably touched with greatness.

"What's in a name?" Shakespeare asked over three hundred years ago. The answer is: "A great deal." The name of Monroe conjures up pictures of the Founding Fathers; it gives the public something tangible on which to pin a rather abstruse principle; it helps polarize the idea of "Hands Off" around a personality; and it provides a convenient catch phrase, which the public so often needs to sustain interest. If no name had been attached to the Doctrine, or a less significant name, there would have been fewer people willing to fight for it without knowing what it meant.

6

Until 1940 the Monroe Doctrine was strictly a unilateral policy of the United States. We had thought it up; it was ours and not the property of any other nation; it was an agreement with ourselves.

The Washington government has often been criticized for the Monroe Doctrine, especially south of the Rio Grande, and we have sometimes been told that we do not know what it means. Such critics overlook the elementary fact that sovereign powers have the right to enunciate and define their own policies. This indeed is one of the most precious attributes of sovereignty. Other nations may charge that our policy is irrelevant, illogical, or unjust, but they can hardly say with good grace that our government does not know what it means, even though this may be true. Yet the accusation has been repeatedly made, and it has filled the air with clamor and the mind of Mr. Average Citizen with confusion.

The ordinary American has been further bewildered by the Protean shapes which the Doctrine has been made to assume. Adaptability is a secret of its tenacity: in the past we could make the Monroe Doctrine mean pretty much what we wanted it to mean, which at times was highly convenient. It started out as a simple statement of the policy of President James Monroe in the field of foreign affairs. What one President says in one message he may unsay in another; what he has said, his successors may unsay, resay, or resay with additions, distortions, or retractions. And they have.

Elasticity has perhaps been the most distinguishing feature of the Monroe Doctrine. It has meant all things to all men; it has meant one thing at one period, another at another. It has been called the "India-rubber doctrine," the "gutta-percha doctrine," "as comprehensive as all outdoors." The elastic clause of the Constitution looks like a piece of sheet iron when laid beside it.

Woodrow Wilson, while swinging around the country in behalf of the League in 1919, made an arresting statement in Spokane, Washington. He said that at Paris he tried to have a definition of the Monroe Doctrine written into the Treaty of Versailles, "but I will confide to you in confidence that when I tried to define it, I found that it escaped analysis." It was, he continued, just a statement of our policy regarding the Western Hemisphere which we felt at liberty to invoke when we wanted to. But, Wilson concluded: "This is not a definition."

Like ivy clinging to a vigorous young tree, the Doctrine grew with our growth, and adapted itself to our necessities. Many corollaries were added, including those of Polk, Grant, Olney, Lodge and Theodore Roosevelt, but the greatest of these was Roosevelt's. What the first Roosevelt gave in the form of a perversion, the second Roosevelt took away in the form of a reversion. One irreverent commentator has said: "The Roosevelts gave, and the Roosevelts took away, blessed be the name of the Roosevelts."

7

A whole cluster of myths, legends and misconceptions have attached themselves to the Monroe Doctrine, and further befuddled the average citizen.

A distinguished journalist, Walter Lippmann, in a best-selling book which attained cigar-counter currency, asserts that the Monroe Doctrine was in effect an alliance with England. The truth is that it was the reverse of an alliance. The British Foreign Secretary, George Canning, proposed to our minister in London that the two nations jointly warn the Holy Alliance to stay out of Latin America. Minister Rush hesitated, then decided to refer the question back to Washington, but before he could get Monroe's negative answer, Canning had lost interest and had embarked upon an independent course.

The brutal truth is that the warning of Monroe was as applicable to Britain as to the Holy Alliance, and Canning, who perceived this at once, was deeply chagrined. Throughout the remainder of the nineteenth century, the British were unfriendly to the Monroe Doctrine, and one must not forget that the most sensational and perhaps strained invocation of the Doctrine (the Venezuela boundary dispute of 1895) was aimed at England, and came perilously close to ending in fratricidal bloodshed.

The erroneous concept about an alliance probably springs from the fact that the British Navy stood between the European powers and Spanish America. James Monroe was wise enough to take full advantage of this temporary parallelism of policy, but parallelism of policy is not an alliance. If there had been no British Navy, we should have had to build a more adequate one for ourselves. As long as the British had a fleet, and as long as we saw eye to eye with them on the question of Spanish restoration, our statesmen would have been stupid indeed not to take cover behind the protecting wooden petticoats of the Mother Country.

Another serious misconception has sprouted from this parallelism of policy. The idea took hold in certain quarters, especially during the post-1898 days of Anglo-American friendship, that the British Navy defended the Monroe Doctrine out of love for the United States, and continued to do so throughout the nineteenth century.*

The truth is that in 1823 the British officials, nursing the stab in the back delivered in 1812 by their intractable offspring, were not overcome with friendliness for the Yankee. They were not overjoyed to see the Americans take advantage of the parallelism of policy and use the British Navy, for which, as in colonial days, they paid no taxes. Until at least the dying months of the nineteenth century, we hated England as the hereditary foe, and a half dozen or so crises with her nearly precipitated war. During most of these years we looked upon the British Navy, not as our protector, but as our most formidable potential opponent. Relations happily improved in the twentieth century, but one does the cause of truth no service by reading back into the nineteenth century the attitudes of the twentieth. Shortly after the Spanish-American War the British, faced with the rising might of Germany, withdrew their fleet to home waters, and left us to defend ourselves, as well as the Monroe Doctrine and common British interests, against the Prussian menace. In this sense, Great Britain belatedly returned the compliment and hid behind the stout steel walls of the United States Navy.

Another common error is to suppose that the chivalrous Monroe issued his dictum primarily to save Latin America from the big bad Holy Alliance. Actually, he wanted to keep the European powers away, not because he loved the republics of Latin America less, but because he loved the United States of America more. Monroe and Adams were vitally interested in saving our own skins, and any protection which Spanish America may have derived from our presumed knight-errantry was largely incidental.

Another tenacious myth is that the European nations—France, Spain, Aus-

* Highly patriotic Americans resented this idea. In 1916 the Galveston *News* wrote: "A London editor lets us know that England will never permit Germany to capture America. Thanks, awfully." Even while France was falling in 1940, Lindbergh and other isolationists sneered at the belief, so distasteful to our dead Revolutionary soldiers, that "the British fleet protects us from invasion."

tria, Prussia, and Russia—recoiled in horror before the paper bombast of Monroe, slunk back into their marble halls, and forthwith abandoned their preparations for trampling down the recently sprouted saplings of liberty. As a matter of fact, the powers had laid no concrete plans for invasion, and they were vastly annoyed at being scolded by an upstart power without formidable armed forces. They might indeed have been aroused to begin active preparations had it not been for the deterring presence of Britain's floating thunder.

8

Another current misinterpretation is that Monroe's message was immediately recognized by the American people as of transcendent importance, and that its principles have continued with pristine vigor to the present.

The Monroe Doctrine, as earlier suggested, is a "crisis doctrine," and it flourishes best when its roots are well manured with insecurity. During those periods of our internal preoccupation, or when the powers had their hands full elsewhere, the Doctrine lay in moth balls. In 1913, the year before the shot sounded at Sarajevo, Hiram Bingham, who knew Latin America well, published a small volume entitled, *The Monroe Doctrine: An Obsolete Shibboleth.* Then came a new set of international tensions, and Mr. Bingham's book and not Mr. Monroe's doctrine became obsolete. One could easily make a rough fever chart showing the rise and fall of popular interest in the Doctrine, and the red line would trace with surprising exactitude the coming and going of international crises.

Another misapprehension is that we have always been quick to resent any challenge to the Monroe Doctrine, just as a jealous husband is quick to resent any attack on his wife's virtue.

The truth is that there have been dozens of violations of the Monroe Doctrine, and many of them have passed completely unnoticed by our people and our government. Much depended on our national mood. When concentrating on the gigantic task of carving a commonwealth out of a continent, we were apt to be unconcerned about the Doctrine. When bursting with energy in 1895, we flared up over the British Guiana-Venezuela boundary line, which involved the Monroe Doctrine in only the most indirect way, and certainly to a lesser degree than other violations that we had conveniently overlooked.

Much also depends on locale. We have never ringingly invoked the Monroe Doctrine south of British Guiana, although the European powers have repeatedly poached on that area. We have seldom overlooked a violation, or even a potential violation, in the Caribbean area, for that is near our Panamanian preserve. "So far as the region of the Caribbean Sea is concerned," said Secretary of State Hughes in 1923, "it may be said that if we had no Monroe Doctrine we should have to create one."

Another enduring legend is that the European powers have come to recognize and respect the Monroe Doctrine. The truth is that all of them were reluctant to recognize it, and most of them have never had any real respect for it. "But they know it when they see it," declared the Baltimore *American* in 1903, "and that is more to the purpose."

Italy and particularly Germany have never been willing to admit the validity or the fairness of the Monroe Doctrine. These two powers did not become unified until the latter half of the nineteenth century, and then proceeding on the theory that all virile powers had to have colonies, they cast about for unpeopled parts of the globe. Their eyes fell upon the riches of Latin America, but here they ran afoul of Mr. Monroe, who in 1823 had officially ended the era of colonization. Tens of thousands of Germans and Italians emigrated to Brazil and Argentina, but as long as the Monroe Doctrine displayed adequate dentures these peoples had to remain orphans. Britain, France, and the Netherlands, all of which by the accidents of politics had become unified early and had got their hands into the colonial grab bag first, might keep their American colonies, but Germany and Italy could not lease, buy or seize a single square foot.

Prince Otto von Bismarck, the Iron Chancellor, once referred to the Monroe Doctrine as "that insolent dogma," and as "a species of arrogance peculiarly American and inexcusable." The German propagandists of his time sneered at it as "a bugaboo fit only to frighten children." The Nazis carried on the Bismarck tradition when, after the fall of France in 1940, they flatly refused to recognize the no-transfer and nonintervention tenets of the Monroe Doctrine. They insisted that nonintervention could be valid only if the American nations on their part agreed to refrain from intervening in the affairs of Europe. The reciprocity argument has much force, and President Truman, in the "Truman Doctrine" of 1947, further weakened our moral position when he declared for intervention in Greece and Turkey, while under the Monroe Doctrine implicitly denying the same right to Soviet Russia in Mexico and Argentina.*

9

One of the most persuasive myths is that Monroe's potent parchment saved Latin America from the fate of Africa.

All one has to do is to place a map of the Americas in 1823 beside a corresponding map of Africa, which was then mostly in the hands of natives. Then compare the 1914 map of the Americas with that of the Dark Continent. By 1914 Africa was completely parcelled out among the European powers, except for Liberia, which was sponsored by the United States, and Ethiopia, which later lost its sovereignty for five years to Mussolini.

* The "Truman Doctrine" was no doubt aimed at Soviet Russia, and certain journalistic commentators, reading the present back into the past, erroneously asserted that the Monroe Doctrine had been directed primarily at Russian colonization rather than at the Holy Alliance.

The Americas were not only spared the unhappy lot of Africa, but the European monarchs in this hemisphere lost enormous holdings after 1823. By 1914 Russia had withdrawn from Alaska; Spain had been deprived of her once magnificent empire; Portugal had been evicted from Brazil; the royal government of Norway and Sweden had transferred Saint-Barthélemy Island to France. And in 1917 Denmark sold her Virgin Islands to the United States.

All this is a magnificent example of argument from false analogy. If South America was rescued from the fate of Africa, that good fortune cannot be traced with any precision to the Monroe Doctrine. Africa was closer to Europe, and, together with Asia, presented easier and richer pickings. The distresses of the European powers—their jealousies, rivalries, and balances of power—did not give a nation like Germany in 1900 a free hand to challenge us. The Atlantic was (and is) wide, and hence difficult for an invading force to cross, if confronted with strong opposition. Within recent decades, some of the South American countries, notably Brazil and Argentina, have developed considerable armed forces of their own. One is prone to forget that twice, in 1806 and again in 1807, the British attacked Buenos Aires with a substantial expeditionary force, and in both instances were repulsed by local armies.

The most ridiculous misconception of all, and perhaps the one most widely believed in the United States, is that the Latin Americans love us and our Monroe Doctrine, primarily because it saved them from the awful fate of Africa.

The truth is that the people south of the border have never loved either *El Coloso del Norte* or the Monroe Doctrine. Those Latin Americans who in 1823 gave any thought to the danger of the Holy Alliance recognized that any presumed "saving" was accomplished by the oaken walls of Britain and not by the paper pronouncement of Monroe. Some of these southern neighbors now concede that once there was a Holy Alliance, and that once there were some storm clouds on the horizon, and that once it was well to have Uncle Sam (and more especially John Bull) hold an umbrella over them. But they saw no need of the umbrella when the Holy Alliance died, as it did more than a century ago. Nations like Brazil and Argentina, which have armies and navies and national debts and other attributes of greatness, resent our patronizing and paternalistic attitude. "We don't want any papa," complained one Chilean in 1908. These sensitive people much prefer the present multilateral arrangement: no longer do we hold a club over them. Together with us, they hold the club over others.

Latin Americans have never loved the Monroe Doctrine of Monroe, but they have violently hated the perversion of Theodore Roosevelt, which is usually what they had in mind when they cursed James Monroe. The Roosevelt Doctrine meant intervention; the Monroe Doctrine meant protection. The Latin Americans resented intervention, but they could not become angered by incidental protection. Only a few educated Latin Americans paid any attention to the Monroe Doctrine when it was enunciated, and these did not attach much significance to it, for discerning persons perceived that the youthful arm of Uncle Sam could not save them from the Holy Alliance, although the muscular naval arm of John Bull could. In succeeding years, and as the United States became more powerful, our neighbors could not become apoplectic if we protected the Western Hemisphere with our fleet. If we did not maintain a big navy, they would have to build bigger navies, and bigger navies cost the taxpayers more money. So three grudging and feeble cheers for the wealthy *norte-americanos*.

10

Monroeism had been intimately connected with Pan-Americanism, which may be defined as the closer association of the American republics for the achievement of common aspirations, whether commercial, cultural, military, or political.

Pan-Americanism has never taken deep root in the United States, despite the proddings of colorful leaders like Henry Clay, James G. Blaine, and Franklin D. Roosevelt. The primary reason is that the ideal never appeared to be very vital; it did not impinge upon the security nerve. Latin America seems so remote; its language and civilization are Latin; and numerous other barriers have caused the two peoples to look to Europe rather than to each other. The various Pan-American conferences have traditionally been long on talk and short on achievement. The cowboy humorist, Will Rogers, once remarked that the best one could hope to do was to patch up the various quarrels that had broken out at the previous meeting.

The Good Neighbor policy of Franklin Roosevelt was the most successful phase of Pan-Americanism, primarily because we recognized, when faced with the Hitlerian menace, that Latin-American sympathy and support were of vital importance to us. Our previous indifference changed overnight to a violently amorous courtship, and we spread our money and affections southward with unstinted prodigality. The Latin Americans were not overjoyed by our too obvious change of heart, and they wished that our love could have been less passionate and better diffused in time. But they were not averse to making hay while the sun of Good Neighborism shone. When the Axis challenge disappeared in the rubble of Berlin and Hiroshima, the honeymoon was over, and we began to slip back into the humdrum bickerings of ordinary married life. The talk about good will and the good neighbor seemed a bit like "wind blowing across the pampas."

Until 1940 the Monroe Doctrine was the greatest single barrier to Pan-Americanism. As Monroeism waxed and brought landings of marines, Pan-Americanism waned and brought heart burnings. As Pan-Americanism waxed and brought a soft-pedaling of intervention under Hoover and Roosevelt, the Monroe Doctrine waned and brought multilateralization.

In the house of a man who has been hanged, the guest does not speak of rope. At the various gatherings of the American republics, the representatives of the United States do well not to mention Monroe, estimable gentleman though he was. He was not officially referred to in the continentalizing of his doctrine at Havana in 1940 or at Chapultepec in 1945. His name has been so frightfully abused, and it has been made to connote so many unpleasant things that he never stood for, that we might do well to forget about the "Monroe" Doctrine altogether, and speak of a new "Hemispheric Security" Doctrine. That would please our neighbors to the south, promote good will and Pan-Americanism, and serve all essential purposes.

CHAPTER TWENTY-THREE

THE MIASMA OF MANIFEST DESTINY

"If there be one principle more deeply rooted than any other in the
mind of every American, it is that we should have nothing to do with
conquest."—THOMAS JEFFERSON, 1791

1

THE AMERICAN PEOPLE were ardent expansionists for roughly the
first three hundred years of their existence. They kept moving in inexorable
stages, and in ever widening circles, to the richer lands beyond the sunset,
until by the end of the nineteenth century they had taken up the last large
tracts of desirable free soil. This magnificent march of empire was primarily
a domestic phenomenon, but where it encroached on the preserves of other
peoples, and led to diplomatic dealings or even war, it became an issue in
foreign affairs.

The American birth certificate—the treaty of 1783 with England—gave us
a tremendous initial endowment, embracing roughly the present United
States east of the Mississippi, except for east and west Florida. We had not
even begun to fill up this princely domain when in 1803 a still-smiling
Providence dumped the Louisiana Purchase into our laps, thereby spreading
the Land of the Free to the Rockies, and more than doubling the original
bequest. We now had the heartland of the richest valley on the face of the
globe, and its vast resources and fertile plains gave promise of eventual
world dominance.

Most of the additional domain that we acquired came in response to
existing strategic demands or future territorial needs, and as a consequence
our population never really caught up with the land, or at least did not do
so until quite recent times. This explains why we have never been swayed
by the living-room arguments of Germany, Italy, and Japan; and why we
have branded as incorrigibly quarrelsome the nations of crowded continents. The Daniel Boones, who became restless when they saw a neighbor's
smoke a dozen miles away, have never realized that the twenty or so different nationalities of Europe, with scores of different languages and dialects,
and with hundreds of hereditary hates, are jammed into a veritable cockpit,
where in certain areas the question is not so much living room as elbow
room.

The great chunks of the continent that we tore off came to us in response
to varied urges. Where we needed to fulfill our "physiographic destiny"—
as in east Florida and west Florida—we seized the territory or purchased it
with more than a show of the mailed fist. Where we needed the area for
strategic purposes—as was true of Louisiana, the Gadsden Purchase, the
Canal Zone, and the Virgin Islands—we acquired it by purchase or lease,

sometimes with a display of force, and sometimes with a connivance at chicanery that definitely weakened our pretensions to moral superiority.

Louisiana in fact was transferred to us with a bad title. Napoleon had no right under the French constitution to sell it, and it was technically not his to sell, for he never fulfilled the terms under which he had acquired it from Spain. Professor Edward Channing of Harvard University went so far as to say that we acted as "the accomplices of the greatest highwayman of modern history." The land-greedy Western pioneer set high store by valid titles, but possession was nine points of the law, and if the title was not good he would make it good, if necessary with his trusty rifle. He was not going to quibble over legal technicalities when they were all that stood between him and the greatest real estate bargain in history—828,000 square miles of land at approximately three cents an acre. Not only did we acquire this vast empire at a fire-sale price, but at the same time we removed the mouth of our great Father of Waters from the clutch of faithless foreigners.

2

We divided Oregon with England, after much bluster and some bulging of our adolescent biceps. We coveted a Pacific frontage in California, and when Mexico would not sell it, we managed to pick a war with her, and then took it, together with the intervening Mexican Cession. This windfall, including Texas, was only one half of Mexico. Like Clive in India we might well have stood aghast at our moderation, for a public demand to take all of Mexico began to gather strong momentum, and was stopped only by the opportune arrival of the treaty of peace.

We did not really want "Seward's snow-farm" (Alaska) in 1867, but on second thought it seemed like a fairly good Yankee gamble. Besides, we did not want to affront the friendly Russian bear, and we welcomed the opportunity to kick the British lion resoundingly in the ribs. We peacefully annexed a part of Samoa and all of Hawaii, in both instances primarily for strategic purposes. We had no real hankering for Puerto Rico, Guam, and the Philippines, but we scooped them in to get rid of Spain, to avoid trouble with other powers, and to do some speculating, which did not pan out nearly so well as Alaska.

The "taking" of the Panama Canal Zone from Colombia, in 1903, delivered a heavy blow to our exalted position, to which we were self-nominated and self-elected, as the most upright on earth. President Theodore Roosevelt, and not Mr. John Doe, engineered this shady deal, but our people generally acquiesced in it or applauded it, particularly if they belonged to the Grand Old Party of their Rough Rider President. The interference of United States naval forces with the attempts of Colombia to suppress the Panama revolt was questionable enough, but the haste with which we recognized the newly propped-up puppet dispelled all doubts as to our disinterestedness.* Not three months, not three weeks, but three days elapsed before Roosevelt extended the right hand of recognition to the Panamanians. A more decent wait would have been possible if the Rough Rider, with the impending election in view, had not been in a lather to start digging the canal. In the early 1930's, when Japan staged a *coup* in Manchuria and set up her puppet regime there, Washington was puzzled by her delay in recognizing her own handiwork. One Japanese spokesman cuttingly replied that Japan was in no hurry; she did not plan to construct a canal there.

Altogether—by inheritance, osmosis, division, annexation, purchase, lease, and conquest—we acquired in scarcely more than a century a domain which would not have shamed the Roman empire in the days of Caesar Augustus, whether one considers extent, method of acquisition, or speed of envelopment.

3

The land-starved peasants of Europe, whose ancestors had for centuries tilled the soil of their lords and masters, could not fail to view the smiling acreage of America with voracious appetites. The natural craving of our people for wider horizons developed into a mental and emotional outburst by the 1840's which is popularly known as Manifest Destiny. Associated with land hunger and democratic bumptiousness was the conviction that the might of America's multiplying millions destined us to become an over-shadowingly great nation, and that it was "manifestly" the "destiny" of our people to spread our democratic institutions from Patagonia to the Pole, by peaceful penetration if possible, by forceful conquest if necessary. Emerson remarked that in a broader way Manifest Destiny signified "the sense all men have of the prodigious energy and opportunity lying idle here."

Manifest Destiny was also associated with the idea that we were God's chosen people, and that we had a divine mandate to spread our beneficent institutions over the broad bosom of this hemisphere. An Edinburgh merchant, traveling in the South during the middle of the century, chanced to say that Providence had ordained that the British and American nations would civilize the globe. "Two nations!" broke in a little sharp-featured man. "Guess there's only one, stranger, goin' to annex that island of yourn one of them fine days; don't know how little Vic [Queen Victoria] will like that, but got to do it, and no mistake about that."

The popular historian-lecturer of the 1880's, John Fiske, used to tell of a legendary meeting of Americans in Paris during the Civil War, where a succession of toasts testified to the stratospheric aspirations of our people. The first speaker declared:

* When Roosevelt said that the people of Panama "rose as one man," the Washington *Post* retorted: "That means that all three members of the junta caught the signal at the same time."

Here's to the United States, bounded on the north by British America, on the south by the Gulf of Mexico, on the east by the Atlantic, and on the west by the Pacific Ocean."

The second speaker protested:

But this is far too limited a view of the subject: in assigning our boundaries we must look to the great and glorious future which is prescribed for us by the Manifest Destiny of the Anglo-Saxon race. Here's to the United States—bounded on the north by the North Pole, on the south by the South Pole, on the east by the rising, and on the west by the setting sun.

The orator sat down, amid gratifying applause. Then arose the third speaker, a very serious gentleman from the Far West (possibly Los Angeles). Said this truly patriotic American:

If we are going to leave the historical past and present and take our Manifest Destiny into account, why restrict ourselves within the narrow limits assigned by our fellow countryman who has just sat down? I give you the United States— bounded on the north by the Aurora Borealis, on the south by the precession of the equinoxes, on the east by the primeval chaos, and on the west by the Day of Judgment!

These were the days when we were at the cock-crowing of our power, and the American was an uncommonly arrogant and disagreeable fellow. He could speak calmly of "the universal Yankee nation," or remark, as one spokesman did in 1851 regarding Cuba: "When we Yankees have once set our *souls* upon a thing, we always have it." The dogma of Manifest Destiny actually played an appreciable role in holding the United States together during the Civil War, and in arousing the North to fight with unexpected tenacity for the abstract ideal of union. How could a disunited United States, broken into two quarreling republics, hope to realize the American dream of democratizing the entire hemisphere?

The sap of Manifest Destiny ran out of American veins on the battlefields of Bull Run, Antietam, Fredericksburg, Gettysburg, and the Wilderness. We emerged from the Civil War physically pinned together by bayonets but emotionally divided by the "bloody chasm," and burdened with cripples, rubble, and debt. Secretary Seward labored tirelessly to interest our people in Caribbean island bargains, and he actually signed a treaty for the purchase of the Danish West Indies. But a hurricane, earthquake, and tidal wave cooled off our lukewarm interest: we did not want even a "shaky" foothold in the Antilles. Seward then turned north and virtually tricked the people into accepting Alaska, but they would have none of his designs on Greenland, Santo Domingo, and other outposts, glacial or tropical. Not even General-President Grant, for all of his Civil War prestige, could wheedle or browbeat the Senate into accepting Santo Domingo as a gift, albeit a somewhat tainted one.

As we approached the sunset of the century, we began to feel stirrings of the old impulse to expand. Reconstruction had ended, the frontier was disappearing, our population was nearing 90,000,000, our factories were going full blast, and our warehouses were bulging with exportable surpluses. Expand or explode is a political law, and we were prepared to obey its dictates. The international atmosphere was tense with alliances and counteralliances, and the miasma of imperialism hung low. France, Russia, and Germany were grabbing territory in the Far East, and our feet, like those of the youth who has yet to sow his wild oats, were itching for imperialistic paths. There is a little Caesar in us all, and besides we had to keep up with the Germans if we were going to merit the title of a great power. The thirst for glory was ready to befuddle our judgment and corrupt our consciences.

4

The American people entered upon the crusade to free Cuba without any conscious thought of conquest. But we were ripe for seduction. When we blundered into the Philippines, and found that we had stumbled into empire, we were puzzled which way to turn. We did not really covet the Islands, but we did not want our commercial rivals to have them. If we turned them loose, the resulting scramble among the powers might touch off a world war into which we would be sucked. The devil was at our elbow; whatever choice we made would be the wrong one. Big Business, which had bitterly opposed the war with Spain, now began to glimpse the riches of the Indies, and drunk with the dreams of aggrandizement the Mark Hannas began to speak of Manila as the future Hong Kong of the Far East. As McKinley retired to pray, Hanna laid plans to prey.

The British, whom we had long berated for land-gobbling, cheered us along the trackless sea of imperialism. Aesop tells of the fox that accidentally lost its tail, and then tried to persuade all the other foxes to cut off theirs. Kipling in his famous poem stressed the idea of *noblesse oblige* and urged the Americans to take up the white man's burden (which all too often has been the loot sack), and wallow with the British in the pompous misery of imperialism. "In other words," as the Omaha *World-Herald* had the discernment to see, "Mr. Kipling would have Uncle Sam take up John Bull's burden." Yet most Americans were feeling friendly toward England because of her unexpected sympathy in the recent fracas with Spain, and for reasons that ranged from the noblest to the crassest, we stepped gingerly into the imperialistic quagmire.

This sudden departure from all previous policy was epochal. Hitherto our expansion had flowed naturally into vacant or semivacant lands that lay adjacent. We could justify all our acquisitions on the grounds of political gravitation (the falling of ripe pears), natural growth, geographical predestination, our superior institutions, or putting the soil to the uses of civilization. Theodore Roosevelt was frank to say that it was best for humanity that the sleepy Mexicans should be elbowed out of their northern provinces.

As for the Indian rattlesnake, he could be brushed aside, exterminated, or put on reservations. "Manifest destiny, like charity," remarked the Salt Lake City *Herald* in 1898, "covers a multitude of sins."

But the Philippines were different. They were located in the debilitating tropics. They were noncontiguous by some 7,000 miles. They were thickly inhabited by a people of alien race, language, and institutions. American critics of imperialism insisted that despotism abroad would develop habits of despotism at home, and that if we subverted the Declaration of Independence and the Constitution by riveting shackles on the Moros and Igorottes, we would doom our own liberties.

The "little brown brothers" in the Philippines bitterly resented the exchanging of Spanish misrule for American overlordship, and an inglorious insurrection broke out which cost more than the glorious Spanish American War, lasted many times longer, and involved far heavier casualties. McKinley's words about duty, destiny, and benevolent assimilation took on a curious ring. "In the clash between the Americans and the Filipinos," sneered the Detroit *Free Press* in 1899, "it is reported that 4,000 of the natives were 'benevolently assimilated.'" The American soldiers were inevitably pulled down to the level of the half-naked and half-visible bushmen whom they hunted, and our lads shocked the civilized world by their water cures and other tortures.

Too late we learned that imperialism brings out the worst phases of the Caucasian character, and that the conquest of peoples with different skins and slightly flatter noses is not a pretty sight. We lost moral face in the eyes of the world, and we began to develop some degree of sympathy for the British in their concurrently vexatious conquest of the Boers. The New York *World* in 1899 wrote a reply to Rudyard Kipling's appeal:

> We've taken up the white man's burden
> Of ebony and brown;
> Now will you kindly tell us, Rudyard,
> How we may put it down?

This is not to say that the imperialism of the United States was as ruthless as that of some other powers, or that we did not pour hundreds of millions of dollars into the Philippines for their defense, education, sanitation, and general improvement. The loyalty of much of the Philippine population after the Japanese invasion in 1941 contrasts glaringly with the attitude of the natives of the Dutch East Indies toward their white masters. But like caged eagles the Filipinos pined for independence, and they expressed scant appreciation of our efforts to gild the cage. The white man's burden sounded fine, but it did not return dividends, so we cast it aside after more than forty years of travail.

The heady brew of imperialism elsewhere turned bitter. Puerto Rico proved to be a small-scale Philippine white elephant, partly because the fertility of the people far outran the fertility of the soil. Even the Virgin

Islands, which we acquired in 1917 for strategic purposes, were branded by President Hoover, after prohibition had ruined the rum industry, as an "effective poorhouse."

5

At the end of World War I the American people wanted no territorial gains; the Spanish War had cured us of that. We were weary of being official nose wipers for little brown brothers who did not want their noses wiped. Our late associates made off with juicy mandates in Africa and the Near East, but we were not particularly disturbed. (If the African Cameroons had been Jamaica, we might not have been proof against temptation.) We would have none of Armenia or Constantinople as mandates; the Philippines had been taken as something of a Kipling mandate from civilization, and we were tired of *noblesse oblige*. All we wanted was peace without having to pay for it. But the liquid "black gold" of Mesopotamia was another matter. Adam and Eve had once held a mandate here, but it had passed to the British after World War I, and American oil interests were fearful that they would be squeezed out by their British competitors. The State Department thereupon made the appropriate protests, which led one American critic to remark: "Blood may be thicker than water, but oil is thicker than blood."

After the collapse of France in 1940, our attention was focused on the orphaned West Indian islands of France and the Netherlands. Strong public support developed for seizing them or buying them or advancing loans for them, but the primary motive was not imperialism but security. Our existing Caribbean poorhouses, under the proud folds of the Stars and Stripes, were worries enough.

In December, 1941, on the eve of Pearl Harbor, and while we were sending huge Lend-Lease shipments to the Allies, *Fortune* asked whether we should get some foreign territory or trade rights for helping to beat Hitler. Approximately six out of ten voted affirmatively, but here trade rights were intermingled with imperialism. There was also a desire, especially among the more ignorant isolationists, to get something in the way of territory for our heavy Lend-Lease outlay, even though the acquisition should prove to be a liability.

After Pearl Harbor the American people had ample time to think of acquiring new domain, particularly the Pacific islands which were wrested at such heavy cost from the Japanese. The various polls showed that only about one American in ten wanted to get as much additional land in the world as could be annexed, and such persons were predominantly in the lowest educational group. Most Americans favored acquiring military bases and nothing else.

6

The Man in the Street, convinced as he is of the wickedness of British imperialism, is apt to feel that our penny-ante venture at the turn of the century was not imperialism at all. It was the white man's burden, or "benevolent assimilation," or something else with a high-sounding and euphemistic name. "Land-grabbing seems dreadfully wicked to the ones that have grabbed enough," observed a California paper in 1932.

We assume that British imperialism has been wholly and unalterably bad, which is not true. British imperialism, although not without its dark side, has conferred many substantial benefits on subject peoples, including the pre-1776 Americans. Even German colonialism prior to 1914 had much to its credit, notably in the field of tropical medicine.

Imperialism on a small scale is nevertheless imperialism, and our escapade in 1898 was motivated by the commercial and imperial motives (with an idealistic frosting) that are associated with large-scale imperialism. Our natural and inevitable expansion across North America was in a different category, for the land was contiguous and sparsely populated. We do not call this imperialism but expansion. Expansion is good; imperialism is bad. Philip Guedalla, the well known British writer, said in 1927: "I have a feeling that imperialism is very much like an open window. If you open it, it is fresh air. If the other fellow opens it, it is called a draught."

The truth is that we expanded our homeland holdings by conquest to a proportionately greater extent than any of the nations of Europe within the same period. The areas acquired by gargantuan gulps were all sparsely settled, but in no case did we consult the wishes of the inhabitants.

We attained our "inevitable destiny" by doing a number of things in the interests of expediency which were later thrown in our faces by other latter-day imperialists. We seized West Florida from Spain in 1810, and when our diplomatic envoy in St. Petersburg attempted somewhat shamefacedly to explain the affair to the Tsar, the response was an understanding smile and the remark: "Everybody is getting a little bigger, nowadays." We also acquired Texas, the Mexican Cession, and the Panama Canal Zone in a manner that will not bear the closest scrutiny.

Over the years we have accused the British of land-grabbing. But the pot should be a bit more restrained in what it calls the kettle. We overlook the fact that while England did more grabbing than we did, she operated out of a relatively small and densely populated island. If she seized things that she did not immediately need, so did we.

The present writer once heard an English lecturer, speaking to a California audience, refer to the American habit of branding the British as "imperialists." He had just toured the Golden State, and he wondered how the Americans had been able to think up so many Spanish names for their towns and cities: Los Altos (the heights), Palo Alto (high tree), Paso Robles (the pass of the oaks), and El Pueblo de Nuestra Señora la Reina de Los Angeles de Porciuncula (the town of Our Lady the queen of the angels of Porciuncula), better known as Los Angeles or L.A. The British visitor knew, of course, that we had wrested this smiling land from the Mexicans, who had inherited it from the Spanish, and he was merely taking a sly poke at a vulnerable joint in the armor of our virtuosity.

7

Most Americans are quite willing to concede that our expansion was not wicked; it was too natural and inevitable for that. Other Americans, more familiar with our history, will confess that perhaps we were a little rough and hasty, but we were merely operating under the morality of the nineteenth century. A new era of morality has dawned, and such rapacity is no longer to be tolerated by decent and civilized nations.

One is reminded of the banker who amassed his millions by questionable means, but in his autumnal years mended his ways, joined the church, passed the collection plate on Sundays, and prepared to meet a forgiving Maker. Now that we have got all the land we want, we are quite willing to kick away the ladder by which we ascended. Not only are we willing to join the church, but we think that the other nations should follow our example.

The "have not" nations after World War I—Germany, Italy, and Japan—were reluctant to join a League of Nations which apparently condemned them to perpetual constriction and poverty. This is one of the basic reasons why the League failed. The Japanese, herded together on islands smaller in area than California, had ideas of their own about inevitable destiny, and they were not willing to adopt the fine twentieth century morality of Uncle Sam until they had acquired more territory by his nineteenth century methods. "Be patient," counseled the Los Angeles *Times* in 1933. "When Japan gets her India or her Panama she will oppose land-grabbing too." Under a system of international "free enterprise" (which also can cover a multitude of sins), there will always be some nations dissatisfied with their holdings, and eager to improve their position by fair means or foul.

Our imperialistic record, while marred by some strong-arm dealings, is on the whole fairly respectable. Although we have done both bad and good things, perhaps the good predominates. Even so, we must remember that, with ample living space and seemingly bottomless raw materials, we have not been subjected to the same temptations that beset less favored lands. We must also remember that we regard ourselves more favorably than do others. "The truth lies somewhere between what Europe thinks of us and what we think of ourselves," observed an Ohio newspaper in the disputatious 1920's.

Nations, like individuals, must beware of the *tu quoque* or "you're another" argument. If a person looks far enough he can always find some sinner more depraved and rapacious than himself. "History," opined the Boston *Post* in 1923, "is what enables each nation to use the other fellow's past record as an alibi." The only hope for the future lies in getting away from this practice and striving toward international organization.

As long as our present mood continues, we are not likely again to try our imperialistic wings. But other peoples, like ourselves, have had their periods of expansion and contraction ("Little Englanders"), and other peoples, like ourselves, pass through alternating moods. We shall always have a dangerous backlog of ignoramuses who, not knowing the cost or counting the cost, will want to grab everything in sight.*

Certain incidents after the close of World War II may have cast long shadows. The Byrd Antarctic expedition of 1946–1947 aroused increasing interest as we perceived the necessity of scooping in all available raw materials for the manufacture of atomic bombs. When radar contact was established with the moon in 1946, there was some talk, perhaps not all of it completely humorous, about staking out a preemptive claim. The use of American money to bolster up tottering "rightist" regimes here and there throughout the world was castigated by the Russian press as "dollar imperialism." And in the spring of 1947, after President Truman had dramatically urged a policy of heavy financial aid to the nondemocratic governments of Greece and Turkey, in the interests of protecting democracy against Communist infiltration, the former Vice-President Henry A. Wallace, speaking in Manchester, England, declared that if such a policy were adopted, the United States was committed to ruthless imperialism and war with the Soviet Union.

Huey Long, the "martyred" Louisiana "Kingfish," was once asked, so the story goes, if the United States would ever succumb to Fascism. "Yes," he replied, "but we shall call it Americanism." If we ever adopt a policy of unabashed imperialism, we shall almost certainly call it by a shorter and less ugly name.

* In 1946 a French opinion poll asked what nations wanted to dominate the world. Russia ranked first with 26 per cent; the United States second with 25 per cent.

CHAPTER TWENTY-FOUR

FREE SEAS AND OPEN DOORS

"The military masters of Germany denied us the right to be neutral."
—WOODROW WILSON, 1917

1

A QUICK GLANCE at popular attitudes toward other historic foreign policies may prove profitable.

As a melting-pot nation, we were from early days strong champions of the right of immigrants to slough off their nationality and become American citizens. But the British clung tenaciously to the rule: "Once an Englishman always an Englishman." The pre-1812 controversy over the impressment of American seamen centered largely about the unwillingness of the British to recognize naturalization papers, whether bona fide or fraudulent. After the Napoleonic wars, the British Navy went back to a peace footing, and subsequently adopted more refined methods of recruiting sailors. At no time since the bitter 1812 days did impressment become a burning issue between the two nations, and in 1870 the British concluded a treaty with us yielding the right to naturalize their subjects.

The policy of commercial reciprocity, though at times reasonably popular, has never commanded enthusiastic nation-wide support. Secretary of State Blaine argued so vehemently for the ideal before the Senate Finance Committee in 1890 that his descending fist smashed his own hat lying on the table. But not until the 1930's was Secretary Hull able to revive some lukewarm interest in the principle when he pushed his trade agreements pacts. Commercial reciprocity will never be genuinely popular until a majority of the American people know what it means.

Disarmament in recent decades has commanded much popular support, primarily because it appealed to the taxpayer and was presumed to lessen the danger of hostilities. The term itself is a misnomer, for during the period after World War I, the most that statesmen could hope for was the "limitation" of naval arms in certain large-ship categories. The great Washington Disarmament Conference of 1921–1922 was actually forced into existence by the pressure of American public opinion, and its results were widely acclaimed as ushering in an era when the lion would lie down with the lamb. But we failed to see that armaments are a symptom of a disease rather than the disease itself, just as fever is a symptom of an internal disorder rather than the disorder itself. We failed to see that unless some means can be devised for removing the causes of the disease, no lasting good will be done by putting ice on the thermometers, or limiting the size of the thermometers, or throwing the thermometers away.

Armaments continued to pile up during the 1920's and 1930's, despite all our high hopes. "It is sad to reflect," said the Kansas City *Star* in 1926, "that most of the friction since the Armistice of 1918 has risen over peace and disarmament programs." The Man in the Street again felt that he had been played for a sucker by white-spatted foreigners, although he had actually "suckered" himself with dreams of a fool's paradise. But the costly lessons of recent years have enabled us to see more clearly that arms limitation is illusory, and that safeguards must be sought in an international organization for putting out small fires before they become big ones.

At the time of Japan's rape of Manchuria, the Hoover-Stimson Doctrine was dramatically announced, proclaiming that we did not intend to recognize territorial changes brought about by force. The formula had so many obvious, if delusive, advantages that in the 1930's it commanded considerable popular support. It was cheap, because it cost us nothing more than note paper; it was moral, because it put us on record as disapproving things which we did not have the power to stop; it was safe, because it presumably would not provoke a war; it was theoretically effective, because nations which wanted loans and other favors from us would do well not to flout our desires. But the record does not reveal that the Hoover-Stimson Doctrine stopped the Japanese for as much as five minutes in Manchuria and elsewhere in Asia, nor the Soviets in Poland, Lithuania, Estonia, and Latvia.* The ineffectiveness of merely scowling at powerful nations was so evident that by the end of World War II the American people were much more disposed to put their faith in international organization, in armaments, or even in alliances.

2

Freedom of the Seas, while much less vital now than formerly, merits attention. It is an excellent illustration of how basic policies can change in the face of changing interests.

We have always been a maritime people, though relatively less so now than in earlier decades. In the formative years of the Republic our hardy sons of the sea wrested a living from the fisheries and the carrying trade, and the historic principle known as Freedom of the Seas arose in response to our vital needs. The large number of diplomatic crises that revolved about ships—from the *Essex* in 1805 to the *Robin Moor* in 1941, attest the significance of the sea in American economic life.

In the early days we were not only a seafaring folk, but we were also too weak to welcome involvement in foreign wars. When the European conflagrations broke out, we sought to carry on business as usual, in spite of

---

* Latvia, Lithuania, and Estonia were reabsorbed by Moscow in 1940, but as late as 1947 the United States still maintained diplomatic relations in Washington with marooned envoys from these places. Subsisting on "frozen funds," they were literally men without a country.

blockades, and reap inflated profits from both sides. We would fatten as feeders while they famished as fighters. Freedom of the Seas for neutrals means in essence the right to do business in time of war, with a minimum of interference from the belligerents, and that within the fluctuating framework of international law.

Like the Monroe Doctrine, Freedom of the Seas does not lend itself to easy definition. The principle at best is a vague one, and much depends on what nation is doing the defining. From Napoleon Bonaparte to Kaiser Wilhelm II and Adolf Hitler, the British used the naval blockade as their chief offensive weapon, and after having purchased it at high cost to the taxpayer, they were not going to blunt its edge simply because some weak neutral carriers, including the money-grubbing Yankee, wanted to work both sides of the street at profiteering prices. In the nineteenth century the Mistress of the Seas generally insisted upon an extreme use of her navy for blockade purposes, and we insisted upon a limited use of it. The British defined Freedom of the Seas their way, and we defined it ours. They would fight before they would give way, and they did, in 1812.

Near the end of the century an American naval officer in Turkish waters remarked to a Turkish official (through an interpreter) that he did not speak Turkish, but—and here he placed his hand fondly on one of his big guns— "this does." In the nineteenth century the big guns still had the most authoritative voices; hence Britain was more successful than the smaller nations in getting her definition of international law to stick.

3

The principle of free seas has been so vital to us throughout our history that we almost fought a half-dozen or so conflicts to uphold it. We actually did fight several undeclared wars, and finally waged four declared wars in which Freedom of the Seas figured among the primary causes. Historians are still disputing among themselves as to why we battled Britain in 1812, but the fact is indisputable that hundreds of thousands of Americans *at the time* believed that they were fighting for free seas, even though many of them had never seen a body of salt water larger than a salt lick. The treaty that ended hostilities made no mention of Freedom of the Seas, but that was because we had not beaten Britain, and she would have continued to fight indefinitely rather than yield her trident.

In the years following 1812 we were so sensitive to foreign tampering with our ships on the high seas that we would not permit British warships to search American vessels for illicit cargoes of slaves.* The result was that

---

* From the 1812 days on, the American people have resented British searching parties. During the Boer War the issue came up again, and the New York *World* warned: "Great Britain's exercise of the right of search may end in her finding more than she was looking for."

the glorious Stars and Stripes were the favorite mantle of slavers, who raised our bunting over floating coffins that could literally be smelled before they could be seen coming over the horizon.

Then came the Civil War, and the United States found itself thrust into the shoes of Britain. As compared with the Confederacy the North was a big-navy power; and only by adopting British principles could Lincoln make the leaky Northern blockade even reasonably effective. We even out-Britained Britain in certain respects: we did to her shippers what she had done unto us, only in some respects worse. The Mistress of the Seas was not overjoyed by this bitter dose, but she made a wry face and gulped it down with as good grace as she could muster. Perhaps at some future date—say 1914—she would be involved in a desperate global war with some European combination—say one headed by Germany—and she would then want to make use of the illiberal precedents established by the Yankees.

From 1914 to 1917, as in the pre-1812 era, we were again the most important neutral carrier, and as such tangled again with big-navy Britannia. "Britain's list of contraband of war," remarked the Indianapolis *Star*, "seems to include almost anything it sees and is likely to want." We lodged protests at Downing Street, which politely threw our own Civil War precedents back into our faces. As the *Wall Street Journal* put it: " 'Made in the United States,' remarked Great Britain as it handed Washington a thesis on the law of blockade."

The German war lords took the issue out of British hands when they announced an unrestricted submarine blockade zone around the British Isles. Henceforth, said the Brooklyn *Eagle*, the Freedom of the Seas would be "enjoyed by icebergs and fish." As in 1812, Western boys who had never seen the oceans flocked to the recruiting stations to fight for the sacred American principle of free seas. But once in the war, we again saw a new light and acquiesced in the British blockade or indirectly supported it.

Woodrow Wilson, in one of the most popular of his Fourteen Points, came out foursquare for Freedom of the Seas. The British naturally entered a reservation, and the principle was lost sight of in the welter of problems at Paris. Wilson was not unduly disturbed, for he reasoned that when the League was adopted, the neutrals would never again have to worry about Freedom of the Seas. There would be no neutrals: only the League violator arrayed against the rest of the world. Unhappily for the Wilsonian dream, the League proved ineffectual, and maritime law remained largely where it was in the "Rule Britannia" days.

The economic prosperity of Britain has long depended on her merchant fleet and imperial lifelines, and her physical integrity has long depended on her naval power. As a consequence, the ocean highways have concerned the British during the last century or so more than they have us. Freedom of the Seas has meant less to Americans than one might suppose, especially after 1812 days, when our industrial tide set in strongly toward manufacturing. Even in times of crisis our indifference has been marked, and early in 1917, when Germany's unrestricted submarine campaign was going full blast, the Philadelphia *North American* complained: "The average Congressman displays less interest in the freedom of the seas than in free garden-seeds."

4

The ostrichlike neutrality legislation of the 1930's, passed in response to overwhelming public pressure, resulted in self-imposed restrictions on Freedom of the Seas. We proclaimed that we were not yielding our historic rights to sail the ocean highways in wartime, but actually we were.

As long as we kept our ships out of the danger zones, and maintained some pretense of neutrality, we had an excellent chance of staying out of the conflict—at least until such time as Hitler saw fit to attack us. But after the fall of France, we wanted to help the democracies by unneutrality short of shooting. When we found that the existing strait-jacket legislation prevented us from helping our friends, we got rid of it, and from there on the slippery descent into war was easy. The neutrality law of 1939 was really too successful for the needs of 1941.

Still we paid lip service to the hoary fetish of free seas. In 1939, together with our sister republics, we established a so-called "chastity belt" around the Americas, within which the belligerents were warned not to carry on their activities. This proved ineffective, primarily because powerful nations fighting for their lives seldom heed the preachments of neutrals. The Atlantic Charter of 1941, like the Fourteen Points of 1918, promised Freedom of the Seas, which was indeed strange doctrine for navy-minded Winston Churchill to be sponsoring.

Freedom of the Seas was used again (in a perverted sense) to justify strong measures by a "neutral" United States against "piratical" German submarines that were trying to stop American Lend-Lease shipments to the British. In the autumn of 1941, following an incident involving the United States destroyer *Greer* and a pursued German submarine, President Roosevelt hastened to the microphone and announced that United States warships, while defending "freedom of the seas," would shoot first. He followed up this "shoot-at-sight" speech with a message to Congress urging modification of the existing neutrality act so that the nation could better uphold "freedom of the seas." Actually Roosevelt's concept had about as much relation to the Freedom of the Seas as it had to Einstein's theory of relativity. Our historic policy related to neutral merchant vessels, and had nothing to do with United States warships convoying munitions (voted gratuitously by our "neutral" Congress), carried on belligerent (British) ships, into German-proclaimed danger zones, which we had by law forbidden our own merchantmen to enter. This tortured interpretation of a time-honored policy is but another example of Roosevelt's determination to use almost any device to awaken the American people to the perils that beset them.

Freedom of the Seas has come to be one of those fighting slogans that have ceased to have meaning. In the days of sailing ships, and before the era of total war, the catchword had some validity, but even that was largely illusory. As was true of the Monroe Doctrine, if we had the naval power with which to enforce our pretensions, we did not need to invoke shibboleths; if we lacked the power, we could gain little or nothing from shibboleths.

In the days of the submarine and the bomber, Freedom of the Seas became defunct, simply because modern weapons cannot be used effectively with due regard for the ancient principles. The embattled belligerents, rather than abandon a winning weapon so as to abide by the rules, will throw the rules rather than the weapon out of the window.

Freedom of the Seas, like arbitration, was the hobble of the strong and the shield of the weak—in some cases the only shield. As the greatest naval power in the world today, we are much nearer big-navy Britain of 1812 than small-navy America of 1812. This is perhaps the principal reason why the hoary ideal has lost much of its vigor.

5

The Open Door, from the standpoint of the American people, is the least fundamental of our historic foreign policies. Unlike such guiding stars as the Monroe Doctrine and nonentanglement, it did not spring from the rugged soil of our needs and aspirations here in the Western Hemisphere, and for this reason it has been a rather sickly plant of hothouse growth. It is one of the most hazily defined and perhaps the most generally misunderstood of all our foreign policies.

The Open Door, in its original and broader sense, meant equality of commercial opportunity for the family of nations in all parts of the world. In short, a fair field and no favors in the scramble for economic concessions.

The principle of the Open Door is associated in the popular mind exclusively with China, although we have been concerned with its application in the Near East, in Morocco, in the African Congo, and elsewhere. All such areas were relatively backward and weak, and subject to exploitation by the imperialistic powers. But China has stolen the spotlight because of our missionary investment there, and because of our potential if not actual trade stake. Our normal commerce with China has, in fact, never been more than 2 or 3 per cent of our total, and our investments have been even less in proportion. But the 450,000,000 or so Chinese, constituting about one fifth of the world's population, have created for our merchants the mirage of a tremendous future market. In 1843 one congressman was impressed with the boom that would come to American producers if the

Chinese could be persuaded to smoke tobacco instead of opium, and the surplus-cursed South has long computed the royalties for King Cotton if the Chinese could be persuaded to add a half inch to their shirttails. But over the years soul-saving has been more important to Americans in China than calico-selling.

The tap roots of the Open Door go down deep into the beginnings of our early trade with China, but the dramatic events near the end of the nineteenth century caused the ancient policy to be headlined in a new form. After elephantine China had betrayed her weakness in the Sino-Japanese War (1894–1895), the powers descended like vultures upon her living carcass, and began to tear away huge leaseholds and spheres of interest. "Europe finds China a foeman worthy of her steal," commented a Pittsburgh newspaper. American merchants and missionaries, fearing that they would be squeezed out, besought the State Department to intervene. The British added their voices, for they had a much larger trade and investment stake in the Celestial empire. With the Irish-Americans particularly in mind, they realized that any move would come with better grace from the United States than from an unpopular "land grabber" like Britain.

Secretary of State John Hay, a colorful knight with an epigrammatic pen, charged forward in 1899 with a series of identical notes to the powers, urging them to accept the ideal of commercial equality in China. After receiving replies from them all, he proclaimed in effect that they had accepted the principles which he had outlined. During the tumultuous Boxer uprising of the next year, Hay announced (without asking the powers to agree) that the Open Door now included the territorial integrity of China, as well as commercial equality within the empire. Thus, on the rushing tide of dramatic events, the new Open Door was floated before the public gaze.

6

The discerning reader will have noticed some striking parallels between the Open Door and the Monroe Doctrine, aside from the vagueness of definition and application, and aside from the fact that the British in both cases helped prod us into an official declaration.

John Hay took an old principle, dressed it up in bright new clothes, added some jewelry, and gave the whole contraption to the American people christened with the catchword "Open Door." James Monroe did the same thing, only his name was not commonly attached until much later. In both cases the catchword was of vital value. The Open Door stood for openness and fairness in a day of crass imperialism abroad and oppressive monopoly at home, typified by Rockefeller's Standard Oil octopus.

Just as the American people needed a personalized peg on which to hang the Monroe Doctrine, so they needed a similar peg on which to hang the Open Door. John Hay was admirably qualified to publicize the policies devised by others. With a flair for popular phrase, a genius for making the headlines, a sure sense of what the galleries wanted, he took full advantage of the tense international drama to publicize his policy. If it had been launched under any other auspices, it almost certainly would have been an even more leaky ship than it actually turned out to be.

A nestful of tenacious myths has grown up about the Open Door, even more perhaps than around the Monroe Doctrine.

The misapprehension is general that the powers all responded affirmatively to John Hay's original request that they adhere to the Open Door. The truth is that Italy was the only nation to accept without qualification, no doubt because she had no leaseholds in China. All the other great nations attached conditions to their approval, except Russia, which in effect responded negatively, and this action released all the others from their commitment. But John Hay publicly announced that the consent of the powers was "final and definitive," and under these circumstances they could not loudly protest that they did not believe in the fair-play principles of the Open Door.

The legend persists that Hay's paper pronouncement "saved" China from the imperialistic powers, just as Monroe is supposed to have "saved" Latin America by his paper pronouncement. Actually, we did not have the army and navy with which to rescue China in 1899, any more than we had the army and navy with which to protect Latin America in 1823. China, like our southern neighbors in the days of the Holy Alliance, was in large measure the beneficiary of Europe's distresses: the jealousies and rivalries of these great nations were such that no power would permit any one of the others to secure an undue advantage. They might pledge themselves to respect the integrity of China, but they did not have much respect for one another's integrity. In 1900 the American humor magazine *Puck* published an imaginary conversation:

"Alas!" said the Chinese statesman, "it is China against the world!"

"That," said his friend, "is our only hope. Singly, any of the powers could whip us; but it isn't quite certain that they can do it together."

Contrary to a popular misconception, we have never had the power to uphold the Open Door by ourselves in the Far East. This explains why we have had to resort to entanglement and cooperation there, in direct contrast to our traditional policy before World War I toward Europe.

7

The Man in the Street is apt to believe, if he knows anything about the subject at all, that the Open Door was pretty faithfully respected until Japan in 1931 upset the Manchurian apple cart.

The Open Door has always been a rather empty phrase. Japan ultimately agreed to its principles in joint understandings with us, but not until 1922, when the Nine Power Treaty was drawn up, did all the major nations (Bolshevist Russia was not invited), agree to define and uphold the Open Door. Even after 1922, the principle commanded more lip service than loyalty, and in 1931, when Japan broke loose in Manchuria, the door was battered off the hinges and trampled under hobnailed boots. Henceforth the archway was increasingly used for the exit of Occidental merchants.

The legend persists that we proclaimed the Open Door primarily because we loved the downtrodden Chinese, just as we supposedly proclaimed the Monroe Doctrine because we loved the Latin Americans. The fact is that the policy was enunciated, not so much because we feared that China would be cut up, as because our merchants feared that they would be cut out. In a commercial sense the Open Door means: "Me too," or, in the slang of the underworld: "Cut me in." Ironically, while John Hay was openly preaching the integrity of China, he was secretly if unsuccessfully aping the European powers by working for an American naval base in southern China.

The myth somehow lingers in America that the Chinese, like the Latin Americans of 1823, are extremely grateful to us for having "saved" them, and that they love us with an abiding love because we took the lead in proclaiming the Open Door.

The position of the Chinese with reference to the Open Door was roughly that of the mat. Every sovereign and self-respecting nation should have the right to confer favors upon those countries which it wishes to cultivate. China was placed in the position of a Mandarin maiden with seven suitors who "gang up" on her and force her to promise that whatever favors she extends to one she must extend to all. Just as Latin America has resented the patronizing overlordship of the Monroe Doctrine, so has China resented the patronizing overlordship of the powers that flocked in through the Open Door.

The ideal of the Washington officials in recent years has been to make China strong enough to be mistress in her own house and to uphold the Open Door by herself. Thus in the early 1940's we undertook to bolster up the Nationalist government of Chiang Kai-shek as a counterweight against a resurgent Japan or an imperialistic Russia or a Soviet-manipulated communistic regime. As steps in this direction both the United States and Britain in 1943 formally renounced extraterritorial rights in China.

One sees here a curious reverse parallelism with the Monroe Doctrine, which began unilaterally and ended multilaterally. The Open Door started as a loosely supported multilateral doctrine, and if things work out as the United States hoped at the close of World War II, it will end a unilateral Chinese doctrine. But the prospects are far from bright, for China emerged from the conflict in chaos. And by a curious turn of the wheel, Roosevelt at

Yalta gave to the Russians a stranglehold on Manchuria, which is the very thing that John Hay sought to prevent by his original Open Door notes.

8

The Open Door has been a hope rather than a reality, an ideal rather than a policy, and in these respects it resembles isolation, and to some extent Freedom of the Seas and Pan-Americanism. Except during those periods when the powers saw fit to accord it respect, it usually rusted on sagging hinges. As early as 1898, the Detroit *News* observed: "There is a widespread disposition to connect the Open Door with the story of the stolen horse."

The ill success of the Open Door has been due in part to the unwillingness of the American people to respect the principle of economic nondiscrimination in their domestic affairs, let alone those 7,000 miles away. Dr. Charles A. Beard has said with some exaggeration that we have been for the Open Door everywhere except at home. We have erected lofty tariff walls against the goods of foreign nations, and our most conspicuous instance of discrimination in the exclusion of immigrants was directed at the Far East, the very area in which we have made the boldest bid for the Open Door.

But the failure of the Open Door, in so far as we are concerned, was due primarily to the fact that the American people have never regarded it as really vital. In an area so far away, seemingly so little related to our security, and involving so little of our trade and investment, it was difficult to arouse or sustain interest.° "One trouble about the Far East is that it isn't far enough," lamented a South Carolina newspaper in 1924. We did not have the power to prop open the Open Door, largely because we did not see the importance of amassing power for that purpose.

Our interests in the Caribbean are primary, and for decades we have assembled the military and naval force with which to protect them. Our commercial stake in China over the years has been not more than tertiary —just pin money. Japan's interests in the Caribbean have not been even tertiary, and she has never had the power to defend them against us. But her holdings in China have been vital: prior to Pearl Harbor they meant the economic life and prosperity of the Rising Sun. She was determined to fight for that stake, and she did, although she would not have fought for Caribbean investments. We Americans as a people were unwilling to wage war for our interests in China, although our government tried to act as though we would, and when Pearl Harbor came we found that we had sent a boy to do a man's job.

° In 1901 the Washington *Star* commented: "The news from China is that the reform program calls for the substitution of the Tsung-li-yamen by the Wei-wu-pu. This news is received with intense interest and satisfaction."

America's economic stake in faraway China was, and still is, of relative unimportance. But little aggressions beget big aggressions, and little wars flare forth into global wars. As long as we were battling for the integrity of China so that our merchants and missionaries might have a fair field, we were on extremely narrow ground. But our stand was more defensible when we took the position that the Far East was not the back door of the world, that what happened there was of vital concern to us, and that the sanctity of treaties and the fine fabric of international law must be preserved if we were to have world peace.

In aiming to prevent wars in which we might be involved, the Open Door was a security doctrine. As such, it may experience something of a rebirth under perhaps a different name. But the old commercial Open Door, assuming that it was even much more than a shadow, has now become unhinged.

CHAPTER TWENTY-FIVE

PROPAGANDISTS AND PRESSURE GROUPS

"When war is declared, Truth is the first casualty."
—ARTHUR PONSONBY, 1928

1

A COMMON ERROR is to confuse public opinion with pressure-group opinion. One explanation is that the "pressure boys" have perfected techniques for making noise out of all proportion to the numbers of their constituents, and in so doing they provide another example of the "tyranny of the minority." Clever operatives can stir up a tremendous pother, particularly when they assail their congressmen with padded petitions, "parrot" letters, and form telegrams signed with names lifted from the telephone directory.

The nervous legislator, ever anxious for his seat, may easily be misled by the aggressive minority that deluges him with telegrams, while the great and apathetic majority tends to its everyday diversions. He may be unduly impressed when a man whom he has never heard of before appears as the alleged spokesman for 22,000,000 people. The congressman in such circumstances would do well to remember the three London tailors of Tooley Street who, in addressing a petition to the king, began: "We, the people of England . . ." The Townsend old-age plan of the 1930's, backed enthusiastically by superannuates with nothing better to do, had thrown a bad scare into the politicians when a national opinion poll discovered that only a negligible percentage of the voters favored it. The poll takers' pencils pricked the vast bubble.

Pressure groups will not here receive the attention they deserve, because this book is concerned primarily with public opinion, not pressure opinion. Nor will emphasis be placed on individual lobbyists, except in so far as they affected public reactions. The prize case is that of William B. Shearer, whose activities were sensationally exposed in 1929. The Big Three Eastern shipbuilding concerns, fearing that naval disarmament would hurt their profits, employed this self-styled "big bass drum" to sabotage the Geneva Disarmament Conference of 1927, at an alleged salary of $25,000 a year for ten years, plus a liberal expense account. The Conference almost certainly would have failed anyhow, but Shearer attributed the result to his "fast and vicious campaign."

The whole sordid story made the headlines three years later, on the eve of the London Disarmament Conference. The American public was aroused, and gave strong support to Hoover's arms-reduction program, thereby defeating the schemes of the armor-plate profiteers. The resulting state of mind contributed powerfully to the dangerous unpreparedness of the 1930's, and played directly into the hands of Senator Nye when he misleadingly spotlighted the machinations of the munitioneers.

The well fed and well groomed lobbyists no doubt have a legitimate role, whether battling reciprocity for the sugar interests, or the St. Lawrence project for the electric power interests, or Argentine beef for the cattle interests, or arms embargoes for the munitions interests. Congressmen need information, and in some respects one-sided information is better than none at all. But the lobbyists in Washington are more numerous than the members of Congress, are often better paid, and are frequently abler men who know more about legislative strategy than the representatives themselves.

2

It is probably fair to say that most Americans belong to some kind of pressure group, whether as farmers, laborers, veterans, manufacturers, or other special interests. A vast number belong to several such groupings. In a broad sense, the American people are a gigantic pressure group, the most powerful in the world. A partial listing of some of the better known organizations will give some idea of the magnitude of the problem.

The hyphenated Americans, through such organizations as the National Jewish Welfare Board and the Ancient Order of Hibernians in America, are better organized to promote the interests of a foreign element than the average American is to promote American interests.

The church groups have formed the Federal Council of Churches of Christ in America, the National Catholic Welfare Conference, and other organizations of huge numbers and impressive power. Their influence, as well as that of the hyphenates, has been discussed in earlier chapters.

The farmers, speaking through the National Grange, the Farmers' Union, and the American Farm Bureau Federation have made their voices heard in regard to tariffs and other matters of primary concern to them. The National Grange, with a membership of some 800,000, threw its weight behind the drive to secure the Kellogg-Briand peace pact.

Commercial and manufacturing interests exert tremendous pressure through the National Association of Manufacturers, the National Foreign Trade Council, and the Chamber of Commerce of the United States. They have not distinguished themselves for a liberal and farsighted approach to the tariff, and some of them, in their desire for cheap sweat, have pursued selfish aims with regard to immigration.

The manual laborer, working through the American Federation of Labor and other groups, has been keenly alive to the fate of his highly perishable product. The only major affiliate of the League of Nations that we ever joined was the International Labor Office in 1934, partly no doubt out of respect for the labor vote. One should also note that labor organizations have consistently opposed unrestricted immigration, particularly that from the Orient. In 1900 the humor magazine *Puck* had a missionary explain to a puzzled Chinese that the latter could go to the white man's heaven but not to his country because there was no labor vote in heaven. At various times labor organizations have favored the World Court; the withdrawal of marines from the Caribbean; the independence of the Philippines with their competing Filipino labor; noninterference by Washington with labor-sympathizing Mexican regimes; the boycotting of Japanese goods (after the attack on China in 1937); and the opposition through boycotts to Communism or Fascism in any form. Labor unions have not fared too well under the Communists and Fascists.

Veterans' organizations, like the Veterans of Foreign Wars of the United States and the American Legion, have been militantly active. They have generally favored narrow nationalism, patriotic textbooks, suspicion of foreigners (especially Communists), nonrecognition of Russia, the exclusion of aliens, a strong foreign policy, isolation ("Keep Out, Keep Ready" was an American Legion slogan in 1939–1940), a "navy second to none," and a formidable military establishment. The veterans who in their earlier days were thrust into front lines without proper training or equipment do not have to be converted to the idea of preparedness.

The women, represented by the National League of Women Voters and the American Association of University Women, have also been vocal. Taking seriously their duties as citizens and mothers, they have generally sponsored a liberal foreign policy, and have campaigned for such objectives as the World Court and international cooperation. Not wanting their sons to die on foreign fields, they have been unusually ardent advocates of peace.*

Anglo-American groups, pooling their strength in such organizations as the English-Speaking Union, have labored for better relations between the Mother Country and the Daughter Country, and in pursuance of their program have published hands-across-the-seas literature.

Preparedness promoters, like the members of the Navy League, have long agitated for bigger and better armed forces. Herbert Hoover, who was both peace-minded and economy-minded, ran afoul of the Navy League, which allegedly contributed money to defeat him in 1932 and elect Roosevelt, who was regarded as more "ship-minded."

The pacifists have also been energetic in time of peace, although forced to soft-pedal their zeal in time of war. The best known of these groups is the Carnegie Endowment for International Peace, generously provided with the gold that Andrew Carnegie made from steel. Much of its activity, especially in published form, may be better classified as educational rather than propagandist. Dr. Charles A. Beard has rather angrily charged that the

---

* In 1947 several hundred members of the Congress of American Women paraded in Washington against President Truman's proposal for strengthening Greece and Turkey against Russia. Banners proclaimed: "Mothers and Wives Reject Proposals That Lead to New World Conflict."

various foundations, through fellowships and other subsidies, have induced academicians to scramble onto the peace bandwagon.

3

The professional patrioteers, such as the Daughters of the American Revolution and the Sons of the American Revolution, have wielded a powerful tomahawk. They have made their pressure felt for big armies and navies, and against the pollution of the Plymouth Rock stock by foreign immigrants, especially those with dangerous ideologies.

The influence of the super patriots has perhaps been most keenly felt in the writing and adoption of textbooks of history, and to some extent of geography. These groups have been especially vigilant in demanding that our forefathers be generously gilded, and that our ancient enemies be liberally blackened. Boards of education and other adopters of textbooks can avoid much tribulation if they favor eulogistic treatment, and particularly if they see to it that foreign ideologies like Communism are mentioned only to be condemned.

All countries do the same thing. The chief difference between censorship by dictators and censorship by pressure groups is that the former is more ironclad. In 1927, when naval disarmament was much in the public eye, the Detroit *News* observed: "Disarmament is a help, but what the world needs is a history schoolbook that reads the same in all countries." Another journal remarked: "Beating swords into plowshares won't help if they keep on beating twisted versions of history into the heads of children."

As the American nation has become more sophisticated and less on the defensive, we have permitted our textbooks to become more critical, although there remains room for improvement. In 1945, when the country was still under the spell of wartime cooperationist sentiment, a public opinion poll discovered that nearly nine out of ten adults would like to see an international agency set up to examine our textbooks. More than seven out of ten were willing to change the texts, even as regards Germany, if the accounts were demonstrably unfair.

Certain other nonpatriotic groups are so definitely nonpartisan that they cannot be fairly classified under the heading of pressure or propaganda. Among organizations of this type may be found the Foreign Policy Association, and the Council on Foreign Relations.

Pressure groups, especially those of a hyphenate or ultraliberal complexion, have often hamstrung the work of our diplomats abroad by emitting loud outcries at most inopportune times. In 1945 the State Department, seeking to forestall subsequent criticism, took the unusual step of inviting forty-two of the most important service, educational, and other organizations to send consultants to the San Francisco Conference. The strategy of inviting potential opponents into one's camp undoubtedly contributed to the snowballing of public opinion behind the United Nations Charter.

4

Propaganda may here be defined as the dissemination of presumed information, frequently with a bias or false twist, for the deliberate purpose of influencing public attitudes and hence action.

In a democracy like ours, propaganda is not necessarily wicked or dangerous. Where there is so much ignorance and apathy, and where the Washington government needs the guidance of an active public opinion,* the spreading of information, even though it be one-sided, stimulates debate and perhaps clarifies thinking. Propaganda is vicious if it is false, if it is used for a patently evil purpose, and if it is aimed at people incapable of evaluating it.

The line between a campaign of propaganda and a campaign of education is admittedly a fine and wavering one. If the crusade is led by a nonpartisan organization like the Foreign Policy Association, the result may fairly be described as a campaign of education. But unfortunately much of what one may call propaganda is disseminated by partisan groups, with narrowly selfish ends in view, and the truth is badly mishandled. Someone has said that if our side puts on a drive, it is a campaign of education; if the other side does so, it is a campaign of propaganda.

Propaganda in foreign affairs is of peculiar importance to the United States. A similar problem does not exist in a dictatorship, except on a secretive basis, for the state controls the press and radio, and foreign agitators are given short shrift. But in America our virtually unlimited freedom of the press is a boon to the propagandist, whether home grown or imported. The United States as a consequence has been, not only the happy hunting ground of the propagandists, but the battle ground of competing propagandists, as was notably true in 1914 and 1941. The results were not commensurate with the clamor, partly because these foreign agents cancelled out the labors of one another, and to some extent left the American voter confused and indifferent.

Even where the campaign of education is free from most of the evils of outright propaganda, one grave danger remains. The crusader is apt to deal with slogans and symbols and other mental stereotypes, and thus delude the people into thinking that they are thinking. A healthy democracy cannot exist without thought on the part of a large number of people, and in so far as a "canned" campaign of education discourages such thought, it is doing democracy a dubious service.

* The Committee to Defend America by Aiding the Allies, by mobilizing opinion in advance, helped to give Franklin Roosevelt the courage to go ahead with his momentous destroyer deal in 1940.

5

An important but dangerous type of propaganda is that disseminated by the Washington government itself. The American taxpayer objects strongly to the use of his own money to propagandize himself, especially in the hands of "bureaucrats" who may be promoting their own ends, as was to some extent true during the days of the New Deal. The congressmen, who do the bidding of the taxpayer, are sensitive, if not violent, on this subject. The administration must proceed with the utmost caution, because Congress holds the purse and may snap it shut if the bureaucrats overstep the line. In time of war, when it is as necessary to mobilize opinion as it is to mobilize men, the government has greater latitude, but, even so, every move must be made with extreme circumspection. The State Department during World War II undertook to explain its work through some innocuous and rather vapid broadcasts, but it was condemned by certain congressmen for putting out propaganda.

Secretary Daniel Webster was forced to sacrifice some territorial claims of both Maine and Massachusetts in the treaty of 1842 with England; and in order to quiet the opposition in these states he resorted to the employment of special propaganda agents. Secretary Seward, after astonishing the entire nation with his treaty for Alaska, spent several hundred dollars of State Department funds in describing for the press the contents of "Seward's Icebox." This was a genuine and much-needed campaign of education, but it would not have fared so well if the public had known that they were being "propagandized" with their own money.

Woodrow Wilson's Fourteen Points address was one of the most potent pieces of propaganda that ever issued from Washington. Wilson deliberately reduced his war aims to these pithy placard paragraphs, so that they could be used to seduce the enemy, unite the Allies, and inspire the home front. He succeeded beyond his fondest expectations when George Creel's Committee on Public Information spread the gospel according to Wilson all over the world in countless millions of pamphlets and leaflets. In Poland, university men met on the streets, clasped hands, and soulfully uttered one word, "Wilson"; in Italy, candles were burned before his portrait. But Wilson and Creel on the whole rather overdid things. Both the American people and outside peoples were led to expect too much, and their subsequent disillusionment more than matched their wartime exaltation.

The Atlantic Charter in World War II was a rather pale imitation of the Fourteen Points, but the Office of War Information carried forward the torch laid down by Creel. This agency served usefully, both at home and abroad, in disseminating information and building up morale. It was not a propaganda organization in the strictest sense, and it generally followed the policy of the Creel Committee that the truth about ourselves and what we were doing was propaganda of the most impressive sort. In the latter stages of the war, the O.W.I. concerned itself with the Negro problem, and the offended Southern congressmen forced the O.W.I. henceforth to direct its propaganda at foreigners. The organization also aroused anger elsewhere when in a magazine distributed in Russia it described the Middle West and Rocky Mountain areas as drought ridden and undeveloped. Following an uproar in Congress, prompt apologies were made to the eight maligned states.

In 1945 and 1946 opinion polls found a majority sentiment in favor of a government organization to explain the policies of the United States to the rest of the world. When the poll takers substituted "our point of view" for "propaganda," the percentage of favorable responses rose sharply, which is a striking commentary on the "sales resistance" that we had developed against "propaganda" following the activities of Senator Nye and others. In 1947 Washington actually began to beam short-wave radio broadcasts through the Russian Iron Curtain and elsewhere, but this activity was viewed with great suspicion by parsimonious and shortsighted congressmen. A slash in the annual appropriation subsequently hobbled the educational activities of the State Department in foreign lands.

6

Foreign agents of various kinds have long been active in the United States. The present discussion excludes the numerous good-will emissaries, like Mlle. Eve Curie in 1940 and Madame Chiang Kai-shek in 1943. The latter made an extremely favorable impression on Congress and elsewhere, and contributed to the ignorant agitation for hitting Hirohito first.

An early instance of foreign intermeddling involved Tom Paine, whose persuasive pen was employed by the French government, at a salary of $1,000 a year, to create sentiment favorable to the recently concluded alliance of 1778 with the United States. During the next twenty or so years various French propagandists and agents, notably the harebrained Citizen Genêt, sought to poison public opinion against the British so as to bring about closer cooperation with France. The British minister in pre-1812 days, "Copenhagen" Jackson, attempted to unpoison the public mind regarding Britain when he spent some 700 pounds on the press and other agencies. The emissaries of Maximilian likewise sought to work up sentiment favorable to his puppet regime by a judicious if inadequate disbursement of money to lobbyists, writers, and newspapers.

In 1879 a French canal company, headed by the dynamic De Lesseps, was organized to undertake geographical surgery on the isthmus of Panama, and it spent about $2,000,000 in the United States in an attempt to quiet American fears regarding an infraction of the Monroe Doctrine. Yellow fever and other obstacles ruined the enterprise, and Philippe Bunau-Varilla, one of the legatees, attempted in 1902 to salvage something by propagandizing in Washington against the Nicaragua route, alleging dangerous volcanic activities. He was not making much headway when Providence came to his rescue with a terrific eruption on Martinique which killed some 40,000 people. Eight days later a Nicaraguan volcano became active, the very mountain engraved on the postage stamps of the Republic. Bunau-Varilla descended upon the Washington stamp dealers, bought ninety stamps, and had one placed on the desk of each United States senator, with an attached message: "An official witness of the volcanic activity of Nicaragua." A volcano-minded Congress finally voted for the Panama route.

The Hawaiian sugar planters in the 1890's spent considerable money in the United States to promote annexationist sentiment. Venezuelan propagandists in 1895 presented their case against Great Britain with unusual success. The ill-starred intervention of the United States in Cuba during 1898 was urged by Cuban propagandists in America, who did yeoman work in exaggerating or falsifying conditions so as to play upon our sympathies.

On the eve of the Russo-Japanese War of 1904–1905, Japanese propaganda pictured unoffending Japan as being wantonly attacked by the ungainly Russian bear. The American public swallowed this version unquestioningly. But after Nippon had won a series of astonishing victories, the Russian propagandists got busy, and by the time of the Portsmouth Peace Conference they had helped bring about a sharp reversal in our sympathy for the so-called underdog.

7

The period of World War I was the heyday of open and unabashed foreign propaganda in the United States, with the Allies and the Germans engaged in a competitive courtship of American opinion. Serious doubts have been raised as to the effectiveness of this propaganda, but there can be no doubt that a vast amount of propaganda was issued by both sides.

The German opinion poisoners were at a serious disadvantage from the beginning, despite our large and noisy groups of German-Americans. During the two previous decades we had become increasingly suspicious of the militaristic and imperialistic Germany, with the sabre-rattling Kaiser cast in the role of villain. During the same years we were enjoying unaccustomed deference from the harassed British, and when the chips were down in 1914 we could not fail to see that blood was thicker than the British blockade. Besides, the land of Lafayette was in the Allied camp, and we could never forget our presumed debt.

The Germans were under the additional odium of appearing to be the aggressors, diabolically bent upon wrapping the world in flames. Whatever the responsibility or intentions of the other powers, the gray-clad German hosts broke into Belgium, despite a solemn treaty binding them not to do so. The entire war on the Western Front was fought on Belgian and French soil, and atrocities against the inhabitants, male and female, were as inevitable as they were susceptible of exaggeration. "What gentle souls Attila and Genghis Khan must have been!" exclaimed a South Carolina editor in 1914, after reading the horror tales. One never heard about Allied outrages on German girls because the Allies never got to Germany until after the Reich surrendered, and then one heard a great deal in America about the lust of black French Senegalese.

With reference to Belgium, the Germans felt that they were completely justified in breaking out of an alleged Allied encirclement, but whatever the truth, they appeared to the outside world as wanton aggressors. With reference to the British blockade, the Germans felt that they were completely justified in breaking out of the Allied encirclement by using the submarine in an unrestricted fashion, but whatever the truth, they appeared to the outside world as wanton aggressors when they ruthlessly torpedoed the *Lusitania* and other Allied ships. The Allies did not need to commit atrocities in Germany or on the high seas; their slow starvation of the civilian population of Germany was quiet, unspectacular, and censored.

Aldous Huxley has said that the propagandist merely canalizes an existing stream: "In a land where there is no water he digs in vain." There was little water for the Germans in the United States. The American people were anti-German and pro-Ally before the war ever began, although they wanted to stay out of it. The invasion of Belgium was a fact, not propaganda; the sinking of the *Lusitania* was a fact, not propaganda; the shelling of Paris by "Big Bertha" was a fact, not propaganda; the shooting of Red Cross Nurse Edith Cavell was a fact, not propaganda.

The case of Edith Cavell is most instructive. She not only helped espionage agents but assisted some 250 Allied prisoners through the German lines, and under the laws of war her execution was justified, as was that of several women disposed of by the Allies under similar, if less highly publicized, circumstances. But she was shot, and to the American people there was little or no justification for executing a woman who was also a Red Cross Nurse. It was worse than a crime; it was a blunder.

All these incidents were facts, but the facts were liberally embroidered and embellished by Allied propagandists. Even when some of the distortion and falsehood were torn away, the unlovely basic structure remained, and "Hunnish" excuses got little hearing.

The Germans, moreover, did not understand American psychology. They were too open, too obvious, too lacking in subtlety, and too prone to adopt the technique of the cave man. They never learned to sell themselves before they sold their product—to get themselves accepted, respected, trusted. They tried to stress the facts as they saw them, but the American people were interested not in facts but in fireworks. The Germans failed as propagandists largely because they were dull. They had no heroine like Nurse Edith Cavell, no hero like "Papa" Joffre, no villain like the Kaiser.

The Allies, notably the British propagandists, were smooth and insinuating. Keeping themselves in the background, they permitted pro-Ally Americans of prominence to be their spokesmen, fully realizing that British noble-men with Oxford accents would be less than successful. The burden of the battle was borne by the press and by American leaders—the preachers, the professors, the patrioteers, and others. Some of these professional people, who should have kept their heads better, wrote and said things of which they were not unduly proud in later years.

8

Disillusionment descended like a heavy fog after the Armistice of 1918. Wilson's ideals were unrealized; the Allies proved to be ingrates and "welsh-ers"; the Germans were found to be not solely guilty in starting the war; and the atrocity stories, with their emphasis on mutilated Belgian babes, were exposed. "Peace is that blessed period," said the Hartford *Times* in 1926, "when it isn't your sacred duty to believe an official lie." In our anger over the exaggeration and falsification, we overlooked the basic facts of aggression and invasion. The American people were pretty thoroughly dis-illusioned even before the Nye committee began its work.

"Propaganda" spelled "sucker" in the American dictionary, and when war again broke out in 1939, we were determined not to be victimized again. Jay Allen, a well known journalist and lecturer, reported: "In the Midwest one gets the feeling that men are waiting with shotguns to shoot down the first propagandist who mentions Belgian babies." One *Fortune* poll in 1940 showed that the people were definitely on their guard against British and French propaganda.

The story of foreign propaganda in the United States is much clearer for World War II than for World War I. Congress, taking a page from our experiences in the first conflict, passed the Foreign Agents Registration Act in 1938, which required foreign propagandists to register.[*]

British agents were much less active in America during the second conflict than during the first. They were keenly aware of the violent Ameri-can antipathy to propaganda, and they did not want to hurt their cause by engaging too openly in it. A center of British activity in America was the British Library of Information in New York, which certainly had an innocuous title. A library is a sleepy and harmless place; information is good; publicity is good. The British officials, to an even greater extent than in 1914–1917, were content to let home-grown organizations carry the banner, notably the well organized and active Committee to Defend America by Aiding the Allies. The emphasis was very cleverly on America rather than on the Allies.

In 1939, to a far greater extent than in 1914, the American people were pro-Ally—the polls indicate by as much as 90 per cent. The chief reason

[*] George Sylvester Viereck, the leading German-American propagandist of World War I, failed to register, and in 1943 was sentenced to a term in a federal penitentiary.

why the British did not engage in extensive propaganda activity in this country is that one does not waste ammunition on a fortress already won. As an Iowa farm journal put it after World War I: "If a cause is just it will eventually triumph in spite of all the propaganda issued to support it."

9

If German propaganda in 1914 was incredibly inept, by 1939 it had become incredibly astute. The master propagandist Dr. Goebbels, having goosestepped the minds of the Germans into line, turned his arts upon the Allies and the Americans. The German Library of Information in New York was quiet and insinuating, and it published an attractive and urbane weekly *Facts in Review*, which kept hatreds pretty well under cover, but which sought to counteract the British. This was the first great war in which radio figured as a major weapon, and the ether was made a town hall for competing ideologies. Dr. Goebbels beamed his message of discord to America by short wave, as did the Japanese through "Tokyo Rose" and others.

The Germans were diabolically clever in stressing those things that would arouse distrust against our potential allies. The British had "suckered" us into the last conflict, said Dr. Goebbels, and they would try to do it again. The sly lion was prepared to fight to the last American in a war which England had started. The Germans were jolly good fellows who wanted nothing more than peaceful trade with us, and the Jews were nasty people. The invincible German war machine could not possibly lose; hence support of the British was a complete waste. Much of Dr. Goebbels's effort was directed at dividing class against class, nationality against nationality, and race against race. He praised men like Lindbergh and Wheeler and even Hoover, all of whom were urging America to stay out. Like the British, the Germans were willing to let American organizations bear the brunt of the battle, notably the America First group, which featured Colonel Lindbergh. Many isolationists whose loyalty no one could doubt were embarrassed by the large number of German Bundists and other un-American characters who flocked to their banners. The anti-Hitler complex had become so pronounced by 1941 that the interventionist leaders were regarded as more patriotic than the noninterventionist leaders, who actually were truer to historic American policy.

In 1945 the Attorney General released a report describing activities under the Foreign Agents Registration Act. From June, 1942, to December, 1944, a total of more than 12,000 different propaganda items in twenty-six languages were filed annually with the Department of Justice. Agents of various kinds were associated with thirty-four foreign governments, although only eighteen of them maintained official information centers in the United States. The British spent the most money in 1944, a total of

$2,143,000, while three governments-in-exile, Poland, the Netherlands, and Belgium, followed in that order.

The Attorney General noted that most of the propaganda was designed to create good will rather than to influence a specific course of action. Much of the information dealt with the history, culture, and problems of the country in question, with special emphasis on its contributions to the common war effort. Propaganda techniques were becoming more refined, and the Attorney General found it virtually impossible at times to draw a distinct line between political propaganda and good-will informative matter.

The motion picture also serves as a potent instrument of propaganda, for it can reach the tired, the illiterate, and the ignorant, who have only to look and listen. The old silent film was used effectively for pro-Ally purposes during the period of World War I, and popular films were *The Beast of Berlin* and *To Hell with the Kaiser.* The tens of millions of American movie-goers are fortunately not exposed to much foreign propaganda, for there are relatively few foreign films. The Hollywood producers are nervous about their overseas market, and they go to great lengths to avoid offending foreign customers. *For Whom the Bell Tolls* was barred from Spain and Argentina even after it had been heavily muffled, and this sort of thing has resulted in an anemic diet for the American patron. Hollywood generally steers clear of subjects offensive to foreigners, and one result is an overstressing of the ranch and the boudoir. Audiences in other countries get a totally false impression of Americans from our movies, which probably constitute the most damaging propaganda against ourselves that has yet been devised.*

As the dictators of World War II became near enemies or open enemies, movie producers were less concerned about Axis sensibilities, as evidenced by *The Hitler Gang* and *Confessions of a Nazi Spy.* The Russian regime was presented in a highly favorable light in *Mission to Moscow. Nurse Edith Cavell* revived pro-Ally sentiment, and *Hitler—Beast of Berlin* recalled memories of the Kaiser. During the war it was customary to have as villains either sneaking Nipponese or snarling Nazis, thus fixing stereotypes in the malleable mind.

When Confucius wrote: "One picture is worth 10,000 words," he did not have in view the animated picture, and above all the animated picture that talks. One clever movie may be worth many more than ten thousand soldiers.

* Heinrich Hauser, in *The German Talks Back,* remembers the effect on hungry German movie audiences of the 1930's when Hollywood actors threw rich whipped-cream pies at each other.

10

Propaganda in time of peace, no matter by whom, is not pretty, but in time of war it becomes downright ugly. In the midst of World War I, the Boston *Transcript* remarked: "Truth is more of a stranger than fiction." The rattling of the presses is no less to be feared than the rattling of the machine guns, and the censor's pen is mightier than the sword.

War propaganda is almost invariably warped, for men's imaginations are fevered, and they are easily persuaded to believe the worst about their enemies. The patriotic propagandist invariably glosses over our shortcomings and magnifies our achievements; he tells only bad about the enemy and good about ourselves. The enemy always plunders and rapes, while our boys are Little Lord Fauntleroys off on a Sunday-school picnic. In 1916 the Chicago *Daily News* concluded: "If either of the belligerents in this war knew the depressing facts about themselves that their opponents know, they would surrender at once."

The history of all great conflicts shows that there are always atrocities on both sides, partly because war is the greatest atrocity of all. From 1914 to 1917 the American people, reading British-censored news stories, got the idea that the Germans were beasts, while the Serbians, Rumanians, Greeks, Italians, Frenchmen, Britishers and Russians never did anything out of line, until of course the Russians turned Bolshevik. The Indianapolis *Star* in 1916 was a bit puzzled to learn that when a German drops a bomb he could hit only women and children, while an "Allied aviator can throw one into a crowd and never touch a soul except soldiers in uniform."

In 1914 we were too naïve and gullible; in 1939 we were too indifferent and blasé. This time the real wolf was on the loose, and we refused to take alarm. We moved with the greatest of reluctance, and then when it was almost too late. The Belgian atrocity stories of 1914, even if they had been wholly true, were but college hazing when compared with the wholesale brutalities of Nazi concentration camps and grisly charnel houses.

Two major safeguards may still be employed in America to combat the wiles of the propagandist. First, education so as to arm the citizen with the facts, with critical attitudes, and with a knowledge of propaganda techniques. Secondly, freedom of speech. Education shades so imperceptibly into propaganda, that if we seek to abolish propaganda we shall imperil legitimate education.

CHAPTER TWENTY-SIX

PRINTING PRESSES AND AIR WAVES

"We live under a government of men and morning newspapers."
—WENDELL PHILLIPS

1

THE THOUSAND-TONGUED newspaper press is a monster with tremendous power. It has long given us the bulk of our information about the outside world, and this is a frightening responsibility. Without sound information there can be no sound public opinion, and without sound public opinion there can be no intelligent foreign policy.

Any criticism of the newspaper must be tempered by a realization that publishing is a business and not a benefaction. The publisher is out to sell subscriptions and advertising space just as the grocer is out to sell eggs and sacks of potatoes. James Gordon Bennett could start the New York *Herald* in 1835 with an office consisting of a plank across two flour barrels. But in more recent years the publishing of newspapers has come to be a big business. Only a Marshall Field, with high principles and inherited millions, could coolly face huge annual losses before the Chicago *Sun* and the New York *PM* might hope to be out of the red.° One result has been that the newspapers are becoming fewer and bigger, with fewer independent, home-owned journals, and with more syndicated, standardized material. The owners are generally "economic royalists" who reflect the conservative, big-business bias of corporate ownership, with correspondingly less freedom of expression. Upton Sinclair's *Brass Check* (1919) inveighed against those "who betray the virgin hopes of mankind into the loathsome brothel of Big Business."

The lifeblood of the newspaper is advertising. When the reader is willing to provide this support himself, and pay substantially more for a copy of his paper, he may expect a better product. But until that time we must recognize that the newspaper is a big business, tied in with big-business advertisers, and that as a consequence we cannot expect the same standards of high-mindedness that we have come to expect from a liberally endowed charitable institution.

Does the newspaper press create or reflect public opinion? In the nineteenth century, when there were journalistic giants like Greeley of the New York *Tribune*, the emphasis was on creating. Someone asked the grandfather of Professor Earl Barnes what he thought about a current problem. "Wait until the *Weekly Tribune* comes," he answered, "and then I can tell you what I think about it." The giants passed, and the emphasis

° After a six-year policy of accepting no advertising, *PM* in November, 1946, announced a reversal of policy. The editor, Ralph Ingersoll, resigned in protest.

began to shift to the reflecting of public opinion. Arthur Brisbane, whose "Brisbanalities" established him as Hearst's most powerful columnist, divulged his secret: "Writing good editorials is chiefly telling the people what they think, not what you think." Yet in 1944 a national survey showed that more than nine editors out of ten regarded the leading of public opinion as their chief function.

The Roosevelt elections from 1932 to 1944 knocked into a cocked hat the assumption that the newspapers are fairly accurate reflectors of public opinion. Roosevelt never did have a majority of the press on his side, and in each of the four succeeding elections he had less support, yet he triumphed each time by tremendous majorities. The explanation is simple. The newspapers, as big businesses, are rightist, and Roosevelt, as the champion of the "forgotten man," was leftist. Many of his following, drawn largely from the lower income groups, did not subscribe to newspapers at all, or read the funnies and ignored the editorials. There is in fact some distinction between public opinion and press opinion. The two may be roughly the same, but often they are not. Editors, like propagandists, can canalize public opinion, but in a land of little water they fare ill.

Within broad limits the newspaper must reflect the predilections and prejudices of its subscribers. The New York *Times* cannot go Communist, and the *Daily Worker* cannot go New York *Times*. If either did, it would lose its subscribers, and with them would vanish its advertising revenue and solvency. Independence of thought is a fine thing, but profits have to come first. Some critic has well said that an editor, unlike a congressman, has to be reelected every day.

2

Some newspapers, notably the Hearst press, editorialize subtly or blatantly in their news columns, which is contrary to the canons of good journalism. Others sin by not printing stories unfavorable to their bias, or presenting news bearing only on their side of the controversy. The power of the press, as someone has said, is the power to suppress. The isolationist Chicago *Tribune*, for example, printed very little that was favorable to internationalism in the decades after World War I.

The headline writer often wields a more potent pen than the editorial writer, especially among the more ignorant classes. We are a nation of headline snatchers who gulp the headlines with our morning coffee before dashing for the train, or who read them while hanging from a strap. The headlines can have some one "assail" or "denounce," when a careful reading shows that there was no assailing or denouncing. They can deliberately magnify inconsequential incidents or minimize important ones. The Hearst press during the Spanish Civil War of the 1930's habitually branded the Loyalists as "Reds," played down their victories, and played up their defeats.

Editorializing has even crept into the so-called "funnies." During the period of World War II the simple-minded and good-hearted Joe Palooka indulged in internationalist sermons, while the pathetic Orphan Annie, syndicated to millions of readers under isolationist auspices, more than countered with isolationist philosophizings. The effect of such propaganda on a host of children, whether of tender or senile years, would be difficult to calculate. In 1933, when Annie lost her dog, the artist was deluged with telegrams, including one from Henry Ford, beseeching a speedy recovery. The artist obliged, and the nation recovered its composure.

Ideally, the newspaper does not present enough foreign news, although in this respect it is improving. The basic answer is that people want to see their own names in the paper, or read about the foibles of their neighbors, and canny editors have long since discovered that this is the royal road to profits. The trouble with foreign news is that it is foreign.

A few editors have been frank to confess that they print material on international relations, not so much because the subscriber is interested in them, as out of a sense of public duty. Such high-minded journalists are apt to fight a losing battle with the debit side of the ledger. The customer is always right, and an opinion poll in 1946 showed that newspaper coverage of foreign affairs was regarded by the readers as quite adequate.

Bismarck once growled that the peace of Europe could be preserved by hanging a dozen editors, which is just another way of saying that the press sins in oversensationalizing foreign news. Many of the topflight newsmen have worked their way up from the ranks, and they cannot quite forget their old police-court days, when there was no news unless there was trouble. During World War II it was proved that rosy headlines sold fewer papers; headlines of disaster worried people into buying more copies. During the San Francisco Conference of 1945, there was a large corps of correspondents but little sensational news, certainly not every day. The newsmen had to write copy, and the pressure was on them to magnify minor differences into crises, sometimes employing the jargon of the prize ring. Thus the conference was represented as a slugfest between Russia on the one hand and the rest of the world on the other. Actually, there were large areas of agreement between the Soviet Union and the other members of the Big Four, while much of the uproar was created by the small nations which resented Big Power domination.

3

Sheer ignorance on the part of the correspondent is perhaps more dangerous than merely getting the picture out of focus. At the Paris Peace Conference of 1919 there were scores of newsmen, many of whom had never left the United States before. A large percentage of them were almost completely in the dark about the background of the infinitely complicated problems they were supposed to discuss. The blind reporters at Paris led the blind newspaper readers at home.

Even more dangerous in its long-run implications is the practice of relating only the bizarre about another country. If a fish catches a man, that is news. If a foreign newspaper says something reasonably favorable about the United States, that is not news. ("Harmony," as Silas Bent said, "seldom makes a headline.") But if the journal is important and it launches a violent attack on the President, that is news. During the Spanish-American War of 1898 the Berlin government was neutral, and the German press on the whole somewhat indifferent. But a certain number of German newspapers printed bitter remarks about America, and these were put on the wires, thus giving our people a warped view of German opinion. Foreign newspapers do the same thing about us, even when not instructed to do so by a Minister of Propaganda. In European eyes, and with the help of American movies, we have become a nation of jitterbugging, love-nesting, zoot-suited, flagpole sitting, two-gun-toting, nigger-baiting degenerates. Many human beings (including Americans) are not so much interested in the good, the true, and the beautiful as in the wicked, the false, and the deformed.

Newspapers and magazines, both American and foreign, often act with a criminal irresponsibility. The abusing of friendly but foreign nations is generally regarded as legitimate fun, and besides it sells papers. Many journals act as though their fulminations cannot be heard beyond the three-mile line, and in almost every international crisis the intemperance of the press heightens the tension and makes more difficult the task of the diplomats. During the Shanghai episode of 1932, the Department of State earnestly admonished the correspondents not to give a sensational turn to the happenings in the Far East.°

In recent years international newspaper feuding has been on the increase, largely because of the intentionally needling tactics of Soviet journals like *Pravda* (Truth) and *Izvestia* (News). In 1945 the world was treated to a not altogether edifying altercation between the well known journalist Walter Lippmann and *Pravda*, and other brave knights, like the Chicago *Tribune* and the New York *Times*, have spurred to the fray.

4

A rapid survey of the role of the press in the history of American foreign relations will illuminate some of the observations already made.

From 1789 to 1815 our people were deeply concerned with the European conflagration, and the pro-French Jeffersonian Republicans were at daggers drawn with the pro-British Federalists. No verbal lashes were barred by the press, and the editors laid on with whips of scorpions, using personal

° In 1935 the magazine *Vanity Fair* grievously affronted the Japanese by publishing a sacrilegeous caricature of the Emperor pulling a ricksha.

vilification to a degree that has happily passed. Federalist editors called the Jeffersonians "filthy Jacobins," a "despicable mobocracy," "Gallic Jackals," "lying dogs," "stinking caitiffs," "tools of baboons," "frog-eating, man-eating, blood-drinking cannibals." The Jeffersonians replied in kind. Well might a man in public life speak of freedom *from* the press.

Foreign agents at various times have tried to purchase our editors. Sometimes their efforts have been merely directed at good will, as when the British minister in Washington wined and dined leading newsmen while negotiating the treaty of 1871. More objectionable than the clinking of champagne glasses was outright bribery, as when in 1868 the Cuban revolutionists offered bond bribes to the press. In World War I certain German interests purchased the New York *Evening Mail* in a futile effort to influence public opinion, and in the years before Pearl Harbor the Berlin government, among other activities, advanced a large sum to the publishers of an isolationist magazine. Another nationally known journal was purchased in 1938 by three Americans with money provided by the Japanese government. During the ensuing four years the owners accepted about $150,000, and during that time some of their articles received additional circulation through reprint media. But on the whole foreign gold has had only a negligible effect on American opinion.

The lurid newspapers, as exemplified by the "penny dreadfuls," appeared before the Civil War, but they were engrossed with local sensations and did not venture far into foreign fields. During the Cuban crisis of 1868–1869 Dana's New York *Sun* and Bennett's *Herald* beat the tom-toms for intervention, but jingoistic journalism was not yet strong enough to prevail. When the blow-up came with Britain in 1895 over Venezuela, the press joined in the uproar, but Joseph Pulitzer's New York *World* (soon to change its tactics) labored manfully to quiet the clamor.

The new era of yellow journalism ("Gee whiz! journalism") was inaugurated in 1895 when young William Randolph Hearst purchased the fast-failing New York *Journal*, and straightway entered upon a titanic struggle with Joseph Pulitzer for what one British critic called the "primacy of the sewer." Hearst employed sensational devices like huge headlines and shocking pictures to appeal to the masses, many of whom were immigrants whose imperfect knowledge of English was flattered by bisyllabic, five-word Hearstian sentences.

The yellow journals are generally credited (or discredited) with having inflamed the public mind to a point where a peaceful settlement with Spain in 1898 was impossible. They snooped, stooped, and scooped to conquer. They screamed for war: when there was no sensational news they invented it; when the government failed to act, they acted. Hearst managed to emblazon the sensational De Lôme letter on his front pages, and his agents spirited the Cuban girl, Evangelina Cisneros, from a Spanish prison.

After the blowing up of the *Maine,* the yellow press sizzled with excitement and public indignation was kept at a white heat. The Detroit *Free Press* ran a banner headline: "MINES IN THE HARBOR!" Below this in small type appeared the revelation that American investigators had been unable to find any. Hearst's New York *Journal* blared: "WHOLE COUNTRY THRILLS WITH WAR FEVER," while Pulitzer, nearly two weeks before Congress acted, proclaimed: "DECLARATION OF WAR." The Spanish-American War in a very real sense was a war for newspapers, by newspapers, and of newspapers. Fortunately this period marked the high point (or low point) of gutter journalism, and in succeeding decades there was usually more restraint.

5

Hearst did not invent sensationalism, and he was not the only publisher to have a chain of newspapers. But his journalistic empire in its heyday was so far-flung, and his position on foreign affairs was so illiberal, that he cannot be dismissed with just a passing word. "In America," Oscar Wilde once said, "the President reigns for four years, and journalism governs for ever and ever." Franklin D. Roosevelt governed for twelve years, but the influence of Hearst has been actively felt in our press for more than sixty years.

Hearst agitated for the Spanish-American clash, and got it. For more than thirty years he clamored for war with Japan, and through no fault of his it was postponed until 1941.* Then Hearst triumphantly demanded that we dispose of Hirohito before finishing off Hitler. He urged the annexation of Canada at various times, and decried the Anglo-Japanese Alliance, as well as its successor, the Four Power Treaty, which one of his editorials in the New York *American* discussed under the heading: "England Recaptures Her Colony." He was opposed to the naval disarmament of the 1920's, and condemned our sacrifices at the Washington Disarmament Conference of 1921-1922 "for the painted rattle called limitation of armaments." Two of the most potent influences in America since about 1890 in stirring up ill will against Britain have undoubtedly been the Irish and Hearst.

Hearst assailed the League of Nations, with its six votes in the Assembly for the British empire, and he carried the fight on against the World Court, which he consistently branded the "League Court." When the showdown came in the Senate in 1935, he labored energetically to encompass its defeat. On this occasion the Hearst press blared: "The way to keep America out of the League of Nations trap—and the only way—is to keep America out of the League Court!"

Revolution broke out in Mexico during 1911, and in subsequent months Hearst violently demanded intervention for the protection of American

---

* During the 1913 crisis with Japan over alien-land legislation in California, a South Carolina newspaper remarked: "In the present hysterical state of our yellow press, we expect to sight a Japanese fleet off Cape Hearst any minute now."

lives and property. (Cynics alleged that his solicitude was prompted by a well justified concern for the fate of his huge Mexican ranch.) He strongly opposed the cancellation of Allied war debts. He became bitterly anti-Russian and anti-Communist; pro-Franco and pro-Fascist. He was consistently antiforeign, proisolationist, and against entangling alliances. He paraded his 100 per cent Americanism on his front pages, with red, white and blue titles and with stanzas of "The Star-Spangled Banner," and he was the first to sponsor the "I am an American" day. An advertisement published in 1946 proclaimed: "The Hearst Newspapers approve the ancient admonition: 'If you don't like this country, why don't you go back where you came from?'"

Hearst apparently regarded international trade as a one-way street, for on newsprint presumably imported from Canada he drove home the slogan: "Buy American." In 1933, from his palatial California home filled with European objects of art and other imported luxuries, he directed his editors to campaign for "patriotic policies," beginning with, "I buy American and spend American."

Nor did the sensational tactics of Hearstian journalism end with the Spanish-American War. In 1927, when Mexican-United States relations were critical, Hearst poured oil on the troubled embers by publishing a series of forged documents purporting to prove that certain United States senators had been bribed by the Mexican government. In 1928 a representative of Hearst was expelled from France for an exposure of the "secret naval accord" between Britain and France, and two years later the publisher himself was ousted when he sought to honor the Third Republic with his presence.

A careful examination of the printed record leads one to conclude that in the field of foreign affairs Hearst's editors have generally championed whatever was narrow, isolationist, antiforeign, illiberal, nationalistic, and chauvinistic. The Hearst newspapers have waxed fat on the carrion of public ignorance, for what they have advocated appeals to the ill-informed masses. "Hearst in war, Hearst in peace, and Hearst in the hearts of his countrymen," wrote the Boston *Transcript* satirically in the days of the Spanish-American War. The writer could better have said, "in the hearts of his ignorant countrymen."

The baleful influence of the Hearst press has probably been exaggerated, partly because so many of its subscribers read the comics and the sports rather than the editorials. In 1936 *Fortune* found that more than six out of ten voters did not know whether Hearst had been a good or bad influence, although those with opinions voted almost three to one that his influence had been bad. But it would be false to assume that he has not done great damage to the cause of enlightenment in foreign affairs. Not only has he helped kill worthy causes, like the World Court, but other worthy causes have presumably not been advocated for fear that the Hearst chain would lash out against them.

Radio broadcasting, like newspaper publishing, is a big business and not a benevolence, and radio executives are reluctant to do anything that will antagonize prospective purchasers of advertising time. Like the newspaper, the radio is an infinite source of entertainment, but unlike the newspaper, it is primarily and avowedly so, and newscasting is more or less incidental. The radio stations, under their federal license to monopolize the airwaves, donate part of their time to the public service of broadcasting and interpreting news, although they are loath to sacrifice their most lucrative advertising hours for this purpose, and although the amount of informational data is painfully small in relation to the total. In fairness one should add that the public probably does not want a greater quantity of solid matter than it is now getting.

The radio brings the news more speedily than the newspaper, and without appreciable cost, except for the pain of listening to the "commercial." Newscasts can be little more than a presentation of the headlines, yet if this type of thing is done without palpable bias it serves a useful function. But from the standpoint of influencing opinion, the news interpreter is of much greater importance.

The nationally known commentators on foreign and domestic affairs have a tremendous following, the more so as they bring to the air the techniques of the tabloid newspapers. Just as the tabloids command a mass circulation far in excess of the more respectable newspapers, so the dynamic but shallow radio seers, with their verbal fireworks and sensational prophecies, command a much larger listening audience than the more careful broadcasters. The public wants a rich voice and sparkling epigrams, but unfortunately a rich voice may be paired with a hot or empty head, and sensational language with an absence of substantial and expert information. The air is daily bombarded with an incredible amount of misinformation, bias (subtle or overt), innuendo, irrelevancy, bad guessing, and name-calling. A kind of Gresham's law operates under which the bad tends to drive out the good.

The radio is an engine of infinite force, and unfortunately many persons engaged in working with it do not have a sense of responsibility that is comparable with their power. The press sins in the same way, but any attempts to control it evoke an outcry about freedom of the press. The radio can theoretically be controlled in the public interest, for the governmental machinery exists to control it. The radio waves, unlike the newspaper, invade the home and partake of the nature of a public utility or a public trust which should be used as a birthright of the people. Many radio executives and commentators are fully aware of their responsibilities, but those who are not merely invite stricter control. Meanwhile one could wish for a sharper differentiation between news and opinion, and the employment of well informed and well balanced commentators rather than overnight experts on world affairs.

7

The magazine press likewise plays an important role in shaping opinion regarding foreign affairs. The more meaty journals, like *Harper's* and the *Atlantic Monthly,* unfortunately do not enjoy huge circulations, and the same is true of liberal organs like the New York *Nation* and the *New Republic.* But such magazines exert an influence out of all proportion to the number of their subscribers, for they are read by leaders in public life, and through them the published ideas are given wide currency.

The baleful "chain" influence has crept into the magazine world, what with the Crowell, Curtis, Hearst, and Luce interests, all of which to a considerable extent reflect the bias of big business, as is notably true of magazines like the *Saturday Evening Post.* The Luce empire of *Time, Life,* and *Fortune,* supplemented by the *March of Time* cinema, wields much more influence than Hearst ever did in his palmiest days, for these organs are read by a more intelligent clientele. The bias of the publisher, as notably revealed regarding China (where he was born), is seen in these magazines, whether through the slanting of the news, or the omission of news, or the selection and rewriting of articles. Even though the Luce chain attains a far higher level than that of Hearst, one cannot agree that in our democracy it is healthy to have one man force his views on so many of his fellow citizens. "Canned thinking," which is the menace of all these chain enterprises, is highly dangerous. "Where all think alike," writes Walter Lippmann, "no one thinks very much."

The *Reader's Digest* has attained phenomenal success by its appeal to the mass mind. Conceived originally in 1921 as a digest of the best current magazine articles, it attracted the hurried citizen, into whose pocket the little magazine so conveniently fitted. It has many other features that appeal to the adolescent or postadolescent mentality, but the real secret of its success is that people in the mass would rather be amused than edified. If they can feel that they are being edified while they are being amused, so much the better. A large proportion of the articles in the *Reader's Digest* are interesting rather than significant.

With success and power, the *Reader's Digest* has broken away from the original and socially desirable ideal of "digesting" the cream of current magazines. The "best" articles are often not the most interesting, and interest must reign at all costs. The management has also followed the policy of "planting" or "slanting" articles to conform to its own political or social philosophy. Discussions often appear on both sides of controversial questions, but the preponderance of material on one side raises a strong presumption that during the years before Pearl Harbor the owners were anti-union, anti-Russian, antibureaucracy, anti-New Deal, and antiinterventionist.

In 1944 William L. White, one of the magazine's roving editors, after making a six-weeks tour of the Soviet Union, published a book, *Report on the Russians,* which was markedly unfriendly to his hosts, and which was "digested" in the *Reader's Digest.* The Russians were deeply annoyed at a time when we and our allies were trying desperately to induce them to cooperate in the all-out war effort.

The *Reader's Digest* was antiboondoggling and hence anti-Good Neighbor policy, and it sponsored a hasty trip by Senator Butler to Latin America in 1943, and published his findings under the lurid title: "Our Deep Dark Secrets in Latin America." The senator belabored our undoubtedly lavish good-will spending, but by adding legitimate defense and other costs he inflated the actual figures by something like 90 per cent. Our friends to the south, whose cooperation we were trying to enlist in the war, were outraged by this unfair attack, and the cause of the Good Neighbor received a serious setback.

Magazines that "digest" the best of current literature have a legitimate place in our scheme of things, and magazines that grind an axe also have a legitimate place in the land of the free. But to do the latter under the guise of doing the former is a species of deception fraught with danger, especially when the vehicle has by far the largest circulation in the world. The *Reader's Digest* has undoubtedly done much good in amusing, uplifting, and educating countless millions, even though the significant information is minimized, skeletonized, and sugar-coated. But unfortunately the evidence is strong that the management has wielded its tremendous power without a commensurate sense of social responsibility.

8

The newspaper press is open to serious criticism in its coverage of foreign affairs, but when one considers the need for haste, the small sum the citizen pays for his paper, and his relative lack of interest in foreign affairs, the better journals have done a creditable job. As we have grown more mature, and as our interest in the outside world has been aroused by the events of the World War II period, the press has presented more adequate foreign coverage. Some journals, like the New York *Times,* print so much that only the most earnest citizen has time to disentangle the forest from the trees. Over a half century ago Lord Bryce observed that if the average citizen would only read and digest what is published, he would be reasonably well informed as to foreign affairs.

A free and critical press is a great asset in the conduct of a democratic foreign policy. It enables the public to keep public servants in the role of servants rather than masters. It throws the white light of publicity on those schemers who would set the ship of state on a course contrary to the desires of the people. Keyhole columnists like Drew Pearson have rather overdone the thesis that the public is entitled to know everything, notably when he published correspondence which forced Secretary of Commerce Wallace from the Cabinet in 1946 over the Russian issue. But the knowledge that the journalistic bloodhounds are ready to bay undoubtedly has a wholesome effect on self-willed intriguers.

The press can never be completely free to tell everything at all times, but one tremendous step forward would be international freedom of news gathering and reporting. When war broke out in 1914, the British cut the German cables, and henceforth most of the news that reached America had to pass by the shears of British censors. American correspondents quickly learned that they had better don British-colored glasses and see things as the British saw them if they expected to get their stories through unmutilated. If the news is distorted at the source by censorship, there is not much that even the most high-minded newspaper can do about it. In 1945 seven out of ten Americans favored the ideal of unrestricted freedom of information, but the Russian Iron Curtain interposed an impenetrable barrier.

We also need abler and better trained foreign correspondents, even though a marked improvement took place during the period of World War II. The foreign correspondent is an ambassador-at-large of the American public, for he is reporting not only to his superiors but to the people as a whole. He provides the facts upon which the newspaper bases its editorials, and the news stories upon which the readers form opinions and as a result of which they may bring pressure to bear on Washington. If the American ambassador serves as the eyes, ears, and nose of his government, the foreign correspondent discharges the same function for the people whom that government serves, and it would be impossible to name a single trait desirable in the ideal ambassador which the ideal correspondent should not also have, including an ability to write incisive and readable English. A correspondent may in fact be more important than the American minister. Frederic Jesup Stimson, while ambassador in Argentina during World War I, found that the Secretary of State either did not see or pay attention to his dispatches, so he advised fellow diplomats to give choice information to the Associated Press correspondents in the confident knowledge that the Secretary (and the American people) would get it the next morning with the breakfast coffee.

One cannot hire all the virtues for a pittance, in either the diplomatic or the newspaper world. We need better trained and better paid men in the newspaper service, as well as a more dignified professional status for them. Coverage of the Far East has suffered in part because the ablest correspondents do not want to "do time out there"; they regard Europe as the main show, and a more pleasant and lucrative show at that. The Oriental languages moreover are extremely difficult, and the translators whom one must employ may be in the pay of Tokyo or some other foreign government and instructed to gloss over or misconstrue important information. Another difficulty is to secure the services of men who know enough about the culture, psychology, and history of Far Eastern peoples to be able to observe as well as to see.

9

Journalistic ethics on the whole have been raised markedly in recent years, but there is still room for improvement. In 1942 the battle of Midway, which marked a turning point in the Pacific war, was won largely because our Navy had "cracked" the secret Japanese code. A large if not great Chicago newspaper later published information which indicated that this feat had been accomplished. The Japanese promptly changed their code, thereby making much more difficult our already hazardous operations in the Pacific. Even if we assume that the people are entitled to know everything, certainly the enemy is not.

Certain columnar calumniators, who make their bread and butter by snooping, naturally wrap themselves in the mantle of free speech and raise the cry that there should be no secret diplomacy. Yet not even Woodrow Wilson, for all of his championing of "open covenants of peace openly arrived at," argued that there should not be confidential bargaining. His point was that the results should be made public so that the people would know wherein they were committed. No negotiator can bargain successfully if he advertises to the world in advance the maximum he will make in the way of concessions. Under the plea of freedom of the press, in whose name many crimes have been committed, the news of the Hoover moratorium was prematurely published in 1931, with the result that France was so deeply offended as to counteract in considerable measure the anticipated effects of the agreement.

More subtly dangerous is the case of the foreign correspondent who reports what he thinks is the truth, but his newspaper, with a bias in the other direction, declines to publish the story. The newsman, fearful of losing his job, quickly perceives that the way to promotion and pay is to see what his superiors want him to see.[*] This was notably true of the Far East before Pearl Harbor. A large proportion of the stories followed the theme: "China can't lose; Japan can't win." The gigantic surprise party that Japan staged at Pearl Harbor and after was in considerable part created by easily duped newsmen or by those who deliberately colored their reports. Heinrich Hauser, an embittered German, claims that the American correspondent in European capitals, before World War II, pounced upon the first copies of European editions of American newspapers so as to discover what the

---

[*] The present writer was told by an American press attaché that many of our correspondents are able men but they are held by their home office to kidnappings and other "human interest" stories.

people at home were thinking, and hence what they would like to have in their foreign reports.

10

If a people get no better government than they deserve, it is no less true that the subscribers get no better newspapers than they deserve. As Oscar Wilde put it: "Modern journalism justifies its own existence by the great Darwinian principle of the survival of the vulgarest." If the masses did not want vulgar newspapers, the alert publisher, ever keen for profits, would provide something better.

In this so-called freest of free countries, we have a crippling self-imposed censorship of the press. The newspaper does not have space to publish more than a small part of the mountain of material that comes in over the tele-types, and the tendency is to eliminate all except what the Almighty Reader wants, or what the editor thinks he wants. Broadly speaking, the subscriber does not want the truth, but a concoction liberally seasoned with his own bias. The radical wants radical material; the liberal, liberal; the conservative, conservative. "Your favorite newspaper," as Bruce Bliven has said, "is your favorite quite as much because of the things it leaves out as those it prints."

The mass of semiliterates, upon which the Hearst journals and the Patterson-McCormick "newspaper axis" feed, is the greatest barrier to a good press, as it is to good government and a sound foreign policy. Newspaper editors have learned to their cost that nothing is gained by getting out too far in advance of herd thinking; they merely antagonize or bore readers and lose revenue. They have learned, as the *Reader's Digest* has learned, that the people do not want problems over which to puzzle their tired heads; they demand interesting and bizarre facts, but nothing that involves a prolonged consideration of causal relationships.

One unhappy by-product of popular education has been the overthrow, with a few notable exceptions, of the sober newspaper aimed at the upper or middle classes. This has been true in England as well as in America, and one can regret that the press escaped the domination of government in the seventeenth and eighteenth centuries only to fall under the domination of the masses in the nineteenth and twentieth. What good does it do to teach the people to read if they demand only comics, murders, sex scandals, and sports, with a consequent debasement of sound journalism? To argue that the subscribers are seduced into reading sound information by these allurements is to argue that vice is the way to virtue.

Newspaper publishing is a business, but the publisher who sells newspapers clearly has a higher social responsibility than the grocer who sells potatoes. The editor won freedom of the press so that he might champion the rights of the people, and if he abuses his dearly-won privileges, the people may impose trammels upon him. With newspapers becoming fewer and bigger, the press is partaking more and more of the nature of a monopoly, and hence a public utility. Those who do not operate quasi-public utilities in the public interest merely speed the day of regulation.

Yet, in the last analysis, the defects of the newspaper are in large measure attributable to the reader, for the editors, like other businessmen, aim to please the customer. The alleged faults of the press are not so much the faults of the press as of democracy itself. As we raise the educational and critical level of the people, we may confidently expect journalistic standards to rise correspondingly. But this is a slow and painful process. An ignorant and indifferent citizenry is not the stuff out of which to make good journalism, a workable democracy, or a farvisioned foreign policy.

CHAPTER TWENTY-SEVEN

CONCLUSIONS

WHEN Emerson said that the Man in the Street does not know a star in the sky, he uttered a profound truth. But it is comforting to realize that our ignorance of the firmament can in no way affect the movements of the heavenly bodies. The same reassuring thought unfortunately cannot be used to excuse our ignorance of public affairs.

Enough has been said to demonstrate that every American citizen is a sovereign, whether he chooses to exercise his sovereignty or not. The question is whether we shall be good or bad sovereigns, alert or apathetic ones, intelligent or stupid ones. "The problem of democracy is not the problem of getting rid of kings," wrote F. C. Morehouse. "It is the problem of clothing the whole people with the elements of kingship."

Many Americans, through sheer indifference or incapacity, have abdicated their kingship. We have set up a representative government, and then all too often have failed to indicate in what way we wish to be represented. In 1776 we needed the consent of the governed; today we need direction from the governed.

One of the most encouraging aspects of American public opinion is that in the last quarter of a century or so we have developed much greater maturity in our approach to international relations. But the increasing complexity of world affairs makes it imperative that we rise more effectively to our responsibilities. With this end in view, and by way of summary and conclusion, the following suggestions are offered.

We should attract our best brains into government service. Leadership of the highest quality is urgently needed.

We should exercise extreme care in the election of our public servants, and in particular give thought to their capacity for a broad approach to foreign affairs. It is much better to vote for the right senator than later to write to the wrong senator.

We should delegate more responsibility to our public officials, after we have gone to pains to select the ablest ones. In a sense we have neither a representative nor a delegate government: not representative, because too many of us are inarticulate; not delegate, because too many of us delegate authority by default.

We should educate for statesmanship at the same time we are educating for citizenship. If we pick out our ablest men, train them from the beginning, and delegate more authority to them, we shall get a relatively quick return on our investment. But even this is only a partial answer.

We should, above all, undertake the Gargantuan task of raising the educational and apperceptive level of our entire population. Elihu Root once said that when foreign affairs were handled by despots, the danger was in sinister purposes; when they are handled by the people, the danger lies in mistaken beliefs.

We should rip away the prejudice-encrusted legends about the past of foreign peoples, and for this purpose we need more critical textbooks, more critical teachers, and a more critical public.

We should develop more tolerance, and realize that in a complicated international situation one side has never had a complete monopoly of the right, and the other side a complete monopoly of the wrong.

We should learn in our thinking to put ourselves in the other fellow's sandals, and view the common problem as he would see it through the lenses of his racial psychology and national bias. To this end we should encourage foreign travel, and the widespread exchange of students and professors.

We should train ourselves to keep our heads in time of crisis, as we definitely failed to do on the eve of the Spanish-American War. The mob is always wrong. Even when it hangs the guilty man, it also hangs Justice.

We should keep vigilant and demand of our government that in so far as possible it take us into its confidence.

We should remember that in unity there is strength. A common complaint of the "little fellow" is that his views do not count. But if he would pool his voice with that of countless other "little fellows," it would count for a great deal. If he does not do this, the purposeful minority will.

Upon every citizen in our democracy rests a solemn obligation to inform himself so that he can direct our foreign policy—*his* foreign policy—along intelligent and farvisioned lines.

BIBLIOGRAPHY

THIS BOOK is based partly on an examination of all published public opinion polls having to do with American foreign affairs from 1935 to June, 1947. The best known of these are conducted by Dr. George Gallup (officially known as the American Institute of Public Opinion), by Mr. Elmo Roper (in *Fortune* and the New York *Herald Tribune*), and by the National Opinion Research Center, at the University of Denver and more recently at the University of Chicago. In summarized form these polls and others have been and are being published in the *Public Opinion Quarterly*. The skeletonized results, which often omit sectional differences, occupational breakdowns, explanatory data, and other significant information, are less valuable than the originals. For present purposes the Gallup polls were consulted either in the newspaper press or in the form of releases to the newspapers sent out by the Gallup organization. In more recent months the author has been receiving these findings directly, through the courtesy of William A. Lydgate, editor of the American Institute of Public Opinion. For the earlier years the San Francisco *News* helpfully made available its extensive back files of Gallup releases. One must bear in mind that many of the newspapers which subscribe to the service do not publish all of the polls, and often telescope the ones published. Through the generosity of Mr. Elmo Roper the author received and is receiving a complete file of the weekly column which has appeared in the New York *Herald Tribune* since October, 1944. These in part draw upon information earlier published in the *Fortune* surveys, which Mr. Roper inaugurated in 1935. The findings of the National Opinion Research Center may be consulted in its special reports, and in the fortnightly *Opinion News,* which has been published since September, 1943.

No particular effort was made to correlate American reactions with those revealed by polls in foreign countries, although this is a subject that will richly repay inquiry. Other fields that could well be investigated at length have to do with preparedness, sectionalism (the South, Middle West, and Pacific Coast), isolation, ignorance, the attitude of women, and the reactions of various occupational and income groups.

The author is aware of the limitations of polling techniques, but as compared with the older method of trying to assess public opinion through localized newspaper editorials, they mark an incalculable step forward. It is regrettable that students of the social sciences tend to ignore or even scorn the vast body of material gathered by the poll-takers.

The bibliographical guides that follow are for the use of the serious research student. The selected reading list is for the classroom student and the general reader. It represents a distillation from hundreds of titles, most of which are already conveniently arranged in the author's general survey of our diplomatic history.

BIBLIOGRAPHICAL GUIDES

The outstanding bibliography on American diplomatic history in general is Samuel Flagg Bemis and Grace Gardner Griffin, *Guide to the Diplomatic History of the United States, 1775–1921* (Washington, 1935). Harwood L. Childs's

A Reference Guide to the Study of Public Opinion (Princeton, 1934), has been superseded by two unusually full works: Harold D. Lasswell, Ralph D. Casey, and Bruce L. Smith, *Propaganda and Promotional Activities* (Minneapolis, 1935); and Bruce L. Smith, Harold D. Lasswell, and Ralph D. Casey, *Propaganda, Communication, and Public Opinion* (Princeton, 1946). The issues of the *Public Opinion Quarterly* (1937 to date) contain many valuable articles and bibliographical suggestions.

Somewhat more concentrated bibliographies appear in Thomas A. Bailey, *A Diplomatic History of the American People* (3rd ed., N.Y., 1946); *Encyclopaedia of the Social Sciences*, XII, 674; H. D. Lasswell and H. H. Cummings, *Public Opinion in War and Peace* (Washington, 1943); and Charles W. Smith, *Public Opinion in a Democracy* (N.Y., 1942).

SELECTED READING LIST

Ray H. Abrams, *Preachers Present Arms: A Study of the War-Time Attitudes and Activities of the Churches and the Clergy in the United States, 1914–1918* (Philadelphia, 1933)

Ephraim D. Adams, *The Power of Ideals in American History* (New Haven, 1913)

Norman Angell, *The Public Mind* (London, 1926)

Howard K. Beale, *Are American Teachers Free?* (N.Y., 1936)

Charles A. and Mary R. Beard, *The American Spirit* (N.Y., 1942)

Charles A. Beard, *The Idea of National Interest* (N.Y., 1934)

D. W. Brogan, *The American Character* (N.Y., 1944)

Jerome S. Bruner, *Mandate from the People* (N.Y., 1944)

James Bryce, *The American Commonwealth* (2 vols., 3rd ed., N.Y., 1914)

C. J. Child, *The German-Americans in Politics, 1914–1917* (Madison, Wis., 1939)

George Creel, *How We Advertised America* (N.Y., 1920)

Merle Curti, *The Growth of American Thought* (N.Y., 1943)

Merle Curti, *Peace or War: The American Struggle, 1636–1936* (N.Y., 1936)

Merle Curti, *The Roots of American Loyalty* (N.Y., 1946)

R. W. Desmond, *The Press and World Affairs* (N.Y., 1937)

Ralph H. Gabriel, *The Course of American Democratic Thought* (N.Y., 1940)

George Gallup and Saul F. Rae, *The Pulse of Democracy* (N.Y., 1940)

Hugh Gibson, *The Road to Foreign Policy* (Garden City, N.Y., 1944)

W. Brooke Graves, ed., *Readings in Public Opinion* (N.Y., 1928)

W. Stull Holt, *Treaties Defeated by the Senate* (Baltimore, 1933)

Walter Johnson, *The Battle Against Isolation* (Chicago, 1944)

Harold Lavine and James Wechsler, *War Propaganda and the United States* (New Haven, 1940)

Walter Lippmann, *The Phantom Public* (N.Y., 1925)

Walter Lippmann, *Public Opinion* (N.Y., 1922)

Meno Lovenstein, *American Opinion of Soviet Russia* (Washington, 1941)

A. L. Lowell, *Public Opinion and Popular Government* (N.Y., 1926)

A. L. Lowell, *Public Opinion in War and Peace* (Cambridge, 1923)

William A. Lydgate, *What America Thinks* (N.Y., 1944)

J. R. Mock and Cedric Larson, *Words that Won the War* (Princeton, 1939)

R. B. Mowat, *The American Entente* (London, 1939)

Peter Odegard, *The American Public Mind* (N.Y., 1930)

Dexter Perkins, *Hands Off: A History of the Monroe Doctrine* (Boston, 1941)

H. C. Peterson, *Propaganda for War: The Campaign Against American Neutrality, 1914–1917* (Norman, Okla., 1939)

Bessie L. Pierce, *Public Opinion and the Teaching of History in the United States* (N.Y., 1926)

DeWitt C. Poole, *The Conduct of Foreign Relations Under Modern Democratic Conditions* (New Haven, 1924)

Julius W. Pratt, *Expansionists of 1812* (N.Y., 1925)

Julius W. Pratt, *Expansionists of 1898* (Baltimore, 1936)

J. M. Read, *Atrocity Propaganda, 1914–1919* (New Haven, 1941)

Bertha A. Reuter, *Anglo-American Relations During the Spanish-American War* (N.Y., 1924)

Clara E. Schieber, *The Transformation of American Sentiment Toward Germany, 1870–1914* (Boston, 1923)

Charles W. Smith, *Public Opinion in a Democracy* (N.Y., 1942)

J. D. Squires, *British Propaganda at Home and in the United States from 1914–1917* (Cambridge, Mass., 1935)

J. E. Stoner, *S. O. Levinson and the Pact of Paris: A Study in the Techniques of Influence* (Chicago, 1942)

Elbert D. Thomas, *The Four Fears* (Chicago, 1944)

Alexis de Tocqueville, *Democracy in America*, ed. Phillips Bradley (2 vols., N.Y., 1945)

Eleanor Tupper and G. E. McReynolds, *Japan in American Public Opinion* (N.Y., 1937)

Arthur Walworth, *School Histories at War* (Cambridge, 1938)

A. K. Weinberg, *Manifest Destiny* (Baltimore, 1935)

Elizabeth B. White, *American Opinion of France* (N.Y., 1927)

M. M. Wilkerson, *Public Opinion and the Spanish-American War* (Baton Rouge, La., 1932)

J. E. Wisan, *The Cuban Crisis as Reflected in the New York Press, 1895–1898* (N.Y., 1934)